POWER AND GREED

POWER AND GREED

Inside the Teamsters Empire of Corruption

ALLEN FRIEDMAN
AND
TED SCHWARZ

FRANKLIN WATTS

1989

New York   Toronto

Library of Congress Cataloging-in-Publication Data

Friedman, Allen.
    Power and greed: inside the teamsters empire of corruption/
Allen Friedman and Ted Scharz.
       p.   cm.
    Includes index.
    Bibliography: p.
    ISBN 0-531-15105-0
    1. International Brotherhood of Teamsters, Chauffeurs,
Warehousemen, and Helpers of America—Corrupt practices—History.
2. International Brotherhood of Teamsters, Chauffeurs, Warehousemen,
and Helpers of America—History.   I. Schwarz, Ted, 1945–
II. Title.
HD6515.T3F74   1989
364.1'6—dc19   89-5653
                                                       CIP

DISCLAIMER

Due to the nature of this book, certain precautions have had to be taken in the writing. In some instances a name has been changed to protect the party involved. In other instances a name has been omitted because the individual involved has been neither indicted nor convicted for crimes they committed. There have also been confidential sources in both organized crime and law enforcement whose identities have had to be concealed because of personal danger and/or pending cases with which they are involved.

ACKNOWLEDGMENTS

Special technical assistance for *Power and Greed* was provided by Robert S. Catz, Professor of Law, Cleveland State University, Cleveland, Ohio, and Inspector Ed Kovacic, Cuyahoga County Sheriff's Office Detective Division, Cleveland, Ohio.

Special thanks to USA Business Computers of Canoga Park, California, and Lee Briggs, without whose assistance this book could not have been completed in time.

Also, thanks to RK and TK of Cleveland, who helped make this dream a reality.

CONTENTS

CHRONOLOGY

1898: Samuel Gompers, president of the American Federation of Labor, notified all teamsters who wished to join with the AF of L to attend the convention in Kansas City in order to form a union of teamsters.

1899: The founding of the Team Drivers International Union, John Callihan president. Headquarters were 213 Franklin Street, Detroit, Michigan, the home of Secretary-Treasurer George Innis.

1902: The founding of a rival teamsters' union called the Teamsters National Union, Albert Young named president. Under pressure from the American Federation of Labor, the two unions were merged in 1903 into the International Brotherhood of Teamsters. The first president of the merged rivals was Cornelius P. Shea. The headquarters were at 147 East Market Street in Indianapolis, Indiana.

1905: What may have been the most devastating teamster strike in history occurred in Chicago. It began with the seemingly unrelated strike of 6,000 special order tailors who found that they were misled by management into thinking that they had contracts calling for closed shops, an end to sweatshop conditions, and the abolition of child labor for those under the age of 16. A lockout occurred and, eventually, the teamsters joined in sympathy. The strike grew increasingly violent on the part of management and the city's political leaders. By the time it was over—105 days later—twenty-one men were dead, 4,600 teamsters had been unemployed, the union lost a million dollars, and the employers lost eight million dollars.

1907: Dan Tobin was elected general president of the IBT and would serve for forty-five years.

1908: The Employees Liability Act was passed to cover government workers injured on the job. The law would be the basis for workmen's compensation laws in various states.

1912: Workingmen were honored with their own holiday for the first time, and Labor Day parades were held throughout the United States.

1912: The first transcontinental delivery of merchandise by a motor vehicle occurred. An Alco truck delivered three tons of Parrot Brand Olive Oil Soap, traveling from New York to San Francisco. The roads were so bad that, in three days of travel through Nevada and California, approximately 100 bridges had to be repaired or given extra support by the Teamsters.

1913: The U.S. government split the Department of Commerce and Labor into two separate departments.

1920: The International Brotherhood of Teamsters affiliated itself with the Canadian Trades and Labor Congress.

1925: The Union Labor Life Insurance Company was incorporated, beginning operations in 1927. It was formed by 400 local, national, and international unions. Dan Tobin was a member of the board of directors.

1932: The Norris-La Guardia Act was passed, which prohibited courts using injunctions to stop labor disputes. It also allowed employees to designate union representation without interference or coercion.

1935: The Social Security Act was passed. There were Unemployment Insurance provisions within the act to allow for compensating workers who suddenly found themselves unemployed through no fault of their own.

1935: The passage of the National Labor Relations Act, also known as the Wagner Act. This also established the National Labor Relations Board, which would investigate charges of unfair labor practices by employers.

1937: Feeling that their problems were different from those of teamsters in Chicago, Cleveland, New York, and other cities to the east, the Western Conference of the International Brotherhood of Teamsters was founded.

1938: The Motor Carrier Safety rules of the Motor Carrier Act determined maximum hours drivers could work. The ruling allowed sixty hours of driving a week, the driver working no more than ten hours after which he had to take a mandatory eight hour rest break every twenty-four hours.

1938: The Fair Labor Standards Act established the framework that would lead to the forty hour week (the act initially established a maximum forty-four hour work week for a minimum 25 cents per hour), time-and-a-half for overtime, and a minimum wage.

1947: The Taft-Hartley Act expanded the authority of the National Labor Relations Board to look into unfair union practices. The law was also known as the Labor-Management Relations Act and outlawed closed shops, certain types of strikes and boycotts, and it created an eighty day "cooling off period" when a strike threatened national health and safety.

1952: Daniel Tobin stepped down after 45 years in the labor movement; Dave Beck became general president of the IBT.

1952: Dave Beck became an adviser to President Dwight D. Eisenhower on matters of transportation.

1957: The IBT was suspended from the AFL-CIO. Jimmy Hoffa became general president of the Teamsters.

1959: The Teamsters Union officially denounced the McClellan Senate Rackets Committee meeting that year. The Kennedy brothers, John and Robert, rose to prominence because of their actions during those hearings, the first to be nationally televised.

1959: The Labor-Management Reporting and Disclosure Act (Landrum-Griffin) forced union members to handle goods manufactured or otherwise related to workers in other unions who were on strike. In effect, teamsters could no longer support other unions, now having to act as strikebreakers. They would also be victims of the same circumstances.

1963: The teamsters launched the DRIVE (Democrat, Republican, Independent Voter Education) political action committee, allowing the International to greatly affect politics through financial support of selected candidates.

1966: Jimmy Hoffa remains president of the IBT but Frank E. Fitzsimmons is elected General Vice President, the first time such a position existed for the union.

1971: Frank Fitzsimmons elected general president of the Teamsters Union.

1980: Jackie Presser asked by President-elect Reagan and his staff to be the senior adviser on economic affairs. He would later be under consideration for Undersecretary of Labor, though opposition within the new administration would stop this from proceeding.

1981: Roy Williams becomes President of the IBT after the death of Frank Fitzsimmons

1983: Allen Friedman indicted for embezzlement and related charges concerning his being a "ghost employee" of the Teamsters Union. As a result of this action, Harold Friedman, Jackie Presser, and Tony Hughes would eventually also be charged. Hughes and Friedman would be convicted (in 1989), shortly after Presser dies of cancer.

1984: Jackie Presser becomes president of the IBT after Roy Williams is convicted of crimes.

1986: The 9,000 member New Jersey Local 560 is placed in trusteeship after its leaders go to jail and the government declares it to be a center for organized crime activities. This is the first move towards the government's effort to place the IBT entirely under trusteeship.

1988: Presser merges the Teamsters with the AFL-CIO for the first time in almost twenty years. The unions had never truly been that separate, but this successfully counters the government's early efforts to place the union in a trusteeship.

1988: Jackie Presser dies of cancer.

1989: William McCarthy becomes president of the IBT.

1989: Harold Friedman convicted on three Federal charges. U.S. government and Teamster leadership settle "racketeering" suit: charges dropped; union leadership will be contested through direct elections; government will appoint officers to oversee some union operations.

PREFACE

The labor movement is supposed to be about the workingman's getting ahead in life, bettering himself with the help of the union. To tell what happened to this workingman and my union is why I'm writing this book with author Ted Schwarz.

I never was much for schooling. I was a hustler, a gambler, and a thief when I was a kid. There was too much action going on in the streets for me to bother going further than the seventh grade. I seldom bothered with the newspapers and never thought about opening a book in those early days of my youth. Yet here I am, doing something I never considered trying before.

I suppose this project started back in the 1950s, when labor unions became my religion. I was working behind the scenes as a slugger, an organizer, and anything else men like Bill Presser, Jimmy Hoffa, and others asked me to be. I was experiencing firsthand what would prove to be one of the most dramatic periods in Teamsters Union history and did not realize it at the time. I was also becoming involved with politics, law enforcement, and other areas where corruption was critical to our success.

Somewhere during this time I began reading. I studied newspapers and magazines. I learned about the contracts we were being offered and ways to negotiate with men who had law degrees and other forms of advanced education. And I began reading about the labor movement, its history, its growth, and the men who emerged from its past. I tried to study every book that was ever published about anyone connected with the Teamsters, the American Federation of Labor (AFL), or the Congress of Industrial Organizations (CIO). I began talking with others who had lived through the important eras of labor's past.

Now I have written a book that is partially from my experiences and partially from research, extensive interviews, and uncovered documents long since buried. It is the first insider's book that has been done where nothing is held back. I am not trying to look like a good guy, and I'm not afraid to tell both the good and the bad about the more important people in the labor movement. By society's standards, I lived a portion of my life as a criminal, yet I am proud to say that I would do much of it again if the labor movement needed my skills as it once did.

Thus what you are about to read might be considered the result of a lifetime's learning, firsthand, through interviews and thousands of documents and numerous books. It is an honest account of both the struggle for human dignity and the violence and corruption at the top. Often the good guys and the bad guys were the same, the working person experiencing the triumphs and the tragedies that resulted from our actions. But no matter what happened, no matter how long it has been kept secret, I have decided to set the record straight.

Only two men have ever truly mattered to me in recent years, at least since Jimmy Hoffa died. One is Bill Presser, the toughest behind-the-scenes fighter since Jimmy Hoffa was second in command to Dave Beck. But Bill Presser, my brother-in-law, is dead and I never again have to worry about his wrath.

The other man is my nephew, Jackie Presser, whose death I deeply regret. He went from a desperate desire for my approval when we were both kids to an arrogant, generally corrupt way of life that led to criminal indictments at the time of his death. He screwed me, abandoned my family when I went to jail, and turned against everyone and everything in the union except the money he could make, both from his salary and from whatever scams he pulled, possibly with the knowledge of the FBI after he became their paid informant.

I never had the chance to face Jackie Presser in court. I never had the chance to show the world the Teamsters I knew and loved. This book is my effort to explain the life I have led, the people I have known, and the labor union that has been called the strongest in the world, the most respected, the most feared, and the most corrupt. It has been all of these things and more, as you will see. Yet given that proverbial second chance, I think that I would do almost all of it once again.

POWER
AND
GREED

1

The Teamsters, the Mob, and the Lawless Years

I NEVER MET an honest person. I'm sure there are some somewhere. It's just that I never met one.

Maybe it's power, maybe sex, maybe money. Some people want a traffic ticket fixed. Others want to meet some broad. Still others want to squeeze out a little more profit in their businesses at the expense of the workingman.

I've been seeing it all my life. A few years ago, Bill Presser handed me a briefcase he said was filled with cash and told me to take it to Edwin Meese in Washington. This was back in late November or early December after Ronald Reagan had become president. I don't know how much was in that case; Bill knew I would never open it. But after Reagan got in, he named Bill's son, Jackie Presser, to his transition cabinet. Then he wanted to make Jackie under secretary of labor, though I guess cooler heads prevailed. Jackie's presence would have been just one more scandal for the administration. After all, though Jackie never did time in jail as Bill and I did, that was only because his father and I covered his ass, not because he was ever an honest man.

Another time I had an envelope filled with money to give to a man running for mayor of Cleveland. He publicly refused the contribution, not wanting to take cash from so "disreputable" a group as the Teamsters Union leadership. But when we left the meeting hall where he had been speaking, he quietly reached into my pocket and took out the envelope. There was no sense in his letting an ethical stand get in the way of unrecorded cash that could help get him elected.

3

I should not have been surprised, of course. From what I saw firsthand and what Bill related, Bill Presser and the Presser family to some degree owned almost every mayor Cleveland had since the 1950s. And their actions were repeated by other Teamsters officials in other major cities throughout the United States.

Even the changes in the ethnic groups that have dominated organized labor over the years occurred, in part, because of a woman. Had it not been for the lust of several Irish labor leaders for an underage girl, Bill Presser might not have so readily dominated the Teamsters Union in Ohio. And it was from that base that Bill, working with organized crime members and others, created the behind-the-scenes power source that ensured that men such as Jimmy Hoffa and Bill's son, Jackie, could dominate the most powerful labor union in the United States.

I was born in Cleveland, Ohio, during one of the most lawless periods the United States has ever seen. The only difference I could see between the criminals and the cops was that the criminals had better clothing, better weapons, and fancier cars.

Take Maxie Diamond, for example. He was a tough independent criminal who made his money from gambling, bootlegging, prostitution, and other activities. Maxie wore expensive suits, smoked the best cigars, and always traveled in a caravan of three cars. The first and last cars would have his bodyguards with their machine guns sticking out the window. His car would be in the middle, more armed men riding the running board. He was better protected than the president of the United States, Warren Harding. But when it came to corruption, the main difference I could see between Maxie and Harding was that Maxie would kill a man who stood in his way. So far as any of us knew, President Harding never used a weapon more powerful than bribery and extortion to get what he wanted.

Actually, it might be said that Harding's administration was the symbol that crime had become part of the American way to success. He was an Ohio boy whose aides were stealing the country blind. Attorney General Harry Daugherty was able to save seventy-five thousand dollars over three years' time from a salary of just twelve thousand dollars, all the time claiming he did not take graft. Almost weekly, until Harding died of a heart attack on August 3, 1923, the papers were filled with stories about the corruption in his administration.

I never read about that corruption when it was happening, of course. I was only an infant when the United States entered what has since been called the "lawless decade." However, it influenced everything I would experience as I grew up.

I was born in an area that was primarily a neighborhood of immigrants in a city of immigrants. Cleveland was a steel and shipping town, a place where an able-bodied man could find laboring work to feed his family even if he couldn't speak, read, or write the language. Construction was extensive throughout the city, including, by 1924, the Terminal Tower, which would become the second tallest building in the United States at the time.

Yet despite the abundance of jobs, most work did not pay very well. Many immigrants had extended families living in their homes: uncles, cousins, and other relatives all working, then sharing their incomes in order to survive. Women were entering the marketplace in record numbers, taking secretarial positions and sales jobs once limited to men.

Some families believed in education and wanted their children to assimilate into the American culture. They wanted the children in school or using the new Carnegie free library system that was slowly becoming a part of the United States. Others saw the children as a resource to be exploited for their earnings potential, taking them out of school if their children could make a few dollars a week on a job.

But no matter what the value system, there was often a self-centered intensity to the immigrants that made many of them willing to exploit their fellow countrymen in order to make a few dollars.

Perhaps much of what I saw around me was the result of the types of people who were migrating to the United States. From the end of the nineteenth century until the period when I was born, Europe was in turmoil. World War I, the "war to end all wars," had gained most of the attention, but it was just one of many periods of violence. There were civil wars and revolutions almost everywhere. The Russians were revolting against the czar, a group of peasants inspired by the ideas of Marx and Lenin trying to create a new society where the uneducated poor took control of the country.

Many cities, and even some of the nations my parents had known while growing up, no longer existed. Some merged with each other. Some were overrun by invading armies. And some were destroyed by the invaders.

Most people accepted the violence and the change. They had lived on the land for generations and saw the revolutions as just another period of hard times that they would survive.

A few were stronger, more courageous, or more rebellious. They wanted nothing to do with the change, nothing to do with the people who accepted and adjusted to whatever conditions were imposed. These were the misfits who could not stand the restrictions they were experiencing. Some wanted a better life. Others wanted to control their own destiny. And a few simply wanted to be able to do whatever they chose, regardless of who was hurt along the way. Such attitudes seemed best suited to some other country than the one where they lived.

Hundreds of thousands of these immigrants found their way to the United States, settling in New York, Cleveland, Chicago, Pittsburgh, and the other major cities. They moved into neighborhoods where they would not have to assimilate. They started their own newspapers, opened grocery stores selling delicacies familiar to them from the old country, and spoke Hungarian, Italian, Polish, Yiddish, French, German, or any of the other languages that were their native tongues. When I was born, there were six local newspapers written in Hungarian, four in Italian, and dozens of others in the numerous languages that could be heard as you traveled throughout Cleveland. The news they read was of their own neighborhood, their own people, as though no one else existed in one of the largest metropolitan areas in the nation.

Each ethnic group was likely to be isolated from the mainstream of Cleveland society. The people dressed differently from the Americans. Their food, their customs, their music all were unfamiliar. They were looked upon as being stupid because they had not yet learned the culture, yet the truth was that they were often far more intelligent than the doctors, lawyers, professors, large manufacturing plant owners, and others who dominated the city. They were also more aggressive, unafraid of giving up everything they had known, the friends and families they had loved, in order to travel thousands of miles for a fresh start.

Before the prohibition of liquor in 1920, there were only a few ways for immigrants to advance themselves. The Irish had the most sophisticated sense of how to gain power. Even though they spoke English, their thick accents and limited education set them apart from the wealthy of the cities. Yet the Irish understood that there were two types of power in a city. If one was closed to you, the other could be used to dominate the community.

One type of power comes from having money, position, and ownership of corporations where others are beholden to you for jobs. A man who owns a steel mill not only becomes wealthy from the products that the mill makes but also has power over the lives of the workers. The ability to hire or fire hundreds or thousands of men and women makes each individual feel helpless in his presence. If the working conditions were not quite right, the owner could fire anyone complaining, knowing that there would be ten more men willing to work under those unpleasant circumstances just to hold a job. And if there were complaints to officials, the boss had the money to pay whatever bribes were necessary to ensure that he would not be continually harassed.

But there was a second kind of power that came from understanding the old-money, white Anglo-Saxon Protestants who dominated big city society. This was the power that came from offering services that satisfied the wants and needs of the wealthy. It was a power based on understanding a man's weakness and playing on it.

The Irish sought this second kind of power, and they did it in a manner that was so subtle that the social leaders never realized what was happening until it was too late. The Irish moved into two primary areas: civil service and labor.

The civil service jobs were positions no one viewed as very important. Many Irishmen became firemen or police officers at a time when a policeman walked a beat. There were few restrictions on the law, each officer having the ability to punish wrong doing on the spot. A teenager who stole from a store might be taken into the back room and beaten with a rubber hose by the police officer on the beat. The youth would only go to court if his offense was unusually bad or he kept repeating it despite the "lessons" provided by the cop. The policeman could control which victimless crimes—gambling, prostitution, the numbers racket, and so on—were protected on his beat and which would be raided. He could close a business for safety and health reasons or leave it open despite any risks to the public.

The Irish also took other city jobs as councilmen, street cleaners, or building inspectors. "Civil service" was not high-paying, nor was it particularly respected. However, by the turn of the century, the established, wealthy social leaders of Cleveland, Boston, New York, and other cities discovered what the Irish came to recognize after holding those menial jobs after their arrival in the United States: With a little organization, the men in those seemingly unimportant positions could control everything that took place within the community.

Whether someone wanted to build a factory, open a restaurant, or avoid being plagued by vandalism, he had to work with the Irish immigrants who had taken the jobs no one thought mattered. Bribes were paid and favors exchanged.

The other area where the Irish quietly took control was the labor unions. At first the unions were determined to help the working man and woman. For example, in 1899 the Team Drivers International Union was formed in Detroit as a division of the American Federation of Labor (AFL). There were eighteen locals with twelve hundred drivers, yet their demands were so reasonable—better pay and working conditions that could easily be afforded by the bosses—that the union had grown to thirty thousand members just three years later.

The labor struggle was a problem because of the way the workingman was viewed. Society at large was distinctly divided by class, which, in most cities, meant those who had money and those who did not. The idea of the middle class was not a strong one, and its development was influenced more by the working individual who managed to better himself than by the natural order of life during that period of time.

There was an attitude among many of the rich that people with money were more deserving than those who lacked it. Somehow being poor was a condition that required neither pity nor correcting. The idea of increasing wages and benefits, and therefore also reducing their profits, seemed to contradict the natural order of life and thus was to be resisted. Surprisingly, this attitude was shared by both the police and the press.

Part of the press's hostility arose because newspapers were in transition. For more than a century, the printers were the elite of the press. They owned the newspapers, sold the advertising, and wrote most of what appeared. They were skilled craftsmen who were generally well paid and deserving of great community respect. Their positions also allowed them to influence both politics and business interests, much as Ben Franklin had in the 1700s.

It was only at the turn of the twentieth century that newspapers began to change in the way the jobs were classified. Reporters were hired independently of the printers, and they were viewed as a less educated, less skilled, inferior class of individuals. The papers became more sensational as the years progressed and some, such as the *New York Daily News,* more attuned to the interests of the workingman. But when labor unions, and especially the Teamsters, were first forming, the elitist attitudes of the printers, publishers, and reporters turned them against organized labor.

The Teamsters of 1902 (The Teamsters National Union of America) had to have far more courage than most modern members can imagine. They were literally the lifeline for America because food was carted fresh each day, the capability of storing foods in frozen form not having been developed. The men drove horses and wagons, delivering meat and baked goods each morning. If they went on strike, everyone turned against them.

The violence was so intense that every strike meant death for one or more of the union members. The public supported the business owners and their use of both police and hired goons to beat the drivers back to work. Everyone wanted his food transported and did not care what had to be done to get it. In fact, during this early period of organization, Teamster membership buttons were two-sided and designed to be reversed as needed. One side had the logotype of the Teamsters Union, and the other side was black, a mourning emblem meant to be worn at the members' funerals. When the Chicago meat-packing drivers went on strike for thirteen days that year, both sides of the buttons received a regular workout.

The International Brotherhood of Teamsters, Chauffeurs, Warehousemen, and Helpers of America, the organization of which I was a member, formed from both the Team Drivers International Union and a second group, Teamsters National Union, which started in 1902. The latter did not last very long, the two Teamsters unions' merging into the International Brotherhood in 1903. The headquarters was Indianapolis, and Cornelius Shea became president, earning $150 per month.

Scandals and violence affected the Teamsters from the start, though through no fault of their own. On December 30, 1903, some twelve hundred livery drivers were on strike for better pay. They were so poorly paid that their lives were plagued with illness and early death, many of their children failing to survive through the teenage years. The strike issue was increased pay (no benefits, pensions, or other sources of aid being considered) to two dollars for a twelve-hour day, usually part of at least a sixty-hour week.

What the Teamsters did not expect when they went out on strike was the fire at the Iroquois Theater, so popular as a source of entertainment that 602 women, children, and a few men would be trapped inside by a fire and burned to death. The Teamsters refused to drive wagons to the fire, and most of the strikers did not volunteer to be a part of the rescue efforts. The fact that circumstances were such that nothing could have been done to save more people than those who survived was irrelevant. The Teamsters were suddenly viewed as murderers who did not care what happened to others.

The employers used this early anti-Teamster sentiment to their advantage when another strike took place two years later. Several hundred black males, so desperate for any job that they would accept employment as strikebreakers, were imported to Illinois, issued rifles, and told to drive the wagons the Teamsters had abandoned. Riots and shootings followed, most public sympathy staying with the bosses.

Dan Tobin, the man who would serve as general president longer than anyone in the history of the Teamsters, was elected head of the organization in 1907. At first he was a leader in the development of the Teamsters Union in the various major cities of the United States. But his first love was the politics of the AFL, and he began spending more time with AFL activities, letting the Teamsters run themselves.

The violence the Teamsters faced during the next twenty years seemed so irrational that the members decided to fight back. All they ever wanted was fair pay for their work, yet they were being attacked by goon squads, the police, and, frequently, the general public. Their answer was to fight back, sending their own men to battle with baseball bats, knives, guns, blackjacks, and any other weapon they owned or could make. They also teamed up with local gangsters who enjoyed being paid to break heads for either side.

It was the influx of neighborhood gangsters that marked a major change in the Teamsters. Suddenly there were men involved who had neither loyalty nor ideology. They began changing the face of organized labor in many communities, taking control and becoming extortionists.

Many of these gangster "labor leaders" collected dues from members to help pay for the fight to improve working conditions and income. Then the same labor leaders took bribes from businessmen either to leave the labor situation alone or to establish contracts that provided less pay and fewer benefits to the workers than the companies could afford to pay. A portion of the money that was the difference between the cost of the contract agreed upon and the contract the labor leaders could have obtained was then kicked back to the labor leaders.

Frequently the children of these men went on to college, becoming judges, lawyers, and doctors. The social prominence denied the first generation of Irish immigrants was gained by their children, in part because their parents knew how to obtain power from laboring and civil servant jobs few others wanted.

Other immigrant groups either understood the same theory of power and influence as the Irish or realized that success came from imitating their actions. Many also went into politics, though the civil service system was so dominated by the Irish that few were successful at first. Others went into labor, the leaders and/or their goon squads frequently using extortion to gain business for their members.

For example, it was not uncommon for the window glaziers to drive down Cleveland streets breaking windows when periods of construction were slow and they were not being hired to install new glass. The police were paid off to look the other way, so few of the vandals were ever arrested. Yet everyone understood the system.

Window washing was another business that was run by extortion. The washers usually staked out their own territory in each section of the city, an arrangement that kept complaints to a minimum. Then the representative of the men involved would walk into a store and ask whether his men could wash the windows. It was generally understood that you agreed or the glass would be shattered by morning. One downtown store owner recalled a short, weasellike "salesman" who would move in and out of the shadows, approaching the store owners with the line "Do I wash your windows or break them?" It was a part of the cost of doing business and was passed on to the customers.

Although I was not born when the Prohibition laws were passed and was a small child during the years when bootlegging was most common, my career in organized labor was actually determined by the ways in which the immigrants were attempting to improve their living conditions. Charles "Lucky" Luciano's decision to have the Mafia take control of the bootlegging business influenced the course my life would take.

The Italian immigrants who came to the United States fell into two categories. There were those who considered themselves Italians and those who set themselves apart because their origins were in Sicily and Calabria. The reasons for their making such distinctions are not important. What matters is that the people of Sicily and Calabria had lived for centuries in a land where both the government and the church leaders were corrupt. They developed a society within a society in order to survive. They gave the impression that they were following the wishes of the politicians and priests though they were actually handling matters of business, law enforcement, and other necessities among themselves.

They would ask for favors, receive favors, and constantly work together to resolve problems that, in other parts of Italy, would have been handled by the government officials.

When the Italians came to the United States they did what all other ethnic groups had done: They settled together, bringing their traditional culture into the neighborhood. For those Clevelanders from Sicily, Calabria, and such towns as Madrice, Naples, and Ripamolisano, among others, this often meant settling on "the hill." This was part of one of Cleveland's "Little Italys" which were five Italian settlements within the city. It is located between East 119th Street and East 125th Street on Mayfield Road and Murray Hill.

In 1911, when the Hill first became Little Italy, it was estimated that 98 percent of the residents either were Italian-born or had Italian parents. Four other Italian settlements were developed in other parts of the city, but when people talk about Italian organized crime in Cleveland—the Black Hand, the Mafia, La Cosa Nostra, and so forth—they are generally referring to the Hill.

Sicilian immigrants to the United States did not realize that they were far safer than they had been in their native land. Because they did not speak English and lived together in ghettoes, it was possible for their leaders to become corrupt quickly. They became involved with extortion and other crimes against their own people.

The Mafia leaders had learned English and understood how the American system of government operated. They knew that they could be jailed for some of their activities, but they also knew that the uneducated peasants would always feel that no matter what crime a man might commit, it would not be so great as the crimes committed by government officials. The peasants feared the police, the mayors, and others in authority. It was easier for them to pay extortion money to the Mafia, the Black Hand, the Cosa Nostra than to expect outsiders to help. Problems were kept among themselves.

It is not certain whether the leaders of the Mafia recognized that eventually the peasants would assimilate into the American culture or whether they just reacted quickly to changing circumstances. What was certain was that if the first generation stayed in an ethnic neighborhood, never learning the language or the culture, the next generation would not tolerate such a life-style. They would master English, get an education, become so assimilated into the American mainstream that they would no longer tolerate extortion. It was time for the opportunists to enter a new business. And when Prohibition became the law, the first such business they decided to enter was bootlegging.

Lucky Luciano went to Cleveland on December 5, 1928, to hold a meeting in the Statler Hotel with a number of Mafia leaders. The meeting occurred at 4:30 A.M. and was observed by Cleveland Police patrolman Frank Osowski. Among those present was Giuseppi Profaci, later known as Joe Profaci, the notorious boss of the Brooklyn Mafia. There were twenty-three men in all, and after a raid of the place, thirteen guns were found. It was at that meeting that Luciano declared his decision to take over the bootleg liquor trade.

The Mafia leaders wondered how Luciano intended to take over the liquor trade. According to reports that emerged over the years, some thought that Luciano wanted to control the sugar trade. Sugar was an essential ingredient in making alcohol, and the sugar suppliers were rich, powerful men.

Others present thought that Luciano would take over the trucks. Without the means to haul the liquor, large-scale operations would be ended. Although many bootleggers sold from their homes, their stores, or their cars, they were small-time compared with those who made hundreds or thousands of gallons which they transported by truck.

But Luciano was smarter than any of them. He said that the way to control the liquor trade was to control the drivers. On that day the Mafia decided to take control of the Teamsters Union. Most of the drivers were not members of a union. Most of them were independent in one way or another. But Luciano had a vision for the future, and the Teamsters were a part of that vision.

It would take more than thirty years for the full influence of that organized crime decision to be comprehended by the general public. My brother-in-law, Bill Presser, would become part of the behind-the-scenes maneuvering that helped them control the most powerful union in the nation. I would become a "slugger," an organizer, an arsonist, doing anything that was needed to help bring about the change. And my nephew, Jackie Presser, would eventually become the head of the International, his lifetime of fraud, deceit, and frequent criminal activities carefully covered up as he rose in power. But organized crime influence within the Teamsters was not a concern in those early days. I doubt that Luciano had any idea of the ultimate impact his decision would have on the union. His only concern was bootlegging, and that was the business in which my father also made his money.

I guess my family had always been what some people would call disreputable. My parents, Louis and Teresa (she was called Toba), were Hungarians who fled both the changing conditions in Europe and possible problems for my father. Although his occupation was listed as "cattleman" on my birth certificate, a reference to his supposed work in the old country, he was actually a horse thief before he entered the army in 1912.

My sister, Faye, and my brother, Joe, had been born in the old country and moved with my mother to Pennsylvania in 1912. My father finished his military service in 1914, joining the family there and having two more children, my brothers Jack and Harry. Then they came to Cleveland, taking a house at 10624 Grantwood Avenue around 105th Street between St. Clair and Superior, two of Cleveland's main streets.

The area where I was born was the most desirable section in which Jews were allowed to live. The city was built like a wheel with Public Square at the hub. Streets came out in all directions like the spokes of that wheel, the Cuyahoga River separating the east and west sides.

The wealthy settlers first lived downtown along the river and the lake. Then they began moving east, mansions being erected along what would be known as "Millionaire's Row."

Zoning restrictions were limited at first so commercial buildings began taking control of the downtown area. Rather than keeping their homes and changing the laws, the wealthy community and business leaders just kept moving. Some of their homes were destroyed to make way for businesses. Others were purchased by members of ethnic groups who could afford the price. It was often said that the eastern migration of Cleveland had the Jews following the Gentiles and the Blacks following the Jews. Certainly this was the pattern in the East 105th Street area where my parents lived.

The areas where the working poor had their homes were further divided and restricted according to ethnic, racial, economic, and religious lines. The Jews had a section called Kinsman Road, an area of multifamily homes. Despite the Kinsman Road Jews and the families who lived in my area sharing a common heritage and religion, we kids often fought each other. There were periodic gang fights, the kids in each neighborhood trying to prove they were better than the others.

My neighborhood was an odd mix of bootleggers and business people. There was a large dealer in eggs and a family that owned a milk company. There were lawyers, bankers, and doctors.

One family owned a scrap metal business, and the husband and wife were constantly fighting. It might be the middle of the afternoon or two or three o'clock in the morning when you'd hear the wife chasing the husband, screaming at him.

Another house near ours had a man who was a small-scale bootlegger. He had a girlfriend who held poker games, cooked for the gamblers, and helped him make and sell the whiskey. When their finances were bad, they burned their home for the insurance.

There was another home where the woman who owned it was a supplier of food, whiskey, and women. Naturally my mother did not want my father visiting her place, though I think she suspected he frequently cheated on her while making his selling rounds to Columbus, Dayton, Troy, Lima, and other communities in the state. You see, my father was also a bootlegger, an extremely successful one.

My parents' home was a wonderful place for a child. It was filled with secret passages and panels where kids could play hide-and-seek. The secret areas were not for fun but for business. They allowed my father to make bootleg whiskey in the basement, then take it to the cars in the garage without anyone's seeing him do it. Or he could take the whiskey to the attic and hide the bottles behind special panels if there was a risk of a raid.

The precautions were typical of those of many successful bootleggers, though they were seemingly unnecessary. He knew all the cops who mattered and supplied them with money to leave him alone. When one of our neighbors was raided, my father handed the lieutenant some money and the lieutenant made certain that 80 percent of the confiscated whiskey ended up at our house.

Police made a lot of money from the bootleggers and gamblers, far more than they made by enforcing the laws. For example, there was an officer named Louis J. Cadek who spent thirty years on the force, a career that ended in 1936 when he was a captain. Cadek and some of the men who worked with him sold tickets to "clambakes." The tickets cost five dollars apiece and supposedly allowed you to attend the parties where everyone would sit around eating clams, corn on the cob, and other food. The clambakes never took place. The money went into the pockets of Cadek and the others with the understanding that if someone did not pay for a ticket, his bootleg or gambling operation would be raided. There was also a higher-priced Christmas dinner at Christmas time, the cost ranging from fifteen to twenty-five dollars per ticket. By the time I was a teenager, Cadek was bolder and his fees for the larger clubs had escalated. But the concept was the same.

Captain Cadek's crimes were not discovered until 1936, at which time he was prosecuted and convicted. It was found that although he averaged approximately $2,300 a year in the course of his career, grossing a total of $67,966, he managed to accumulate savings of $109,000.

My father's success as a bootlegger reflected more than his ability to pay bribes to the right people. He understood the business and set himself up in a way that assured the greatest possible profits. He specialized in only the finest liquor money could buy, or so his clients thought. They paid well for the privilege of buying his stock.

There were several sources for bootleg whiskey during Prohibition. Liquor production and sales never stopped. Companies could sell it to drugstores, where the pharmacists were allowed to sell it to anyone who had a prescription. Although only thirst could be cured by whiskey, doctors obligingly wrote orders to the druggists to supply their patients with alcoholic beverages for "medicinal purposes." Thousands of gallons were sold across the country in this way, and thousands more were sold through the back door by pharmacists who wanted to increase their sales beyond what the doctors provided. In addition, alcohol could be used for religious purposes, the sales of kosher wine soaring dramatically.

A second source of alcohol was bootleg gin (or rye or anything else you wanted). This was made in bathtubs and washbasins and sometimes in large-scale operations involving truck loads of alcohol. Companies that used alcohol legally before Prohibition, such as the perfume manufacturers, were often purchased so that bootleg whiskey could be made there after hours.

Bootleg whiskey ranged in quality from a drink that tasted like the "real" whiskey tasted before Prohibition to drinks that were actually poison. Many people died from bad batches. Others were made seriously ill. Unless you were certain of your supplier, you never knew what you might be getting.

A few people made arrangements with chemists to have the bootleg whiskey analyzed before they tried each new batch. There was a story that may have been true or may have just shown the attitude many people had toward cheap bootleg whiskey. It was about a judge who had a batch of liquor, the liquid having a rich yellow color, analyzed by a chemist. The chemist called him and said, "I'm sorry to say that your horse has diabetes."

The third source of whiskey was Europe. There were rumrunners who brought everything from cheap liquor to the finest of champagnes from France, Italy, and other countries. Sometimes it was smuggled directly to the coast. Other times it came by way of Canada. And always it was readily recognizable because of the labels on the bottles and the way it was packed in boxes with mud and straw as cushioning against breakage.

My father decided to cater to the wealthier whiskey buyers, the ones who could afford the bottles being smuggled from Europe through Canada. This was the most expensive liquor available because it was made professionally, not by amateurs working from backyard or basement stills. However, my father either lacked the connections to get the genuine European liquor or realized that the greatest profits would come from making it himself. He obtained counterfeit labels and bottles similar to the type used in Europe, then filled the bottles with home made brew carefully colored to look like the expensive brands. Finally he placed the whiskey into boxes packed with straw and mud. Then he made the rounds of judges, lawyers, doctors, and other wealthy business leaders who could afford to buy what they thought was the finest liquor available.

Life was good for us. In addition to the rest of the staff, my father had a former boxer as a bodyguard. We also owned five cars: a Cord, a Packard, a Pierce Arrow, a LaSalle, and a DeSoto convertible. We kids wanted for nothing.

My mother was actually the stronger of my two parents. She was bigger than my father, but it was more than that. She had had the courage to come to America alone with two small children. She had survived with limited education and little ability to speak English. In fact, neither of my parents could read or write the language. And my mother had learned to fear no one.

For example, there was the time my father was kidnapped. There was a Jewish organized crime group in every large city that had a good-sized Jewish population, but most of them were weakened or destroyed by the Mafia. The Jewish Combination of New York, for example, had almost everyone killed but Meyer Lansky, who became the financial genius for the mob. In Chicago, one of the leaders of what the Italians called the "Jewish Mafia" and we called the "Jewish Combination" was kidnapped when the Italians were challenged over territory. While he was tied to a chair, his wife and daughter were shot, sexually molested, and then killed in front of him. Only then was he shot to death. The brutality so horrified the other Jewish criminals that their challenge ended. Instead they worked around the Italians in areas where there would be no conflict or they worked with the Mafia, acting as "soldiers" instead of trying to dominate.

It was only in Cleveland that the Jews and the Italians worked side-by-side for a prolonged period of time. Both Jews and Italians were a part of New York City's Murder, Incorporated, but that organization was short-lived compared to the work relationships in Cleveland. Bill Presser, for example, worked under two generations of Mafia leaders in Cleveland. Each respected the other and they frequently worked together. My mother knew this and that was why she was irate when she received a telephone call from some Italian men in Youngstown, Ohio, who were holding my father and his load of whiskey for ransom.

One reason for buying alcohol from Maxie Diamond was to receive protection from the Italians. The bootleggers he supplied were not supposed to be harmed. The idea that this rule had been violated infuriated my mother. She immediately called Maxie Diamond and demanded that he get both my father and the whiskey back. There would be no reasoning. There was no respect. Maxie was to act, or else.

Maxie Diamond normally could not be threatened. He was a proud, tough man who once shot a man in a barber shop on 105th Street, a commercial strip near our home. We all knew about it, though we never did learn why he did it since he was well enough connected with law enforcement not to be charged with the crime. Most people, men or women, who made the demands my mother did would have been beaten or killed. In Mother's case, Maxie listened and promised that my father would be home by morning.

It must have been 7:30 or 8:00 the next morning when Maxie and his bodyguards arrived at the house. They brought my father and the whiskey, along with the Italians who had kidnapped him. The Italians attempted to apologize, explaining that if they had known who he was, they never would have taken him. Mother just swore at them, slamming and locking the door in their faces.

Stories of my mother's temper were frequently told to me by my aunts. She would argue with family members, then throw them out of the house, only to make up with them later. Because she was superstitious, she insisted that they always make peace the same way they had parted in anger. If mother threw somebody out the side door, the first time the person returned to our home, he or she had to come in through the side door. If the person went out the front door, then the first visit back after the fight had to be through the front door.

My father never seemed to get into serious trouble despite his criminal activities. The one time I remember his being arrested was in Troy, Ohio, a small community where the sheriff threw him into jail to serve ninety days for bootlegging. When Mother and I drove out to visit him, we found that he wasn't being kept in a cell. He was out back, resting in a hammock the sheriff's deputy purchased for his pleasure, a glass of whiskey in one hand, a corned beef sandwich in the other. As usual, he had paid off the law.

My father was a show-off about his money in other ways. There was a barber shop where he'd get a shave and a shoe shine every day. He'd also get regular haircuts, though he was 90 percent bald. He used to buy LaPalina Cigars, which, at $.25 each, were the most expensive you could smoke. However, that wasn't good enough for him. He would take out a $100 bill, light it with a match, then use the money to light his cigar. He would take a few puffs, then turn to the man shining shoes and say, "Look, Bill, this cigar just cost me $100.25."

My father also showed off through me. When I was in school, we had a postal savings program for children. We would buy stamps for the amount we deposited, the money going into a savings account from which we could make withdrawals. It was a savings and loan program for children.

Many children involved with the program in the different schools would deposit five or ten cents a week in the program. Because I was in a wealthier neighborhood, it was fairly normal for the children to be given fifty cents or a dollar to deposit. My father gave me thirty or forty dollars, a good week's pay for the average workingman. By the time I was ten years old, I had approximately five thousand dollars in the postal savings program. After the Depression hit, and my father lost almost all of his money either through failed investments or in bank closures, the money I had saved became extremely important for the family's survival. It was like having two years' income for the average workingman.

Although I'm talking about the ethnic neighborhoods, the country as a whole had changed during this period. Movies often had religious themes, not because the producers were trying to sell the Bible but because they could show half-naked women in the scenes that told how the people were sinning. No one censored them so long as the "evil" was punished at the end. And the songs people used to sing had lyrics that shocked the conservative people. One popular song of the twenties, written by Harry B. Smith, Francis Wheeler, and Ted Snyder, was "The Sheik of Araby." Although pretty tame by today's standards, the sheik's claim on the love of a young woman, and his promise to creep into her tent while she slept shocked many listeners.

Ridiculous statements by moralists helped fuel the rebellion of the young. One evangelist wrote in the *Portland Oregonian:* "Social dancing is the first and easiest step toward hell. The modern dance cheapens womanhood. The first time a girl allows a man to swing her around the dance floor her instinct tells her she has lost something she should have treasured."

Unmentioned was the biggest concern at parties: women slipping out of their corsets. The heavy foundation garments were uncomfortable and unnecessary, yet viewed as assurances of chastity. Girls going to parties would first stop in the ladies room, remove their girdles, and return to their dates. They would return for this infrastructure before going home, but by then they were considered sinners.

One professor went so far as to suggest that couples should have trial marriages to find out whether they were compatible. They would have a brief ceremony that would make it legal for them to live together for a year. After they had had sex and tried to pay the bills together, they could either go their separate ways, perhaps living with someone else the next year, or could marry for life.

It was as though all past values were no longer going to be followed. Everyone was doing what he wanted, and I grew up without once meeting an honest person.

BILL PRESSER

I was five years old when Bill Presser came into my life. His parents and my own had been close. And this was before he truly became family and, eventually, almost a surrogate parent.

Bill was nineteen, Faye just sixteen. They were little more than kids, though in those days, marrying before completing high school was not unusual.

Bill had been apprenticed as a hatmaker when he was fifteen, then became a journeyman when he was seventeen. He did not get involved with the labor movement until he and my brother, Joe, needed jobs and my mother arranged for them to work in organizing through Maxie Diamond.

The wedding was a gala affair, my father sparing no expense. It was one of the biggest weddings ever held in Cleveland to that time, my father taking over what we called the Jewish center, a building located at the corner of our street. The Jewish center had a big ballroom, an area for praying, a basketball court, a swimming pool, and other recreational facilities.

School, as an institution, was not important to my parents. They had discovered that America during Prohibition was the land of opportunity where the hustle and the scam meant more than an education. Although they did not care about education, they took pride in our good grades. As a result, one of my brothers, Harry or Jack, would periodically wrap up a bottle of whiskey and hand it to me to give to our English teacher or the shop teacher, or the coach, or someone else. Sure enough, no matter how little we had done in classes, we always had good grades.

My older brother, Joe, was a kid who was big for his age, strong, and a great athlete. He also warned me about the problems that might occur in junior high school.

For example, there was an attendance counselor whose job it was to discipline the kids who skipped school. If he had a boy he wanted to discipline, he would take him into the gym, where he and the gym coach would push him around. Joe warned me about the beatings, telling me never to let the attendance counselor get me into the gym. He also let me know that he had beaten the counselor, though I have long forgotten the reasons behind that beating.

I stayed in school only through the first half of the seventh grade. I never had an interest in school, though I've been a reader all my life, probably because I was embarrassed that my parents never could read and write English. Anyway, I was cutting classes whenever I felt like it and the attendance counselor called me to his office. He asked me why I wasn't in classes, and I must have answered with some smart remark. All I know is that he told me he wanted to take me to the gym to meet the coach.

It was just the situation Joe had warned me against. I swore a lot then, so I told him that I was Joe Friedman's brother and asked him whether he remembered the beating Joe had given him. Then I said, "If you get within an arm's length of me, I'll knock your head off."

And that was when he backed off, teaching me the next to last important lesson I would carry through life. I was a big kid, powerful, but that wasn't what was important: What was important was the fact that I was not afraid of him. I learned that violence or the threat of violence could often get you your way in this life.

I say that it was almost the last lesson I had to learn as a kid because I learned the last one shortly after that. I don't know what I would have been like had things been different. I just know that I have yet to overcome the experience.

My father was forty-eight when I was nearing my thirteenth birthday and he was almost a magical figure in my life. I don't know why we were so close. My brothers and sister helped him make bootleg whiskey, yet the time I spent with him when he wasn't making his selling rounds throughout the state was precious. He would take me to the gambling spots. He showed me off when Faye got married. Maybe I was his favorite child. Maybe I exaggerated my importance in his life in order to feel special compared to my older brothers and sister. I really never knew. All that was certain was that I loved him and felt like his special friend.

There was the time when he bought a perfume factory in Cincinnati for what, today, would have been $2 or $3 million. My father planned to let the business carry on as usual during the day. Then, at night, he would have a source for alcohol as he turned the plant into a giant bootleg whiskey operation.

The idea was brilliant but it was not unique. The federal agents also understood the concept and began looking into the operations of all such alcohol-intensive businesses. Within a couple of months my father's business was closed and he was out his money. That was when he took me to the bank to withdraw my postal savings money. It was also when he had to admit his personal shame and humiliation over having gone broke.

I did not mind that he had lost his money. I also did not mind giving up the savings I had accumulated. I knew that my father had given me that money and I looked upon it as being his. Yet I also knew that it took courage for him to admit defeat and I felt closer to him for the experience.

There was more stress on my father than any of us realized. He had never given much thought to problems because, once he became a bootlegger, everything he touched seemed to work for him. He ate what he pleased, drank what he pleased, gambled, enjoyed the horses, and delighted in having women whenever he desired.

My father never cheated openly. He didn't parade his women past the house or take them to places where my mother might see them. Still, it was obvious that he got more pleasure from the opposite sex than was healthy for a married man, and my mother knew it. One time she grabbed me, put me into the car, and drove to Dayton, a trip that amazed me.

My mother never seemed able to function outside the immediate neighborhood. She spoke Yiddish and never traveled without my father, except when we went to Troy, Ohio, after he was jailed. Even that trip was remarkable for her ability to find the place.

Anyway, we began driving and apparently took all the right roads because suddenly we were at a strange hotel. She got out, her body tense, looking like a hand grenade whose pin has been pulled and whose timing mechanism is about to explode at any second. She went to a room, knocking and yelling until my embarrassed father came out. He was there with another woman. Someone must have called my mother to tell her. My parents got into a violent fight I could only watch in horror. Yet as upsetting as that was for everyone involved, my father never changed his ways.

Life changed for all of us after my father lost his perfume company. The Depression had struck in 1929. The banks had failed and many people, including my father, discovered that it was possible to lose most, if not all, of the money they had entrusted to the banks. He could no longer support the life-style we had once enjoyed and that fact must have caused him great pain. All any of us knew was that one moment he was healthy, the next he had collapsed with a serious heart attack.

My father was taken to St. Luke's Hospital, where they kept him until his recovery. The fact that he was able to leave spoke strongly for his health. Although much progress had been made in medical care by the early 1930s, hospitals were still viewed as places sick people went to die. Most older people were terrified of them, and even those who survived what was then state-of-the-art health care often contracted other diseases while being treated. My father was lucky. He came home to relax, the doctors assuring him that he would completely recover if he took the time to rebuild his strength.

There was no way that my father was going to change anything he did once he left the hospital. A man who has the nerve to womanize after being caught by someone as strong and feisty as my mother was certainly not going to listen to the doctors. He returned to drinking, eating anything he wanted, and gambling.

It was raining one day when my father went out. He did not worry about getting wet because he was only going to go to a gambling joint at the corner. It did not seem all that far, and he knew a little water wouldn't kill him. What he did not expect was that he would catch a severe chill from the drenching he received. The chill led to a fever and then to pneumonia. A short time later he was dead.

I have never gotten over the death of my father. In my mind, he had no right to leave me. I loved him, wanted him, and needed him, and he died.

Of course I know better. I had a heart attack myself when I was forty-eight, and the doctors have said I've been living on borrowed time for more than a dozen years now. But I was a child when my father died, and I guess I've carried that child's pain with me all of my adult life.

My brothers were older and had a better sense of life and death. I turned inward then, becoming angry with an intensity that lasted more than fifty years. That anger was the reason I could become cold enough to take a baseball bat and willingly break a man's collar bone just because he wanted to cross a picket line and go to work to feed his family. That anger was the reason I could happily burn down a building, doing thousands of dollars in damage and maybe destroying someone's livelihood because Bill Presser or Jimmy Hoffa told me that it was for the good of the union. There are plenty of men who were bigger than I am and tougher than I am, including my brother Joe, who never had the stomach for the actions I took over the years. And I know now that one reason I was capable of such brutality was that I never tried to accept my father's death. I developed a chip on my shoulder. Only now can I understand and quiet the rage that formed within me.

Everything began to fall apart in my life after my father died. The Depression was on and jobs were scarce. Bill Presser was having trouble finding work, as was my brother Joe. In addition, my father's family, his brothers and sister whom he had personally brought from Hungary, then set up in business, refused to assist my mother. They would not pay for my father's funeral, nor would they do anything that might put food on our table. They abandoned my mother even though it was her husband who ensured that they would have a new start in life in America.

The only man who came through for my mother was Maxie Diamond, in an action that was typical of many of the organized criminals of the 1930s. People wonder how criminals of that time could be beloved. These were men who ruthlessly tortured and killed. I had grown up seeing violence on the streets caused by Maxie and his men, though my mother taught me never to get involved, to become deaf, dumb, and blind so no one would ever question me. I knew men such as Maxie were killers. Yet everyone also knew that when widows and orphans were in trouble, members of the Jewish Combination, Sicilians in the Mafia, and other ethnic crime group leaders were liable to come through and help them. Rent might be paid for one family, bags of groceries delivered to another. Whatever emergency assistance was needed was only a request away from being provided, a better situation than we got from our family or the government.

My mother called Maxie, who arranged for both Joe and Bill to become involved with the unions. They would go to work for the three Salupo brothers, violent youths whose activities amounted to extortion.

The union activity had nothing to do with what unions have become, though one of the Salupo brothers eventually became a respected labor leader who helped the members. What Bill and Joe were doing was organizing businesses, then taking payments from the owners. No dues were collected from the members and the members received no benefits from the money that was paid. It was an extortion racket in which heads were broken if the business owners failed to pay. It was also an activity that Joe left very quickly. Bill was able to do whatever was asked of him, but Joe, as tough as he was, did not believe in fighting unless someone else started the violence.

Maxie helped my mother a little, but with no family support and a teenager to feed and clothe, my mother decided to take me to Chicago, where we would live with her sister.

In Chicago there was a farmer's market that had a food stand that sold breakfast and lunch to both the merchants and the customers. Mother used what little money she had to buy the stand, and the two of us went there to work each day.

I had always been a wild kid. I would steal milk bottles from the neighbors' porches to drink the milk and commit other petty crimes. But once we reached Chicago, my anger led me into any crime that I thought could generate a buck.

At thirteen I began a pattern that would be a part of my life until I grew too old and sick to "score."

There was a lot of work to do at the food stand during the early morning and noon time rush. The rest of the time things could be handled by my mother working alone. Thus I took an off-hours job working for a fruit stand in the market.

I learned quickly that if you were going to steal from a business, a cash operation like that fruit stand was the perfect place to do it. Most people paid more than the cost of the fruit, and I made change from the cash register. But sometimes people gave me the exact change and walked away. When that happened, I took the money, usually a few cents, and started toward the cash register as if to put it where it belonged. Instead, I busied myself waiting on someone else, slipping the money into my pocket. The customer never knew, and I figured that if I were quick enough, the owner of the stand wouldn't either. I was wrong, and when the owner of the stand discovered I was stealing, he took me to my mother, who beat me with a stick.

My mother was always hitting us kids when we did something wrong. Something about her prevented you from arguing when she was going to punish you. I remember one time she was angry with my married brother, took a coat hanger, and began beating him with it. He was a big man, strong, and on his own. Yet he let her do it to him. In fact, his wife was shocked by his standing there, not understanding the great respect we had for her. Finally he just told his wife to shut up, that if his mother wanted to hit him, then he was going to let her do it.

We were living on Roosevelt Avenue in Chicago, again a Jewish neighborhood, though a rougher one than the one I grew up in Cleveland. I began getting into crap games with the other kids. I also learned how to steal things from trucks, then sell them for a few dollars. I liked the excitement. I liked the money. And in that anger I carried with me throughout life, I did not care that somebody else might be hurt by my actions.

The stress of all the change was too great for my mother. She had been courageous all her life. She had done everything necessary to stay alive and take care of her children. But there were physical limits: the loss of my father, the move to Chicago, the work from early morning until late afternoon at the market in the lunch counter, where it was open, exposed to the cold weather, all took their toll. Like my father, she developed pneumonia, and, within a few days of getting sick, she was dead.

Remember that this was in the 1930s. Penicillin and most of the other antibiotics that have made diseases such as pneumonia a minor problem for the majority of people were not invented until the war years. There was no treatment that routinely worked. Survival often depended upon the general health of the person who came down with the disease. My father had had a heart attack shortly before he became ill. My mother was physically and emotionally exhausted when the diagnosis was made.

My brother Jack was able to get to Chicago to see my mother. Faye kept in touch from Cleveland. When the death occurred, Jack rode home with the coffin so that Mother could be buried next to my father.

And then my life, as I had known it, was over. Both parents had abandoned me through death. Sometimes I think that each time I used a golf club, a baseball bat, or my fists to hurt a man who challenged me in the labor movement, I was striking out at my parents. I hardened myself against everyone. I tried not to be vulnerable to my emotions ever again.

Back in Cleveland, no one really wanted me to live with him. My brother Joe took me in for a while, but he was extremely strict and the situation did not work for either of us. Then my brother Jack and his wife offered me a place, though again that was not really satisfactory. Finally Faye and Bill Presser took me in and I returned to a living arrangement that was the closest thing to a home and family I would have.

I was still in school at this time, but I would not last for very long. Bill and Faye seemed as casual toward school as my parents, though Bill loved reading. I dropped out of Patrick Henry Junior High before the second semester of seventh grade.

THE GREAT DEPRESSION

For me, the 1930s were an exciting time to be alive. Much was happening that affected my life, either directly or indirectly.

The Depression years after 1929 not only took money from many people but also became a time to make money. A lot of people lost their jobs, their homes, and their valuables as the stock market crashed, banks shut their doors, and businesses could not sustain an adequate cash flow to retain their employees. Yet the truth of human existence is that most people seem to have three desires in times of crisis. They want to stay alive. They want to run away from reality. And they want to cling to the hope that tomorrow will be better for them.

In Detroit, a man who would influence my life many years later understood the idea that people must stay alive during even the worst crisis. The man's name was James R. Hoffa, and his background had a few parallels with my own.

Hoffa, eight years older than I, was born on St. Valentine's Day in 1913 in Brazil, Indiana, a small mining town. His father, John Hoffa, operated a steam-powered drilling machine that dug core samples. It was difficult work, and, like so many other miners, he quickly grew old before his time. He became sick when Jimmy Hoffa was seven and died four months later.

Hoffa's mother, Viola, was a strong woman who was similar to my mother. Jimmy later discussed how strict she was, the type of woman who believed in the razor strop and the bottle of foul tasting castor oil to cure any problems her kids might have.

Like my mother, Viola Hoffa took a job in a restaurant, though she worked as a cook in a real restaurant, not a short-order place located in the cold open air. She also did housework for the community's wealthy families and took in washing. The latter became a family business, with Hoffa's sister's doing the ironing and Jimmy and his brother's handling deliveries.

Hoffa's family moved to Detroit in 1924 and things became a little better. His mother was able to get a job in the auto industry, where she earned her living polishing radiator caps.

Jimmy began working at the age of twelve. He took a job bagging potatoes in a grocery store and then graduated to delivery boy. Two years later, after completing the eighth grade, he left school to get a job.

Hoffa left the food business to go to work at Frank and Cedar's department store. He was a stock boy working a sixty-hour week for twenty cents an hour. The money was good for a teenager, and he hoped to move on into management in a few years. However, instead of moving up, he was forced by the stock market crash to rethink his future. He realized that survival even in the worst of times required food. People had to eat, and a job in the grocery business was the key to work stability. The sixteen-year-old Jimmy Hoffa took a job on the loading docks with Kroger food stores.

The Kroger job was Hoffa's first encounter with exploited workers. Each man was paid thirty-two cents per hour, almost double what he had been earning, for a twelve-hour shift that ran from 5:00 P.M. to 5:00 A.M. His job was to work the loading docks, sweeping, loading and unloading freight cars and trucks, and doing anything else that was necessary. However, the rules for employees required both long rest breaks and periods of idle time when there was nothing to do. These were also periods for which the men were not paid. Hoffa determined that he and the others were making approximately $15.36 per week for forty-eight hours of actual labor. They were also forced to be on the docks without pay for an additional thirty-two to forty-two hours each week. (Seven-day work weeks and twelve-hour days were not unusual for many men during this period.)

The problem was made worse by a foreman who was nasty to the workers. Had the man been friendlier with the help, Hoffa probably would have tolerated the situation. But the foreman's attitude was so bad that when one of the older workers suggested that the men organize and strike, Hoffa readily agreed.

The idea of the workers' organizing for better conditions seems an obvious one today. But in 1931 when Hoffa and the others made their decision to act, it was illegal in Michigan for anyone to strike against his employer. Even worse, the companies often retained armies of goons who were willing to come in and beat up the workers. Remember that many men were out of work and that any job, even one so violent and unpleasant as beating up workers complaining about unpleasant conditions, earned money to live. It was always easy to find strike-breakers.

The Depression also made the men on the loading docks fearful of losing their jobs. It was one thing to talk of organizing. It was something else to do it.

The change among the men came in May 1931. Hoffa later related the story of two loading dock workers' making the mistake of leaving the dock long enough to eat at a lunch cart. The irate foreman fired them upon their return. The action was so unjustified that the men at last had the courage to unite.

Two days later the men on the loading dock had a chance to take action. They wanted to wait until a refusal to work would cost Kroger money and the shipment that arrived that night was perfect. There were several special boxcars, all designed for the cold storage of fruits and vegetables, that had to be unloaded. The load that night was fresh strawberries, which would begin to spoil the moment the train cars were opened. They had to be unloaded immediately.

Hoffa and the other loading dock workers unloaded almost half the strawberries, then set a crate down in the middle of the dock and walked to the end. Other men on the crew, including Sam Calhoun, the man who first talked of organizing, and Hoffa's friend, Bobby Holmes, who would later become one of the heads of the Teamsters, followed Hoffa's example. Within moments, all 175 workers were idle and the night supervisor had been summoned. He listened to the complaints and agreed to arrange a meeting with company officials at ten the next morning. In exchange, the men agreed to finish unloading the strawberries.

The talks took place as agreed, lasting for several days. They ended with a contract that was revolutionary for that period of time. The hours were still long and there would still be idle time, but no matter how much work was available, the dock workers would receive a minimum of a half day's pay. They were also provided with a lunchroom, and the foreman lost the right to fire the employees at will. In addition, the negotiating committee Hoffa created was recognized as the bargaining arm of the dock workers. Jimmy Hoffa had entered the world of trade unions.

Hoffa continued with his efforts, organizing the day workers. Then an organizer from the Teamsters Union talked to the workers, who decided to affiliate with the union. They would have to start paying dues to both the local and the International, but they would have greater support and benefits in the event of a strike. Hoffa and his men agreed to become members of Teamsters Joint Council 43. The Teamsters activity led Hoffa into contact with other men who would play roles in Cleveland organized crime activity and the unions. Most important of these were Moe and Lou Dalitz.

The Dalitz family was involved in a number of businesses, the most important being the ownership of laundries. Lou, the older of the brothers, was involved with bootlegging, but he also formed the Dalitz Brothers Company, Inc., which ran laundries in Detroit. Later the firm became Colonial Laundry, merging with Michigan Industrial Laundry in 1951. Then, in 1959, it merged again to become the Michigan–U.S. Industrial Glove and Laundry Company.

Hoffa's first action with the Teamsters involved a strike against a laundry. He was brought in to act as muscle by Joe Wilder of the International Laundry Workers Union. The Teamsters had the four drivers as members but were working with the women who were employed there to affiliate them with the union.

The situation was similar to the one that had existed at Krogers. The women were paid seventeen cents an hour to operate mangles, but they were only paid when they had work to do. The rest of the time they were expected to be in the laundry, waiting for work. When they organized for a strike, the owner attacked them with a shotgun. The women retaliated by attacking replacement "scabs" hired by the owner. As these new women stepped off the streetcar, the striking workers stripped them naked and chased them down the street. It was a situation that was likely to become violent, so Hoffa and other Teamster muscle were brought in to handle the matter.

During this same period of time, Moe Dalitz was involved with the Purple Gang, Detroit's version of Cleveland's Jewish Combination. It was a group of Jewish gangsters who were involved in extortion and other rackets against their neighbors. Because they preyed on their own kind, they were viewed as "off-color" and eventually called the Purple Gang.

The Purple Gang often fought with the Mafia, and Hoffa was asked to be muscle in some of their battles. In the early 1930s, the Mafia allegedly put Hoffa on trial for his actions against them. They supposedly found him to be both knowledgeable about the various criminal alliances dividing the city and also willing to work with them for everyone's benefit. As a result, he was not hurt and gained his first behind-the-scenes backing by organized crime.

Later Moe Dalitz would be named as part of the Cleveland Syndicate (also known as the Cleveland Gang), which included Morris Kleinman, Sam Tucker, and Louis Rothkopf. Later the Syndicate would include Chuck Polizze and Tommy McGinty. Together they were alleged to be involved with numerous rackets in Cleveland in addition to going out to Las Vegas in 1950 to build the Desert Inn.

The Hoffa/Dalitz relationship was an interesting one. Hoffa helped organize the laundries Dalitz owned in Detroit, then was involved with loans to Dalitz through the Central States Pension Fund. Hoffa provided the money needed to build hotels and casinos in Las Vegas. Dalitz also would become involved with a $17,500 payoff to Hoffa to bring peace to the Detroit Institute of Laundering in 1949, a payoff meant to ensure labor peace and influence through the acceptance of a sweetheart contract.

But all these connections and behind-the-scenes activities meant little to me then. I was still a kid, not yet involved with the labor movement. For me, the greatest excitement came from activities such as gambling, which are related to the other two ways many people react to hard times. Some try to escape through alcohol and drugs. Others involve themselves with gambling.

As a kid I had seen small-scale gambling with my father. I was in the smoke shops and other locations. Being out of school and on the streets, I became more aware of the private clubs that made Cleveland famous as a gambling center. My brothers did some work for them, and my sister, Faye, was a regular visitor.

Perhaps the most famous of the gambling operations was the Harvard Club, which opened in 1930 and finally closed in April 1941. It was primarily located on Harvard Avenue near East Forty-second Street in Newburgh Heights, a suburb of Cleveland. There were several owners and at least six different addresses for the club, though the owners for the longest period were Daniel T. Gallagher, Arthur Hebebrand, and James "Shimmy" Patton.

The Harvard Club was not alone. Other gambling clubs were the Arrow Club and the Pettibone Club. However, the Harvard Club gained national recognition for two reasons. The first was its immense size. This was a place that can only be compared with the casinos in Nevada and New Jersey. As many as one thousand gamblers a night enjoyed roulette wheels, slot machines, all-night poker, and crap games. When you consider the volume of business and the number of people who went there, as well as the fact that gambling was completely illegal in Ohio, you can see how widespread the corruption had become.

My brothers Jack and Harry each owned seven passenger cars, which they used on regular routes, taking housewives to the clubs for an afternoon of gambling. The shuttles were actually the forerunners of the buses used for transporting gamblers to Las Vegas, Atlantic City, and similar gambling spots today. The Cleveland business was so good that altogether there were probably fifty guys with seven passenger cars working around the clock. There were both regular pickup spots for the different clubs and pick-ups made to order when someone called for a ride.

During this period Bill Presser was becoming extremely active in the labor movement. Bill worked with the Salupo brothers under a charter from the laundry and dry cleaner's union, a connection that would give him a background somewhat similar to those of Moe Dalitz and Jimmy Hoffa. The Cleveland operation that Bill was involved with had no connection with labor as we know it now. There were no contracts and the dues were collected from the boss. Any store owner who did not pay off, either by joining the union or by paying a bribe, would find that his shop was dynamited or firebombed.

One of the big stories of 1936 involved the attempt to raid the Harvard Club. It was January 19, and Eliot Ness had become the safety director of Cleveland.

The Harvard Club had nothing to do with Ness. Located in a suburb, he had no jurisdiction. However, County Prosecutor Frank Cullinan did have the power to close down the club, and he had the cooperation of the entire Newburgh Heights Police Force: one patrolman.

Cullinan, after alerting the patrolman that he was raiding the club, knocked on the door, only to be faced with "Shimmy" Patton, who informed him that a machine gun was trained on his chest. If the prosecutor entered the building, he would be shot.

Cullinan withdrew to a gas station across the street and called Cuyahoga County Sheriff John Sulzmann, who had known about the illegal gambling and other crimes for the previous five years. He had allegedly been on the take the entire time since he had the manpower and the authority to raid the club at any time.

The sheriff said he could not help the prosecutor. He said that he had to follow "home rule," meaning that he could not act in any manner, including providing armed support for the prosecutor, without the authorization of the Newburgh Heights mayor. The mayor had not provided authorization and was conveniently unreachable.

Desperate, Cullinan called every official he could think to call, including Ness. Although the reputation Ness developed as a fighter of organized crime during the Prohibition era and beyond was greatly exaggerated (men who worked with him said he never carried a gun and would sometimes seek a stiff drink and the company of an attractive woman when he was off-duty), he did stop most of the major organized crime figures in Chicago and Cleveland during his day. He could not be bribed and delighted in the challenge of fighting the criminal element.

Ness said that he would bring bodyguards for Cullinan, though he could not force the sheriff or anyone else to take action. He went to the police station, where he found eight Cleveland police officers just coming off duty. He asked them to volunteer to serve as bodyguards, warning them that they probably had no legal police powers in Newburgh Heights. They would be there strictly as an armed show of force.

What happened next was humorous and demonstrated the realities of the times. Cullinan arrived at the club in the early evening. As he spoke on the telephone trying to obtain assistance, cars pulled up to the club and all gambling paraphernalia was removed. Money, slot machines, and all other evidence were taken out. It was not until 10:30 P.M., an hour and a half after all the gambling equipment had been removed, that he was admitted.

No one left a machine gun behind, but there was violence from an unexpected source. Byron Filkins, a five foot two inch photographer for *The Press,* one of several newspapers in the city at that time, decided to photograph the empty club. He stood on a stool and began adjusting his Speed Graphic when a five foot eleven bouncer, annoyed by the interruption of the normal night's activities, walked over. The bouncer knocked Filkins from the stool, an action that enraged a reporter for the rival *News.* The reporter, an inch taller and somewhat stronger than the bouncer, decked the man who had struck Filkins. Immediately the other reporters and photographers got into the battle, tangling with the employees of the club. The police Ness had arranged to serve as bodyguards for Cullinan spent the evening restoring order among the combatants.

A second raid during that same period was made at the Thomas Club. This was a smaller operation and no one resisted arrest. As a result, a better picture of such an operation emerged. Among the items seized were thirteen slot machines for dimes and quarters, three "costly" roulette wheels and layouts, seven crap tables, and four chuck-a-luck cages and tables. There were more than a thousand silver dollars, half dollars, and quarters and a .32 caliber revolver, a sawed-off shotgun, a tear gas pistol, a blackjack, and a large sheath knife. In addition, they found a telegraph switch panel, key, resonator, and loudspeaker set to allow for the receiving and announcing of racetrack results from around the country.

Another newspaper, the *Plain Dealer,* noted that the Thomas Club had other interesting aspects:

> Along one of the walls was an immense racing chart on which were posted results at Santa Anita, Alamo Down, and Fair Grounds. The board occupied half of one side of the immense room. Along another side were twelve payoff windows—nine of them open and three closed.
>
> The moving van—a ton-and-a-half truck—had to make two trips to remove the equipment, which included a desk and two large safes found in the office.
>
> A sign over the payoff windows in the club listed seven locations in Cleveland from which seven-passenger sedans left with customers for the club every fifteen minutes from noon to 6 P.M. each day.

The raids fascinated Ness as much as they did the public. By February 1, he was able to announce that gambling in Cleveland alone was a $200,000 per week business. Policy gambling was estimated at $7 million per year, primarily in the area from East 9th to East 105th Street, and from Cedar Avenue south.

On February 14, 1936, *The Press* gave a hint as to the gambling joints that existed, none of which was legal and none of which was closed as a result of the disclosure. Among those listed, along with the newspaper's comments about them, were the following:

Old Arcade. The fruit merchant at the Superior entrance has no bananas but lots of betslips.

Gale's Restaurant, 408 W. Superior. Caters to newsboys, takes bets from 10 cents up, employs solicitors to collect them from the youthful customers.

Columbia Smoke Shop, 111 High Avenue, run by Jackie Price. One of the biggest downtown places. Cards are played as camouflage, a wee button shifts the loudspeaker from music to the more esthetic cries of the tracks.

"Slimey's" Place, 819 Vincent, Room 434. Cards and craps are offered. The password is: "The Dago sent me."

Hotel Gillsy, George (Yellow) Abbey moves from room to room, but anyone standing around will direct you to his latest location if you have a nice, gentle face and are kind to your mother.

Whitman's Place, 1700 E. Ninth, Cherry 8816. William May is manager. (Note to anyone interested: He keeps the slips in his left-hand pocket, the money in his right.)

I didn't have the sophistication of the men who ran the big joints, but I had the same desire to make money any way I could. Nothing mattered to me except that. My parents were gone. I was out of school. And all I had ever known were gamblers, bootleggers, corrupt cops, judges on the take, and people out for themselves. I wanted my own piece of the action.

A kid who wants to be a tough guy both becomes a user and is used in turn, though he never understands that at the time. I adored Bill Presser. He was part father, part brother to me. When he was seriously ill and in the hospital 10 or 11 years before he died, I wept with him. Yet when I was busy being a punk in the thirties and he was running with some tough Italians, working the so-called union business, he was frequently in danger. There was always the chance that someone would bomb his car as the car of Sam Salupo, one of the brothers with whom he worked, had been bombed.

In Sam Salupo's case, the bombing was quite clever. He had been in jail when Bill first became involved with the brothers. After he got out, he began stepping on too many toes. He did not realize that he had made enemies who would finish him off.

Sam was driving his seventeen-year-old girlfriend to work in Shaker Heights, a wealthy Cleveland suburb, when he used his car horn. The horn was attached to a bomb hidden in the car, a bomb that killed both Sam and the girl.

More common were bombs connected with the ignition that would explode when you started the engine. Bill never said that he was afraid of being blown up; he just paid me anywhere from fifty cents to two dollars each morning to start his Studebaker. That was a lot of money for a fifteen-year-old kid, and I never thought that Bill was actually paying me to get blown up if his car had been wired. It probably wouldn't have mattered if I had known. I wasn't afraid of anyone or anything. I knew nobody could hurt me with all the wisdom of a punk teenager.

Bombings were never very organized when I was a kid, though they were the standard way to deal with anyone who gave you trouble. A stink bomb would force the owner to spend hundreds or thousands of dollars to strip the floors and replace wood, clean, and do whatever else had to be done after the foul-smelling chemical got into the woodwork. A firebomb might destroy a business or home. And dynamite was used in a variety of ways, for everything from terrorism to murder.

Later there would be a language of bombs. First there was the warning, which might come in the form of a stink bomb released in a home or business, or a stick of dynamite left on a car. Maybe the person had refused to cooperate by paying a bribe. In that case, the dynamite served to indicate that the person who left it was angry. The recipient had to start doing whatever was asked or there would be a serious price to pay. Or perhaps the person receiving the stick of dynamite had become involved with rackets in which he did not belong. For example, there might be one person handling shakedowns in the building trades, another in charge of west side prostitution, and a third who controlled gambling. If the man who ran illegal gambling joints decided to offer a few girls to the gamblers, an action that would cut into the territory of the man who controlled prostitution, the man who controlled prostitution would place a stick of dynamite on the gambling king's car. It was a friendly warning: the dynamite not set to explode.

The next level of warning involved the exploding of a bomb that was not meant to kill the person who was being given a warning. His business might be dynamited late at night when no one was around to get hurt. Or his car might be blown up when no one was inside. This type of bombing indicated the seriousness of the victim's action and was the final warning the person would receive. The third level of bombing was meant to kill.

We didn't do things that professionally back in the 1930s. Bill Presser hired my brother Harry to throw bombs into the businesses that were not cooperating with the union shakedown racket. Harry had me go along and wait behind the wheel while he went into the shopping area and heaved the firebomb into the business. Then he'd race to the car and we'd make our getaway.

What I wanted most in those days was one big score. I had no real talent for anything, no training to take the available jobs that might have a future. I could work in a gas station, but that paid between twenty and thirty dollars a week for what might be sixty hours or more. Such straight jobs were just too slow.

A friend of mine and I obtained an old postal truck. We'd use it to go where there were truck trailers loaded with merchandise, stealing whatever we could. I was a strong kid, so I used to grab whatever was on the truck—furniture, furs, clothing, or anything else—while my friend kept watch. We never ran into the police back then, but if a truck driver or night watchman showed up, we'd threaten him to get him to leave. Once in a while we had to punch someone out, though no one ever had us arrested.

We sold things through a fence, a guy named Al who ran a pawnshop and could get rid of most things. What he couldn't handle was taken by guys we learned were specialists. I suspect that we received 20 to 30 percent of the resale value if we were lucky. We really didn't care. We were kids who didn't know anything, who only wanted money. If we found diamond jewelry when we broke into someone's house, Al could have told us it was only glass and we would have believed him.

Most of the kids looked up to me in those days. I had been having girls almost from the time I was old enough to have sex. And I was one of the ones who got some of the younger ones their first lays.

I also was seen as a tough guy who would stand up to anyone. Thus a lot of the kids wanted to live adventures they knew they'd never dare have through what I had the guts to do.

For example, I had always been involved with petty theft. I'd go into gas stations to steal batteries, chains, and anything else I could sell quickly. Sometimes I'd spot new cars, follow them, then steal their parts.

I'd also roll drunks who had been gambling. I'd go to a crap game or poker game and, because I was always big for my age, everyone assumed that it was all right for me to be there. I'd watch to see a big winner who was also drunk. Then I'd follow him out, beat him, and take his money. I certainly didn't advertise that I was rolling drunks, but I had the money, word got around, and a lot of kids knew I was doing it.

Pretty soon it became a big thing for kids to tell me about scores I could make. "I have an aunt who's loaded. She has all this jewelry and furs" would be a typical greeting.

The score I was promised was always a big one. Usually we were told that there were thousands of dollars hidden in the house. One kid told me that a relative had fifty thousand dollars, for example, but when a friend of mine and I searched the place, there was only eight hundred dollars.

One kid told me about a barber on Cleveland's west side who gave illegal abortions to desperate pregnant women. I was told that he was always paid cash, and again the kid who fingered the barber said that we would get at least $50,000.

The barber was home when we got there, but we didn't care. We knew it didn't matter whether he could identify us because he was never going to report us to the police for stealing the money he made committing a crime like performing an abortion. We tied him up, then discovered that his wife was in the bathtub, taking a bath, the door locked. We kicked in the door, grabbed her out of the tub, tied her up, then began torturing him. We used matches on him to make him talk, eventually getting everything he had at home—twelve hundred dollars. It was a good score, but it wasn't what we expected. We also never gave the kid who fingered the barber a fair share, though we gave him enough so we knew he'd come to us again.

One kid, Blackie, probably gave me three or four tips a year, none of them very good. In fact, only once did I make a really big score and that was when I got lucky by following a jewelry salesman. I took five or six thousand dollars off the guy, then spent it on girls, gambling, and clothes.

Had I been caught breaking into homes, I would have gone to jail for a long time. There was a stiff penalty for entering a place that was occupied, but I didn't care. I was both good at what I did and lucky when there was a chance someone would complain. When the money I was stealing came from crimes the home owner was committing, like the $1,200 from the barber who performed abortions, there was no chance that a complaint would be filed. Everybody had too much to lose.

The fact that the police were corrupt also helped. I remember one time when I hijacked a truck and was going to sell the contents. It was loaded with radios, a popular item back then since the radio was the main source of home entertainment. Soon after the score, I was contacted by the police department's labor squad. The detectives had figured out that I was the kid who stole the radios and they wanted me to do them a favor. They wanted six radios for themselves and six for the chief of police. The ones for the chief were to be in different colors, an easy request to fill.

Everywhere it was going on like that. Gambling joints were raided regularly on what might have been a schedule. At least one was hit every two to three months, the cops smashing a card table or some other equipment while the newspaper photographers took their photographs. The place was always tipped off and would always be able to operate a minimum of six months before the next raid.

Judges who liked gambling, drinking, and women were provided whatever they desired. If a horse race was fixed, the judge would be tipped off as to how to bet so that he could brag to his friends that he got lucky.

One city councilman paid me and a friend, Harold Friedman (no relation), to tear down his opponent's signs when he was running for judge. He liked to gamble and saw nothing wrong with people who made their living running gambling joints. Once he won the election as judge, he had a habit of finding anyone who was charged with gambling offenses innocent.

Everybody was tied in to everybody else, and the only person who seemed to care was the Cleveland safety director, Eliot Ness. Ness would change the face of the city during the period when I was in the army during World War II. He went after the people involved in the labor union protection rackets, attacked the bootleggers, and cracked down on gambling. He used a group of handpicked men, some legitimate law enforcement officers and some involved as private investigators, in order to accomplish his ends. He also restructured the Cleveland Police Department, adding patrol cars with radios, a police academy for proper training, and other improvements that made it a professional force. By the time Ness left Cleveland in 1942, the old rackets that dominated Cleveland had been radically changed. They were far from eliminated, just more sophisticated and careful about where their activities took place.

While I was hustling for money and my teenage years were coming to an end, Jackie Presser was growing into manhood. I never thought much about Jackie, though I loved my nephew even when he turned on me when we were older. But when you're sixteen and seventeen years old, an eleven-year-old kid can be a nuisance, especially when that kid idolizes you. My friends were not his friends, and he was too young to hang around the places I liked to go. However, the kids who were running with him then, men and women who are now in their sixties, talked about Jackie to me.

Bill Presser had taken me in, and Bill was becoming quite successful financially, but Jackie and I were quite different in our attitudes. I was born to great wealth, greater than Jackie knew as a kid, but the money came with a street toughness even before my parents died.

Bill and Faye were tough people who were always attacking each other, yet deeply in love. One of their friends, now living in retirement in Florida, spoke of double dating to go see westerns at a movie theater in downtown Cleveland.

Traffic was heavy near the theater as Faye, who was driving, looked for a parking place. A policeman was guiding the cars to keep everyone moving and he made them drive to a lot where Bill did not want to go. After they passed the police officer, he began cursing the man to the other occupants of the car. He swore quietly at the cop, suggestions some obscene actions the man could perform on himself for preventing them from parking more conveniently.

Faye listened to this tirade, then proceeded to continue driving around the block. She returned to where the policeman was standing, pulled to a stop, rolled down the window, and said, "Officer, there's something my husband would like to tell you." Bill, red-faced, was unable to speak.

Another time Bill and Faye went into a Chinese restaurant, where Faye decided to steal some of the silverware. When the staff was not looking, she hid the silverware in her bosom. Then they walked to the cashier to pay for the meal.

Suddenly Bill grabbed Faye's blouse, pulled it from her skirt, and jerked on it. The silverware fell from her bra and went tumbling to the floor, clattering together.

As Bill began making good money in the 1930s and Faye was heavily involved with gambling, she began going through his pants pockets to look for money. She was in the habit of stealing from him whenever she could, thinking he was asleep and would not realize what was happening. However, she discovered otherwise when a small mousetrap snapped shut on her fingers, startling rather than hurting her. Bill had written on the trap, "Ha Ha! You think I don't know what you do?"

Bill spoiled Jackie when he was a kid. My sister and brother-in-law were making money then, so Jackie never wanted for anything. There were pinball and game machines in the basement where Jackie's friends claimed they lost all their money. In fact, they used to call it the "12000 Club" because the home was at 12000 Scottwood Avenue.

Jackie was always considered the life of any party as a kid. His closest friends used to refer to him as the "little Lou Costello," comparing him to the fat comic partner in the team of Abbott & Costello.

Friends talk about the petty crimes Jackie used to plan. They would break into gumball machines, cutting the chain that secured the machine, then taking it to the roof of a gas station, where they could empty the change without being seen.

"One time we took all the cases of empty bottles from an RC Cola truck," said Mario, one of Jackie's friends from the time they met at Patrick Henry Junior High. "We could get a nickel for each bottle and I wanted to take the cases in and get all the money. But Jackie had more sense. He knew we'd be caught for stealing them. So Jackie had us hide the cases, then take a couple of bottles at a time for refunds so we could get a dime and go swimming. We went swimming all summer with the money."

The day Jackie decided to become a gangster was when he learned about a wealthy woman who was living at the Alcazar Hotel. The Alcazar had a number of wealthy, long-term residents in addition to high-income transients. The woman was supposed to be out of town, leaving jewelry and other valuables in her rooms.

Jackie talked his girlfriend and a boy named Howard into going to the Alcazar to rob the woman. Jackie and Howard obtained guns, the girlfriend being used to get them through the lobby. The staff would not be so suspicious of a young female as they would two young men.

His former girlfriend, speaking of herself, Jackie, and Howard, said, "We got into the Alcazar and we got in front of this woman's apartment door, and I was between the two of them. I looked at both of them and I said, 'Are we crazy? We can go to jail. What if somebody comes in?' And I turned around and I ran. I mean, I literally ran, and two seconds later the two of them were right behind me."

Jackie's first big-time caper came to an end before it started. Later he would hit drunks and bookmakers on the head when he and some friends wanted to steal their money, but at that moment, the fear his girlfriend expressed infected him too badly to continue. They all ran from the Alcazar, the woman's possessions undefiled.

There were other things taking place during that period. There were gang fights, such as the Parkwood riots, in which a group of Polish kids attacked some Orthodox Jewish rabbis, pulling their beards and generally harassing the old men.

The Jewish kids in the neighborhood were upset with what was happening and wanted to fight. Jackie spread the story that he rounded up all the kids into a gang so that they could avenge the neighborhood. Years later his public relations people and some of his close friends who were beholden to him for favors promoted the "tough guy" myth that he and the other kids went after the Polish kids with bats and other weapons. It sounded impressive, a little like a fight in the play *West Side Story*.

What really happened was that a bunch of us older guys hung around the poolroom all the time. When the trouble went down, one of the younger kids let us know. We had our pool cues and just went out, beating the troublemakers and sending them back to their neighborhoods. We were bigger than most of them, were used to street fights, and handled the problem in a few minutes. The truth wasn't as dramatic as the myth, though, and Jackie encouraged the local legend.

And there were girls. Jackie was a great womanizer who always had one girlfriend or another. He was fat, but there was something about him that attracted girls, even when he was a teenager.

The hustles, the gambling, the girls, all meant very little when the war years came. We had been attacked by the Japanese at Pearl Harbor. There was a war in Europe against Hitler. All of us boys were aware that we would soon be leaving our neighborhoods to fight in the war.

THE ARMY

I'd like to say that I did something heroic, but I never charged a group of Nazi machine gunners or single-handedly slaughtered a battalion of crack Japanese troops. Instead I joined the army like so many other guys because I truly believed in supporting my country and we were at war. I enlisted, though that probably would not have mattered. A friend of mine, Harold Friedman, also planned to enlist, then backed out at the last minute. Yet he was soon in the military, having been drafted.

I took my basic training in Cheyenne, Wyoming, then was sent to Omaha, Nebraska, where they wanted to train me to be an auto mechanic. I knew at once that the army gave no thought to what a soldier was capable of handling. I have trouble unscrewing a light bulb without detailed directions. The idea of my fixing a Jeep or truck that had to carry soldiers into combat was ridiculous.

Omaha came as a surprise to me. Our camp was just outside the city limits, but the attitude of the people of that community was such that it was as though we had just freed them from occupation by the Nazis. They couldn't do enough for us.

People talk about the way communities take advantage of soldiers. Each weekend, when we'd get passes to go into town, the moment we left the base there must have been a line of cars a mile or two long lined up, waiting for us. The cars were owned by families in Omaha who would invite one or more soldiers to their homes to spend the weekend. "Soldier, you want to come home to dinner with us?" they'd ask. There was nothing they wanted from it. They'd have us to dinner or for a weekend in their homes just to be nice.

I wouldn't go for that. I wanted some broads. So I took the bus into Omaha, then found a cab driver and said to him, "Where's a place that really jumps?"

I was taken to a bar where a lot of hockey players hung around. It had the same excitement as some of the spots in Cleveland where the mob and the politicians used to hang out. Yet even in that place, I'd sit at a table for two or a table for four and, because they were crowded, I'd be asked whether I'd mind sharing. I always said no, and then some stranger would sit down and take the check. You couldn't pay for anything in Omaha because the people were so grateful to the soldiers for what they were doing.

There was this really pretty waitress working in the nightspot and I began kidding her. One night she said, "What you doing tonight, soldier?"

"Anything I can get my hands on," I told her.

"Then you've got your hands on me," she said, and she took me home to her place. The next thing I knew, I was living with her on the weekends. She'd give me spending money and I really fell in love with her.

I still didn't know what to do about being a mechanic when there was a sign posted on the bulletin board at the camp. There was a paratrooper who was holding a meeting, looking for volunteers to enlist. Curious, I decided to attend.

There were only four or five of us who showed up to hear the paratrooper, a sergeant who was dressed like a higher-ranking officer. He had an officer's uniform shirt with all sorts of patches and medals on it. His pants were secured at the ankle by a rubber band, then inserted into the high boots he wore. Those boots had a shine so bright that you could see your reflection in the leather.

Everything about him was unconventional. There were no khaki pants of the kind we all wore, not even regulation bootlaces. He wore white laces made from the cord used to hold parachutes. It was the most impressive uniform I had ever seen, and when I finally joined the paratroopers, I dressed just as he did when I was home on leave. I didn't dress like that on the base, though. Neither did he. The uniform was a false one put together with clothing he had purchased and clothing that was government-issued (GI). We didn't look much better in training than I looked in my uniform when I was studying to be a mechanic. But when he was recruiting, he was the sharpest dresser I had seen in the military.

The paratrooper was a big guy who impressed me with his toughness. I also liked hearing about the great pay.

A GI serving during World War II was paid $50 a month. But according to this recruiter, pay was $50 a jump for the paratroopers. He said we'd jump at least five times during our training, so that was $250 right there. Then he mentioned that if I became a sergeant, my base pay would jump to $96 a month and I would still receive that $50 per jump.

I didn't fear death or injury. If all I had to do for the equivalent of a month's pay was jump from an airplane, then that seemed to be the perfect work for me. Certainly it was better than being a grease monkey trying to fix a truck with my two left hands. I immediately signed up.

I went back and told the girl I was living with that I was going to enlist in the paratroopers, and that would mean going to Fort Benning, Georgia, to train. She wanted me to marry her, so we talked about maybe doing it after I finished my paratrooper training.

For a while my personal life got more exciting than my training. I had been dating a girl named Doris in Cleveland and she wanted to get married. I guess she figured that she could force my hand if she announced our engagement. All I know is that suddenly the Cleveland papers had the announcement of our forthcoming marriage. In fact, much later, when I went home on leave, I discovered that there was a surprise engagement party being thrown in our honor. I had to take Doris aside, explain that we would go through with the party, but that later we would quietly explain that we decided to call off the wedding. That way she could save face, since there was no way I was going to marry her.

The training was much harder than we expected. We'd jog five miles every morning, often with a full backpack. We constantly worked out and I was in the best shape of my life. However, I quickly learned that the base pay was the same and that there was no bonus for making the jumps. Still, it beat trying to be a mechanic and having my hands greasy all the time, though almost half the guys never finished.

Oddly my regiment was 507, an ironic coincidence because, many years later, I would belong to Teamsters Local 507, the power base that would launch Jackie

Presser to national attention. But at that time the idea of my being involved with unions or politics was not something I could imagine.

I was lucky when I was in the paratroopers because I met a second lieutenant who took a liking to me. He also began getting promotions, taking me with him each time he moved up in rank. When he became a first lieutenant, he made me a private, first class. When he became a captain, I was made a corporal. And when he made major, I became a sergeant.

I got in good with the officer when my brother, Harry, brought me a quantity of gasoline ration stamps to use while I was stateside. My brother Joe was driving a gasoline truck, and I guess he was stealing ration coupons he gave to Harry. I had a car I didn't need very much so I would let the officer use it, giving him some of the coupons so he could go pleasure driving with his wife. I gave him enough rationing stamps so that when he went out in another officer's car, he would supply the stamps to buy gas.

There was a lot of rationing during the war, sugar, gasoline, and other products all being scarce. Everything was being diverted to the war effort, though there were different coupons you could use for your authorized share. Gasoline was in such short supply that the coupons were carefully controlled and it was a real luxury even to be able to go for a Sunday ride. Most of the other stamps were sold to the few guys who had cars, giving me a few extra bucks while I was in camp.

I've always been lucky in my life. There have been a number of times when I would have died had things gone a little differently, something I first discovered when I was in the army.

It came time for my outfit to move out and go into combat, but the officer I befriended was asked to stay behind to train a group of Mormon boys arriving from Utah. He asked me to help him teach them to jump instead of shipping out with the 507. I would see action later, the delay only being the length of one more training camp. I agreed.

The 507 was sent to Italy for combat, but somebody made a mistake. Instead of their jumping where they were supposed to go, the plane dropped them into a red zone.

A red zone was a section no American soldiers were supposed to enter. It was a section of intense combat where it was presumed that everyone who entered was an enemy. No one realized that American boys were being dropped into the territory, a section close to the ocean. As they came down, American battleships, assuming them to be enemy paratroopers, blasted the men from the skies. Most of my unit was killed, as I probably would have been had it not been for the chance request to stay behind.

I was eventually sent to Columbus, Georgia, and then to Fort Bragg, North Carolina, where I worked in a variety of positions, training other paratroopers, running a recreation area, and, in Columbus, working Chute Patrol. Each branch of the service had its own police force. The Navy had Shore Patrol, the Army had the Military Police, and the Paratroopers had Chute Patrol. We'd go to areas where there were a lot of our guys and try to keep them in line.

I was assigned to an amusement park near the base, a place where a lot of the guys went to relax on weekends. I liked to stand around with my chest sticking out, my muscles showing. I was big and strong and the girls thought I was good-looking.

As I was standing, just watching the crowd, the most beautiful girl I had ever seen in my life walked by with a blond and two soldiers. Then, two or three minutes later, she walked back and went by me again. The third time she did it, she was looking at me and I told her to come over. This was the woman who would become my first wife.

I was making a lot of money from my gambling, so I bought a car down there. My brother Joe was sending me more gasoline ration stamps so I was doing well. I rented an apartment off the base and we began living together.

The one thing I didn't realize was that she was a heavy drinker. That would eventually cause me problems, but in those days I was young, she was beautiful, and that was all that mattered.

Eventually I went to Scotland, England, and finally France. We traveled by boat to Europe and the trip to Scotland was miserable. We went on the *New Amsterdam,* a cruise ship converted for war use. It was supposedly the fastest ship in the world and could outrun any of the enemy ships. I don't know whether that was true or not, but they didn't give us an armed escort.

The trouble with the ship was that it had to take an evasive pattern of movement. We would zig and zag across the ocean, the constant movement making the seas even more choppy than normal. Everybody got sick, most of the guys unable to keep any food in their stomachs, and two of the men died on the trip. When I began vomiting bile, one of the other men told me I had to force myself to eat or I might die as well. Finally some of us sneaked into the lifeboat area to sleep at night so we could have more fresh air. With five thousand of us on board, and all of us sick, there seemed to be no room to breathe and I think that made us worse. Once I had been in the open air for a couple of days, I began to feel better.

I did a lot of training before I had to see any action, and sometimes I was surprised by the men. There was one guy I was trying to teach to throw hand grenades. But the guy couldn't throw a grenade to save his life. He'd toss it and it would never go far enough to protect his own men. Finally I became disgusted and told my commanding officer that the guy was just no good. I said that he should go into the kitchen to work because there was no way I was going to be in a foxhole fifteen feet from him and risk his tossing a grenade into my foxhole instead of the enemy's. He was that bad.

It was not long after that an incident occurred that showed me you can't always tell about someone unless he's under pressure. One of the pilots was flying an old wooden plane when he lost control and crashed near us. We were warned to stay away because the fuel tank was likely to explode and burn at any moment. The officers realized from past experience that with a crash like that, it was best to let the pilot die, if he wasn't dead already, because otherwise the rescuers would probably be killed. Everybody obeyed except one man, the guy I thought was worthless. He ran to the downed plane and dragged the pilot to safety. I thought he was a jerk for the way he couldn't throw a grenade and he turned out to be a hero.

I was eventually assigned to the 1288th Combat Engineers, which was both a building and a fighting unit. One of my jobs was to clear fields of land mines. We weren't in direct combat zones but were just ahead of the troops who were doing the heavy fighting. Land mines—explosive devices that were set to blow up when someone stepped on them—were left behind by all sides as they retreated, and they had to be removed before the combat forces moved in pursuit of the fleeing enemy. Otherwise a lot of lives might be lost.

Cleaning out the mines was dangerous because, if you made a mistake, you would be killed. I used to take a grappling hook, a large device with four prongs, that was tied to one end of a rope. The other end was tied to the bumper of a Jeep.

I would take the hook on the rope, spinning it around my head like a lariat, then heave it as far as I could. Then my partner would slowly drive the Jeep forward while the hook dragged through the dirt, exploding any mines with which it came in contact.

We also had metal detectors we could use, especially when we were flown a few miles ahead of the troops, then dropped into an area to clear out the mines. However, when it came to the river area, the normal devices did not work. Ore boats used the river, dropping bits of metal that gave false readings. We had to use long probes to check for the mines.

Again I got lucky. I was supposed to check for mines in an area where no one thought there was a problem. However, I had been working for three or four days without a break and I was tired. We were also getting sniper fire at a time when another outfit, in the clear and not so overworked, was located just a quarter mile down the road. I suggested to the major, my friend from the training days, that he send some men from the other outfit because the risks seemed less for them.

The major agreed, but the men who went didn't take normal precautions. Instead of using a long probe as they approached the shore, they went right to the beach and jumped out—onto some mines. All of them were killed because of their carelessness.

Despite the work, much of my time was spent making money. The war had cost many of the French people all of their possessions. We ran into many of them who had money but no way to buy shirts, shoes, and other necessities. They were always offering to buy our blankets, uniform clothes, and anything else we had that they could use.

I knew the supply sergeant and the sergeant who ran the mess hall, so I set up a small business. I went to the motor pool and got a truck, then the supply sergeant loaded the truck with blankets, sheets, shoes, shirts, caps, sweaters, and other things. A few of us drove into town and sold it all, splitting the money with whoever stole the merchandise.

We'd do the same with food, selling butter, flour, bacon, or whatever else the mess sergeant could steal. Everything sold and we all made a lot of money.

The biggest sale I got was with a guy who came to me and asked whether I could get him a Jeep. I told him I could, but warned him that he might get caught with it. He didn't know my name so he'd take whatever penalty they gave him.

The man said he could handle it. He lived on a farm that was quite remote, and he planned to paint the Jeep so that it could not be spotted.

I went back to the motor pool and stole the Jeep, and he gave me a lot of money for it. The French francs were worth twelve and a half cents in American money so that every American dollar was worth eight francs. My pockets were bulging after the sale.

I did get into a little trouble during this time. I always had a lot of money on me and I was sending a lot of money home. The army discovered what I was doing and realized that something was wrong. I was called in and accused of working the black market.

I've always been pretty good at covering myself in a bad situation. I told them that I had nothing to do with the black market, knowing that none of the guys who were helping me steal would talk. I said that they should drop around on payday and see what was going on. I told them about all the gambling and crap games that went on, and the fact that I was lucky gambling.

I knew that the gambling I did wouldn't account for the twelve to fifteen thousand dollars I had in my possession, but they didn't. A lot of guys gambled and the stakes were pretty big. It probably was against regulations, but no one cared about that, only about the black market.

My friend, the major, backed up my story. They couldn't prove I was lying and I could have made that money gambling for all they knew. They decided to let me go, warning me that I would have trouble with the IRS when I got back. "I'll worry about that if I live," I told them.

Although there were high risks checking for mines and danger from snipers, the only serious action we anticipated was when we were sent to clean up the German soldiers in Dusseldorf. Our unit was working with the British, who performed a softening-up operation. What that meant was that, for five days and nights, they constantly fired rockets, mortars, and cannon shells into the city, which was one of the last holdouts of German soldiers in our area. After the five days of shelling, we were to go in and take control of the men.

All of us were nervous, waiting for the action to happen. This would be large-scale, direct combat, something we had not experienced before. We knew that if our number was up, this was probably where we would get shot. However, the shelling had been so intense that, when we entered the city, the soldiers threw down their weapons and surrendered. Most were in shock and many had bloody ears because the noise of the explosions had shattered their eardrums. They all stood, terrified, shouting, "Me no Nazi. Me no Nazi."

I was discharged from the army in 1946, married and with a healthy bankroll. The marriage was a folly of youth that I would soon regret. Bill Presser was becoming a major behind-the-scenes figure in organized labor, and the roll of the mob was becoming entrenched in the movement. The names of mobsters, labor leaders, and politicians on the rise would all soon become familiar to me. I would become a slugger on picket lines, an arsonist, and a bomber, taking orders from men like my brother-in-law Bill and Jimmy Hoffa.

But for the moment, all I knew was that the world had changed. I was married, had seen men die, had been to several countries, and had enjoyed the favors of dozens of women, many of whom could not speak English. I never imagined that, as I fought and schemed my way through life, I would be helping to make a part of American labor history.

2

The War Years

As I LOOK BACK on the war years, remembering my own experiences, interviewing men and women who were slightly older during that time, and reviewing the newspapers and magazines of that period, it is obvious that there were three profound changes in American society during the war years. The first was the end of the illegal whiskey business, a situation that began in 1937, a time when Americans only knew of turmoil in Europe secondhand and were still naive enough to think that we would not be drawn into violence.

The Cleveland Syndicate (also known as the "Combination") made the decision that they would have no more whiskey deals. Prohibition, the Eighteenth Amendment to the Constitution, was officially repealed on December 5, 1933. Yet the transportation and sale of liquor remained a good business for organized crime for several years following repeal. It was only in 1937 that the decision to abandon such business was reached.

The second major change was the entry of women into the work force. Prior to the war years, the "ideal" woman, according to much of the popular press of the day, was the good-time girl of café society who did the Lambeth Walk, the rumba, and other popular dances of the day. Her dress was the strapless evening gown with the new under-wire bra. It was a daring type of outfit, a challenge to the conventions of the past.

"Proper" behavior for women in society was often determined by Elsa Maxwell, a woman who, under other circumstances, might be described as a "fat broad" with no particular talent other than a quick tongue. Maxwell came from Keokuk, Iowa, with nothing but an obvious lust for food, drink, and a good

45

time, coupled with a skill at self-promotion. She held parties where the rich and famous were regularly present, and she once defined her idea of the ideal woman for Inez Robb, a columnist who quoted Maxwell in *The New York Mirror* for December 16, 1938. Maxwell stated:

> First, I want a woman guest to be beautiful. Second, I want her to be beautifully dressed. Third, I demand animation and vivacity. Fourth, not too many brains. Brains are always awkward at a gay and festive party. Brains are only a requisite when the party is limited to a handful of persons, say six or eight.
> And fifth, I expect obedience. It's ruinous if guests refuse to cooperate with a hostess if she asks them to dance, play games, go on a treasure hunt, tell stories, guess riddles or whatever she has planned for the occasion.

When war came, some women followed the patterns of the past, though they did things with older men. Frequently a woman in her twenties was drawn to a man twenty years her senior because he was available and not eligible for the draft. Marriages of convenience were relatively common, eligible young men entering the military either by choice or by orders of Uncle Sam.

But most women simply went to work. Many were hired by defense plants which needed workers to keep up with war material production. Others filled in on jobs that once would have been the exclusive domain of males. There were jokes and songs about "Rosie the riveter" by men in uniform who thought the circumstances were temporary. They would fight the war, they would return home, and the natural order of life would be the same. What they did not expect was that women would like being independent, would enjoy having their own money, would want careers.

And the third major change was in the field of entertainment. This was an era of gadgets, the forerunner of the video arcade phenomenon that seemed to sweep America in the late 1970s. Pinball machines, Ski-Ball, and numerous other gaming devices held a fascination for the public. The vending machine industry became a major success, and coin-operated jukeboxes were installed in bars, restaurants, diners, and other businesses throughout the country. Millions of dollars were being earned in an industry that seemed ready-made for organized crime. The return was in cash, a situation that allowed for skimming, kickbacks, and still enough volume to assure that everyone profited.

The millions of returning servicemen and servicewomen did not care who was involved in the jukebox industry. All they knew was that dancing to the records, whether in a soda fountain or in a restaurant, was the ideal way to spend an evening. By 1946, both the Decca and RCA record companies were selling 100 million singles each. Five billion nickels were "officially" put into 400,000 jukeboxes throughout the nation. An unknown number more, perhaps half again as many, were "skimmed" before the official count began.

During the war years Bill Presser entered the vanguard of this new industry. He was given a charter by the Electrical Workers' Union and began organizing the men who worked with jukeboxes and pinball machines.

Bill owed his charter to his partnership with John Nardi, the nephew of Tony Milano. It was only one of Bill's several links to organized crime.

To understand how all this occurred, you have to go back to an earlier time when a pair of brothers, Frank and Tony Milano, were first involved with Luciano's plans to dominate the Teamsters.

Frank Milano, along with a business partner of his, Chuck Polizzi, was among the men present at the infamous Mafia grand council meeting that was held at the Statler Hotel on December 5, 1928. At the time, Frank owned a saloon and social club at 12601 Mayfield Road in Cleveland, an area that was considered part of the Hill.

Frank was protected by the police, who knew he was running an illegal operation. The only time he was bothered by anyone was after a July 5, 1930, shooting that took place in Milano's saloon. The victims of the shooting were Joe Porello and Sam Tilocca, Porello shot three times in the head, Tilocca shot five times before crawling into the street to die. Tilocca's insensitivity to the ways of the corruption in law enforcement forced the police to violate past procedures and investigate the murder. Too many people had seen the corpse and everyone knew that Milano was present, along with three friends: John Angersola, Charles Colletti, and Alfred "Big Al" Polizzi. However, the four men explained that they heard nothing, saw nothing, and knew nothing, an unlikely situation but one which the investigating officers accepted as gospel. No charges were filed.

There was still the issue of a saloon's being operated during Prohibition. In order to give the appearance of following the law, the police searched Milano's home, noting that he had beer, whiskey, slot machines, automatic rifles, shotguns, account books, and canceled checks. The public assumed that such a search meant an arrest would be made if warranted. They did not realize that the police could only investigate, then present their findings to the county prosecutor. It was ultimately the prosecutor's decision whether or not to bring formal charges. Thus when nothing happened with a case, the public was expected to believe that the evidence was inadequate.

Milano's account books and canceled checks made fascinating reading for the county attorney, Ray T. Miller, who later became mayor of Cleveland. The books revealed that payoffs had been routinely made to numerous politicians and bootleg dealers. Miller, a realist in the ways of corruption, recognized that such knowledge could be used for his own advancement in Cleveland politics.

Prosecuting would make headlines, might gain a conviction, and would be the end of his own career. By not prosecuting and not releasing the specifics of what he found to the general public, he could make a number of extremely important men willing to show their gratitude by supporting his candidate for higher office. He quietly announced that there was no reason to prosecute Milano or any of the others involved.

Milano had a previous history of violence in his places of business. On October 8, 1927, for example, Frank Milano was operating a restaurant on Hough Avenue. He had previously run a speakeasy at 7310 Lexington Avenue, but that had been closed.

The Milano restaurant was visited on the eighth by Jack Brownstein and Ernest Yorkell, whom the Cleveland Police Department identified as Philadelphia gangsters. The Pennsylvania men had been running a shakedown operation against area bootleggers and planned to squeeze Frank Milano next. Although he was never linked to the murders, his restaurant was the last place the men visited before their bound corpses were found in Cleveland Heights.

Tony Milano, Frank's brother, was also in the restaurant and bootleg whiskey business, though his place, the Mayfield Road Inn, was at 12020 Mayfield Road back in 1928. He was the less aggressive of the two brothers, tough enough to be respected yet content to be a front man for Frank. He would eventually become one of the leading Cleveland Mafia figures, wealthy, powerful, deadly, yet never doing anything that Frank would not approve.

Frank Milano recognized that Prohibition would not last but that gambling was forever. He became involved with slot machines in 1930, often working with Gameboy Miller, who was then running the Thomas Club.

Miller introduced Milano to a technique that the Mafia would eventually use in other cities. It was also one that Jackie Presser relied upon, in a slightly different manner, to gain extra support from the Teamsters Union membership when there was pressure against him.

Miller knew that it was important to maintain a positive image in the community where he worked. He realized that it was not enough just to pay off the police: He also had to ensure that he would have an early warning system for any problems. Thus he began providing coal for twenty indigent Maple Heights families who would otherwise be likely to freeze during the winter, and he provided both food and shelter for an additional thirty poverty-stricken families.

Naturally, the community came to appreciate the gangsters. People knew that the police and other government officials were not helping them stay alive during hard times. Thus they felt a loyalty to the members of organized crime which was reflected in their willingness to help in some minor way when asked.

This relationship between the mob and the poor developed a carefully structured organization of its own in many Mafia-controlled communities over the next several decades. In Providence, Rhode Island, the Mafia leader placed two metal lawn chairs in front of his business during the warmer months, then sat on one and waited for someone to sit next to him. A favor would be asked by a poor person or someone seeking help for the poor. The favor would be granted and the person would then be in debt, a debt that might not have to be repaid for many years, the repayment at times being as simple as providing an alibi to cover a man's involvement in a crime.

In New York's Little Italy, numbers houses were placed in lower-income sections near the Bowery. Then elderly widows who would otherwise not have enough money to survive with dignity had their groceries supplemented, gained assistance with heating bills, and had help with anything else that proved a burden. Sometimes the elderly would approach the organized crime leaders themselves. At other times, friends and neighbors would make the appeals on their behalf. Either way there was a sense of gratitude and loyalty which was translated into an early warning system concerning police raids. Whenever anyone unfamiliar entered the area, the elderly women, often clad in black, stooped and troubled, would suddenly become animated, shouting warnings that the police had come. The women even took the trouble to learn the faces of the winos so that they would not be fooled by an undercover vice squad officer dressed in rags and carrying what appeared to be a bottle of liquor in a brown paper bag.

Cleveland, like Rhode Island, frequently used the patron/client arrangement of granting favors and establishing indebtedness. Bombings and murders would take place in front of witnesses who were somehow "distracted" just long enough to see nothing. Restaurant owners who had accepted favors from the Mafia would declare that a killer had been dining during the time a murder took place. And if enough patrons either owed favors or thought they might wish a favor in the months ahead, the police might encounter a room full of "honest" citizens who could give the killer an unshakable alibi.

When Jackie became a high Teamster official, he and his vice president, Harold Friedman, utilized a variation of this mob concept by taking special care of the retirees. They made certain that they had good pension checks, parties, and other benefits so that if there were a power play against them, they could be assured that the retirees formed a strong bloc vote in their favor. But that would come years later. We were just teenagers when we first observed the way the mob went out of its way to assist the elderly.

Frank and Tony Milano moved into other areas as well. They formed the Mayfield Importing Company to import such ethnic foods as olive oil and tomato paste. The business also served to cover the smuggling of any illegal substance.

The Mayfield Importing Company was linked with New York Mafia figure Joe

Profaci. It was also connected with the Brotherhood Loan Company, which formed a business called the Ohio Villa. The name of the company was an inside joke. The "Brotherhood" was alleged to be another name for the Unione Siciliana, which was supposedly run in Cleveland by the Milano brothers. However, most of the men and women who remember the Milano family say that they were from Calabria, an origin that would separate them from the Unione. However, in many areas, including Cleveland, the Unione was corrupted by members of the Mafia, making it into an organized crime outfit identical to the Brotherhood.

The Unione Siciliana had an interesting history. At first it was a legitimate secret society that was a fraternal organization for Sicilians living in the United States. Any city that had a decent-sized Sicilian population was likely to have a branch of the Unione, an organization not much different from similar groups in other ethnic areas.

When immigrants first came to the United States, they were not economically organized. If a man died, his friends and neighbors passed the hat to obtain enough money to pay for a burial. Otherwise the man would be relegated to a pauper's grave.

Groups such as the Unione Siciliana were formed, among other purposes, to establish insurance that would take the place of passing the hat to help the widow and children. The organization and the insurance were both legitimate and filled an important need within the community.

When Prohibition came, some of the members became bootleggers and alcohol cookers, working for organized crime figures. Making illegal liquor did not seem to be a serious crime, and the money from the mobsters was good. However, the membership and goals of the organization were slowly changing. In 1931, Lucky Luciano took control of the Unione Siciliana in some parts of the country and, within a few years, only racketeers could be members in those areas. (The Unione Siciliana still exists in some communities as a legitimate social organization. The comments about the changes refer to a large number of these groups but certainly not to all of them.)

Luciano had the sense to expand the Unione's membership so that it would go beyond the majority of the new members who were Mafiosi. He would not allow "straight" citizens to join where he was in control, and he also dropped the Sicilian heritage requirement. As a result, Meyer Lansky and Bug ("Bugsy" was not a nickname routinely used by his friends at the time) Siegel, both leaders of a powerful mob organization, joined because they were partners in the alcohol business with Joe Adonis of Brooklyn and Luciano.

J. Richard "Dixie" Davis, the lawyer for Dutch Schultz back in the 1930s and the man considered the most important outsider to be involved at the top of an organized crime ring, wrote at length about the Unione and other activities in

1936. His story was printed in six issues of *Collier's* magazine, the articles running from July 22 through August 26. He wrote, in part:

"I know that throughout the underworld the Unione Siciliana is accepted as a mysterious, all-pervasive reality, and that Lucky used it as the vehicle by which the underworld was drawn into co-operation on a national scale.

"Repeal of prohibition speeded up the centralization of control. Bootlegging had greatly increased the resources of the underworld and speeded its growth, but it also had created anarchy."

He later added:

> What had happened in the underworld under Lucky might be compared with the modern developments in trade associations, the NRA idea. The big fellows got together, whacked up territory, and agreed to eliminate the cut-throat competition of gang warfare and the competition of any outsiders. The Unione Siciliana served, you might say, as a sort of code authority.
>
> Power naturally stemmed from New York. In the first place, the old New York gangs had been a breeding ground for boss mobsters. Al Capone and Torrio had gone from New York to take over Chicago; also New Yorkers were the Bernsteins of the Purple mob [*sic*] of Detroit. And the natural weight of New York man power had been augmented by Lucky's alliance with the mobs of Lepke and of Meyer and the Bug.

Davis explained how the cities were divided, Moe Dalitz of the Cleveland Syndicate heading Cleveland, leaders of the Capone empire gaining control of Chicago, and so forth. "Gambling was a mainstay of the mobs that lived on after prohibition, and it was soon brought into control on a national basis," Davis explained.

Despite his rising power, Frank Milano was uncomfortable with the changes that had come to Cleveland in the early 1930s. He was not so strong as his brother, Tony, and did not want to fight men he could not bluff. For example, Frank Milano decided to declare an Italian neighborhood at East 116th Street and Kinsman to be off limits to federal officers. He informed a federal agent named Bob Bridges that he would not tolerate federal intervention in his business. He even went so far as to arrange a meeting with his attorney and several federal agents he felt were harassing him.

The agents wanted nothing to do with the deals Frank Milano wanted to make. They arrived at the meeting with submachine guns, then quietly explained to Frank Milano that if any of Milano's men tried to interfere with their work, they would shoot them.

Frank Milano was so intimidated that he moved to Vera Cruz, Mexico, in 1934. There he purchased coffee plantations and went into the lumber business.

He also formed a transportation network allowing him to smuggle men who had been deported from the United States back into America. He developed a route for smuggling people and contraband, running from Vera Cruz, through Arizona, a state that had been given to the Cleveland Mafia to dominate.

Frank Milano was good at smuggling. So many supposedly deported gangsters returned this way that the phenomenon was called smuggling "wet Italians." One such individual was Frank Cammerata, the brother-in-law of mobster Pete Licavoli, a bank robber who was deported in 1937. With Milano's help in 1939 Cammerata managed to sneak back into the United States, where he hid in Cleveland for the next seven years. Then, in 1946, having been discovered in the United States, he persuaded Jimmy Hoffa to intercede for him with the governor of Michigan in an effort to gain a pardon for past crimes. Hoffa failed, but the two did create a lengthy delay for him.

Tony Milano was the man who helped Bill Presser and John Nardi, though he may have acted on orders from his brother, Frank, the more respected of the two. Whatever the circumstances, the timing was excellent for everyone. The United States was putting together war plants, most of which would soon be operating on a twenty-four-hour-a-day schedule. These plants needed electrical workers, and Bill and John had their offices in the same building as the electrical workers' union. They knew the union organizers, and their contacts helped me get one of my first jobs in construction.

A plant was being built in Sandusky, so Bill got jobs for my brother Harry and me. He also arranged for a few Italian guys to go on the payroll, all of us having to look busy, though never actually doing anything for our money. In fact, Harry used to find a place to hide, then go to sleep all day or find an open area that was hidden from view where he could get a suntan.

I didn't know a pliers from a screwdriver, but we were paid journeyman's wages, taking home $169 and some odd cents, which was a lot of money. We also did a lot of gambling on the job, holding crap games and betting on sports. Nobody cared because there were kickbacks to everyone who mattered, including the head of the electrical workers' union, who eventually went to jail for income tax evasion.

Not all the union leaders were like Bill and the man who headed the electrical workers. When I was still in school, I lived on Ninety-ninth and Pierpont, getting to know a kid on the next block whose name was Harold Friedman. Although we shared the same last name, there was no family relationship between us.

Harold was a kid who was about eighteen months younger than I was, just enough of an age difference so that, at first, he followed me like a puppy dog. We were both big, tough kids, afraid of nobody, but when you're teenagers, the age difference means a lot more than it does later on in life.

Harold's father, Harvey Friedman, was a baker by trade. Conditions were rough for the bakery workers—the pay low, the benefits nonexistent—and he wanted to do something to correct this matter. He decided to enter the union movement, a decision that resulted from his desire to improve the lot of all the men in his trade. He was involved with unions long before Bill Presser.

There were other men and women interested in a bakers' union, but few were so stridently militant as Harvey Friedman. They used to take streetcars to various members' homes, holding their meetings in the basements.

Harvey's strikes often became violent, but not just for the sake of violence as often occurred with the Teamsters. I remember one strike I went to see because I thought there might be some excitement. It was at Rosen's Bakery on 105th Street, a major bakery at the time, and a woman made the mistake of trying to cross the picket line to buy something from the store. Several of the women pickets grabbed the woman, took her to the streetcar tracks, and held her down so her body was across the rails. They knew that it would be quite a while before another streetcar came by, and they had no intention of letting the customer get hurt. But the woman did not know that, becoming terrified of what she thought might be impending death. The pickets had made their point.

The union involved with that strike was Bakers' Local 56, which was then a Jewish bakers' union. As I have mentioned, Cleveland was ethnically divided and this division carried over into the unions.

Harvey was so radical during the meetings that he was expelled. But he was sincere in his belief in unions and was determined to fight for the bakers, regardless of their religious or ethnic backgrounds. He began organizing the bakeries where the workers were Gentiles, bakeries such as Ward's and Laub's. He was quite successful, able to buy new cars, furniture, and other items he had never been able to afford before.

The Pressers and the Harvey Friedmans had mixed feelings about each other. Bill Presser was in the unions, but he was considered a rackets man. He was tied in with Milano and had been involved with strong-arm tactics, shakedowns, and extortion. Harvey Friedman, on the other hand, was seen as a legitimate labor leader trying to improve the lot of the workingman rather than stealing from anyone he could.

Harvey Friedman and his wife did not like Bill and Faye Presser. Many was the time I was over at their house when they did not realize I might overhear them. Harvey Friedman would often say, "I wouldn't sit in the same room as Bill Presser." Then he would spit and add, "He's nothing but a gangster."

Harold Friedman and I were never really friends as kids and, by the time the war was over, we had both been exposed to all sides of the union activity of that time. We knew the violence and we knew the dedication. I, personally, liked the excitement of the violence and enjoyed the money that could be made in the way Bill worked his way up in the field.

Tony Milano remained a major force in Cleveland, not joining his brother, Frank, in Mexico. Bill Presser and John Nardi had switched from handling Wurlitzer jukeboxes to taking on the line of Rockola, a rival manufacturing company. I don't know what caused the falling out with Wurlitzer, though I do remember that, because Bill ran the owners' association, he could strong-arm the members into getting rid of their current machines and taking the Rockola line.

Bill had also become involved with Moe Dalitz. It was Dalitz who helped firm relations among Bill, a former boxer named Louis "Babe" Triscaro, Mickey Cohen, and Jimmy Hoffa. It was also through Dalitz that Jimmy Hoffa came into contact with Frank Milano.

The unions in those days were an odd mix. The Teamsters was not independent then; it was part of the American Federation of Labor (AFL), which would later merge with the Congress of Industrial Organizations (CIO). As with all labor, the AFL leadership was predominantly Irish. Strangely enough, it had been founded by Samuel Gompers, a British-born Jew. Gompers was succeeded by William Green, the son of Welsh immigrants and president from 1924 to 1952.

Just prior to the war, the Ironworkers International leader was Tommy Lenahan, a powerful force in what was then known as the Cleveland Federation of Labor/AFL. He was so powerful that he was able to talk to Franklin Roosevelt at the White House or have an audience with the pope whenever he desired. Lenahan used a "slugger" named Bill McSweeney. McSweeney's job was to break heads until the union gained what they were after. For example, McSweeney used to hire Jimmy Fratianno, a friend of Babe Triscaro and, later, a member of the Mafia, to commit violence during organizing efforts. He later talked of being hired to help organize parking lots, an effort during which he broke windshields, slashed tires, and poured muriatic acid on car bodies. For this Fratianno was paid fifteen dollars a day plus a ten-dollar bonus for each man he was able to find who would commit violence for five dollars per day as part of the violent crew.

Lenahan's days would be numbered by the time the war years were over. There was a revolt brewing within the AFL/Cleveland, a revolt led by Ed Murphy, who eventually would join forces with Harvey Friedman, Bill Finnegan of the stagehands' union, and Tommy McDonald, who was also in the ironworkers' union. When it came time to vote Lenahan from office, Harvey Friedman cast the deciding vote.

Lenahan was so angry about being kicked out of the labor movement leadership in that manner that he vowed not only to outlive his enemies but to "piss on their graves." Bill Presser brought Lenahan into the Teamsters, giving him a paycheck though he never had to do anything to earn it. However, Lenahan's anger continued over the years until, one after another, his four major enemies were dead.

I still remember the day that I was in a restaurant where some men were expecting Lenahan to join them. He arrived late, explaining that he had been making the rounds of the graveyards where three of his four enemies were buried. He had gone to the headstones, unzipped his pants, and pissed on each of their graves. Only Harvey Friedman sidestepped Lenahan because he died in California and his son, Harold, buried him there. Harold has never told me the reason, but since he knew about Lenahan's determination, and, though the Friedmans had a daughter in California, I've always suspected that Harvey was left there to prevent posthumous humiliation.

Bill Presser was not yet involved with the Teamsters Union, but his many connections would soon enable him to take a leadership role. In the meantime, he was involved with the fastest growing business in the entertainment field, a business the mob also enjoyed because of the cash that it generated.

After I left the army, Bill arranged for me to go to work for his company, the one which handled the Rockola phonograph machines. I wore a suit and went to work each day. The job was a phony. There was nothing for me to do except draw a paycheck. Once in a while I might help the guys load one of the machines onto a truck, but that was about it. Bill saw the job as a way of taking care of me.

Payday came and I was paid what I considered a small sum. It was forty or fifty dollars—I don't remember how much anymore—but it was enough for a man to live on if he were frugal. It was especially fair because I hadn't done any work. However, I wasn't there to be treated fairly. I was there because Bill wanted to give me spending money and, by making me an employee of the company, he could take it from the company payroll. In a sense we were both stealing, but it was Bill's company and I didn't care.

The manager at the business was shocked when I complained about how little I received. I told him that I wouldn't work for the forty or fifty dollars. I wanted more money.

The manager laughed in my face. He told me that I hadn't done any work. He knew that Bill never expected me to do anything more than draw a paycheck. However, he had no idea how well Bill wanted me to be paid for doing nothing. Angry with him, I went into his office; picked up the telephone; called Bill, who was in Florida at the time; and arranged for the manager to pay me what I wanted, a sum several times what I had been given.

John Nardi, Bill's partner, had little interest in the vending business so long as it seemed to be making money. He seldom came around, even though Bill was in Florida, so the manager began making decisions on his own. One of these was to purchase several hundred fairly expensive Ski-Ball machines.

Ski-Ball is a game you may have seen in penny arcades. You take a ball, roll it up a sloped ramp, and try to get it to bounce into one of several circular rings. The rings look a little like a hunting target, the center one being the smallest and thus worth the most points if you can get the ball into it. As the surrounding rings get larger, the points you earn are lower. If you have not seen it, the best way to describe it is to say it looks a little like an odd mix of bowling and basketball.

The trouble was that the manager had given no thought to outlets for the machines that had cost $300,000. He was convinced that the game would be extremely popular, and eventually it was, but he made the purchase without authorization. He also had no place to put the machines he had purchased.

Bill was extremely angry with the manager, stalking out of the office certain that the man had cost him a small fortune. However, when I looked at the machines, I realized that I could get rid of them. I went to Bill later that evening and explained that I knew how to do it.

"What? By starting a fire?" he snorted. "Burn down the joint? I can't afford to do that."

"No," I said. "I'll sell them for you."

I explained to Bill that I was going to go to West Virginia, to the towns that still had what we then called hillbillies. I knew that the boys liked to hang around bars when they could, drinking and looking for entertainment. I figured the Ski-Ball machines would be perfect for them.

The term *hillbilly* has changed over the years. Originally it was used to mean the isolated farmers in the hill regions of West Virginia, Kentucky, and similar areas. Some of them had lived in such rural locations for so long that the people and their settlements were unknown for years. Eleanor Roosevelt, the wife of President Franklin Roosevelt, was one of the first prominent individuals to visit one section where the people still spoke Elizabethan English. They were hard-working, powerful people with limited education and fairly simple lives. Yet I always respected them because they were tough, honest, and good fighters.

I had gotten to know boys from the hill regions during my time in the army. I thought that with a seemingly good product, a sales pitch that sounded straight, and a good con, I could move the machines in some of the cities.

My first stop was one of the larger West Virginia cities, where I took a suite of rooms in an old hotel. Then I took an advertisement in the paper which read, "SALESMAN WANTED. HIGH COMMISSION."

What I was hoping was that one of the hillbilly kids would answer the ad. I wanted a guy who was both hardworking and a regular customer of one of the bars in the area. I figured that a regular customer would have no trouble convincing the bar owner to take one of the machines for his place.

In two days, fifteen to eighteen men had come to see me at the hotel. I explained that I wanted them to put the machines into the bars they used and they all felt that that would be no problem. I also told them that they would receive 50 percent of the first week's take as their commission.

The men went out and worked hard. By the second night I had commitments for sixteen to eighteen machines.

I had no idea how good the machines were, but they were electrically simple so I wasn't worried when I began getting service calls a day or two after the machines had been installed in the bars. I remember one call from a place. At the back of each machine was a big door I had to open to see what was going on. Now these were nickel machines and they had a coin holder that was six inches long, three inches deep, and three inches wide. The size should have been more than adequate to hold the number of coins that would be used under normal circumstances. But when I opened the machine, the box was overflowing with nickels.

I went to a couple of the other joints and found that all of them were loaded with coins. I had a goldmine on my hands, though I knew it would not last.

The Ski-Ball machines were not complicated to use. If someone had been playing for a while and wasn't too drunk, it was easy to bank the machine and start getting high scores. At that point the novelty would wear off and the revenue would decrease. I figured that within three or four weeks the take would start to drop heavily.

The second week I was in town, I put an ad in the paper which read, "GOOD GOING COIN BUSINESS FOR SALE." Then I waited.

By the fourth week, the nickels were drastically down. Yet even then the receipts totaled two hundred to four hundred dollars per machine.

That first week I gave half the take to the bar owner and half to the salesman. After that, I was locking up the money until I got a customer; that usually occurred by the fourth week. At that point there was also a heavy drop, sometimes from a three hundred-dollar gross to a fifty-dollar gross.

When I got what I called a "mooch," I'd always tell him that my collection day was the next day. I explained that I had to make the rounds, taking out the nickels, counting them, then giving the bar owners their shares.

Next I got five or six hundred dollars' worth of nickels and went around to the places I knew were no longer doing well. I'd throw as much as one hundred dollars in nickels into each of the machines where the take was drastically down. Then, the next day, the first guy came to the hotel and we had breakfast together. When we were done, I said, "Okay, you ready to go to work?"

"What do you mean 'work'?" he asked.

"Counting money, pal," I replied. "That's going to be your business and you're going to make a lot of money."

We worked ten or twelve hours that day, and the take he saw was enormous. There were sixteen machines that yielded between eight thousand and twelve thousand dollars. Half went to the owners, but the rest would be his if he took the machines.

The man was impressed. I explained the price of the machines, a figure that was always a couple of hundred dollars more than they had cost Bill and John. Then we arranged for financing, the man using whatever credit he had. The sale was consummated within three days, and my brother-in-law was thrilled. Bill knew then that I would be able to move the other machines and turn a profit and that he wouldn't have to take a $300,000 loss.

The arrangement we made was that a number of salesmen would be turned loose in those rural areas that were similar to the section of West Virginia where I made the first sale. They would go into Pennsylvania, Indiana, Kentucky, and so forth. They would follow the same approach I had, though I also took some territory for myself.

I went south again, by Christmastime reaching a small town which I will not name because some of the innocent people involved in what happened are still alive. I was sure of myself, having made a second sale just like my first and developed a sense of how much I could sell in a given area. In fact, as I approached this town I arranged for a truck to have twenty Ski-Ball machines of varying lengths at the ready. I knew I was going to place them.

It was during this period when I received a telephone call from a sergeant on the police force in the town where I had been selling. My truck driver, who had stayed behind for the holidays, had been arrested for drunk driving and hitting a car. There was no serious damage and he was all right, but I was called because he worked for me.

I talked with the sergeant, explaining that I would be setting up a business in his community after the first of the year. I asked whether the driver could be released on bond with my guaranteeing the money. I also offered to send money by Western Union.

The sergeant was pleased with my cooperation and told me that none of that would be necessary. He would keep the driver overnight so he could sober up, then release him.

When I returned to the area, I met with the sergeant and gave him $250. I told him it was not a bribe but my way of thanking him for his kindness during the holiday. The man was extremely grateful and I knew he was corrupt.

I opened the business as I had before, putting an advertisement in the paper. To my surprise, the first person to respond was the police sergeant. He told me that he was looking for some extra money and wanted to buy some of the machines.

I told the sergeant that the purchase was not for him. I said that it wasn't a scam; the buyer would not go broke. The problem was that it was a novelty and the take would go way down after the first few weeks.

The sergeant was surprised by my honesty. I told him that I didn't want any trouble with the police and that I thought he seemed to be a pretty nice guy.

"What other machines do you sell?" the sergeant asked.

"Jukeboxes, slot machines, pinball machines," I told him.

Then the sergeant asked me how I'd like to open a business in the area with jukeboxes, slot machines, and pinball machines. He said that the American Legion, the VFW, the Moose Club, and the Elks Club all had slot machines with the approval of the police. There was also what he called a "nigger hotel" that had slot machines, as well as whorehouses with both jukeboxes and slot machines.

The sergeant said that he would be able to kick out the other machines and put only my machinery in the places. However, if he did that, both he and the chief would want a piece of the action.

"How many units are you talking about, pal?" I asked.

Then the sergeant started counting the number of slot machines in town, listing the bars, the whorehouses, the cheat spots, and the other businesses in both the white and the black areas. By the time he was done, I knew that a man supplying the machines for all the action could get quite rich.

"I'll have to talk with my brother-in-law," I explained, knowing that I would need Bill's approval for that kind of volume. Then he said something that surprised me.

"You're Jewish, aren't you?" he asked. I told him I was.

"Good, because if we go into business here, we don't want any Italians. We don't want no racket people. The first thing you know dope will come and then there'll be a war with the whorehouses."

"I'm with the Jewish people," I said. "I don't even know any Italians." As soon as he started bad rapping them, I knew I was going to go along with him. I was going to speak against the Italians. I wanted to be certain that we made the sale.

I placed the machines, but I didn't put an ad in the paper to sell them. I figured that if I could get jukeboxes, slot machines, pinball machines, and punch boards, I would just wait until the Ski-Ball units died out, then replace them with the slot machines.

I went home to Cleveland to tell Bill Presser what happened. He was shocked, yet delighted. However, I warned him that the men would not work with the Italians because of troubles they had had in the past.

Bill and I talked about the possibility of persuading the chief to come to Cleveland, then decided that Bill would go back with me. We went to breakfast, the chief in a business suit, the sergeant in uniform. They began talking about the number of slot machines, pinball machines, and jukeboxes they would need, the figures indicating that their area alone could net hundreds of thousands of dollars.

Bill was concerned with trying to put machines in all the possible markets in the community at the same time. His cost would be extremely high despite the profit potential.

The chief suggested that Bill might want to start slowly, placing his machines in a few spots, then moving on to another group as such a move made sense. He also explained that he and the sergeant would want 50 percent of the action for their involvement, each man taking 25 percent. Bill tried to argue with the fee split, but the chief said that they knew the potential take and that the split would ultimately make a lot of money for everyone.

As I made the rounds of the bars and restaurants, I was accompanied by the uniformed police sergeant. Either the town was so corrupt or the police were so accepted as being corrupt that there was no effort to lie about what we were doing. The sergeant said that the pinball machines and jukeboxes already in place had to be removed. The owner could no longer do business with the guy who had those machines. He said that I was going into the same business and that they were only to do business with my machines.

I did compromise. I told the bar owners that I would take out the Ski-Ball machines since the profits were down. This made me something of a good guy, though what they didn't know was that we had enough guys in other states selling the Ski-Ball machines to different markets that we had no trouble getting rid of them again. They were making more money for us when I removed them than they had when I sold them in the first place.

I had to take back twenty Ski-Ball machines, though I replaced them with an initial order of a dozen jukeboxes and eighteen pinball machines. The places did well with pinball so some wanted two machines and one wanted three. We also installed punch boards, which were cheap gambling games that had a hidden big winner.

The punch boards were all rigged so that we knew where the jackpot was hidden. The jackpots varied from fifty to two hundred dollars, depending upon the type of board, and we wanted to make certain that we took the payoff as often as possible.

By that time I was no longer just working with the sergeant. The chief was accompanying me on my rounds, as was the mayor. The cops never told me why the mayor was with us, though it was obvious to me that he must have had a piece of the action. There was no other reason for him to keep quiet while we were taking over his town that way.

There were different ways the slot machine business worked. Usually the owner of the business owned the slot machines. When that happened, I would either buy them from him and change the locks on the boxes or I would replace them with newer models. It was obviously an offer the owner couldn't refuse because if he did not buy my machines the cops would raid the place and destroy what they had. Using my machines meant that business would continue as usual, the payoffs going to different places than before.

We had the black hotel, the American Legion, the Elks Club, the Moose Lodge, the whorehouses, the various lodges, all the places in town. Over one hundred slot machines were installed, the money coming in so fast that I had to hire several girls to spend every day doing nothing but wrapping nickels, dimes, and quarters. Everything was going beautifully. The town was sewn up. We had whiskey joints, cheat spots, and every other place where people went for a good time.

To show you how much money was being made, I was stealing between four and five thousand dollars a week off the top by not giving the chief and the sergeant a fair share of the take. Yet they were happy with what they were getting and my share was based on the take they knew about, not the skimmings that had to go to Bill's partners.

I was doing quite well with my 25 percent of the take after all the splits. I rented a nice house. I attended some of the different churches in the area. I gave money to charities. I also became a softball player with a team sponsored by the Elks and, because players who were good were local celebrities, I got my name in the paper a lot. Everyone knew me, smiling, waving, and speaking to me on the streets. I had become a major part of the community during the nine or ten months I had been there.

It was when everything was going so well that Bill Presser asked me to go back to Cleveland for a meeting. He took me to see Tony Milano, who greeted me in the European manner, grasping my shoulders and kissing me on each cheek. "You're making a lot of money for us," he told me.

"That's my job, Mr. Milano," I told him.

"Well, it's about time we want a gambling joint there." What Milano had in mind was a small casino like the Pettibone Club, the Arrow Club, or one of the other places that existed in the Cleveland area. The place would not be showy, like the Las Vegas clubs, but rather a location that could do a steady business with minimum overhead and maximum profits. There would be a good dining room serving high-quality food, and the customers could feel that they were having an enjoyable evening on the town instead of throwing their money away. The take would be much higher than the profit from all the machines we had placed, and that take looked as though it would soon reach nearly a million dollars a year.

I was a little concerned with the way the conversation was going because I knew the bias in the community. "Mr. Milano," I said. "I don't know if my brother-in-law ever told you this, but I'll be quite frank with you. Now please don't take this wrong.

"I'm very close with the mayor. I'm very close with the chief of police. I'm very close with the sergeant. And they always bad rap Italians. They had trouble with Italians a few years back.

"Mr. Milano, I respect you and I must tell you the truth. We're going to blow what we have up there now."

I explained about the great potential of the area without changing what we were doing. The town itself only had a few thousand people, but it was the major shopping and business area for a county where most of the people were miners, farmers, and workers in other trades that kept them fairly isolated. Every two weeks when the residents of the county were paid, several million dollars came into the town. It was that money we were tapping and it was that potential I did not want to lose.

"Mr. Milano, we've got something very good here. Why don't we open up an amusement park or a drive-in theater (there was none in the town at that time) and go that way?

"I can't run a big casino with big-time gambling. I'm too busy with the slots and pinballs and jukeboxes. If I neglect them, we'll start losing money there.

"But I don't think the gambling casino is a good idea, Mr. Milano, because I think we'll blow the whole thing if they find out Italians have anything to do with this."

I chose my words carefully. Tony Milano was an old man, one of what we called the "mustache Petes," the old-school Mafia leaders. I knew that I had to talk straight to him, but that I also had to treat him with respect. He was a powerful and potentially dangerous man.

Tony's nephew, John Nardi, was a very pleasant man who made friends easily. People liked him. But John did not fully understand the potential for trouble we were facing.

"Is there a place available?" John asked, still talking about the possibility of opening the type of casino we had been discussing.

There was. Four or five miles out of town was a building that had once held a big, fabulous restaurant that could not do the volume of business it needed to stay afloat. When I saw that I couldn't win the discussion, I mentioned this former restaurant.

"You will go buy it," said Tony Milano.

"Mr. Milano, I don't know. It's outside the city limits. We'll be involving the state troopers and the sheriff's department."

"I want it done!" said Milano. Then he said good-bye and he walked away.

I turned to my brother-in-law and John Nardi and said, "John, we're going to fuck up the whole deal. I want you to know that. You know how I feel about you, John. I don't have to pull my punches like I do with your uncle. We're going to fuck up the whole deal."

"Allen, don't worry," said John. "I'll handle it."

The next step was for me to go back to find out whether they even wanted a gambling joint. I said that I wouldn't mention the amusement park or drive-in theater. Maybe they wouldn't want a gambling joint despite the millions of dollars coming into the area every two weeks from the payroll.

I returned to the town and took the chief and the sergeant out to dinner. I said that I had talked with my brother-in-law, who told me to tell them that they were making so much money, they might want to make even more.

"Whatever you want to do, Allen. You made us a lot of money," they replied.

I then explained about the restaurant I wanted to buy to convert to a club. The chief agreed but said that we would have to cut in the sheriff and the state troopers. He said that arrangements could be made, but we'd probably have to throw a piece of the action to the governor.

I told the chief that if all those additional people had to be cut in on the action, there would have to be a reduction in the percentages. The chief reminded me of how much additional money would be made, then said he would look into it.

I let matters drop for ten days. I didn't like the idea and felt it could only hurt us. I hoped that somehow nothing would happen if I did nothing, but at the end of the ten days John Nardi called to find out what was happening.

I explained to Nardi how many people were becoming involved. John said it did not matter. He knew the potential and I was to go ahead with things.

A short while later the chief came to my office. He made arrangements for us to talk with the sheriff, who knew me from my softball playing. "What's my end?" asked the sheriff, the first thing.

The chief told the sheriff that he had no idea how much would be involved but assured him that he would get a good chunk of money each month. That was good enough for the sheriff, and the next day the same situation occurred with the captain of the state troopers. The only difference was that the captain had to talk with the governor, who, two days later, approved the action.

The only thing I didn't do that I had been asked to do was buy the building where the casino would be installed. It was fortunate because once I got the go-ahead, John Nardi told me that he and Bill were going to come down to meet with the chief.

There was nothing for me to do. John told me to use his real name with the chief, and the name Nardi was obviously Italian. I could see disaster but figured that it was out of my hands. I would do what they wanted. I had told them everything I knew, given them all the warnings, so it was time just to let things happen.

The chief came to the suite of rooms Bill and John rented in the best hotel in town. "Are you Italian, Mr. Nardi?" asked the chief after being introduced to John.

John was extremely smooth. He said that he was of Italian descent. He was born in America and was 100 percent American despite his Italian origins. He certainly wasn't connected with the Mafia. In fact, he couldn't even speak Italian.

Everyone was laughing, talking, enjoying pastry and coffee. I thought everything was fine, so I excused myself from the conference. I had service calls to make and work to do. I left, knowing that Bill would tell me what happened.

Four hours later the chief came to my office. "Friedman," he said. "I liked you, but you're a fucking liar! You've got twenty-four hours to pick up all your slot machines, your pinball machines, and your jukeboxes or we're going to smash them."

"Come on, Chief," I said. "Get off that shit. Don't go around threatening me."

"I'm not threatening you," he said, coldly. "I'm telling you. We don't want no fucking dagos up here, okay? We had enough trouble."

I tried to smooth things over. I said, "This guy isn't even a true dago. He's married to a Jewish girl." That was a lie, though apparently John had said the same thing.

"Yeah, I know," said the chief. "He was telling me. But we don't want no fucking dagos up here. You've got twenty-four hours. Okay?"

"Okay, Chief. You sure I can't talk you out of it?"

"Out!"

I ran to the bank and withdrew twenty thousand dollars from my account. I was angry about what was happening. Had they just listened to me, we would have had no trouble. They didn't, everything was over, and I was hot.

I took a list of all the places that had the various machines. Then I called my brother-in-law and told him I was coming to see him. Then I took the list and all the master keys and went to the suite where Bill and John were staying.

I called them every name I could think of, then I handed them the list and the master keys. "The chief told me to pick up all this shit within twenty-four hours or they're going to confiscate or smash them."

Finally they listened. Bill wanted me to call the chief, but I refused. I told him that I had taken twenty thousand dollars from the bank and was leaving. I told them that they had better hire people and a couple of trucks if they wanted to get the machines safely out of town. Then I left, returning to Cleveland for my wife before moving out to California for the next several months.

I was angry and frustrated. What I did not realize was that the actions of Bill Presser, John Nardi, and Tony Milano reflected something else that was taking place throughout the United States.

Bill was not yet involved with the Teamsters Union, yet his connections with the mob and with the vending industry were putting him into a position to be a part of some major changes in organization. As I later learned through investigating Hoffa and this time in Detroit, shortly before the end of the war, Teamsters Local 299 and Local 337 loaned a man named Eugene James two thousand dollars to reorganize the car wash and garage workers' union local. James immediately broadened the local's power base by organizing the coin machine industry employees. He also brought Jimmy Hoffa into the action by putting Hoffa's wife on the payroll, though using her maiden name, Josephine Poszywak, for the records to hide the family's involvement.

At the same time, various jukebox companies were being purchased by the Detroit mob. Interestingly, the president of that same car wash workers' local realized what was happening and told Hoffa that he could not work with the criminals who had taken over the jukebox industry. Hoffa sent in one of his lawyers to serve as assistant to the president. He was mob connected through marriage and family ties. However, he stated that he had no control over the family connections of either his cousin or his wife. He would also eventually prove to be well respected as an honorable attorney.

During this early period the lawyer was moved into a position where he was used by Hoffa to force out a dissident president involved with the car wash workers' local. The involvement with the corrupt jukebox industry continued. In fact, during a congressional investigation of the local (*Investigation of Racketeering in the Detroit Area, Joint Subcommittee Report, 1954*) it was alleged that Hoffa had arranged for the systematic destruction of the local's records. They also said that "there existed a gigantic, wicked conspiracy to, through the use of force, threats of force and economic pressure, extort and collect millions of dollars not only from unorganized workers but from members of unions who are in good standing, from independent businessmen, and, on occasion, from the Federal Government itself. . . ."

Extortion charges were eventually brought against the lawyer and others in the fall of 1953. Typically, they went before a judge who, in 1952, earned $100 a week for his appearances on a radio program sponsored by the Teamsters. In addition, the judge was provided with a sixty-two-hundred-dollar campaign contribution when he had to run for office again in 1953. Approximately five years later, the investigative committee headed by Senator John McClellan would eventually uncover all of these facts (*Committee Report* 621), but by then the judge had acquitted the lawyer and the others of all charges.

The players were coming together while I was busy getting rid of those Ski-Ball machines, then taking over the small town where we made so much money before greed overcame good judgment. It was like the early stages of a spider web where the intersecting lines have yet to form an obvious pattern. But I was caught up in my own concerns and had no sense of the bigger picture that was unfolding. Bill Presser in Ohio, Jimmy Hoffa in Detroit, organized crime figures, unions were all moving inexorably closer together in ways that would alter not only my life but American history. Yet all I knew was that I was angry. It was time for my wife and me to move on to the West Coast, a trip that only served to delay my future involvement in what was taking place.

The Teamster's Union was just beginning to become a power during this period. Teamsters in general have influenced all aspects of American life from the time we abandoned self-sufficient agricultural living. The move to cities meant that teamsters, originally men or women who drove a team of horses in front of a cart or similar conveyance, were needed to deliver food, clothing, furniture, and other items. Teamsters moved goods to and from shipyards, railroad depots, and urban warehouses. Teamsters provided the public transportation that allowed low-income men and women to obtain jobs that were often far from their homes. If the teamsters ever organized effectively, it would mean that they could paralyze the nation or hold it for ransom just by choosing when to work and when to strike. Yet the Teamsters Union had only 135,000 members in 1937, when men like Jimmy Hoffa began to recognize the potential of such organization. Through him; through Dave Beck of Seattle, Washington; and through the efforts of many other men around the country, there were 530,000 members in 1941. However, even those figures did not anticipate the growth that would begin in the immediate postwar years and reach its high point when Jimmy Hoffa became International president in the 1950s.

There was another factor coming into play. The Wagner Act of 1935 affected labor conditions throughout the United States. This act was passed after a number of violent strikes by longshoremen on the West Coast; workers for Auto-Lite in Toledo, Ohio; and Teamsters in Minneapolis.

Many observers of union history feel that the Wagner Act, though allowing the orderly establishment of unions, was actually a means of defusing the potential strength of the union movement. According to these observers, rank and file members were led to believe that their power came from the federal government since the federal government established strict rules and regulations for establishing a union. It also forced the employers to bargain with the unions in good faith so long as everyone obeyed the laws. Strikes would not be necessary and business could continue uninterrupted. In addition, the act protected management by making it almost impossible for workers to decertify a contract that had been ratified if they found that their representatives had been dishonest and had not helped them obtain the best possible contract. Decertification required 30 percent of the employees to sign a petition ninety days before the contract went into force. Sixty days after the contract there could be an election for employees to decide whether or not to decertify the union. It was complex enough that few were able to do it.

The Wagner Act also established the National Labor Relations Board

(NLRB) to oversee the relations of workers, unions, and employees. The board was appointed by the president of the United States and was viewed as a vehicle for stopping labor since the members were perceived to be pro-management.

Because of the Wagner Act, unions were able to flourish, but the union members became potential victims of deals between the labor leaders and corporate management. The wording was such that the members had little recourse against their leaders if bad contracts were negotiated or if grievances were not processed. Decertification was possible, though not easy.

At first the Wagner Act was viewed as giving workers so much power that many of the large corporations refused to abide by it. Earl Reid, the counsel for Weirton Steel Company, headed a group of attorneys who felt that the act was unconstitutional. However, in 1937 the Supreme Court upheld it in the case of the *NLRB* v. *Jones and Laughlin Steel Corp.*

While the issues were being resolved, labor found a new tactic that seemed to do more for unifying the members than anything tried before. This was the sit-down strike in which workers simply refused to leave their places of employment.

The sit-down strike, like so much else that was taking place in the labor movement, is believed to have begun in Cleveland on December 28, 1936. There were a thousand workers inside a General Motors (GM) plant who wanted to become members of the United Auto Workers. Instead of the usual procedure of walking off the job, a tactic which would allow management to hire scabs to take their place, they laid down their tools and sat down. There was no way to make them work. There was no way to make them leave.

The sit-down strike spread to GM, then the third-largest corporation in America. Workers on the night shift in the Flint, Michigan, plant also refused to continue working. Eventually another fifteen plants had the same problem, until 140,000 of the company's 250,000 workers were engaged in a sit-down strike.

There was violence, but it was not the same type that occurred when workers were outside on picket lines. Flint police arranged to have the heat turned off inside the plant, block food shipments to the strikers, and use tear gas and buckshot on the few men who picketed outside the plant. However, the men inside the plant fought back against the police by turning on a fire hose, then hurling their coffee cups, pop bottles, door hinges, and anything else that could serve as a weapon.

The drama came to a head when Michigan Governor Frank Murphy asked United Mine Worker leader John L. Lewis what would happen if he sent in the National Guard. Although Lewis was not connected with the UAW, he was the toughest, most prominent labor leader of his day. He did for all the unions—

American Federation Of Labor, Congress Of Industrial Organizations, International Brotherhood Of Teamsters, and so on—what Jimmy Hoffa later did just for the Teamsters.

Lewis, a charismatic leader with massive bushy eyebrows and a flair for the dramatic, knew that the governor's grandfather had been hanged during the Irish Rebellion for his activities against what he viewed as corrupt authority. According to Saul Alinsky in his book *John L. Lewis* (Putnam, 1949), he alluded to this fact in his response:

> You want my answer, sir? I give it to you. Tomorrow morning, I shall personally enter General Motors plant Chevrolet No. 4. I shall order the men to disregard your order. I shall then walk up to the largest window in the plant, open it, divest myself of my outer raiment, remove my shirt and bare my bosom. Then when you order your troops to fire, mine will be the first those bullets will strike. And as my body falls from that window to the ground, you listen to the voice of your grandfather as he whispers in your ear, "Frank, are you sure you are doing the right thing?"

Governor Murphy not only abandoned plans to send in the National Guard but also refused to allow the General Motors management to prevent the delivery of food and other necessities to the strikers. As a result, the strike lasted forty-four days at a cost to the company of $1 million per day, before GM agreed to negotiate with the UAW.

The UAW fight for recognition helped all the unions because the abuses were so blatant. Currently a top executive in the auto industry earns from twenty-five to thirty times the average salary of a factory worker, more than double the ratio of management/employee income in competing companies such as Japan. Yet when the strike occurred at GM in the 1930s, the ratio was approximately 200 to 1. The average factory worker earned $1,000 per year. The top executives took home $200,000 per year.

Next came the fight against U.S. Steel. Again the offenses were blatant. Efforts were made to keep the men on part-time status to reduce payments to them. As a result, the average worker was likely to make $369 per year in order to support a family that averaged 5.92 people. Temperatures in the mills rose to 220 degrees near the open furnaces, carbon monoxide poisoning was common, and pneumonia was a major cause of death for the workers. The equipment was not replaced, regardless of its age and condition, so long as it was cost-effective to keep it working. As a result, there were 22,845 people hurt in accidents each year, including 1,435 either killed or permanently disabled.

In Cleveland where Republic Steel workers joined the fight, the deaths in the industry offered the only hope for advancement in some families. The men did not earn enough money to live decently, but many had some form of accidental death benefits from the company. Families living in such extreme poverty that their children would never have the opportunity to learn more than basic reading and writing skills before having to quit school to work looked upon the deaths as a mixed blessing. The loss of a beloved husband and father was emotionally devastating. At the same time, the benefits from the death were enough to enable the family to move to a better neighborhood. The result was that some sections of Cleveland were filled with single-parent families and children who would complete their educations only because their fathers had died in the mills.

By 1937, the combination of the Wagner Act and a total of 22,658 strikes by laborers in all walks of life during the previous decade resulted in 7.7 million workers organized into unions. Yet the truth was that there was an odd situation taking place that would first be exploited during the war years. Although the average worker was receiving better income and benefits than ever before, his fate was now in the hands of the labor leaders and the bosses of industry who understood each other's needs and desires.

There were two types of corruption in the labor movement. There was the extortion racket of which Bill Presser was a part. There were also sweetheart deals with employers through which the employees received lower pay and benefits than a legitimate contract would have given them. For a kickback the Teamsters' leaders might negotiate a contract less valuable to the workers than what could have been achieved.

The members of the labor movement were unaware that they were being hurt because they were also gaining benefits. For example, with the support of Teamster General President Dan Tobin and AFL President William Green, the Fair Labor Standards Act of 1938 was passed. Workers no longer had to be on the job more than forty-four hours a week. In addition, the minimum wage was established at twenty-five cents an hour for all industries involved with interstate commerce.

The war years also caused a change in the relation between labor and management. Tobin was a strong supporter of Franklin Roosevelt and worked closely with the president in motivating labor not to strike as part of the war effort. Roosevelt even sent Tobin to England to learn how the government had motivated labor there.

The Teamsters became active in conservation programs, war bond drives, and other efforts. At the same time they began recruiting members outside their previous areas of control, including agricultural industry personnel on the West Coast. Teamsters also went to war, serving in areas such as Africa as noncombatant truck drivers, not soldiers. General George Patton, talking about the African campaign, said:

> You should have seen those trucks on the road to Gabes. The drivers were magnificent! All day and all night they rolled over those terrible roads, never stopping, never faltering from their course, with shells bursting around them all the time. We got through on good old American guts.
>
> Many of these men drove over 40 consecutive hours! These men weren't combat men but they were soldiers with a job to do. They did it—and a whale of a way they did it. They were part of a team. Without them, the fight would have been lost. All the links in the chain pulled together and that chain became unbreakable.

Obviously no man drove forty hours straight, though teams of drivers, usually black and usually quartermasters, did put in that kind of performance.

When the war was over, Tobin worked to assure that Teamster veterans would have their seniority maintained at jobs they left. In addition, there was a campaign established both for the public and within the Teamsters correspondence with their members, to encourage having purchases delivered to assure more jobs. As one ad, showing a woman trying on a new hat in a clothing store, stated:

> EASTER BONNET OR BATHROOM SCALES; NO MATTER WHAT YOU BUY, HAVE IT DELIVERED. BUT, MORE THAN THAT, BUY ONLY WHERE UNION TEAMSTERS ARE EMPLOYED. IF ALL TEAMSTER WIVES WOULD INSIST ON NOTHING BUT UNION GOODS AND SERVICES, THE CAUSE OF UNIONISM WOULD ADVANCE TREMENDOUSLY! DON'T TAKE IT HOME; HAVE IT DELIVERED.

The rank and file did not pay close attention to the allegations of kickbacks to various state and local Teamster leaders from the various companies with which they were negotiating. Because of their intense patriotism, their primary concern was winning the war, not reviewing contract negotiations. There was full employment for most of the members, though conservation efforts forced some changes, including the return to horse-drawn vehicles, where possible, to save rubber.

In addition to the corruption in contract talks, there were other alliances being formed during those war years. Louis "Babe" Triscaro had worked his way into the Teamsters Union after starting as a "slugger" on the picket lines back in the 1930s. He earned fifteen dollars a day to beat up cops and men who were hired to work in the place of the striking workers. The scabs were usually hardworking guys who were unemployed because of the lingering Depression and would do anything to feed their families. Babe was used as muscle by Tommy Lenahan, then the head of the local ironworkers' union, which was a small operation for its day. Lenahan let Bill McSweeney handle the day-to-day chores of recruiting the sluggers, but he knew what was taking place.

Most of the sluggers came from the Hill, and many were either Mafiosi or friends of the organized crime families. As a result, Triscaro formed the right connections, eventually making friends with both the mob and Jimmy Hoffa. Later Joey Glimco, a Chicago Mafia family *caporegime* with a long record of arrests, including one for murder, explained Babe's position to Jimmy Fratianno, who became a government witness against the mob. At the time of the conversation, Glimco was in control of at least fifteen Teamster locals in Chicago and by the 1950s, a behind-the-scenes power broker for the union nationally. He was quoted by Ovid Demaris in the book *The Last Mafioso* as saying: "Hoffa knows that Babe's got an in with made guys. Listen, if you ain't got the made guys with you in the Teamsters you've got nothing. We're the guys who crack heads for them assholes, the guys who get things straightened out. So when Babe goes to the president of a local and says I want so-and-so to be the business agent of your local, the guy knows that's what the family wants. That Union guy ain't never going to meet Johnny Scalish or Tony Milano, but he knows they're calling the shots through Babe."

Bill and Babe became close through Moe Dalitz, who was also a friend of Frank Milano. Although Milano supposedly lived in Mexico the rest of his life, the truth was that he spent at least seventeen years in California, extensive time in Las Vegas, and remained the man to see for problems with Cleveland. Dalitz was also considered the final connection between the Teamsters leadership and the non-Mafia men who were on the fringes of organized crime or accepted into that part of the inner circle reserved for well-trusted non-Italians.

The Mafia was working several areas at once during the war. They were involved with the black market, handling stolen gasoline ration stamps and other valued items. A pattern of payoffs to various government officials was being formed, and new businesses were being explored. Carlos Marcello of New Orleans and Santos Trafficante, Sr., in Florida, were working on dope deals involving both American cities and such locations as Cuba and Marseilles. Frank Costello and Meyer Lansky, starting with their New York base, moved into New Orleans and then to Las Vegas, where they handled the financing of the Flamingo Hotel. Lansky also became involved with Fulgencio Batista and helped set up the Cuban gambling operations.

At the same time, Charles "Lucky" Luciano agreed to help Navy Counterintelligence fight sabotage in the New York waterfront area. Luciano had served five years of a thirty- to fifty-year sentence for running a prostitution racket, but his power was as great in prison as out. Luciano and Lansky ordered their racketeers to watch out for sabotage. This was not only a patriotic act: It assured that anything the Mafia wished to do along the waterfront—theft, gambling, prostitution, and so on—that would not hinder the war effort would be tolerated by the government.

Luciano also helped the Office of Strategic Services (OSS) with the invasion of Sicily in 1943. He arranged for Mafia underlings in Sicily to risk their lives acting as guides for the Allied forces. They were able to accomplish what could not have been done by an outsider during the time left for training.

The reward for Luciano was release from prison and deportation to Italy. There he was able to establish a narcotics trade route to America working with Frank Coppola and Salvatore Vitale, both former Detroit residents and friends of Jimmy Hoffa, as well as Antoine d'Agostino. The latter was not a deported American like the others but a Nazi collaborator who had run a French-Corsican criminal organization.

No one realized at the time the far-reaching results of all these various alliances that were becoming known in the late 1940s. First, Jimmy Hoffa was consolidating his power by working with both members of the Mafia and criminals who were trusted by the Mafia inner circle. So far as I know and research has determined, Hoffa was not connected with the drug dealing that became a major business in Detroit. He also looked upon the mob figures pragmatically. He needed them to rise to power. He needed their help to strengthen the union, work picket lines, handle intimidation and extortion. Yet he also dreamed of eventually running a completely clean union free from such influence.

It was as though Jimmy Hoffa saw himself as a building contractor with a blueprint for the most flawless high rise ever constructed. He did not care about the backgrounds of the laborers. He did not mind if the men were criminals, killers, or corrupt political leaders. All that mattered was that they not compromise the materials so that the building, when completed, would be a monument so strong, nothing could corrupt it.

The trouble was that the mob did not work that way, and his naive belief that he could throw out the mob he had used for so many years was a contributing factor to his eventual murder. In addition, the Cuban connection that was indirectly being developed and would later be nurtured when he and Bill supplied weapons to both sides of the revolution would be a factor in the Kennedy assassination. And that assassination would be linked with the attempt to murder Castro by some of the same mob figures connected with the Teamsters as well as the Robert Kennedy vendetta against the union.

Yet we were all naive in this postwar period. We had no idea how any of the actions or the men involved would eventually have so much influence on so many facets of history.

The other racket that was taking place during this period was seemingly minor by comparison, though it showed the way Bill Presser operated. Bill worked behind the scenes as the primary power for an association of jukebox and pinball machine owners that was the most lucrative in the area. He also had the jukebox company I mentioned that was the partnership with John Nardi. He used his power and influence with the association to ensure that his jukeboxes were installed in the restaurants and bars. If there were problems or grievances, he was the one who would handle the matter for both sides. Thus the only people who were fairly represented were Bill Presser and the men from the Hill who backed him.

3

Grabbing a Piece of the
Postwar Action

JIMMY HOFFA'S MOVE into Ohio, Bill Presser's territory, would be a major step forward in his effort to become the International's president. It began in December 1946. He had engaged in illegal activities that were similar to Bill Presser's actions with the jukebox industry during the war. A year after the peace, he was elected president of Detroit's Local 299. Frank Fitzsimmons was vice president, and Dave Johnson was recording secretary. Sam Calhoun and Frank Collins, associates from the Kroger strike, were named as trustee and secretary-treasurer. Neither Hoffa nor 299 was unsullied of reputation before his ascendancy.

Before the war there were a large number of family-owned groceries in the Detroit area. These grocery stores were common sights in most large communities. A husband and wife ran them, often with the help of the children. The more successful allowed the family to live away from the business. Others had living quarters either in back or on an upper floor of the building that housed the grocery store.

The grocery stores had joined together to handle the hauling of the goods they sold. None of them had very much money so they formed an association to share the cost of a nonunion driver and truck, as well as to allow them to make bulk purchases of various products. Service improved without expenses increasing.

Hoffa, working with members of the Mafia, decided to extort money from the association of family-owned grocery stores. He forced them to pay for "permits" to allow them to keep using a nonunion trucker. The money that allegedly went into union funds instead apparently lined the pockets of Hoffa and his associates. Thousands of dollars were involved, and a felony indictment was issued against Hoffa. He blustered about his innocence, but when his lawyer managed to reduce the charges to a misdemeanor, he pleaded guilty and paid a fine.

Hoffa faced a different charge in 1941. He had been involved with the wastepaper industry, working with union companies to prevent nonunion companies from competing. He was indicted on antitrust charges because of labor racketeering, charges to which he pleaded "No Contest." Such a plea is essentially the same as a guilty plea insofar as the court's sentencing action. However, it is not a direct admission of guilt, nor is it a claim of innocence. Hoffa escaped jail once again, though.

The International Brotherhood of Teamsters president, Dan Tobin, was impressed with Hoffa and offered him a job as an organizer with the international office in Indianapolis. This recognition was important in light of Tobin's position with the Teamsters.

The Team Drivers International Union was formed in 1898 with twelve hundred members and a charter from the American Federation of Labor. The Teamsters National Union, with a membership of eighteen thousand, was founded four years later by rebels in Chicago. The following year, in 1903, Samuel Gompers, the president of the AFL, helped the groups negotiate a single union known as the International Brotherhood of Teamsters (IBT), which was headquartered in Indianapolis.

Cornelius Shea, the first president of the IBT, was voted out of office in 1907 after winning a court case in which he was charged with extortion. He was also disliked by Chicago dissidents who formed a group called the United Teamsters of America a few months before Shea's ouster.

Shea was replaced by Tobin, a Boston man who had emigrated from Ireland and had little interest in exerting power over the widely varying locals. He also had no interest in healing old wounds. He refused to readmit the United Teamsters of America, allowing them to fold in every community except Chicago, where the dissident union maintained one last local.

Tobin's leadership was limited. There were 125,000 members in 1933, yet Tobin allowed so much local autonomy that there were frequent problems with rigged elections, misuse of finances, and other crimes, mostly in Chicago and Detroit. Eventually Tobin was forced to intervene in some of the affairs of locals, including placing Detroit Local 299 in receivership. Among the members of that union were Rolland McMaster, a city cartage driver; Frank Fitzsimmons, a long-distance driver for National Transit Corporation; and David

Johnson of United Truck Service. All of them would eventually be important players in Teamster history.

By 1937, a man named Farrell Dobbs was gaining great respect for his leadership in Minneapolis, Minnesota. Dobbs was a socialist, a fact that would get him into trouble with the coming of the war years. However, his insights into the needs of organized labor quickly changed both the union and society as a whole.

Dobbs realized that the Teamsters could not succeed by organizing truckers only. They had to reach out to others, bringing in not only transportation but also warehousing and the food industry. When he met Jimmy Hoffa and expressed his ideas, Hoffa immediately agreed because of his own background in the grocery field.

Tobin had a love/hate relationship with Dobbs. He admired the man's skill, but he feared Dobbs's "Trotskyist" philosophy. This concern did not prevent Tobin from encouraging Dobbs when the latter established the Central States Drivers Council: forty-six locals in twelve midwestern states.

Dobbs was the man who created the idea of regional contracts, something Hoffa would eventually embellish with his national contract plan. He handled such matters in Chicago during negotiations with representatives from three hundred companies. The only problem was that he inadvertently obtained a better contract for the owner/operators than for the drivers, a problem that would be subject to controversy for some years to come.

Tobin was against owner/operators in the union and wanted nothing to do with helping them better themselves. Dobbs became insistent, refusing to yield to Tobin's desires, and thus causing the IBT decision to crush him.

Tobin was a close friend of President Roosevelt and had forced a resolution through the IBT expelling Communists from the ranks. By 1941, Tobin had made his decision to use the anti-Communist decree to get rid of Dobbs. Jimmy Hoffa, a friend of Dobbs, was proving his value to the union and was wise enough not to fight for Dobbs despite the friendship and mutual respect that had developed between the two men.

The war in Europe was taking place when Tobin clamped down on Dobbs. Tobin wanted to attack Dobbs in any way necessary and needed a man who both knew Dobbs's thought patterns and also was loyal to the IBT. Jimmy Hoffa became the field marshal, using Local 299, by then under Tobin's firm control, to supply the muscle.

Hoffa was next offered an organizing job in Indianapolis. He felt that although such a job offer was an honor, it would also prevent him from building his own power base. He preferred to stay in Detroit, though he did succeed Dobbs as negotiating chairman of the Central States Drivers Council. In 1943, Dan Tobin appointed him one of the three trustees who examined the International's books.

Not only did this role increase his prestige, it also gave him a full understanding of the Teamsters financial potential.

Hoffa used the war years to create a number of changes that would be important later. Before doing anything, though, he had his 1-A draft classification quashed by claiming that his work with the Teamsters was vital to the transportation industry.

Despite his criminal convictions, much of what Hoffa did was legitimate. He continued organizing members of the Teamsters, adding approximately one thousand new men to the organization. He also followed the government program to prevent strikes; keep the trucks rolling; conserve gasoline, rubber, and other essential materials; and cooperate with other shipping approaches, such as using Great Lakes ships instead of trucks for longer-distance hauls to locations where such a move was possible. Many union members also joined the U.S. Truck Conservation Corps, which assured that they were following preventive maintenance procedures for longer truck life.

Hoffa organized throughout the state despite the fact that his local was in Detroit. This meant that when the war was over and it was no longer unpatriotic to strike, he could fight for new contracts anywhere in Michigan. He had the power to strike anywhere, forcing companies such as those in the auto industry, with several scattered site plants in the state, to negotiate with him, as would not have been possible in the past. Instead of the union's threatening one location, all plants could be closed until a settlement was reached.

Hoffa also had a second goal which could not be reached until after the war. This was to have a uniform contract for both urban and rural trucking. Ironically the difficulties he had stemmed from Ohio, where the Teamsters were not doing well. This was before Bill Presser's involvement with the Teamsters, but Bill's success in labor would impress Jimmy in this all-important state. It was another reason why Bill would become an important ally and friend to Hoffa in the next few years.

Hoffa explained the problem in his autobiography, *Hoffa, The Real Story,* which he wrote with Oscar Fraley:

> Take as an example a bakery in Chicago. They engaged in different types of trucking, using large vans to move big loads of bread to their warehouses and supermarkets. But they also used smaller driver-salesman trucks to make home deliveries or small-store deliveries.
>
> Now when they entered into a Teamster contract in Chicago the contract was geared to big-city living costs. So they'd move their business offices to, let's say, a small town in Ohio. There they'd ask for a local contract. The chances were pretty good that the terms and conditions they'd get from a small town local would be a hell of a lot lower than they were in Chicago.

Now they'd start cutting wages and increasing hours in Chicago. They'd claim that, even though the bakery still was in Chicago and deliveries were being made from there, they'd have to pay only as much as the contract called for in the small town where they had their headquarters.

It was a sweet dodge and you'd be surprised how many companies started picking up and moving their headquarters to Ohio, setting up offices there so they could enter into a local contract and avoid paying the higher scale.

Hoffa's idea—and he would still be fighting for it in 1952 when Dan Tobin, the second International president, finally stepped down in favor of Dave Beck—was to have a uniform contract for everyone in the Midwest. He forced two problems.

The first problem was one I saw when I became active in the Teamsters. This was that a uniform contract did not allow the locals freedom in negotiations. I've always maintained that even a bad union is better than no union at all because I've seen the abuses of working people by the bosses over the years. As an organizer even in recent years I've seen sweatshops where conditions were both unsafe and unhealthy. I've seen people give five years, ten years, even twenty years of good, dedicated service, only to have the boss announce that his nephew or niece needs a job and that good employee is being let go. Unions stop that abuse of the dedicated worker.

On the other hand, unions have gone too far, a problem I'll go into later in detail. Instead of looking at what each business does, how much it can make, and what it takes to earn a profit, the workers sometimes think only of themselves. They demand bigger and bigger contracts. They demand more and more benefits. And eventually the company has to go out of business or relocate to an area where they will not face those outrageous demands. The workers suffer because the union leaders refuse to deal realistically with the employers.

Hoffa's uniform contract idea was one that caused us problems. Sure, the bosses were playing games when they moved to Ohio as he described. But the locals needed the freedom to be flexible in their negotiations with different companies. The national contract might not be fair for everyone and, when it wasn't, a business might fail or have to relocate to survive.

Hoffa had another concern during this period. He resented a phenomenon that was quite common in Ohio: the owner-operator, the man who was both boss and employee.

The idea of being an owner-operator was a dream of a lot of guys during the war. They would buy their own rig, then work independently, hauling whatever they wanted, wherever they wanted to go. It was the type of job that formed part of the myth of both the long-distance and the short-haul trucker. A man could do what he wanted to do, set his own hours, and know that he would earn according to the time he put in.

Eventually some guys went into partnership with their wives. They alternated driving, sleeping in the cab in shifts. They were able to see America together and they made a lot of money. Some of them made four or five times what they would have made as employees. They felt proud of themselves and were fulfilling what for them was the American dream.

Hoffa didn't want the drivers owning their own equipment. You cannot organize bosses. He said that they hadn't owned it before the war so they had no business owning it afterward. There were numerous freight hauling companies that avoided negotiating with the Teamsters entirely just by using nonunion owner-operators.

Another problem facing Hoffa was the ease with which a man could buy his own rig. The government was selling off the large number of trucks it had required for wartime but which would go to waste in peace time. They were sold for a fraction of the cost of new equipment and enabled men of relatively limited financial means to feel that they could afford to work toward what many hoped would eventually be fleet ownership.

The largest group of rebels was in Ohio, where the laws were in their favor. These were the owner-operators who hauled for the steel companies. They discovered that through independent negotiations with the companies, they received better pay than as union drivers working for someone else. There were many reasons for this, including the fact that they had to pay their own maintenance and benefits so the steel companies could be more generous in their base pay. Also the men could work whatever hours they wanted as independents, not being forced to take rest breaks as others were required to do. If they violated any federal guidelines, they often doctored their books or team-drove to allow for nonstop work.

Union drivers and rig owners who had previously gone along with Hoffa saw what was happening in Ohio and began to relocate there. They realized that they could make more money by taking advantage of the Ohio benefits. Their actions were a personal affront to Hoffa, who would lose face if the practice were not stopped. The fact that such actions were occurring just sixty miles from Detroit increased his embarrassment.

The Interstate Commerce Commission (ICC) established rates that had to be followed by any driver who drove both interstate and intrastate. Many of the owner-operators found a way around the ICC regulations by only hauling within Ohio. There was plenty of work for them, and the discounting enabled them to take business from the larger companies. Since the men only owned one or two rigs in most cases, their overhead was next to nothing. They made greater profits undercutting the ICC rates than many of the larger companies made staying within the ICC guidelines.

The steel companies and other large businesses decided to take advantage of this situation and of the desires of the men for independence. They either got rid of all their trucks and worked only with owner-operators or arranged for their drivers to buy the trucks the company owned, working out a split arrangement for the fees the drivers earned while paying for their rigs. Again the companies saved money because their drivers were paying their own maintenance, enabling the companies to eliminate mechanics and work areas set aside for maintenance.

Once Hoffa could have relied almost solely on strong-arm tactics to deal with the problems he was facing, and Hoffa never did reject such tactics completely. However, outright violence could no longer be an automatic tool. In 1946, the Hobbs Anti-Racketeering Act made it a crime to stop the transportation of goods involved in commerce or to threaten violence that would lead to such a stoppage.

The Taft-Hartley Act was passed in 1947. Jurisdictional strikes and violence against the self-employed were outlawed. More important, the penalties for violating these acts were stiff: ten years in jail and/or a ten-thousand-dollar fine.

The laws never stopped Hoffa or any of the Teamster leadership. In the end, unions are about money. The employer wants to make the most he can for himself, paying as little as possible to others. The worker knows that he will never take home more than an amount fixed by his hourly wage. He sees that the only way he will ever get ahead is through an increase in his wages. And the union must demonstrate its worth to the membership or the leaders will lose their high salaries and all their benefits when the rank and file replace them. With each side under so much personal and economic pressure, violence is inevitable. Maybe the new laws reduced the openness of that violence, but they did not eliminate—and have not eliminated—violence as a tool of or the result of a bitter strike.

Hoffa sent two men into Ohio during this period to begin to force a change in the way the owner-operators were thriving without yielding to the Teamsters' desires. All manner of secret deals were made. Employers who cooperated with the Teamsters were allowed to make illegal shipments using city drivers who were union members to travel improperly between states. Also, union members gave a break to those steel mills that loaded and unloaded company-owned trucks before loading and unloading the rigs of the owner-operators. This meant that the owner-operators often had long waits which were extremely expensive, even if they arrived at the mills ahead of the company-owned trucks.

Problems began building intensely in Toledo, Ohio, because the owner-operators, including those who had joined the Teamsters Union, were irate about the city drivers' being used illegally. They threatened to shut down the steel hauling industry if the practice continued, and Hoffa had to send Frank Fitz-simmons, who would later succeed Hoffa when Jimmy was jailed, to try to straighten out the problem.

For the first time the Teamsters leadership saw that they could go too far. Fitzsimmons was shouted down every time he tried to justify what, to the men, was unjustifiable. Hoffa had to give in, and the situation was never fully resolved. In fact, it was 1952 before enough of the owner-operators went along with Hoffa that he could claim even a partial victory.

Essentially the Teamster leadership had been sent a message that the members' concerns could be strong enough to override the desires of leadership. Hoffa and Fitzsimmons learned that they could not be certain of blind obedience. As much as we controlled elections and other actions in the years that followed, the failure to defeat the owner/operators completely would be a reminder to the leadership that their pursuit of power and personal gain had to be more subtle.

There were other changes taking place during this period. Bill Presser, Jimmy Hoffa, and others who either were part of the Teamsters or would soon become part of the union were becoming involved with Las Vegas.

There are many stories about the history of modern Las Vegas. Perhaps the most ironic is that the community was originally earmarked as a major religious center for the Mormon Church. Brigham Young sent a group of Mormon missionaries to the Las Vegas desert in 1855 in order to convert the Paiute Indians to the faith. However, the Paiutes were not interested and ignored the missionaries. It took three years for the Mormons to understand the message the Paiutes were expressing, but they finally realized there was no choice other than leaving as failures.

The next time there was an attempt to change Las Vegas radically was in 1905, a year when the forerunner of the Union Pacific Railroad, then known as the San Pedro, Los Angeles and Salt Lake Railroad, extended tracks to the city. Gold and silver had been found in nearby mountains, boomtowns were constructed, and the rail line was meant to help the area do a thriving business. However, the lodes were not so great as everyone thought, playing out quickly before the miners and their families abandoned the region.

The one good point about the Las Vegas region was that it was almost a wasteland and thus ripe for the development of cheap property. Water was desperately needed and a number of workers came to build Boulder Dam thirty miles from the city. Then the army wanted to train American soldiers to fight in the Sahara Desert and decided that the territory just outside Las Vegas would be perfect. In addition, the Hollywood community was growing, the stars notorious for having large incomes and limited morality. They delighted in traveling to Las Vegas every time they wanted to get married without a waiting period. Then, when the marriage soured in a few weeks or months, they could go to the Reno, Nevada, dude ranches for six weeks of pampered relaxation while establishing enough of a residency to be divorced.

But the real potential of Las Vegas was not understood until the Moe Sedway arrival in 1941. Sedway understood big-time gambling and was sent to establish the Trans-America wire service in Nevada. The wire service would provide racetrack information to bookmakers. Control would rest with both the Capone gang in Chicago and a man named Benjamin Siegel in Los Angeles.

Siegel was a handsome man who dressed in the latest styles of the day. His clothing was monogrammed, his shoes handmade in the Italian style. He wore pin-striped suits, tailored overcoats with fur collars, and snap-brimmed fedoras. He was seen in the finest restaurants and night clubs, traveling in a chauffeur-driven limousine. His friends were such Hollywood stars as George Raft, Jack Warner, Cary Grant, and Jean Harlow, and his recreation of choice was golf on the major courses of Florida, California, and Acapulco.

But Ben Siegel, as he was known to the public, had another side. The press nicknamed him "Bugsy." The most intimate insiders sometimes referred to him as "The Bug," but not to his face. He was willing to kill any man who used the nickname.

The fear that Benny Siegel generated in many mobsters was due to the way he earned his money. He and Meyer Lansky handled most of the contracts for the New York and New Jersey organized crime families. If you wanted someone killed, you called Benny and the matter was handled.

The work came naturally to Siegel, who was considered one of the most precocious criminals of all times. American history is filled with stories about young criminals such as Billy the Kid. These are usually young punks whose careers involve a couple of shootings or perhaps a series of dramatic robberies. Siegel was far superior to such nonsense. He was a brilliant psychopath who, before he was twenty-one, was considered highly skilled at white slavery, rape, drug dealing, bootlegging, bookmaking, extortion, robbery, hijacking, bur-glary, murder, and the numbers racket. He put together his first gang at age fourteen, then teamed with Meyer Lansky at twenty in order to make murder a respected business in the underworld. Had the two men been only slightly more sophisticated in their business knowledge, they probably would have incorpo-rated and sold stock in the thriving concern. As it was, they were emulated seven years later by the organization known as Murder, Incorporated.

Siegel and Lansky went so far as to form a board of directors which also included Lucky Luciano, Al Capone, Lepke Buchalter, Longie Zwillman, Joey Adonis, Johnny Torrio, Gurrah Shapiro, Augie Pisano, Willie Moretti, Dutch Schultz, and Frank Costello. It was a Who's Who of organized crime.

Siegel was viewed as a man who could organize the various mob factions. Organization on the East Coast had enabled the various families to move into highly profitable crimes without wasting their time in constant warfare with one another. This was not the case on the West Coast, so Siegel was sent to

California to bring some order to an area where in thirty-seven years there had been forty-one murders officially linked to organized crime. Although almost meaningless by today's standards, such violence at that time was considered out of control. Since the state had a limited population at the time, the numbers were actually greater in proportion to the number of people living there than in better known areas of violence such as Chicago.

Siegel formed a coalition of the various factions, making Jack I. Dragna his right-hand man. This preceded a series of violent incidents in which small-time operators—gamblers, bootleggers, and so on—were beaten, murdered, or had their businesses destroyed if they refused to cooperate. In addition, Siegel helped coordinate a method for smuggling narcotics through Mexico and for transporting prostitutes up and down the West Coast.

The prostitute trail showed Siegel's brilliance. He studied the business and realized that most of the money came from regular users of the girls. But the customers paid for sex because they liked variety, not just in what they did but in the women who were available. He put together a stable of the most desirable women, then kept them moving up and down the coast. They might work in San Diego for a week or two, then move up to Los Angeles, Sacramento, San Francisco, Portland, Seattle, and back down the coast. They stayed only long enough to work the regulars, then moved on, a new batch of prostitutes taking their place before following the same trail north and south. Not only did this fact excite the customers seeking variety, it also prevented the police who had not been paid off from building a case against any of the women.

Siegel had a tremendous arrogance, fueled, in part, by his success. By the end of the war, he had turned California crime into a well-run business. He had managed to unite the seemingly disparate elements, showing them that by working harmoniously, they could make more money for themselves. The ultimate monument to his genius would be the most fabulous entertainment spot ever created, and he wanted it to be legitimate. He would have gambling; a hotel, nightclub, bars, restaurant, swimming pool, exquisite service, and well-landscaped grounds; and no one trying to arrest him. The logical location was Nevada, where Moe Sedway had formed the highly successful wire service.

Sedway was never a threat to Siegel, even though he was several years older than the man for whom he worked. He was a small man who seemed to blend into the woodwork. People were comfortable talking in front of him, never realizing that he was listening to everything that was said, then passing it on to Siegel.

Sedway's skills and ambition seemed to grow after he hit Las Vegas. Siegel was busy coordinating the big money in California, the wire service being essential to the gambling casinos that were legal in Las Vegas, yet bringing in relatively small profits. However, most of the gamblers who wanted to work with the bookmakers hung around the various clubs that had slot machines, black-jack, crap tables, and other activities that did bring in large sums of money. If the bookmakers could not have a reliable wire service, the more lucrative aspects of their business were jeopardized. As a result, Sedway found that he could blackmail the bookmakers, threatening to cut off the wire service if they did not pay him a piece of the bookmaking action.

Sedway triumphed, but still would not go up against Siegel. He let Benny know what he was doing and brought him into it. By 1942, a number of casinos were providing Siegel and Sedway at least two-thirds of their bookmaking income. Because they made their fortunes from the table operations and ma-chines, no one seemed to care. Yet Siegel's take alone was a minimum of twenty-five thousand dollars per month. In addition, he acquired small pieces of both the Frontier Club and the Golden Nugget.

Without Siegel, and with large sums of money coming in, Sedway decided to become a pillar of the community. He supported church projects and various developments. He was feted by the politicians and the wealthier, more respected citizens. He even went so far as to start to enter politics himself, though Siegel quickly stopped that by saying, "We don't run for office. We own the politi-cians." The break between the two men left Sedway so embittered he became an FBI informer.

Siegel moved to Las Vegas in 1946, apparently planning to operate on his own. He did build his casino. "The fabulous Flamingo Hotel" eventually cost a record $6 million because of Siegel's pretentiousness. For example, there were private sewer lines for every bathroom, a needless extravagance that cost $1 million at a time when the entire operation could have been constructed for $1.5 million. The hotel had marble, imported woods, and a constant change in plans whenever Siegel discovered something he thought would be more elaborate.

The expenses mounted and Siegel went broke, losing $1 million of his own money in the project. Shares of stock were sold for fifty thousand dollars each, yet the bill he owed the Del E. Webb Construction Company of Phoenix, Arizona, which handled the construction, was $2 million more than he had raised.

The Flamingo Hotel opened on December 26, 1946, with a number of Hollywood celebrities in attendance. Jimmy Durante, Eddie Jackson, Xavier Cugat, and other big-name entertainers provided the show. Yet the hotel was not finished, and there were problems with the heating, the air conditioning, and even Siegel's own penthouse apartment.

The hotel lost money from the first day. It also provided a contrast in styles. Everything appeared flawless, the male staff members often wearing tuxedos while handling even relatively minor tasks. Yet anyone who was not a celebrity was likely to be bullied by the violent men who acted as "security," observing everything that took place. There were numerous stories of guests' tossing their cigarettes onto the lawn, only to be attacked by one of Siegel's thugs, who berated them, then forced them to pick up the cigarette butt.

There was a $100,000 loss of funds the first two weeks the casino was in operation, forcing Siegel to close the place until the hotel section was finished. At the same time, Lucky Luciano was in Cuba and called a meeting of the board of directors as well as the top American Mafia ("Combination") figures other than Siegel.

Needing money and not realizing how badly he had jeopardized his position with the mob, Siegel and six of his men flew to Havana to try to arrange a private meeting with Luciano. He wanted time and money. Luciano ordered him to make the hotel work at once.

The Flamingo Hotel reopened on March 27, 1947, and by May it was $300,000 in the black. Siegel was elated, but he would never know how successful he could have been. Three weeks later, on June 20, he was murdered at the home of Virginia Hill, one of his girlfriends, in Beverly Hills, California. The assassin used a 30-caliber rifle with a nine shot clip, firing rapidly and striking Siegel four times. Twenty minutes after the killing, Moe Sedway and Morris Rosen walked into the hotel and took control of the operation.

As unusual as the circumstances surrounding the "fabulous Flamingo Hotel" happened to be, Siegel effectively showed the mob how successful Las Vegas could be as an entertainment center. There were other hotels by then, but the publicity surrounding the Flamingo greatly boosted interest in the area. Siegel created the idea of a fantasy world for adults where gambling, lavish entertainment, luxury service, and low-cost, high-quality dining could lure men and women from throughout the world. The only problem that existed was a need for risk-free money, and that was where the Teamsters were going to become involved.

The man who made the connections that brought Teamster investment to Las Vegas was Moe Dalitz, and his actions actually began when he was running a chain of laundry facilities in the Michigan area.

Isaac Litwak was the head of Teamster Local 285 in Detroit. Litwak was a dedicated union man who believed in aiding the workers. He genuinely wanted to better their lot, and, in 1949, the biggest issue he faced was the desire for a five-day workweek for the laundry company driver.

Moe Dalitz had no intention of providing the Teamsters with such a fair contract. The arrangement would cost him and every other laundry owner more money than he was willing to pay. He decided to fight the strike by utilizing the laundry owners' association, the Detroit Institute of Laundering.

During this period Dalitz was well known in several areas. He had been a member of the Purple Gang and later operated out of Cleveland, where he helped organize the Cleveland Syndicate division of the National Crime Syndicate run by Meyer Lansky and Lucky Luciano. Dalitz was also a gambler who enjoyed the action in both Las Vegas and Havana, Cuba, and built the Desert Inn in 1950. In addition, Dalitz was a friend of John Paris and his wife, Sylvia Pagano O'Brien Paris, the alleged former mistress of Jimmy Hoffa. As a result, Hoffa and Dalitz became friends.

Hoffa understood that Litwak was an honest man, a troublesome fact during the labor negotiations. He sent his own men, Joseph Holtzman and Jack Bushkin, to Carl's Chop House to negotiate with the representatives of the Detroit Institute of Laundering.

It was explained to the laundry people that there was no need to worry about Litwak if they wanted to pay a fee for a favorable contract. The idea was to split the fee among all the laundry owners, minimizing their personal costs. So long as the share of the fee for each laundry owner was less than the cost of limiting drivers to a five-day week, the money would be well spent. The "fee" would be twenty-five thousand dollars.

Hoffa had not considered that many of the laundries did a volume of business such that almost any major increase in costs would force them into bankruptcy. Finally Dalitz's and Hoffa's men settled on a bribe of $17,500.00 to be paid in three installments. The first payment, to be delivered in 1949, would be $7,500.00. Five thousand dollars more would be paid in each of the next two years. This came to an assessment per laundry owner of $45.00 for each truck the first year and $22.50 per truck for each of the next two years.

Litwak was not told of the secret arrangement. He continued bargaining with the Detroit Institute of Laundering representatives, convinced that he could win his drivers a five-day week. Yet at the end of the bargaining session, when Litwak realized that he would have to call a strike, suddenly Jimmy Hoffa entered. He announced that those portions of the contract with which everyone was in agreement would stand as the final contract. The five-day workweek would not be included, and there would be no arguments. It was a power play which both Hoffa and Litwak recognized as unnegotiable.

Hoffa liked to repay the people who had been good to him. Ten years later, Dalitz would begin receiving multimillion-dollar loans from the Teamsters Pension Fund. Among these was a loan to build the one-hundred-bed Sunrise Hospital, a facility that opened despite thirty-nine serious building code violations. Bill Rardon, the county director of building safety, was edged out because he had allowed the hospital to open, though he claimed he had fought such an action and been overruled by the chairman of the County Commission.

Money connected with Sunrise Hospital went through another firm known as Congress Factors, which was run by Milton Dranow. Milton's brother, Benjamin, borrowed $1.2 million from the Teamsters Pension Fund in order to invest in a Minneapolis department store which went bankrupt through fraud. Benjamin eventually went to jail for that crime, in addition to being convicted of income tax evasion.

Another loan, this one for $1 million, was made by the Teamsters Central States, Southeast, and Southwest Areas Pension Fund to A&M enterprises, a firm whose members were long time Dalitz associates. A&M's loan was also connected with Sunrise Hospital, with the equipment's serving as collateral.

Eventually Hoffa made certain that Sunrise succeeded by arranging deals that forced both Teamsters and members of the Culinary Workers Union to use Sunrise even though the quality of care, at the time, was considered worse than at other facilities. In addition, Dalitz personally helped raise money for cancer research grants to the hospital through his involvement with the Damon Runyon Cancer Fund and the Desert Inn's Tournament of Champions charity golf event. The fact that the hospital, at the time, was not involved with cancer research or equipped to start any was not important.

Perhaps the most humorous of the Las Vegas Teamster corruption stories involved the time when fifty-two cabdrivers in one local wanted a formal agreement to be allowed to participate in the prostitution business. It happened with Roxie's Resort, a motel in Formyle, four miles outside Las Vegas. The motel was owned by Roxie and Eddie Clippinger. The place had thirty-five girls, who were moved in and out enough that there was always someone new to try, some variety. The standard charge in the early 1950s was five dollars for each fifteen minutes and you could stay as long as you liked. The location was well known to the sheriff and his deputies, but no one cared. Roxie's was grossing more than a million dollars annually, truly big money at the time, and payoffs were made wherever necessary. Thus it went ten years without a raid and was a standard destination for the cabdrivers who felt that they should be rewarded for taking clients there.

According to testimony that was brought out in the trial of the Clippingers during a rare period of social reform, at one Teamster meeting, a driver read the following speech after referring to himself and the other drivers as "pimps" for Roxie's.

> We members of Teamsters local 631 would like to call a special meeting and have a vote on subjects mentioned about Formyle.
> It seems that at different times we have had some union members working there. We recommend that all men have a paid up union card. It seems that we are helping to build a business there which isn't appreciated.
> We ask that the house use one price for every 15 minutes or whatever is suitable, whether he comes in a cab or not. If he does come in a cab the driver gets $1 out of every $6 spent. If a driver sells the customer in the beginning and he ever goes out in a private car the driver is ruined forever in

getting a so called "kelly" which is always expressed several times. Several drivers have had people that would make regular customers but after one or two trips they wind up with no "kelly." This does not cover a full discussion but we would like to call a special meeting for all drivers and vote and discuss this subject.

All of this would occur later, and I mention it only so you can understand how these early deals would eventually have an impact on many other aspects of the union's business deals. In 1950 Bill was just starting his power rise and I had returned to Cleveland from California. I would soon be going into the unions along with Harold, Jackie, and Bill, but for the moment I was involved in a business enterprise that was going to send me to jail.

I did not stay in California very long because I had no way of earning much money. Cleveland was the place where I had connections, where I would have the easiest time making a score. But I wasn't certain what to do, other than knowing that I needed to get a job.

The first work I did was legitimate. I wanted to drive a soft drink truck because it would pay well and the work was easy. I went to see a friend who could get me a drive with Coca-Cola. The friend tried, but in those days the local Coca-Cola Company would not hire Jews to work as driver/salesmen.

Next I went to Bireley's Bottling Company, a fruit beverage soft drink company whose Bireley's Orange was extremely popular, and there I got a job as a driver/salesman with a route of stores to service.

My route took me to the Jewish neighborhood of Kinsman Road, where many of the store owners were immigrants. Coke was the most popular soft drink anyone sold, and there were cases stacked floor to ceiling. Bireley's, though probably the most popular fruit drink of the day, did not do anywhere near the volume of business that Coke did. Most stores had only a couple of cases of orange, grape, and the other flavors I handled.

I realized that I was not going to make any real money if I couldn't move a larger volume of the soft drinks. I went to the owners and said, in Yiddish, that it was a shame they didn't buy more Bireley's. They asked me why and I told them that I was a Jewish boy and had tried to get a job with Coca-Cola, only to find that Coke didn't hire Jews.

The store owners were people who had fled the persecution caused by anti-Semitism in Europe. When they discovered that, in those days, unlike today, the Coca-Cola people would not hire Jews, they refused to stock more than a minimum amount of Coke. There would be twenty to thirty cases of Bireley's purchased per store, yet only one or two cases of Coke.

The Coke people were irate, even to the point of sending two supervisors to follow me around and see what was happening. I finally went over to their car and told them the truth. I explained that I was letting the customers know that they wouldn't hire Jews and that was why their business had been damaged.

The supervisors were irate, telling me that what I was doing was against the law. I mentioned that Coke's hiring policy was illegal. I told them that I would go to the papers and tell them that Coke was trying to hustle me if they didn't let me alone, and they backed off.

The route was built up and I was making a lot of money on commission when my boss called me in to ask me to take over a route in the Polish neighborhood. I didn't like the idea because I was making so much money, but the company needed the other area built up and offered me an extra hundred dollars a week to do it.

I figured that if my story were good with the Jews, it would be good with the Polish. I knew a Polish guy who taught me how to say "It's a shame" in Polish. Then I told the people the same story, that Coke wouldn't hire the Polish and that's why I had to work for Bireley's.

I didn't know whether Coke discriminated against the Polish and I didn't care. The story worked when there was discrimination. I figured it would work in the Polish neighborhoods as well, and it did. The only problem was that now it wasn't legitimate and, though I began to increase the route, Coke had a legitimate complaint against me. The union head called me to tell me to stop and I said that not only wouldn't I, but I was planning to go into the Hungarian neighborhood and do the same thing.

The business agent laughed and said he would have to switch me. He was going to arrange for me to have a beer truck so I could make a better living without the scam.

But I had no interest in a straight job. Even when I was delivering Bireley's, I used to steal an occasional truckload of soft drinks and get rid of them on the side. What I really wanted was a way to make a good score.

I was living with my wife in an apartment, and a lot of the guys in the neighborhood knew who I was. They respected me and knew I was always looking for a good score. That was why one kid I had met a few times in a bar came over to see me. He said that he had something he wanted to show me and took me outside to look at a 1947 or 1948 car with a couple of thousand miles on it.

"Where the hell did you get that?" I asked him.

"I stole it," he replied. "I've been driving it around for a month."

"I don't want anything to do with this," I told him. "I don't want to fuck around with cars. It's too complicated for me. Why don't you do yourself a favor? Park it on the next street and leave it go."

There was a park behind the area where I had him leave the car and I used to go there twice a day to walk my Dalmatian dog. I kept an eye on the car, waiting for the cops to pick it up. A week went by, then two, then a month. After it had stayed there two months I realized that it wasn't going to be moved. No one noticed or no one cared.

I had an old clunker car that was falling apart. I decided to switch the license plates from the one I owned to the stolen one I persuaded the guy to abandon. Then I began driving the new one as though it were my own.

I knew a few used car dealers so I went to them, told them I had a stolen car, and wanted to know how I could sell it. Most of the guys had no idea and didn't want anything to do with it. But one man told me that there was a way to get rid of it. He explained that in the South—Georgia and Tennessee, for instance—there were no titles for cars, only bills of sale.

I went down south to Tennessee with the car, drove to the city hall, went inside, and told the clerk that a policeman stopped me while I was driving because I had Ohio license plates on my car. I explained that he told me that since I would be down there more than ten days, I had to register my car.

The clerk asked for my title, so I told her it was back home. "What's the difference? I just want to register."

The clerk gave me a registration and a license plate. Then she said I would also need a bill of sale.

I started to hang around a couple of used car dealers' lots until I was able to steal some of their stationery. Then I typed out a bill of sale using a phony name.

I returned to Cleveland, now with a Tennessee plate, registration, and bill of sale. I went to the Department of Motor Vehicles and used the same story: that I had been stopped by the police and had to register my car since I was a Cleveland resident. I also had to pay sales tax, making a show of complaining about the fact that I had already paid sales tax and resented the extra charge. By the time I was done I had to pay $138 or $148 for registration, but that gave me a legitimate Ohio title, registration, and plates.

I realized that I could make a lot of money stealing cars if I did it right. I followed the same pattern each time, taking the stolen cars south, getting local forms, then returning to the North, where I would have them legitimately registered. Finally I drove to car lots in Michigan, Illinois, Pennsylvania, and West Virginia, where I sold the cars I stole. Each time I averaged twenty-six hundred to twenty-nine hundred dollars, big money for that time. This was 1949 and I stole only 1947 and 1948 models.

My success was quickly noticed by my brother and my friends. Harry asked me what kind of score I had made, but I didn't want to tell him the details. I had an easy time of it, stealing one or two cars a month, getting all the money I wanted. If I cut anybody else in on what I was doing, nothing would be so easy.

Eventually, I ignored my better judgment and told Harry what I was doing with the cars, and agreed to cut him in on the action.

Now things were changing and I was getting uncomfortable. Instead of stealing one or two cars a month, I was stealing three cars a month. I had the keys, so I took the major risk. Then, when I had the cars, Harry would help drive them down to Georgia or Tennessee to arrange for the changes in registration that would make them "legitimate" for resale. We only drove a few because we didn't like driving the stolen ones any more than we had to. Usually we would just take the paper work down there because that was all we needed to have to get the right documents.

Harry didn't want to drive alone so he approached Jackie Presser, offering Jackie a few bucks to drive him south. Then Jackie got a guy to drive for him. Soon there were four or five guys involved in the car theft ring that had been so comfortable when I was working alone. Instead of stealing a couple of cars a month and enjoying myself, I was suddenly in big business, having to steal a car every few days to cover everyone with a cut. It was like having a straight job and the work was rough, though there would be times when we all had plenty of money and would lay off for three or four weeks.

The only thing that worried me during this time was the fact that only Jackie owned a legitimate car. Harry and the others had been too broke to buy a car so their only transportation was the cars I had stolen. Driving a hot car offered too great a risk because they could get a ticket or something and the whole deal would go bad.

At this point our car theft ring involved five people. I worked alone, stealing all the cars. No one ever saw me take one, and I never would have been suspected of any crimes if I had continued to work alone. The driving, the paperwork, and the other details that were necessary after the initial theft were handled by two teams. Harold and Jackie were partners, and we had two other guys who acted as a separate team. In addition, Harold Friedman was hanging around us, watching us split up the money, fully aware of what we were doing.

I never really liked Harold Friedman, and, as we got older, I watched him do things that hurt a lot of the union men. But he was not the kind of guy who would go out and steal something. His father was doing well in union work and had given Harold a car. He didn't have to worry about things like the rest of us, yet he still wanted more. Finally he came to me and asked to be cut in.

I told Harry that, beginning the following month, I'd cut him in on the car thefts. I'd take an extra car for him, and he would do the kind of driving and paperwork that the others had been doing. Unfortunately, before we could get that far, everything fell apart.

I stole two 1948 Pontiacs, which the last two guys to join the ring were handling. One of the guys was stupid enough to carry the titles to both of the

Pontiacs with him when he went to see the car dealer in Columbus, Ohio. He had one title in one pocket and the other title in the other. The trouble was that he couldn't remember which pocket had the right title for the car he was trying to sell. He finally pulled out the wrong title, then switched when he discovered his mistake.

The dealer never let on that he was suspicious. He just told the guys that he was not in the market to buy used cars right then, carefully noting the license plates and description. As they pulled out of the car lot, suspecting nothing, the dealer called the state troopers and had them arrested. They were terrified when they were locked up, telling everything about our car theft ring.

The minute I heard about the arrests I knew that I had to go on the lam. There were no witnesses to what I had done, yet the two kids had finked on me and enough cops knew I was a thief that I could be in big trouble. I took Harry's kids and gave them to Bill and Faye, asking them to take care of them for a while because I had to go out of town and my wife couldn't handle them without help. I didn't tell them why I was leaving, though. The FBI began looking for me. Although I stayed hidden for three or four months, they eventually found me living in a West Virginia motel room.

Apparently either no one brought Jackie Presser's name into the case or there was a cover-up. I never knew which. Bill Presser was becoming an important and powerful figure in Cleveland. He had either bribed or done favors for so many politicians, judges, lawyers, and cops that the Presser name had power. No one wanted to embarrass him or get on his bad side by going after Jackie.

The problem was that there was one way Jackie's name could come up in the case and that was if I went to trial. Apparently if that occurred, the whole story, including all the names, would get out and Jackie would have to be indicted.

I don't believe in pleading guilty. I don't care what I've done. I figure that if they want to send me to jail, they're going to have to work at it. And in this case, no one ever saw me steal anything. They saw the money I had, but there was no one who ever saw me take a car.

The county jail was located on Twenty-first Street and Payne Avenue in Cleveland at the time. The cells were divided into blocks where from eight to a dozen men were held. The blocks were separated from each other so you could not reach anyone in a different block. They were also segregated by race.

In a nearby cell block was Shondor Birns, who was given almost complete freedom within the jail. He was not actually allowed to enter different cell blocks, but he could walk anywhere else the guards normally went. Birns acted as a mediator among the men, including the time I got into a fight with the fat mobster who was bringing in the food and the girls.

Birns would go in and out of my life and the lives of almost everyone in Cleveland who was involved with either organized crime or organized labor. He came to America from Austria-Hungary when he was two years old in 1907, yet for some reason he never became an American citizen. He was raised on Woodland Avenue between East Forty-fifth and East Fifty-ninth streets, gaining a reputation as one of the toughest kids in the area.

Alex "Shondor" Birns had a different childhood from mine and that of most of the men I knew. I was typical in that I was raised in an ethnic neighborhood that was closed to outsiders. Shondor was raised in a location where there were Jews, Italians, Hungarians, blacks, Germans, Slovenians, and members of other nationality groups. It was probably the most integrated of all the areas where immigrant groups lived in Cleveland. Shondor made friends with kids who would grow up to head various criminal organizations normally closed to outsiders. He was the rare individual who could mediate disputes between the blacks and the Mafia, or between the Jewish Combination and the Mafia, or between whatever other large factions were fighting.

Birns also had the sense not to become too greedy. He sometimes seemed to have a piece of everyone's action, working in numbers, prostitution, and other rackets. He also had businesses such as the Alhambra Restaurant and the Ten-Eleven Club.

He was a friend of judges, lawyers, cops, and journalists. He was delighted when someone called him "Public Enemy Number 1" in the press. And he accepted serving time on those occasions when he went to jail, for example, after his 1925 conviction for car theft. There was much violence in Shondor's life, though almost never related to business. The violence—and it included murder—was generally personal, the result of his quick temper. However, he managed to avoid jail for most of the violence because he was so well connected.

I had to stay in jail until the trial, and I told my lawyer that I was not going to plead guilty. He gave that message to Bill Presser, who came to me, all upset, explaining that I had to plead guilty.

Apparently Bill had made a deal with the prosecution to protect Jackie. He told me that if there were any waves—meaning if I pleaded innocent—his son would be implicated in the case.

I didn't care what happened to Jackie. No one had seen me. They would have a tough time building a case against me since the others had handled all the paperwork and two of them had been caught with the cars.

Bill went to my brother, Harry, and made a deal without telling me. He had Harry write out a statement against me, detailing my actions as a car thief. In exchange, he agreed to adopt Harry's children as his own, raising them, sending them to college, and including them in his will. Then he would use the sworn statement against me as pressure to plead guilty and prevent a trial that would raise Jackie's name.

It might seem that Bill was using Harry's children, but the truth is that there were always two sides to Bill. He was a vicious user, a man who would screw anybody in business given half a chance. When he was given money for someone, including a family member, he took a cut for himself before passing it on. Men who respected him, such as Jimmy Hoffa, knew this and always made certain they paid me directly when I worked for them. The Presser family was notorious for taking advantage of people.

Yet there was a second side to Bill Presser. He loved children and he loved his family. For years I always thought that it was Faye who organized family gatherings, who made certain we all spent time together, who introduced my wives to the various members of the family. But the truth was that Bill was behind all that, something I did not realize until he died and many past relationships fell apart.

Bill did not take Harry's children as collateral in some deal. He wasn't planning on turning them over to Faye, letting her raise them, and considering them a burden he was stuck with as his part of a bargain. Bill was committing himself to being a full father, a man who would truly love those children and treat like his own and, in some ways, better than his own. Harry's kids were almost young enough to be Bill's grandchildren. Bill's own sons were grown, and Jackie, in Bill's eyes, was something of a failure who was pushing too hard and accomplishing too little. He was determined not to make the same mistakes when he raised Harry's children. He was going to be as much a father to them as if they were his natural children, and he was going to do it with the greater knowledge he had gained raising Jackie and his brother. In fact, Bill probably would have taken Harry's kids, regardless, had Harry asked, but Harry did not know this and Bill took advantage of that lack of awareness to ensure Harry's full cooperation.

Bill came to me the next day and told me that Harry, my own brother, had written a statement that named me as being guilty of the car theft. He said that he had worked a deal in which I would plead guilty in exchange for two years' probation. That seemed fair to me, especially since I wouldn't have to serve any time.

Once I decided to plead guilty, I went to Harold Friedman, who was in jail with me. I told him to instruct his lawyer to put me on the witness stand and I would clear him. I would explain that he never received any money and that he never stole any cars.

Harold's father, Harvey Friedman, hated me and wouldn't make any deal that involved my testimony. I figured that telling the truth about Harold wouldn't matter since I was getting probation anyway. But Harvey was too stubborn to allow his son's lawyer to do what I asked, so Harold was sentenced to two years for conspiracy though his only crimes were knowing what we were doing, hanging around as we split up the money, and keeping his mouth shut.

The others got three years, and then it was my turn. I'm still not certain exactly what happened. The Judge may have been annoyed about one thing or another, but even an angry judge goes along with the fix when the money has been paid. No matter what else was going on, I knew that when the sentence was handed down, Bill Presser had screwed me. He hadn't made any deal for probation. He had protected his son and didn't give a damn about me. I was sentenced to twenty years.

The sentence was based on four counts, each worth five years in the can. The only decent thing the judge did was to run the sentences concurrently so the maximum time I would spend was five years. Both Harold and I were going to Milan, Michigan, to the Federal Penitentiary.

I never realized what type of men end up in jail before I went to Milan. A federal penitentiary is different from a state pen. You get a lot of extremely bright men in a federal pen, such as an illegal Russian immigrant I met who had stolen diamonds and had them hidden and waiting for his release. He also was able to sneak in watches and, when I broke mine, he was able to fix it. In fact, this man could fix any type of machinery.

There was one machine that broke down and the part to fix it cost eighteen thousand dollars. The immigrant took a look at the problem and told me that he could fashion a part from scrap that was already available. I believed in his ability, so I convinced the captain to let him try. He used two assistants, and the entire cost to the prison, including the price of the materials he shaped to make it work, was only a couple of dollars.

Another time a decision was made to move the bake shop, a much more elaborate problem because of the large commercial ovens that also had to be relocated. The prison got a bid on what it would cost. Then the Russian showed them how they could break down some walls, use maybe eight or ten men, move the ovens, and repair the walls, all the same day. No baking time would be lost, and I convinced the captain to listen to the man.

Then there was an artist whose work was quite successful. His only problem was that he had a three-hundred-dollar-a-day heroin habit that forced him to steal.

And there was a mathematician who could do anything with numbers. However, he was one of those caught during the investigation into corruption in the offices of Louisiana Governor Huey Long.

But no matter how privileged I might have been, no matter how distinguished the company, I was in trouble. I did not make parole because the government was out to get me for the auto theft ring that they thought was much bigger than it actually was.

The government agents were convinced that I was the mastermind of a multimillion-dollar operation and that I had large sums of money stashed somewhere just waiting to be enjoyed when I got out. This was because one of the last of the guys to join the ring exaggerated my role when he was questioned. He told of a time he got into trouble selling a car in Chicago and I had to get him out. We flew back together on a regular commercial airline, got the car, and straightened out the problem. But when the cops got to him, he lied and said that I had a chartered plane.

I was mad when Bill Presser lied about the probation. I was even hotter when I wasn't given the parole.

It turned out that Faye did not realize that Bill had screwed me. She was all upset about my serving time in jail, especially when it turned out that I would have to do at least forty months: two-thirds of the five-year sentence. Faye talked with me and promised that I would be home by Christmas 1951.

I was angry and didn't believe Faye. Then I was called into the associate warden's office to receive a telephone call from an Ohio congressman who had either been paid off by Bill or was mob-connected. I never knew which. As Faye shouted in the background, telling me that she loved me and that I would be coming home, he tried to explain that he had arranged for a parole. As promised, I was released.

Bill had become a part of the Teamsters Union by the time I was released from jail. His involvement, which began in 1950, was the first break in the hold of the Irish. Bill entered the Teamsters after Ed Murphy's death. Murphy was one of the few labor leaders who did not let ethnic background stand in the way of maintaining a power base.

Ed Murphy was a tough Irish labor leader who disliked Italians and most Jews except for Harvey Friedman. He did not like Bill and would not have wanted to see him gain any power.

Murphy had a background a little like my own. He was born in 1891 in what amounted to an Irish ghetto on Cleveland's near west side. Typically the family was very large, very poor, and beset by early deaths. There were eleven children in all, Murphy being the sixth, and the kids were orphaned when Ed was thirteen. No matter what plans or dreams he may have had, Murphy's world turned to one of work and survival. He drove a horse and cart for General Cartage Company, then switched to driving a dray, a low, heavy cart that had no sides and was more difficult to handle with a load. He worked long hours for little pay, a fact which made him decide to try working with the newly formed Teamsters Union in 1911 when he was twenty years old. Five years later he was vice president of Local 407 and, in 1924, he became president.

Murphy was a lot like Hoffa in that he believed in the idea of the union's bettering the life of the workingman. He may or may not have been completely honest at the time—Hoffa certainly wasn't as he rose to power—but he was not like Bill Presser. He wasn't interested in extortion and bribes. He was interested in improving conditions for the worker.

There were seven Teamster locals in the Cleveland area with a total of 3,500 members. Murphy felt that there would be more power if they worked together so he and John Rohrich formed Teamsters Joint Council 41. He then became general organizer for the International in 1931. This led to his having power over 125,000 drivers in four states and Canada.

Murphy developed the strategies necessary to cripple plants where a strike was taking place. Before Murphy brought so many men together, a strike was not always successful. One group of employees might be on the picket line at a manufacturing plant, but deliveries would be made by members of a different local of the same union. Still other union members might be on duty inside. It was Murphy who found the way to shut down the plant completely. By affiliating drivers of various locals through Joint Council 41, it became a simple matter to shut down an entire plant by not allowing any drivers to take supplies to the location.

Murphy was respected because he was considered to be one of the most honest Teamster officials. He was a skilled negotiator who used strikes as a last resort. He also was praised for keeping "racketeering," another way of saying organized crime influence, out of the union.

Another factor in Murphy's success was his refusal to be caught up in power politics within the Cleveland Federation of Labor (CFL). He chose to work behind the scenes, letting other men take positions of leadership. As a power broker, he actually had more influence than the men in front.

In 1938, Murphy worked to change the CFL by limiting the former dominance of the building trades officials. Through his influence, Tommy Lenahan became executive secretary. Lenahan was the Teamster candidate (though he was actually an iron worker), but he arranged for both the Teamsters and the Building Trades Council to work together within the CFL.

Lenahan stayed in power until 1947, when Murphy decided that he had been in office too long. There was a rising antilabor bias in Cleveland caused by the postwar prosperity. Lenahan did not seem able to handle the problem but William Finegan did. Through Murphy's support, Finegan won by a tiny margin.

Murphy died in 1950, having previously suffered such severe injuries in a car crash that he had been forced to retire. Without Murphy's power, it was a simple matter to bring in Bill Presser and Babe Triscaro, respected labor leaders who were also seen as representing an element that could join with Finegan against the Lenahan faction. Bill would not have been welcome in the old days, but now he was assured of a power position that would soon be a factor in the suspension of the Teamsters from the AFL-CIO after the two groups merged.

The other major change that would take place in the Teamsters Union once Bill was in power was the forming of the Central States Conference of Teamsters. Ohio and eleven other states created this new organization in 1953, also merging their pension funds. Suddenly anyone seeking money had a source for loans that was larger than the reserves of many banks. It was that money that would eventually be used for both legitimate business loans, including the establishment of casinos in Las Vegas, and loans that were highly questionable and the source of numerous government inquiries.

In 1950 Murphy's death left an important opening. At first it seemed logical that Murphy's son would succeed him at Joint Council 41. The son, Joseph Murphy of the Service Employees International Union Local 47, thought he was going to get the position, as did John Felice, Sr., and Tony Cimino, up-and-coming leaders of two other locals. The position was finally offered to Babe Triscaro.

Babe refused the job, though I never learned his reasons. It may have involved the different organized crime families and their views of who should move into the union leadership. Or Babe may have meant it when he said that he felt he could not handle the position. Babe then said that Bill Presser was the right man for the job. Bill was well known in the labor field and could be moved into the Teamsters to take over Joint Council 41.

Everything was a setup when Bill joined, though I didn't know it at the time. Bill came to me the day of the election and asked me to get my brother Joe because we had a meeting to attend.

Joe was a member of Local 410 because he was working as a mechanic in the jukebox business. He was a big man, strong, a better fighter than I, who never feared anyone. But Joe lacked the violent streak that was in me. I was comfortable going out and breaking heads on a picket line. Joe was not. He would fight back if someone attacked him. He would defend Bill Presser when Bill was cornered. Yet he didn't enjoy fighting, didn't want to use his fists unless it was absolutely necessary. Still, Joe was a good man to have with you if trouble was unavoidable.

I was told to pick up Bill around 6:00 or 6:30 in the evening and take him down to Joint Council 41. Joe was to be there, too, and Bill wanted to make certain I was armed. I told him that I would be carrying a gun and my blackjack. Joe would be unarmed. He'd use his fists if he had to, but he wouldn't carry a weapon.

At the meeting hall when we arrived were presidents, vice presidents, and other members of the various locals that Joint Council 41 comprised. Twenty-two different locals from Cuyahoga County as well as a few from Akron (Summit County) were represented.

I took the aisle seat, with Bill Presser next to me. Joe sat two rows behind. If trouble started, it would probably come from someone who was trying to reach

Bill from the aisle. That person would have to get by me, and Joe would be behind for a backup if things got too rough.

Nominations opened for president, vice president, and secretary/treasurer of Joint Council 41. Different men got up to make speeches, some talking for Bill Presser and some talking against him. The ones who were against him discussed his Mafia connections. They called him a gangster and said that they did not want him in the organization.

Oddly, there were very few Italian locals. The Bakers' Drivers' Local was split because some members were German and some were Jewish. Perhaps four other locals were Italian, and all the Italians were told to vote for Bill. This meant that four and a half locals would vote for him, but I knew that the remaining locals, all ethnic, would vote against him. For example, he had no chance against the Irish, who dominated; the Polish; or the others.

There was a guy sitting within arm's length behind Bill who suddenly got up and began bad rapping Bill Presser. He talked about Bill's being Mafia and stressed that he shouldn't be in charge of Joint Council 41. He even said that it was wrong to allow Bill to bring his Electrical Workers Union charter into the Teamsters Union.

The man began making sense. He questioned how Bill could rise so fast after entering the union. He came in as a nobody, and suddenly there were people trying to make him president of the Joint Council. They were all good questions and ones I might have asked if I had been in what I thought was his position.

"Now, Bill?" I asked him, wondering whether to hit the guy to shut him up. He was just continuing to speak, constantly talking against Bill for fifteen or twenty minutes.

Bill told me to shut up, an action I didn't understand. Finally someone else interrupted, requesting a time limit on the speaking for fear that the man would go on for hours. It was obvious that the guy truly hated Bill.

Finally the speeches were limited to ten minutes, one of the Irish guys being the next one to talk against Bill. "You haven't got a chance in hell," I told Bill.

Then it was over. They took the vote and, to my surprise, Bill won.

You could hear the rumbling all around: "Fucking Jews and Dagos are taking over." I knew we were in for trouble, certain we were going to be jumped in the parking lot outside. I was tensing for action, getting ready to take Bill out, knowing that Joe and I would have to fight all the way.

"Sit down. Sit down," said Bill, his voice calm as he watched many of the people leave the building. He was in no hurry to go, completely unconcerned about the reaction.

It was finally nine o'clock at night. Bill looked at me and said, "Come on. Let's go to my new office."

We went up the stairs to where there was a small office, sort of like a reception area, and a larger office that would belong to Bill. I still did not understand what was happening until we stepped inside and there was the man who seemed willing to talk for hours against Bill. There was also the acting Joint Council 41 leader, an Irishman, along with two or three guys who had been making speeches against him. In addition some of the Italians who had voted for him were present.

Suddenly one of the Irishmen said, "Well, Bill, you were right. We did it! Everything came out the way we planned it."

Then the guy who had been sitting behind me said, "God, Bill, when you told me to bad rap you, I was scared to death. I thought your brother-in-law was going to punch the shit out of me because he turned around three or four times."

Then everybody began shaking Bill's hand and the Italians kissed him on each cheek. It wasn't until later that I fully understood what had happened—in the debate, no one had wanted to be seen as pro-Jewish or pro-Bill to hide the fact that the election was rigged.

Babe Triscaro had used his muscle and his connections to rig the election in Bill's favor. There were enough Irishmen who could see that they had more to gain earning favors with organized crime than they had staying with the old Irish leaders so that they voted for Bill. It was the first test of just how powerful mob-connected union leaders, still a minority in the Teamsters, could be.

When it was time to leave, there remained a risk of trouble. Even with the setup, most of the members were hostile to Bill. There was a risk of shootings, and Bill told me to have my gun ready when we went outside. Joe was to bring the car around and Babe Triscaro said he would go with us, letting someone else drive his car home.

There was no violence; no one was waiting for us. We drove Bill home, took Babe Triscaro to his house, and then I took Joe to pick up his car. Bill had succeeded in taking over Joint Council 41.

Moving Bill into position was the culmination of the plan that Lucky Luciano had discussed more than twenty years earlier. Bill was comfortable with the Mafia involvement; indeed evidence indicates that he received all the deference, respect, and involvement afforded only to the inner circle of non-Italians. This inner circle had men like Bill in Cleveland and even more involved individuals like Meyer Lansky in Chicago, men trusted to do any task assigned and to coordinate money-making programs. Their power flowed from the top. They were given almost complete freedom to act as they wished so long as they never forgot to whom they ultimately owed their loyalty and respect. Yet I didn't understand how smart Bill was. He understood what was happening and how to position himself for the power he wanted.

To me, Bill had always been a nice, tough, dumb motherfucker. I had no respect for his mind. I used to see him constantly reading pulp novels about Doc

Savage, Buck Rogers, and Flash Gordon. He loved to talk about space travel at a time when such travel was impossible. But Bill wasn't dumb, as both union and aeronautical history have shown. I never understood how carefully he had manipulated himself into a position that would lead to great power. Yet he had pulled off something that should have been impossible, given the circumstances involved.

The Mafia was common knowledge in the 1930s and 1940s, but it was not until 1950 and 1951 that many of the men working with Bill Presser, Jimmy Hoffa, and others were identified publicly. This was the period when Senator Estes Kefauver, from Tennessee, traveled to six major cities with his Committee to Investigate Organized Crime. Kefauver began in Miami and held the first nationally televised investigation in American history. Television was such a new medium that there were even questions about the legality of broadcasting such an investigation. It was also so new that most Americans did not yet own television sets, a situation rectified by many businesses that turned on sets so the public could watch. In New York, for example, one theater invited the public to go inside and watch the Kefauver televised hearings instead of first run movies. They also dropped all admission charges as a goodwill gesture.

For the first time in American history, the public was forcibly made aware of organized crime. They witnessed the major gangsters in the United States, politicians who admitted to corruption (former New York City Mayor William O'Dwyer, speaking about why he appointed friends of Mafia leaders to city posts: "There are things you have to do politically if you want to get cooperation"), and nearly everyone's announcing that he would refuse to answer most questions on the grounds that his answers would tend to incriminate him.

Reports from the committee made for fascinating reading. But one of the most quoted passages was on page four of the Second Interim Report:

> There is a sinister criminal organization known as the Mafia operating with ties in other nations, in the opinion of the committee. The Mafia is the direct descendant of a criminal organization of the same name originating in the island of Sicily. In this country, the Mafia has also been known as the Black Hand and the Unione Siciliana. The membership of the Mafia today is not confined to persons of Sicilian origin. The Mafia is a loose-knit organization specializing in the sale and distribution of narcotics, the conduct of various gambling enterprises, prostitution, and other rackets based on extortion and violence.

Hoffa was playing a dangerous game during this period. He was protecting mob interests, engaging in shakedowns, and trying to build a legitimate labor organization: a combination of actions that was impossible to achieve.

For example, there was one mob-owned company that Hoffa deliberately aided. This was a company that supplied coveralls, as well as laundry and repair services for the coveralls, for companies employing mechanics. The primary clients were gas stations, auto dealers, and truck maintenance shops, yet Detroit, being the Motor City, had far more such businesses than it could use. After the war, numerous firms thought that coverall supply and repair would be big business and soon overcrowded the market.

Hoffa made certain that the mob's operation succeeded. An organizer from Joint Council 43 was dispatched to make it clear to businessmen that they would use the mob's coverall company. If they didn't, the Teamsters would go on strike, picketing their businesses and preventing anyone from getting through.

Hoffa was also considered the brains behind the extortion racket in the local jukebox industry as well as the problems that evolved when the Teamsters organized the car washing business in Detroit. The latter resulted in car washers' complaining directly to the Kefauver Committee that the union severely hurt them. They said that organizing efforts of Local 985 resulted in their pay dropping from thirty dollars per sixty-hour week to just eighteen dollars when they joined the union. They also claimed that though they paid seventy cents per week for union dues, they never received a union card and never were informed of when union meetings were going to take place. The business agent who was supposed to go around and check on their problems and concerns never appeared.

Hoffa also either had intimidated the police or paid them off. Whatever the case, the Detroit Police Department, although hearing complaints against Local 985, never took much action. Usually they just advised the person being troubled to get a gun.

The Irish still dominated the union, and it was Bill Presser who began to change that. Not only had he taken control of Joint Council 41, he was about to be involved with gaining the support and respect of most of the union locals— the city workers, the milk drivers, the ice and coal men, the scrap iron workers, and others—who were either Irish or tied in with the Irish. Almost half of the locals referred to Bill as "the fat Jew." If they didn't hate Bill personally, they hated him for being Jewish. Either way he was not going to get their support or respect even though he had pulled off the feat of winning the Joint Council presidency.

Despite the hostility toward Jews, the Irish labor leaders were looking for Jewish workers to join the union and increase their membership. This was a time when some of the trades of the past were no longer meaningful. Coal furnaces were being replaced by gas. Iceboxes were being replaced by refrigerators. Old professions were being lost and that meant a loss of union members.

There were several trades that were not unionized at the time. The junkyard workers who separated scrap iron and other materials for resale had not belonged to the Teamsters. Likewise, the barrel makers and restorers of used barrels were both predominantly Jewish and unorganized. This meant that the Irish leadership had to enter areas they had previously avoided.

During this period I was working for the Hotel, Restaurant Workers, and Bartenders Union along with Jackie Presser. We were one of five locals that would later merge, but we were not part of the Teamsters despite Bill's new position.

I knew some of the Irish organizers who approached the Jewish groups and one was extremely big. He was taller than I, with shoulders that were bigger than mine. He was a little flabby, but what you noticed was the sheer size of the man. He also had a gruff voice and a crude manner so that he intimidated some of the people he tried to organize.

There was one man who called me after a visit from the organizer. He was terrified that he was going to be killed by the organizer if he did not allow his business to unionize, yet he could not afford union pay and wanted to pay a bribe to be left alone. However, he was too frightened to try to bargain and had no idea whether or not offering the bribe would be acceptable or cause him more problems than he already had.

I told the man I would handle his concerns. Then I went to the organizer's office and told his secretary who I was. She checked, then told me that the organizer would not see me. He was one of those who hated both the Jews and the seemingly sudden rise to power Bill Presser had achieved.

There was no way I was going to stand for that attitude. I barged into the union president's office. He looked up from his desk and said, "What do you want, *Jew*?"

I got mad. "I came here to do you a favor, you Irish motherfucker. Now do you want a favor or do you want to fight? Any way you want it."

At that point the president burst out laughing. "I heard about you," he said. "I heard that you don't scare."

"And I heard about you. I heard that you don't scare."

The president stuck out his hand and we shook. Then I explained about the problem with the company he was trying to organize. I explained that I could fix it so that he got some money, the company got a contract the owner could live with, and everybody would be happy. I said that he could pay me something for what I was going to do for him or he didn't have to, whatever he wanted.

The president was pleased with the offer. The company had sixteen or eighteen workers, and that was more than other places where he had only organized five or six people per location. We went to see the company, where I explained that the organizer was the most decent Irishman he was going to meet, that he should sign a letter of union recognition, that he should sign the contract.

The president wanted fifteen hundred dollars as his bribe. He kept a thousand dollars and I received five hundred for my trouble. We also became quite close.

The president and I left the company and went to see a couple of Irish labor leaders. I was introduced as someone who was a good man, and I offered to help them with their organizing of the Jewish scrapyards. I also said that I would be happy to supply muscle for their picket lines or other needs.

The three of us went out to drink and we hit it off. They explained that they didn't like my "fat Jew brother-in-law." I said that I didn't care. We got along and I was willing to help them with their work. I said that I saw where I could make a little money. As I came to be accepted, they gradually introduced me to many of the top Irish labor leaders.

Although this was the 1950s, it was still a time of great prejudice. Ethnic neighborhoods were firmly entrenched in Cleveland. It was still dangerous for someone who was Polish to go into a working-class Italian bar. The Hungarians would not welcome the Italians. The Slavs, the Germans, and all the other groups that populated the city kept themselves segregated from one another. If they became successful and were fortunate enough to move into neighborhoods that were wealthier and willing to have them, then those neighborhoods developed their own restrictive standards based on income.

The idea that a Jew would become involved with Irish labor leaders was unheard-of. The Jews had broken new territory with their alliance with the Italians. But not only did the Irish hate both groups, they also felt threatened by events they did not understand. How could Bill Presser, a Jew, become such a powerful labor leader? How was Jimmy Hoffa's influence spreading when Dave Beck, an Irishman, was the man who headed the International? The country was changing, labor was changing, and they had trouble relating to any of it, which caused them to close in all the more, letting their hate blind them. That I could become an insider to any degree was a remarkable change. It would ironically also bring about their downfall in a way that none of us could have planned or predicted.

Before the decline of the Irish, I began talking to the various Jewish businesses to help them join the Irish-led labor unions without breaking the business owners. We were giving the workers a nickel an hour raise a year on a three-year contract or, at times, a dime an hour raise each year (known as a 5, 5, and 5, or a 10, 10, and 10 in the industry). It was affordable and the business owners felt comfortable that they could always call upon me as an intermediary if they had trouble with the Irish. It was a good deal all around.

The arrangement worked both ways. There was an Irish-owned restaurant where I had signed up all the workers to be unionized. Under such a circumstance, the owner was expected to sign a letter of intent to negotiate with the union and accept the union leadership as the bargaining arm of the workers.

However, this man refused. He told me that if I kept coming around, he would take his shotgun and blow my head off.

I was irate. I decided that I would return when the restaurant was closed and blow up the place.

By chance I had to meet with some of the Irish labor leaders for lunch, and they wanted to go to this restaurant before the time I planned to retaliate. I went, but I told them what had happened and that I didn't feel comfortable eating in the place.

One of the men with me was the president of the local I had helped get the first of the Jewish companies. He called over the owner and raised hell. He told him to bring the shotgun to the table so that he could shove it up his ass, pull the trigger, and blow his head off.

The owner was shocked by the wrath of a man he considered a friend, especially since the matter involved the way he treated a Jew. Yet when he realized that his friend was serious, he agreed to sign the letter of intent that I carried in my pocket. I had the restaurant officially organized and the debt the Irish felt to me had been repaid.

A few weeks later everything changed in ways that completely altered the power structure of the Teamsters. I was with some of the Irish organizers at the Ascot Raceway, a horse racing track that once existed between Cleveland and Akron. During the races we went to the clubhouse to eat, spotting an extremely good-looking girl who appeared to be twenty-two or twenty-three years old sitting at the bar. The organizer asked me to see whether I could persuade her to join us, so I bought her a drink, then convinced her to join us at our table. I told her that the men were big spenders who liked her and would bet horses for her, maybe making her a little money.

The girl was very friendly, not objecting when the men started touching her, putting their hands between her legs. She let them do what they wanted and responded by kissing their necks and mouths and cuddling up to them. We didn't realize that she was a prostitute working out of a place called the Haddam Hotel. She was being friendly because she was anticipating the money she would get for handling several tricks. Yet they would have acted the same way even if they had known. It was what they enjoyed doing.

I was involved because I had approached the girl to come to the table and I was supposed to pick her up that night and take her to the 216 Club in the Hollenden Hotel. Room 216 of the hotel, which has since been torn down and replaced by one with no connection with the former activities, was an after-hours joint. You could go there at any time for food, drink, and a good time, though the place was always unlicensed for liquor. The Irish liked to hang out there and that's where they wanted the girl.

I got involved in a card game and couldn't break away. I called the president at the hotel, gave him the telephone number and room of the girl at the Haddam, and told him to call over there to have her take a cab to the Hollenden. He could meet her when she arrived and pay for the cab. In that way everyone would be happy.

About two or three weeks later I saw a newspaper headline that said something like "TEAMSTER OFFICIAL CAUGHT WITH 15 YEAR OLD GIRL." As it turned out, the local president, about half the men from one suburb's fire station, and this girl were caught together. She looked twenty-two or so, but she was actually fifteen. The fact that she was a prostitute didn't change anything. They had had sex with a minor, and that was statutory rape. Both men could be ruined and jailed.

The local president was terrified and angry with me. His family were devout Irish Catholics, his wife a schoolteacher. Every year he and some of the other men went away for a retreat, where they reflected on their lives, prayed, and tried to come back better people. He was a drinker and womanizer, but that didn't change anything, though such actions were certainly not approved by the church. He had never been caught and now he was facing public humiliation.

My telephone rang and it was the president, screaming out of control. "You fucking Jew! You fucking set me up! You ruined me! You . . ."

I finally calmed him down and agreed to meet him at a private club to talk about what happened. When I got there, he was drinking heavily and weeping. Some of his friends were also there, equally angry but more controlled.

For the first time I learned the whole story. Until we talked I hadn't realized that the girl was fifteen. I reminded him that she looked older. I also reminded him that I had never seen her before and that I approached her only because they thought I was the best-looking of the men sitting together in the Ascot clubhouse and they figured she might like me. None of us had any idea what was really taking place.

That seemed to quiet his anger but make him even more despondent. He took out a gun, announced that he was going to kill himself, then asked one of the other guys to take it from him.

"I can get you out of this," I told him. "All you have to do is go to the fat Jew [my brother-in-law, Bill Presser] and he'll get it squashed. There won't be any more trouble with the papers, the police, the judge, anybody."

"I'd rather die than go see the fat Jew," he whined, and there was no reasoning with him. Finally I told him that he knew how to reach me. If he wanted help from the fat Jew, he should give me a call. Otherwise there was nothing I could do.

The building that housed Joint Council 41 was run as though it were a series of ethnic neighborhoods. The leaders of the various unions kept their doors tightly closed, only welcoming their own kind. The Irish stayed with the Irish. The Italians would mix with the Jews, though they often stayed by themselves. Anyone who encountered someone from a different ethnic group either didn't speak or was hostile. At one point, one of the Irish leaders got drunk, then stood outside in the parking lot, shouting up at the office of one of the Italians that he could beat any "fucking dago" in the place. I had to go downstairs, put the guy in my car, and talk to him until he calmed down.

Everyone's temper was always on edge. When Bill read the story of the arrest in the paper, he found it hilarious. He was delighted that the Irish were in trouble.

The organizer did call me that night, drunk and crying. I told him that he would have to go to the "fat Jew," but he kept arguing with me. He said he was going to kill himself, and I told him to go ahead. He could listen to me or he could kill himself if he wanted. I didn't care which. By the time the night was almost over, he had called crying about ten times and I was exhausted. At 5 A.M. he agreed to see Bill.

It took quite a bit of effort to convince both parties to get together. Bill was the more reasonable, recognizing that helping the Irish was a way to reduce their power. They would owe Bill, in a sense, and that might stop the hostilities in the building.

The organizer needed more convincing. He didn't want to have to come to Bill on his knees, an idea I explained was ridiculous. Bill was eager to get in with the Irish, I said. He didn't like the way everyone was at each other's throats. He would be happy to squash things as a favor. It would do everyone some good.

We had a 9:30 A.M. appointment with Bill, at which time he heard the story from the embarrassed organizer. Bill said he would handle the problem and did: Nothing further ever appeared in the newspapers, and the legal case was officially dropped.

After the indictment of the organizer was quashed, everything changed. Bill asked for no money, no favors in return. But the Irish recognized that Bill was one of their own, a man who would do what was necessary to protect the leaders of organized labor. Suddenly all office doors were open and everyone wandered freely through the halls, the "fat Jew" being accepted as one of their own.

I never learned what happened throughout the country during this period and I have not been able to find any records that indicate what might have taken place behind the scenes. Knowing now how powerful Bill Presser had become before taking over Joint Council 41, I suspect that the information was spread to the powerful union cities of Detroit, Chicago, New York, and similar locations that had Cleveland's ethnic structure. The Irish talked among themselves just as the Italian/Jewish coalition of labor activists talked. Bill Presser was to be respected and, with that change in attitude, the organized crime elements gained a stronger national foothold.

Now all the players were in place in key cities of the country. It was only a matter of time before organized crime dominated the Teamsters, Jimmy Hoffa could be moved into power, and I would be traveling the country in order to commit arson, assault and battery, and other acts of intimidation.

4

Power Bids in the 1950s

THEY ALL CAME together in the 1950s: the Teamsters, the mob, the politicians, Las Vegas, the greed. Everyone was a user. Everyone had a scam. And the only ones who would eventually prove to be the losers were the rank and file, though not in the way most people ever imagined.

The Teamster leadership knows where its money comes from. They needed the support of the rank and file, if only from the dues that were paid. As a result, they worked to get better contracts with higher hourly wages. Eventually there would be locals whose members told their leaders that they did not need much money. What they needed were more benefits, and these came as well. The men and women became extraordinarily well paid, no one bothering to explain to them that there were limits to what companies could handle. Eventually some businesses folded because of the contracts, as the cost of help became too great. Unemployment for Teamsters would increase in some areas as the unions went too far in their demands on behalf of the members. But few people saw such a problem in the 1950s.

It is probably safe to say that it was the Central States, Southeast and Southwest Areas Pension Fund that gave the Teamsters the real power in the United States. The fact that, for a time, we were the largest union in the nation with over two million members meant less than the money.

There has always been talk about the danger to America if the Teamsters all struck at once. People create the nightmare scenario of a nation where trucks no longer deliver food, clothing, and other merchandise. Bus drivers stop driving. Cabdrivers refuse to get behind the wheel. Hospital supplies, parts needed for manufacturing, even rigs that bring gasoline to service stations throughout the country come to a halt, paralyzing all commerce. People run rampant through supermarkets, desperate to stock up on rapidly dwindling supplies. Those who lack the funds to buy stockpiles of food suddenly find themselves starving. People begin dying for lack of essential medical and surgical supplies. And the cost to the economy is greater than anything experienced when cities fall victim to earthquakes, hurricanes, tornadoes, and similar disasters.

The problem with such a scenario is that it will not happen. Teamsters are among the most patriotic people in this nation. These are men and women who support the country, are concerned with leading a decent life, want to give their children a better life than they've had. They have served with honor in World War II, the Korean War, the Vietnam War, and elsewhere. They want a fair deal; they want to feel a part of the American dream; and they will fight against any leaders or employers who try to stop them. Yet the idea that they will suddenly stop working, deliberately bringing the nation to a standstill just because a labor leader asks them to do so, is nonsense. Most members would consider it to be a step similar to a revolution unless there was such overwhelming provocation that they felt it was the only way to save America, not to hurt it.

The real power of the Teamsters is money, as exemplified by the Central States, Southeast and Southwest Pension Fund. The pension fund is so large that its assets are greater than those of most lending institutions in America. There is close to $8 billion in the fund today, and in the 1950s the fund was approaching $200 million, a large sum for the day. Jimmy Hoffa once commented that it didn't matter how many bad deals they had—and their percentage of successes was greater than that of most financial institutions—because the interest alone on all of their money ensured profitability.

What did the money mean? For one, it meant Las Vegas.

Everybody knew that gambling was profitable and not considered particularly criminal, even where outlawed. I live in the Cleveland area, for example, where it is understood by most police officers that gambling joints are to be left untouched, despite their being against the law. The days of the big gambling clubs are over, though not the backroom joints frequently known to vice cops and beat officers. Sometimes there are payoffs. Other times the joints are not considered to be worth raiding. And sometimes the officers enforce the law, often to the surprise of both other officers and judges.

Nevada began as an open state. Gambling was welcome, of course, but there was more to its popularity than that. All members of the Mafia were also welcome. The state was declared "open," meaning that all feuds among the families had to be put aside when you crossed the state line. Business could be negotiated even among warring factions. Everyone was free to invest, Chicago families made as welcome as those from New York, Rhode Island, or New Jersey.

Nevada also had legalized prostitution in almost every county and "approved" prostitution in those areas that "officially" did not wish it. For example, Las Vegas does not allow prostitution, though there are numerous "chicken ranches" (legalized whorehouses) just outside the city. At the same time, a high roller who wants a woman by his side both at the tables and in his complimentary suite can have his choice among dozens of professional beauties. You will not find streetwalkers or formal houses of prostitution in Las Vegas, nor will families be embarrassed by the husband's being accosted in front of the wife and children. But the girls are readily available, and many even advertise that they have health certificates proving that they are disease-free, at least as of the last inspection date.

Prostitution and gambling are ideal businesses for the mob. They are vices greatly in demand and are relatively inexpensive to operate. Las Vegas prostitution requires little more than a decently maintained building with a number of private rooms, some security personnel, and an attractive greeter. It is a low-cost hotel operation with a high profit margin.

For the men and women who own the houses of prostitution, the business is a money machine. In the early days of Las Vegas, when $40 a week was as much as some men earned to support their families, the Nevada prostitutes were grossing $20 an *hour* in the better brothels. With just a dozen girls and a fifty-fifty split, the management was taking in $120 an hour during the active periods. Since most were open twenty-four hours a day and the only salaried personnel were the managers and security, the cash business was clearing thousands of dollars a week. A large portion of this could be skimmed and divided among the owners, the rest reported on their income tax, and no one would know the difference. Prostitution was a money machine.

The gambling casinos were more of a risk at first. They had to be elaborate, a fantasy of sensual pleasure, in order to attract the customers. This was still a period when many larger cities had their own clubs so there had to be an allure not found elsewhere. This meant elaborate rooms, great food, extravagant floor shows, machines that had all the "bells and whistles," high-quality roulette wheels, expensive crap tables, and a well-trained staff who could make you happy while taking your money.

The seven passenger cars that carried people to and from the Pettibone Club and the other joints we knew in Cleveland suddenly became Greyhound buses and charter planes. People were brought to the casinos from all over the country, given money for the slots and coupons for food, just to help them make casino gambling a regular habit.

The idea seems like a gold mine today, but no one was positive it would work, and there was no way to compensate for the losses. The prostitution paid for itself, yet its success was dependent upon visitors to the casinos, not just the locals. Every city had a place to find girls so the only reason to use the facilities in Nevada was that you were already there for the gambling. Thus there were risks, and the Mafia does not like to take risks.

The pension fund seemed the ideal way to cut the losses to the mob. At the time the casinos were built, the men involved worked out a legal way to open the gambling facilities without risk. They decided to use accepted business practices that favored borrowers which already existed.

The idea was a simple one. The mob builders (and there were others who built casinos using the same practices but who were honest in their efforts) would create a corporation for the sole purpose of building and running a casino. Then they would borrow all the money they needed for the business. If the business succeeded, they would pay off the loan and make handsome profits. If the business failed, they would walk away and let the lending institution "eat" the loan.

All lending institutions, including the pension fund, require collateral for loans. This means that you have to pledge property, cash, or anything else of sufficient value to the company giving you money. The collateral must equal or exceed the value of the loan. Then, if you default, the company takes control of those assets, sells them, and pays itself from the proceeds so the corporate assets are protected.

The mob put a different twist on collateral. They would borrow a sum of money—$5 million, for example—and say that the casino and its furnishings would be worth $5 million after completion. (Actual costs were usually higher, even then. Today a casino runs between $120 million and $160 million. The $5 million figure is a hypothetical one.) They would give the deed to the business to the pension fund as collateral for the loan. Then, if the business failed, the pension fund would own the business.

The problem was that a failed business is seldom worth the money it cost to build it. The retail cost of gambling equipment is much higher than the resale value. The cost of construction is much higher than the value of a building that was custom-designed for a business that was unable to succeed. And even more important, when all of this started, there was a good chance that a city devoted to gambling as its primary industry would not succeed. Las Vegas might revert to its origins as a little-desired desert community with the "Strip" where the casinos were located becoming a ghost town.

When the mob entered the casino business, they didn't want the risk that a legitimate loan would have. They wanted to make money or walk away by having the casino serve as collateral. And the only lending institution that would cooperate was the Central States, Southeast and Southwest Areas Pension Fund under the primary control of Jimmy Hoffa. Dave Beck may have headed the Teamsters, but Jimmy was controlling the financial shots from behind the scenes.

According to Jimmy Fratianno, a Mafia member who became a government witness, Babe Triscaro discussed the fact that Dave Beck's presidency was part of a deal that had been made well before the election. Dan Tobin, the incumbent president of the Teamsters, had come to dislike Jimmy Hoffa despite his respect for Hoffa's abilities. It was obvious that Hoffa was putting himself into a position to take over through the power he was wielding within the Central and Southern Conference of Teamsters. However, it seemed most sensible for Hoffa to buck no one. Instead, a deal through which Beck would move into office for a single five-year term, then retire, was cut. At the same time, Hoffa would broaden his own power base, including being elected vice president, the youngest man ever to hold that position.

New York's Tom Hickey was also going to get a seat on the board, though this idea worked against the desires of Joey Glimco, a Sicilian union leader who was part of the Chicago mob family and a self-made millionaire from his businesses. He also had an extensive record for assaults and other crimes of violence. He did not want to become a member of the Teamsters board, a fortunate situation because his extensive police record made him ineligible. All he wanted was behind-the-scenes control, and that included putting his own man, John O'Rourke, in power.

Eventually a compromise was reached in which Hoffa had to show key areas such as Pittsburgh, Chicago, New York, and St. Louis that he was able to lead effectively. At the same time, during that year's Teamsters convention, Hoffa not only backed Beck but also wined and dined Glimco and other alleged Mafia leaders who were present.

The mob had other ways of maintaining a stake in Las Vegas. Frequently they bought existing operations, using a legitimate front so there would be no challenge to the gaming license. The front would be a man with a clean reputation and no direct ties with organized crime. Often the front man would be operating with a loan from the mob, an arrangement that gave him the impression that the casino would be his once he repaid the money. However, the moment profits were less than anticipated by the mob backers, he would find himself without a job.

The Strip began developing quickly in the fifties. Gus Greenbaum began managing the "fabulous Flamingo," making it a profitable showplace that drew other casinos: the Last Frontier (renamed the New Frontier), Wilbur Clark's Desert Inn, the Sands, and the Sahara, the latter two opening in 1952. The Riviera, the Dunes, and the Royal Nevada all opened in 1955.

The fears about the success of Las Vegas and other Nevada areas were unfounded. The casinos' cash business was such that they were able to take from five thousand to twenty thousand dollars per day from the receipts. Then the remainder of the funds would be declared income, reported to the IRS, and taxes paid on the money. So much was involved that no one felt the need to check more closely on the real take. Everyone was happy.

We know today that anybody could have made money backing the casinos, but no one knew that then. Instead, the mob saw that there was a gamble, worked out a way to cover their possible losses, and the Teamsters Union Central States, Southeast and Southwest Pension Fund went along with them. The mob and the Teamsters leadership had shown their loyalty to one another, a link in the future. What nobody expected was that Jimmy Hoffa would later decide to get rid of the mob influence, a factor in his being killed.

I didn't know all that was happening during this time. I was still trying to find my own way, building my own reputation. It was only years later, when I pieced together conversations I had with Bill, Jimmy, Harold, Jackie, and various guys I knew from he Jewish Combination, the Irish Combination, the Italian mob, and others, that I learned the whole story. Reports from the Kefauver Committee and similar investigating groups, as well as documents not previously available, have also helped. But for myself, I was busy making a buck and establishing a reputation. And, in my opinion, Jackie and Harold were still nothing but punks in those days. They wouldn't have any direct knowledge of Hoffa and what was taking place at the top of the Teamsters until the late 1960s. Only Bill mattered, and he didn't talk Teamster business with his son.

There was a man I'll call Frank who was one of the most brilliant men I knew. He was also a business genius, but he always wanted to be a gangster. He and I used to wear the broad-brimmed hats and the styles of coats that were worn by gangsters in the movies back then. He figured the clothes made people afraid of him. For example, one time we walked into a bank and he told me that he suspected the tellers would think that we were there to rob it. We weren't and no one looked at us twice, but in his mind, the guards were sizing us up for a possible shoot-out.

Frank moved to Chicago with eleven hundred dollars in his pocket and a chance to become involved in what was known as the gray market.

Steel was in short supply in those early postwar days and the gray market for steel involved eight or ten brokers. Normally a company that needed steel orders directly from a manufacturer. But in those days the manufacturers either could not keep up with the demand or were not able to get it on time to fulfill their contracts. Yet there were other individuals who had quantities of steel they did not need and willing to sell to another company. It was the gray market broker's job to match the holdings of steel with the companies that needed it. They would sell it for the fair market price plus a small markup that would be their profit.

I never thought you could make much money in a business like that, but Frank showed me otherwise. He went to work for one of the brokers until he learned the business. Then he went on his own, stealing ten or eleven of his former employer's customers. By the end of his first year in business, he had parlayed that eleven hundred dollars into a net profit of $1.2 million.

Frank never handled any of the steel at first. He just acted as a middleman, selling and buying over the telephone. Eventually Frank had the money to expand. He bought his own giant warehouse in Chicago and began buying steel wherever he could find it, storing it in his warehouse. Then he leased space to other brokers who also wanted to store steel but had no place to put it. The operation became so large that Frank had no idea exactly what he had in storage, a situation that made him a perfect target for a rip-off.

Frank asked me to come to Chicago to help him. He needed some protection and figured I was the perfect person. My brother, Harry, was already up there so I knew that one way or another we would be able to score. Besides, I was just out of the joint, had nothing, and Frank bought me a complete new wardrobe after I arrived.

The first thing we did was get keys to the warehouse because of our work, then become involved with one of the men who ran the place. We knew that no one checked the steel as closely as he should and we also knew that there was equipment available to turn the cold rolled steel into sheet steel. We began going to the steel Frank was storing, cutting off a chunk from the different holdings. We usually took around five hundred pounds of steel from each pile, a quantity small enough that it would not be noticed. Then we set it in a corner of the warehouse which everyone ignored, accumulating more and more until we had at least a truckload (thirty thousand to thirty-five thousand pounds). At that time we picked up the phone and called around until we could sell it.

We never stole from Frank. We stole only from the guys who were storing with Frank, and they never knew what was happening.

During this period a scientist talked to Frank about a scheme to make galvanized steel from his holdings. Galvanized steel was a type of zinc-coated steel that did not rust and did not need additional coatings to protect it. The rest of the steel had to be sprayed with oil to prevent it from rusting.

The scientist told Frank that if he bought some machines that he was selling, the oil would be cleaned off the steel. Then a special solution he had formulated would be used to soak the steel before spraying it with some other compound that would make it look and act exactly like galvanized steel.

Frank had several million dollars at this time and decided to begin using this process to produce the equivalent of galvanized steel for far less money than the true product. He told all the brokers who were storing their steel that they would have to move it because of the business he was going to enter.

The other brokers wanted to get involved, even going so far as offering to underwrite the costs. But Frank wanted nothing to do with the others. He was determined to become a billionaire using the process that would revolutionize the steel business.

Frank got a contract from Montgomery Ward for more than $600,000 and another from Sears Roebuck for over a million dollars in order to make gutters from his rustproof steel. What he did not realize was that galvanized steel does not rust. The steel coating the scientist invented prevented surface rust but did not stop the steel from rusting from the inside out. Six months after his product was in use, the customers found out that it was not what they thought they had purchased. The result was a backlash that cost Frank just about everything he owned. He was also arrested and tried for fraud and, I believe, tax evasion.

Frank did have $675,000 left, though it was really not his. It was money that belonged to his creditors, and he wanted to try to find a way to keep it.

The answer, for Frank, was to go to Las Vegas. He was not a gambler, and he knew that playing straight in Vegas would cost him everything. He decided to gamble enough of the money that when the IRS came after him, he could claim he lost everything on the slots, the cards, and the other games. In the meantime he would hold back enough to get started again after he left jail. That money would be placed in a safe deposit box and no one would know he had it.

I told Frank that he better lose big at the tables because the IRS would find out. The guys who worked at the tables "counted down," meaning that they kept track of the big winners and losers. When Frank discovered this fact, he asked me to go with him to handle the gambling since I knew what I was doing.

The two of us went to Las Vegas, where he and I made big lay-downs. Whatever we bet, we put a lot of money on it, winning some and losing some. This went on for several days, at the end of which he had between $130,000 and $140,000. Yet he had gambled so much that I thought he had lost everything and I was certain that his lie about losing would be believed. I also made out, keeping some of the winnings I had made with Frank's money.

The money was good, but it would not restore Frank's life-style when he got out of jail. He wanted to get all the money he could, and this meant collecting an old bad debt for thirty-five thousand dollars from a broker who had received steel but not paid for it. He told me that I could have ten thousand dollars of the money if we collected it.

We went over to the broker's office, where Frank talked with him awhile. The guy was crying the blues so I took over, acting like a tough guy. "Lookit, motherfucker, I don't want to hear your shit no more," I told him. "You write out a check for thirty-five thousand dollars that you owe Frank or I'll throw you out of the fucking window."

"Who are you talking to?" the man demanded. We hadn't been introduced and he had no idea who I was. He didn't know that I was there to shake him down for the money he owed.

"He's a man from Cleveland," Frank explained. "He's a bad guy."

The man asked for permission to make a telephone call. I thought he was going to call some men to help him so I warned him that he could call anyone he wanted, but I had a gun in my pocket and, if anybody came through the door, I would get him first.

He explained that he wasn't calling Chicago. He was going to call a man he knew in Cleveland, apparently to threaten me.

The broker called Morris Kleinman's office. Kleinman was one of the members of the old Cleveland Syndicate and had the power to kill me if he wanted. The broker figured I could be scared off by him.

Morris Kleinman wasn't in, but his son was there. The father was living in Las Vegas, involved with the Desert Inn, and the son was trying to act tough on the telephone. He knew that his father would want a favor done for a friend, and apparently the broker was a friend of Morris.

The Kleinman boy didn't know me but tried to talk tough. I told him that I didn't care who his dad was, that he had better tell the broker to pay immediately. And before he started making threats, he had better call his dad to find out who he was messing with. I explained that I was going to give the broker the telephone and that the Kleinman boy was to tell him to make out a check for the money he legitimately owed Frank. Then I said that if the check paid to Frank was no good, I would return to Cleveland and put him into the hospital. He had no right to interfere in my business.

I guess the boy was scared because, when I put the broker back on the line, he listened for a minute, then made out the check he owed. Oddly the broker apparently admired my technique. He explained that he was also owed money by two other steel brokers and wondered what I would charge to help him collect it. I told him that I wanted 30 percent plus all expenses, and that I wanted a G-note (one thousand dollars) plus expenses if I failed.

I had a friend I asked to go with me, and we soon found that when you collect from one guy, that person sends you to collect from someone else. For the next several months we traveled the country, collecting money for the various brokers.

The only time I had trouble was when I went to Providence, Rhode Island, to collect from a guy who was Italian and, I suspect, mob-connected in some way. For that trip I didn't go with my friend. I took a girl with me, promising her a good time on the trip. I was feeling too self-confident and that almost got me into trouble.

The Italian broker convinced me that he didn't have the money the day I went to see him, but he would have it the following day. Then he asked me where I was staying and, like a fool, I told him. Immediately after I gave the name of the hotel, I knew I was in trouble. I also knew I would be in more trouble if I let on that I knew I had made a mistake.

After I left the broker's office, I began to think about what I should do. Should I leave Rhode Island and forget about the debt? Should I change hotels where the girl and I were staying? I finally decided to play it out and see what would happen. I had a gun with me, a German P-38 I always carried, and warned the girl that whenever I told her, she was to go into the bathroom and lock the door until I told her she could come out.

It must have been after 11:00 P.M. when there was a knock at the door. I was in bed in my underclothes, holding the pistol under the blankets. I had also left the door unlatched so anyone could come in.

"Who is it?" I called, getting out of bed.

"Room service" was the answer, and I knew I had trouble. We hadn't ordered room service so I figured that this was the guy who was sent to take care of me. I told the girl to go into the bathroom, then told the guy to enter.

There were three of them, but they weren't expecting me to be ready for them. One had a set of brass knuckles. A second had a blackjack. The third had a gun, but he wasn't ready to use it. I suspect they just wanted to give me a good beating, then get out of there, but I disarmed them and made them lie on the floor.

The guys were terrified. They begged me not to shoot them. Then the guy with the gun admitted that he was the broker's brother, who had been sent to teach me a lesson for trying to collect.

I put the gun to his head and told him to call his brother. I told him that I wanted a certified check by ten o'clock the following morning or I would blow the brother's head off. Then I tied up the three men and sat up all night, watching them, wanting to be certain that they wouldn't get loose and come at me.

In the morning the girl took care of the room bill, rented a car, then waited for me with the motor running. The broker showed up at ten, terrified that I might kill his brother. He had the check with him, but I took the brother hostage anyway, keeping the gun under my coat so we could go through the lobby without anyone's noticing. I figured that there might be other guys waiting for me, and I was determined to shoot him if I were jumped.

That was an approach I used whenever I wanted to muscle some guy. I always said that I'd take my beating if it came to that, but I'd take out the guy I was sent to get first. And if there were any way to do it, I'd try to send at least some of the others to the hospital with me.

I also used to say that if I were beaten before I could get the guy I was after, I'd come after him later. He probably wouldn't see me coming, but I'd beat the shit out of him no matter what he did to avoid me.

I meant it, too. I was driven like that. If I said I was going to get a guy, I'd do it. I wasn't afraid of anybody, and I didn't take a job unless I had the guts to do whatever was necessary to finish it.

The girl drove us around the area while I watched to see whether we were followed. Then, a half hour after we started, I told her to stop the car, threw out our hostage, then drove to the airport in Boston so we could fly home. It was the only time I had to use force when running the collection business.

It was during this period that I married again. I made a lot of money doing the collections, but I spent a lot of money in Vegas and elsewhere, never setting anything aside. Frank was heading for jail, so before he went, he and I visited a tough neighborhood in Chicago where he introduced me to a woman I thought was half owner in a bar.

The woman was in a bad way. Her kid had been taken from her, and she needed a stable home life to get the kid back. She was from an ethnic background that considered women who lost their children unfit mothers.

I started dating this woman, meeting her family. Her father was dead; her mother, sisters, and one of her two brothers liked me when I visited their homes. Only the older brother hated me, and that made it harder for him when I visited and was placed at the head of the table. That position was traditionally reserved for the father or, if there were no father, the head of the family, usually the oldest son. My sitting there was robbing him of his inheritance, though it really made no difference to me.

There was no real affection between the woman and me, though we got along well and most of her family liked me. What she really wanted was to get married in order to get her child back. She said that she would give me money and buy me a new Hudson automobile, one of the pioneering sedans from the company that merged with American Motors (the Hudson name disappeared in 1957). Then I could return to wherever I wanted to live, get a divorce, and get on with me life.

We got married, she got her kid, and only then did I learn that she had no money coming in. She had no half interest in the bar; the money she spent on me came from savings.

I didn't divorce her then. I took a job in Chicago driving a beer truck for a company owned by her former husband.

Everybody was on the take in that town. One of my new brothers-in-law shook me down for ten dollars a month to give to the cops so I wouldn't go back to jail for violating my parole. It cost another ten dollars a month to the neighborhood cop to prevent my parked car from being keyed. Anyone who didn't pay had a key scraped along the side, removing the paint along a narrow line, forcing the owner to have the car repainted.

Driving a beer truck gave me a license to steal. Chicago supermarkets sold liquor by the bottle in those days. You could buy expensive liquor at the same time you bought your groceries. The liquor was in such demand that there was a big market for stolen bottles sold at a discount.

A number of us drivers did the same scam. We'd wheel in the cases of Global Beer we were delivering. Then, instead of just taking out the empty cases, we'd slip in a few bottles of expensive stuff, stealing it in broad daylight. Nobody ever worried about the beer drivers' taking things so we were pretty much left alone. They were too busy watching for regular shoppers who might try to conceal a bottle under a coat.

Each afternoon the Global Beer drivers who were stealing would meet the supervisor who showed up with a truck to be loaded with the liquor. Then he sold what we stole, dividing the money according to the number of bottles we had each taken.

It was while I was in Chicago that I did some of my first work assaulting someone for pay. I had established a reputation for violence by then, through the work I had done for Bill and the collections I had handled for Frank. He had a man who was going to testify against him in court and offered me seven thousand five hundred dollars to handle it.

The job was similar to the types of things Jimmy or Bill Presser eventually would ask me to do. The Mafia had a reputation for murdering anyone who got in the way of business deals, and the Mafia was in solid with some of the Teamsters. But labor violence tried to avoid murder as much as possible. Instead we went for pain and intimidation. We found that we got further putting a guy into the hospital with broken bones he could feel and remember than anybody got killing someone. We put a bomb on the back porch of someone's home, firebombed a factory when it was empty, or blew up a car. A guy who has seen a little violence and knows things can only get worse is more likely to agree to your demands than a guy who has lost everything at once and is pushed to the wall.

Frank understood this and wanted to apply the same reasoning to a man who was going to testify against him in court. But the man was careful, never letting himself get into a position where someone could take care of him. Yet Frank wanted him beaten and I didn't want to disappoint the guy. I finally went to a family member of my wife's who was a precinct captain. He had the right connections, arranging to have two homicide detectives handle the job. They would be paid $2,500 of the $7,500 that Frank had offered me.

My friend picked the two best guys he could find: a pair of trusted detectives who, like so many people in power in Chicago, would do anything for money. They were able to reach the man who planned to testify since he had no fear of the police. The detectives beat the man in public, knowing that no one would stop them and no one would arrest them.

The story grew more interesting a few years later when I happened to see one of those true detective magazines. There was a story about a pair of Chicago homicide detectives who were highly decorated heroes. Taking a close look at their pictures, I discovered that they were the same men who beat the man Frank wanted to get.

My first real taste of the power of the Teamsters and the corruption they could breed came with the story of George Bender, an Ohio Republican politician. Bender was a pain in the ass for Bill Presser, who, in 1953, was executive secretary of the Tobacco and Candy Jobbers Association. This was the same kind of scam he had pulled when he was head of the association of owners of jukeboxes as well as the union for the drivers and delivery men. His actions were a criminal misdemeanor based on the restraint of trade. As a result, he was fined fifteen hundred dollars. Because Bill was obviously doing something less than proper, the House of Representatives decided to investigate both him and the Ohio Teamsters in general. The committee that would do the work was headed by Congressman George Bender.

Senator Robert Taft of Ohio died in 1953, and a man named Thomas Burke was being supported by Bill Presser, Babe Triscaro, and the Ohio Teamsters as Taft's successor. I never knew much about Burke except that he probably would have been Ohio's next senator at the time had it not been for the investigation.

Congressman Bender made a dramatic tour through Ohio with Cleveland hearings in September 1954. Bill Presser and Babe Triscaro, then the vice president of the Ohio Conference of Teamsters, were asked to appear. They were questioned about their income, much of which came from kickbacks and other illegal actions. They each took the Fifth Amendment, preferring not to testify to anything which might incriminate them.

Sometimes there is a humorous side to the Fifth Amendment issue. Several years later, during the McClellan hearings into Teamster Corruption, Rolland McMaster, a top organizer for Jimmy Hoffa early in Hoffa's career, was asked whether Yvonne McMaster was his wife. It was a seemingly innocuous question asked by Senator Sam Ervin, but McMaster took the Fifth Amendment.

A rather bemused Sam Ervin said, "Did I understand you correctly when I understood you to testify that you honestly believed that it might tend to incriminate you in the commission of some criminal offense if you admitted that you were married to your wife?"

McMaster leaned over to speak with his attorney, then straightened up and again pleaded the Fifth, at which time Ervin said, "I will leave it up to you to answer her when you get home."

Congress does have two ways of getting information when someone takes the Fifth Amendment. The first is to grant the person immunity from prosecution for whatever is revealed during the hearings. This technique is usually used when the person's information can provide evidence leading to a more important person's being charged with criminal conduct. The second method is to charge the person with being in contempt of Congress for refusing to answer. The person can then be arrested and jailed for the duration of the hearings or until he or she cooperates.

Congressman Bender and his committee did none of those things. Bender was obviously angry with Bill and Babe, determined to make an example of them if he could find a way. At least, that was the impression he gave that September. He scheduled another appearance for Bill on November 9, and he also announced his intentions to bring Dave Beck to the hearings.

November came and Bill had to go to Washington for the new hearings. Once again Bill invoked the Fifth Amendment; this time Bender made no show of trying to get him to talk. Instead he declared a recess just two days into the hearings.

Suddenly there was great tension in the air. It was presumed that the hearings would be resumed with a vengeance. The recess seemed to be a way for the investigators connected with the committee to locate the additional evidence needed to put Bill into jail. The public and the press eagerly awaited what they assumed would be startling revelations. What they did not realize was that forty thousand dollars in behind-the-scenes bribe money had been paid to stop the congressional investigation. In addition, Bill agreed to support George Bender rather than Thomas Burke in the senatorial election.

The bribe was well hidden from both the press and the Teamster rank and file. Just after Bender's November election, the Joint Council was told that the $40,000 was needed to pay the expenses incurred by Babe and Bill. It was not mentioned that the legal bills had already been paid. Instead, it was stated that the additional funds were needed to manipulate the politicians behind the scenes.

For me it was an example illustrating that everyone has his price. George Bender wanted to be a senator. He wanted to have one of the most powerful political positions it is possible to hold in the United States. Integrity, ethics, his duty to the investigating committee and the nation were all meaningless in his drive for power. The election was important to him and he was not about to lose. The offer to compromise his integrity—to stop investigating men he considered crooks—showed me just how easy it is for a man of power and influence to corrupt himself.

The outcome of the Ohio senatorial election that year was so close—the candidates were just six thousand votes apart—that it is easy to see how important organized labor had been in Bender's success. Equally obvious was Bender's willingness to change his tactics the following year. He agreed to be the guest speaker for the Ohio Conference of Teamsters at their quarterly meeting in 1955, a meeting where Bill acknowledged his debt to the politician: "To you George Bender, the Republican whose name has been handed around as an anti-labor Senator, if it weren't for this one man, and his advice and the constant pounding we would have a lot of problems that do not exist . . . and Bill Presser is committed to George Bender anywhere down the line."

We never had to solicit the cooperation of George Bender so far as I know. I think that he approached Bill with the offer of a deal to get the support he needed in the election. However, in every other case, the politicians came to us, wanting our money, our support, or our muscle.

The rank and file has no sense of the corruption at the top. The Teamsters has an organization called Democratic, Republican, Independent Voter Education (DRIVE) that is seemingly objective about whom it supports. The primary criterion in the minds of the members is that DRIVE support candidates who support labor. In the minds of the members, a good politician is one who helps assure them of jobs and a bad one is someone who may cause them to be out of work. They generally don't think about the bribes, the compromises, and the actions that may be harmful that are taking place. They generally don't question the endorsements. They don't know that a Bill Presser would rather cover his own ass in the way he supports a candidate than look out for the members' good.

Yet as greedy as the Teamster leaders have been, they do take care of their own. George Bender accepted bribes, including the change in endorsement, but he was not able to remain in the Senate. Ohio voters dumped him despite Teamsters Union support in 1956. However, he maintained close ties with Jimmy Hoffa and the other leaders.

By 1958, the corruption in the Teamsters Union was so obvious that the general public was equally divided in their attitude toward the organization. Those who were not eligible to join primarily saw the union as little more than an organized crime group. Those who were eligible often were thrilled by the tough guy image. I used to ask people why they wanted to be a part of the Teamsters and was told that it was because they were the toughest union there was. Never mind the corruption. Never mind the stories appearing in the press. If a worker felt he or she was getting shafted by the boss, the Teamsters was the union of choice.

I remember watching members of other unions clench their fists and wave their arms in a power salute when truckers drove by during periods of labor strife. They would cheer the Teamsters, taking pride in the image.

Jimmy Hoffa was a crook who arranged violence throughout the United States, extorted money, and played both sides, working with organized crime and legitimate business leaders. He was short and squat and had the body of a muscular fireplug. Yet there was something about Jimmy I'll never forget. I'm not the kind of man who cheers in a crowd. I don't get enthusiastic about speakers. I don't shout and jump around at football rallies. I tend to sit back and watch, noticing the reactions of others.

But not with Hoffa. Jimmy could just walk into a room where he was going to speak and I'd go crazy like the rest of them. I'd be clapping and whistling, stamping my feet. The man had something about him—charisma, leadership ability, I don't know what. I just know that if you saw him speak, you wanted to follow him. You knew he was on your side. He was one man I would have backed for anything.

Hoffa was also seen as fearless, a tough guy who would fight for the workers. He had a policy of taking calls from members that brought him closer to the rank and file than any president since. When Jackie Presser and Harold Friedman ran the Teamsters, for example, Harold avoided the members almost entirely and Jackie was only comfortable with public speaking. It was only with Jimmy that you had the feeling that if you had a problem, you could call him and he would talk with you and then take care of it.

Because of all this, Hoffa knew that he had to make a show of getting rid of the corruption, but he also knew that he, Bill, and the others could continue business as usual if they had the right front. The man who was selected to clean up the union was none other than former senator George Bender.

In August 1958, George Bender was hired to head a committee investigating racketeering in the Teamsters. At first he was given all expenses, office rental, secretarial help, telephone, travel, and so forth, plus $250 per day. Later, after his outrageous pay was discovered—a senator's pay that year was $22,500, or approximately $80 per day; an excellent income for a family of four that year was $200 per week—his daily fee was reduced to $125 per day, though all perquisites and expenses remained the same.

George Bender was called before the Select Committee on Improper Activities in the Labor or Management Field. This was the committee chaired by Senator McClellan. Robert Kennedy was the chief investigator; his brother, Jack, was a member, along with Goldwater of Arizona, Erwin of North Carolina, MacNamara of Michigan, Butler of Maryland, and Mundt of South Dakota.

Bender had been paid $58,636.07 for his union work from August 18, 1958, to May 4, 1959, and the committee wanted to know how he had earned his money and which criminals he had removed from the union. Robert Kennedy mentioned Sam Goldstein of Local 239 in New York, a Teamster official who was receiving $375 a week plus $25 per week for expenses. Bender acknowledged that Goldstein was "a good man" but was not able to explain why the salary was being paid while Goldstein was in the penitentiary convicted of extortion.

Senator Barry Goldwater pushed the issue of Goldstein, saying: "George, let me ask you a question. Take the case of a man like Goldstein. Suppose you went to Mr. Hoffa and said, 'Jimmy, you ought to kick this fellow out.' Do you think he would do it?"

Bender replied: "Last week I went to him regarding a man, a matter came to my attention where a man was having relations with a 16-year-old prostitute and speaking very bluntly, he said, 'Well, frankly, that son-of-a-bitch should be kicked out.' He said, 'He is no good. No man should be in this union who is doing that kind of thing.' "

But when Goldwater asked whether the man had been expelled, Bender did not know. More important, his answer had completely bypassed the original question.

Bender then decided to turn the discussion against the committee. He said that many members of the Republican party were disreputable. He mentioned that he had once appointed a prostitute to the post of Republican committeewoman for the area where he worked. Then he went on to say that a politician has to work with all kinds of people in order to gain their votes. It was as though he were justifying his overlooking criminals within the Teamsters because that was part of his job. He never addressed the issue that his job was supposedly to rid the union of such scandal.

Kennedy tried to find out about my brother-in-law, Bill, as well as Babe. (McClellan Committee Hearings, page 19437) Kennedy asked, "Did you recommend that William Presser be ousted?"

Bender replied: "No, I did not. . . ."

Kennedy: "You have not recommended him. Have you recommended anything on Mr. Triscaro, that he be ousted from the union?"

Bender: "I have not."

Bender was of no further help. He explained to Robert Kennedy that he would not talk about his recommendations for removing anyone from the Teamsters. He explained that he had come as a voluntary witness but that he would only discuss the work he was doing with Jimmy Hoffa. Then he made a comment about the Teamster headquarters: "I have been so impressed with the manner in which that building is run, it reminds me of a church office. There is no gambling, and no liquor drinking or nothing of that kind going on there, and it is run very efficiently."

Bender became quite wealthy through his association with the Teamsters. He was cut in on the take from the pension fund loans, in most instances, the loans were provided in such a way that kickbacks to the board were assured.

The criminal activities in which the Teamsters engaged in the 1950s were made possible by a number of carefully planned deals as well as the dishonesty, naivete, and ambitions of key law enforcement officials during this period. George Bender provides a dramatic example, but there were many others who had comparable roles.

J. Edgar Hoover, the first director of the Federal Bureau of Investigation (FBI) and its most famous leader, was an American hero during this period. Hoover, it is now known, was a power-hungry man who carefully hid his homosexuality at the same time that he was demanding that his agents be morally "pure." He created a propaganda apparatus that made him and, secondarily, his men, look like the toughest law enforcement officers in the nation. He created the "Ten Most Wanted" list, exaggerated the importance of some of the federal criminals arrested (rather crude bank robbers, for example, though more sophisticated and efficient white-collar criminals were ignored), and encouraged anything that would add to the myth of FBI invincibility. There were radio shows about the "G-Men," movies, comic book heroes, and even Junior G-Men clubs.

The truth was that Hoover was a criminal himself. He illegally gathered intelligence information on senators, congressional representatives, presidents, cabinet members, and anyone else who might cause him trouble. Then he blackmailed anyone who might challenge him or try to replace him. With the favorable publicity his public relations efforts generated, everyone knew that to challenge him was futile.

Hoover undoubtedly knew as much about the existence of the Mafia as other members of law enforcement. Victor Navasky, the author of the book *Kennedy Justice,* revealed that in the fall of 1958, for the first time in his reign as head of the FBI, Hoover had a report on the Mafia. Only twenty-five numbered copies were prepared, each to be circulated to a different top government official concerned with law enforcement. Navasky explained that "The day after they were circulated, J. Edgar Hoover had each copy recalled and destroyed. He denounced the report as 'baloney,' and it was never heard of again."

Then there was the case of Paul Dorfman. Dorfman was introduced to Hoffa at a time when Hoffa was seeking organized crime connections and other influence in the Chicago area. Dorfman had been involved with Al Capone and was close to Anthony Accardo, one of the most powerful of the Capone successors. Dorfman, at the time, was president of the Chicago Scrap Handlers Union, which was considered to be rife with organized crime.

Hoffa and Dorfman found that they could have a mutually beneficial arrangement. Hoffa helped Dorfman solve trucking problems in Chicago, and Dorfman helped Hoffa develop alliances with Joseph Glimco of the cabdrivers' Local 777. At the time Glimco had an arrest sheet that indicated more than thirty confrontations with the police, two of which involved arrests for murder. Hoffa also met with Paul DeLucia, also a former Capone lieutenant, and with Sam Giancana. Giancana would eventually be implicated in a number of major crimes, including the assassination of President John Kennedy.

In 1951, Hoffa convinced the trustees of the Michigan Conference of Teamsters Welfare Fund to place the assets in a newly formed company called Union Casualty Agency. Hoffa also arranged for the Central States Health and Welfare Fund to be transferred to Union Casualty, a new and unproven company whose executives were Rose Dorfman, Paul's wife; and his stepson, Allen. Allen Dorfman, who became the primary money manager, had no background or experience in money management or insurance.

At the time the deal was made, Union Casualty could call upon total assets of $768,000 according to information gained by the McClellan Committee. Bidding against Union Casualty was Pacific Mutual Life Insurance Company, a firm both reputable and financially solid, with assets of $376 million, almost five hundred times the capital of Union Casualty. Pacific Mutual also offered to handle the work for far lower fees than Union Casualty promised to charge, yet Pacific Mutual was not considered. Hoffa had made a deal that would pay off his friend.

The payoff was excellent. During the first eight years, the Dorfmans made more than $3 million in service fees and commissions. According to insurance experts, this amount included $1.25 million in excessive commissions and another $400,000 in excessive fees. Hoffa allowed the Dorfmans to increase their premium rates and commission fees each year from 1952 to 1954. In addition, at one point Allen Dorfman took $51,000 worth of premiums and deposited them in his personal account without the Teamsters ever complaining. None of the members had benefit problems, but Hoffa's action resulted in higher than necessary rates for their services.

In theory there was a control over the pension fund money: the Taft-Hartley Law, which stipulated that there could not be more union leaders than industry representatives on the pension fund board. In theory, the industry leaders could dominate the board if they wished, but Hoffa insisted that the board comprise equal numbers of men from organized labor and industry.

Hoffa also insisted upon a large board consisting of at least six men from each side. He felt certain that his power was such that he could force the union members to vote as he chose. He also thought that there were enough differences among the more independent business representatives that the more he had on the board, the easier it would be to sway at least one of them to side with labor, giving him a simple majority.

The industry representatives asked to serve on the board disagreed with Hoffa. They wanted a small board to prevent Hoffa's domination and assure that they could avoid the scandals such as the move to transfer health and welfare funds to the Dorfmans.

Hoffa had a power move ready for just such dissent. He quietly informed the representatives from industry that either they went along with his plans or he would attack the companies they headed. He would arrange to have grievances planted and then wage selective strikes. The representatives immediately agreed to his demands for the twelve-man board with equal union/nonunion representation. Then he forced a decision allowing all actions to be binding with a simple majority, unlike the procedure other pension fund boards followed—a majority vote of both sides. In Hoffa's case, that would have meant that eight of the twelve would have had to agree instead of just seven, an easier victory for him.

Hoffa had a good business sense despite his corruption. He always said that the pension fund backed a larger number of financial winners than most banks, and I think that was true. But his real genius was understanding what was happening in America.

Hoffa wasn't only getting better contracts for the workingman. He knew what the extra money would mean for their families. They would have increased leisure time and ability to enjoy themselves in ways that had not been possible.

For years most working people never really had a vacation. They would spend their time off fixing up their home, working in the yard, maybe going to the beach or some other inexpensive recreation place. Some people camped in tents in state parks, but eating in restaurants more than a couple of times cost too much for most families. They had to find recreation that didn't cost any money.

The new contracts meant that people could afford to take a real vacation. They could stay in hotels. They could eat in restaurants. They could gamble a little in Las Vegas.

This was a time when leisure activities were becoming important in America. Bowling alleys were built in record numbers. Companies like Holiday Inn were expanding across America. Station wagons were becoming extremely popular for hauling kids and luggage from state to state.

As a result of all this, Hoffa began looking for real estate investments that would match the leisure-time interest. He wanted the Central States Pension Fund to invest money in casinos, hotels, and resorts, among other properties.

However, Hoffa still wanted to help his friends. For example, Bill Presser convinced him to provide a $1 million loan to Cleveland Raceways in 1956. The loan was for ten years at 6 percent interest and was one of those loans that were not properly secured, at least in the eyes of investigators for the McClellan Committee. When Robert Kennedy mentioned the loan, Hoffa got nervous and arranged to have it repaid to the pension fund. Later, upon reflection, he made the decision not to back down again.

There were other Hoffa deals that were suspect. For example, he arranged for five different 6 percent interest rate loans for the Miami, Florida, Castaways Motel. The loans totaled $3,705,000, an amount in excess of what would have been proper to loan the business. By splitting the total into five pieces, Hoffa managed to prevent anyone from getting wise to his ultimate goals—taking the money.

Kickbacks were also common during this period. Hoffa had a friend named Benjamin Dranow who had a department store and provided such bribes as $2,000 coats to the wives of two close friends of Hoffa. The pension fund loaned the Dranow store $1 million, only $234,000 of which was paid back by the time Dranow deliberately bankrupted his business in 1961. This time the secret deals had gone a little too far because Dranow was convicted on eighteen counts of fraud for stealing $100,000 from the store's accounts before declaring bankruptcy. Then Dranow was convicted of tax evasion, followed by a conviction, along with Jimmy Hoffa, for conspiracy to defraud the pension fund. The latter involved a total of $25 million in fourteen different loans. The money was meant to help Hoffa get out from under some bad land investments he had made in Florida (including the Castaways Motel), but the ruse was discovered.

Numerous other loans may or may not have been good, but certainly the people who received them were questionable. All the loans were for 6 percent or less at a time when higher interest rates could have been charged. Jay Sarno received $1.8 million to build the Atlanta Cabana Motel, which was to be the first in a chain. He later received money to help him build such Las Vegas operations as Circus Circus and Caesar's Palace, as well as a loan to build the Dallas Cabana Motel. Allen Dorfman helped Sarno get the loan, Sarno allegedly acting as a front for Chicago mob figures in the ownership of Circus Circus. In addition, Sarno had offered to pay a higher interest rate than was ultimately demanded by Hoffa and the board.

One loan for $800,000 at 5 percent was to a trucking company owned by one of the trustees of the pension fund. And another, for $735,000 was to a business partner of Ben Dranow. The actions, which became blatant as early as 1958, gave a hint as to the direction the fund would take whenever friends of Hoffa and his associates were involved.

Bill Presser was getting a piece of the action himself. He arranged for Jackie to obtain $850,000 to build Eastgate Coliseum, a mammoth recreation complex in the Cleveland area. The Pressers pocketed some of the money and mismanaged the rest, but that did not matter. The pension fund kept pace with their needs until they borrowed a total of $1.6 million for the project.

Jackie eventually owned other bowling alleys, places I would occasionally run for him and he always bankrupted. Jackie liked to skim the money off the top and not bother paying the various purveyors, guaranteeing that they would fail. But he learned a number of different ways to make extra money by having companies like Brunswick handle most of the financing so, even bankrupt, he made a profit.

The best example was the Coliseum, where the loans and other support brought Jackie plenty of money before the bankruptcy. After that a sweetheart deal was made with Sam Klein, who worked for the Bally Corporation and was a close friend of both Bill and Jackie. Klein took over the company, loans and all, for an investment of $1 million. Ironically, for the investment Klein made, the Coliseum could turn a profit. It was a good business deal for Klein, and it was good business for Jackie, who made plenty of money before unloading the place at a bargain price.

Even with all the other deals and side deals, it was the Dorfmans who were receiving some of the greatest benefits. In 1954, a Special Subcommittee to the Congressional Committee on Education and Labor headed by Republican Wint Smith of Kansas issued a report on its investigation of welfare funds and racketeering that was conducted at the end of the previous year. The committee found that Hoffa, acting without the knowledge of other trustees on the Central States funds, invested approximately $250,000 in Union Casualty's preferred stock. At the time of the hearings Hoffa was defending the investment as a good one although neither dividends nor interest had been paid during the previous two years.

When it was time to audit the Central States fund, Union Casualty handled the matter, discovering that the union still owed insurance premium payments totaling $249,000. The subcommittee found that the money was paid despite concern about the accuracy of the figure and the self-interest of the auditor.

The committee called both Paul and Allen Dorfman to testify; the men invoked the Fifth Amendment 135 times. Yet so great was Hoffa's power and the influence of both the Teamsters and the mob that the Dorfmans were never cited for contempt of Congress, an action that normally would have been taken with so many refusals to talk.

The profits Allen Dorfman made came into question during the McClellan Committee hearings. Martin Uhlmann, an accountant for the General Services Administration, showed that Allen Dorfman had been reimbursed by the Mount Vernon Company for $182,000 in expenses incurred from 1953 through 1957. This would not have been a problem had his agency not received an additional $158,000 for expenses. More important, only $78,000 of the money paid was connected with receipts submitted, and some of the receipts were false. For example, it was shown that between 1956 and 1957 Allen Dorfman purchased $7,300 worth of furniture for both his home and his mother's. The furniture came from a Chicago furniture store, and false receipts were used so that the money appeared to have been spent on office furniture.

The payroll of the Dorfman agency was also padded with relatives, including one who was found to be working full time for another business that Dorfman owned. There was also an indication that, along with numerous other financial improprieties, Dorfman may have diverted money to Jimmy Hoffa. This was a charge that Hoffa denied, though one which both Paul and Allen Dorfman never discussed, taking the Fifth Amendment when questioned about the matter.

The Dorfmans expanded their business into other states, though not all of the states allowed them to operate. New York state, for example, withdrew permission for them to do business. The State Insurance Department found that the parent company, Mount Vernon Insurance, paid Union an additional twenty-six thousand dollars in expenses without adequate documentation. There were also commissions that were generous at best and seemingly excessive at worst. Dorfman was denied the right to sell in New York when he failed to supply investigators with documentation for his claims. The parent company in Mount Vernon was censured for continuing to work with Union, but they were allowed to continue operating in New York. However, this did not occur until after they had helped Hoffa's influence expand into that city.

John Dioguardi, a close friend of Paul Dorfman, was sent to New York in order to establish what were known as "paper locals" for Jimmy Hoffa. These were locals whose main purpose was to help Hoffa take over the New York City Joint Council. More important in terms of the organized crime links Hoffa was forging at this time was the fact that Dioguardi, better known as Johnny Dio, was a convicted labor racketeer and the man who allegedly ordered the acid blinding of Victor Riesel, a columnist specializing in the labor movement.

Years later Allen Dorfman became a controversial figure in the 1972 campaign of Richard Nixon, showing a receipt for $100,000 to a number of people during a trial that led to his conviction for receiving pension fund kickbacks. Russell Sackett, a reporter for *Newsday,* broke the story, relating that his sources said that the receipt was signed by John Mitchell. Supposedly this was an illegal contribution to the Nixon campaign that was meant to gain undue influence. However, nothing on the receipt indicated the purpose of the money, nor was the receipt connected with any company or business. It was simply a standard form of the type available from any office supply store.

That 1972 campaign would also be noted for other improper and illegal contributions which Hoffa claimed to be $1 million while Frank Fitzsimmons said were only fifty or sixty thousand dollars. There were also a number of large individual contributions from men such as Salvatore Provenzano, a Teamster official with alleged organized crime connections.

But all of this was just starting in the 1950s. Dorfman, father and son, were becoming extremely important to Hoffa and the Teamsters, and their reward was being allowed to participate in the corruption.

You probably are wondering how Jimmy Hoffa could have so much power during the 1950s since he was not yet at the top of the Teamsters Union. Again this is an example of the power that Jimmy knew how to handle.

Hoffa always thought ahead, just as my brother-in-law Bill did. These were men who had patience, who understood how to gain power. They had studied the Irish and learned their weak points. They had watched the changes in power throughout government and labor, learning how to reach the important players. They studied organized crime and participated in ways that would help them.

For Bill, becoming involved with organized crime meant being much like a soldier, proving himself by exchanging favors, cutting the leadership into any scam he had in mind, or otherwise getting as close as he could without being Italian. He worked with old man Milano, John Nardi, and others. He acted as muscle for them and they supported him.

Jimmy Hoffa worked differently. He worked with the mob, but not in the same manner. He tried to find ways to exchange favors, to gain mob influence, without ever accepting the fact that any involvement can bind you for life. Thus he was laying a groundwork for favors by protecting organized crime members wherever he could.

Many people have heard of the story of the French Connection, which was eventually stopped through the actions of men such as Detective Doug Reid of the New York City Police Department in the late 1960s and early 1970s. At that time a combination of Mafia members and Argentine criminals such as Louis Caesar Steppenberg, Jaime Cohen, and Jacobo Grodsky (aka Jack Grosby) was running the operations. But the French Connection actually began in 1954 under the direction of Giuseppe and Vincent Cotroni. They manufactured narcotics in Marseilles and shipped them by way of the Atlantic Ocean and the St. Lawrence Seaway to Montreal, Canada. From there it was a simple matter to spread the drugs throughout North America.

Carmine Galante was the primary American contact for the Cotroni brothers. He was underboss of the crime family run by Joseph Bonanno and had previously worked for Vito Genovese. Through his connections he developed a route for bringing the drugs into the United States through Buffalo, New York, as well as taking them from Toronto, Ontario, into Windsor and then down into Detroit.

Some of the drug dealers were connected with Hoffa in legitimate business activities. Others were given union jobs. Hoffa was never connected with narcotics trafficking in any way. He would not become personally involved with such matters, nor would he try to profit from them. However, he understood the financial importance of narcotics to organized crime members who were friends of his. By helping the men in ways outside the drug importation activities, he was winning their gratitude. He gave them a certain amount of respectability and, in that way, protections from some of the investigators. He also knew that they would feel obligated to him, willing to help him win and maintain power, no matter what the cost.

By the time the 1952 International Brotherhood of Teamsters convention took place, Hoffa was the most powerful man in attendance. He had the behind-the-scenes power on a national basis that Bill Presser had learned to wield regionally. However, whereas Bill was always content to stay behind the scenes, doing the bidding of Mafia leaders such as the Milano brothers, Hoffa wanted complete control. Yet he understood that it was not time to make his move against the

Irish. It was time to be a kingmaker, holding enough power so that, when he was ready, he could topple the king.

Dave Beck was a close friend of Dan Tobin and popular with Teamsters on the West Coast, a group independent of the Midwest. In fact, when I went out to California to live and work for a while after Bill became prominent with the Teamsters, I found that my position gave me no power. I would have had a job in a second anywhere in the country except out there. The West Coast guys were autonomous and hated men like Hoffa, who came from Detroit. Beck, from Seattle, was one of their own and the fact that Beck looked upon Hoffa as his chosen successor was fine with them.

Beck was not popular enough to win the election as the new president, a fact that only Beck, Tobin, and a few others realized. There was a powerful "stop Beck" movement, and there was a good chance that enough men were involved to prevent Beck from winning. Hoffa, who could have taken over as a candidate and won, knew that it was best to wait and truly solidify his power. He went behind the scenes, talked with the men who opposed Beck, and convinced them to be quiet. Beck won immediately, then was so grateful that he named Hoffa an International Brotherhood of Teamsters (IBT) vice president and appointed him to the Teamsters general executive board.

Beck did not understand the labor movement as Jimmy Hoffa did. Beck liked the attention his power gave him. He had become an important figure in the United States at a time when the news media had changed radically. A few years earlier he might have been written about in *Time* or *Life* magazine or discussed on the editorial pages of publications such as *The New York Times,* but that would have been the extent of it. His name probably would not have been a household name, at least not for those families unconnected with the labor movement. Certainly, his opinions concerning anything outside labor would not have been taken seriously.

Now television was becoming available to almost every home in America. News programs, broadcasts of congressional investigations, and other fare, all of which would be considered boring today, were immensely popular. Dave Beck found a willing audience for his opinions. He began making foreign policy speeches, enjoying a friendship with President Dwight D. Eisenhower, and generally promoting himself.

Hoffa recognized the self-centered arrogance of Dave Beck and knew that such actions and attitudes would not go over well with the rank and file. He became the man who was assigned to be Beck's troubleshooter. Beck never realized that he was assuring his own downfall.

Suddenly Jimmy Hoffa was in a perfect position. He had all the power of the Teamster presidency without the title. If anything went wrong, Beck would take the flack. Yet the members only knew Jimmy.

Hoffa developed a number of new organizing tactics because he was sensitive to management's problems as well as those of the business community. For example, Hoffa recognized that an industrywide strike hurt everyone, including the workers, and did not always result in the settlements he wanted. He analyzed the companies within an industry to discover those doing the largest volume of business. Then he would selectively strike the biggest, ignoring the smaller ones. This meant that the bosses faced two problems. They had their workers on strike so they could not work. But they also had competitors able to pick up the business slack. Either they agreed to Hoffa's demands or their business would be eroded by their competitors. They could no longer ride out a strike secure in the knowledge that no one would profit. They had to settle more quickly than in the past.

Another tactic was to hit a company where it mattered most, which was not always at the source. For example, suppose a company were in one state, but its business in another. Hoffa wanted a contract with the parent company, but the owners would not sign. Instead of striking the plant, he would arrange the strike so that it stopped the drivers in the state to which they delivered. They might not stop the manufacture of a product, but they would stop the delivery of that product to the customer base and, at times, create a greater economic impact on the company than would otherwise have been possible.

The third weapon Hoffa used was one with which I would also become involved. This was terrorism. If a guy won't do what you want, you burn his business, dynamite his car, beat him up, or do whatever else you have to do so that he is running scared. Unless a guy has a death wish, strong-arm tactics often work, and Hoffa knew how to use them.

Rolland McMaster was assigned the position of unionizing areas such as Tennessee. Hoffa placed Frank Fitzsimmons in charge of Detroit Local 299, making Fitzsimmons his second in command. Both men liked McMaster and trusted his abilities, so they declared him to be an "administrative assistant." The title meant nothing, though almost everyone realized he was officially the third in command.

McMaster's "traveling partner" to Nashville indicated what uncooperative Tennessee business leaders could expect. The man was Frank Kierdorf, a business agent for Flint, Michigan, Local 332. He was also an ex-convict and Teamster torch, who was well connected.

In Nashville, McMaster and Kierdorf teamed up with Nashville Local 327 head Don Vestal who had an arrest record for assault and battery. (He had been charged with attempted murder, the charge being reduced.) Because of Vestal's loyalty to Hoffa in 1952, he was also made head of Tennessee Joint Council 87, becoming the spokesperson for seven locals.

Vestal was provided the money necessary to form his own goon squad. The acts of violence against those opposing Hoffa's plans are unknown, though Tennessee trucking battles seemed to turn the state red with blood. What is known is that 173 deliberate acts of violence were directly connected with the organizing efforts. Then the goon squads were moved into other southern states including Georgia, Mississippi, and Florida. By 1953, the muscle was led by William A. Smith, a Local 327 "assistant business agent," a title you will not normally find in the Teamsters. Smith had a reputation as an explosives expert along with twelve prior convictions for crimes of violence.

McMaster, working under orders from Hoffa, carefully supervised the target selection. Some of the companies in the area were owned, directly or indirectly, by Mafia figures in Chicago. Whenever such a company was found, there would be no violence against it.

Hoffa recognized that he needed good men helping him, not just those loyal enough to be willing to go out and break heads without asking questions. One of the most important aides he took to Washington was Harold Gibbons, a man who was the complete opposite of both Hoffa and Frank Fitzsimmons. In fact, if Gibbons had had the ruthlessness, the power drive, and the support to take over the International, the Teamsters Union would have been the finest workers' organization in the world.

Harold Gibbons understood the problems of the workingman. His father, Patrick Gibbons, was a miner, and the family lived in the coal mine camp of Archibald Patch in northeast Pennsylvania. Harold was the youngest of twenty-three children, in which all of the brothers began working in the mines as soon as they were old enough to help support the family. There were frequent strikes because of the dangerous conditions and low wages, strikes that left the family so poor that Harold remembered meals consisting of a single potato for each child.

Harold Gibbons, as the youngest in the family, did not have to go to work full time until he was seventeen years old. He found a dishwashing job in Scranton, Pennsylvania, where he worked an eighty-four-hour week for ten dollars in pay.

The family left the coal mining region, moving to the Chicago area, where Harold gained better jobs, first as a short order cook and later in a machinery warehouse. This was during the Depression years, yet instead of just trying to survive, he determined to better himself. He won a scholarship to an industrial workers' summer school educational program at the University of Wisconsin. Later he would attend a worker education program at the University of Chicago.

More was happening than a Horatio Alger story of a poor kid trying to better himself through an education. Harold Gibbons was an intellectual who delighted in campus discussions about economic theories. He began reading about the differences between capitalism and socialism. He was struck by the ways in which socialism seemed to have answers for poor families such as his when capitalism hadn't had any impact on their ability to survive the grinding poverty.

Gibbons decided to devote himself to bettering the lives of the people at the bottom of the economic scale. In 1932, after becoming an adult education teacher, he formed a union for the other teachers. He was just twenty-two years old, but already writing textbooks for the classes he was teaching.

There was a national teachers union whose annual meeting Gibbons attended for the first time in 1934. Despite his youth, he was immediately elected vice president. In 1936 he became actively involved in the Chicago area branch of the CIO.

Gibbons had found his place in the world. Like me, he had unions as his religion. Unlike me, he was never out for himself in anything he did. He organized textile workers by day and taught school at night. This pattern continued until 1938, when he became a full-time textile worker organizer for five states. He moved to Louisville and was paid a salary of thirty-five dollars a week, usually drawing just half that pay to ensure that there would be enough money to pay other bills.

Gibbons kept moving up in union activities. He became the head of the St. Louis branch of the Retail, Wholesale and Department Store Employees Union of the CIO in 1941. Then, six years later, he merged the six locals in his union into an independent union separate from the CIO because he thought that he could serve them better.

It was 1949 when Harold became a part of the Teamsters, though. He signed an agreement that merged his distribution workers independent union with the Teamsters Local 688, which had eight thousand members. He moved into the position of head of that local when its president retired and expanded it to sixteen thousand members, among whom were brewery and soda factory workers.

Success in organizing was not important to Harold Gibbons. Guys like Jackie Presser and Harold Friedman looked at the numbers. They wanted the money that came from having thousands of members. The more men they had, the wealthier they could become. They were users; Harold Gibbons never was.

He wanted workers to have benefits that would prevent them from suffering as his family had when he was growing up in the coal mining camps. By 1951, although some of the workers were earning as little as thirty-five cents an hour, they had free, prepaid medical care from the employers. Gibbons created the Labor Health Institute, a forerunner of contemporary health maintenance organizations, which employed fifty-seven full- and part-time physicians for the employees. All dental care was free, with the exception of bridgework and dentures, though those were supplied at cost. They also received free legal advice, free home nursing services, and both prescription drugs and eyeglasses at cost. In addition, they had pension benefits, something that other Teamsters would not learn about for four more years. It was the most progressive union in the nation and treated the workers better than anyone else ever had.

Gibbons did not stop there. Food prices increased rapidly in 1951 and workers with large families could not keep pace. Gibbons's answer was to provide an alternative, a Teamsters Union grocery store where all items were sold at cost.

Eventually Gibbons convinced St. Louis area employers to finance a recreation center for his members. They were able to enjoy both indoor and outdoor swimming, golf, and a gymnasium and numerous other resources which were similar to those found in the most expensive country clubs. However, not only were many of the country clubs segregated at the time that Gibbons built the complex, they were also beyond the social or economic capability of the members. Many Teamsters were living in ghetto areas, and many others were just getting by in decent neighborhoods. The recreation facility was a force not only to better the lives of the workers without cost to them but also to fight segregation, a major problem in the St. Louis area.

In the 1950s even the better Teamsters locals were generally insensitive to racial bias or had leaders who hated minority groups. Gibbons was so progressive that in 1952 he presented the St. Louis public schools with a plan for desegregation despite the fact that the Missouri state constitution required racial segregation in education. This was two years before the Supreme Court desegregation order which began the civil rights era in the United States.

If it was unusual for a union leader to fight for unpopular causes, it was even more unusual for the rank and file to throw their support to him. Local 688 began an activist campaign to allow blacks to attend movie theaters, use public restrooms while shopping, and eat at the restaurants of their choice. Then Gibbons created the "community steward" idea. He placed a steward in each neighborhood where twenty-five or more members of Local 688 were living. Just as stewards on the job agitated for better working conditions, the community stewards helped the people organize to gain full community services, including garbage collection, street lighting, and properly maintained public playgrounds.

The activism extended to the city at large. Through Gibbons's community organization, using the community stewards and rank and file members as activists contacting their neighbors, the Teamsters radically changed St. Louis. They gained community colleges and a state university branch to provide low-cost education. Their work improved the transit system, the sewage system, and other services that needed to be changed in some manner.

Gibbons could have demanded any salary he wanted and the members would have given it to him. His contracts brought greatly increased wages along with the benefits, yet he was a confirmed socialist. He arranged for all staff members, including himself, to receive ninety dollars a week and five dollars a day for expenses. Raises had to be approved by the stewards, an elaborate system that eventually involved five hundred men and women. No one resented the money spent for salaries for the administrators because there was a genuine feeling that the rank and file truly were involved in all that was taking place.

There was a toughness to Gibbons when it came to negotiations, though. He was not afraid of strikes and generally had as many as three dozen picket lines active in any given week during the 1950s. The business owners knew that the men would do anything he wanted and that he would not hesitate to shut them down. At the same time, he was completely honest during negotiations. He wanted to know the company's financial picture: what they could afford and what would create a genuine problem for them. Then he negotiated a contract that was fair to all sides. There were no kickbacks. There were no under-the-table deals. The terms he negotiated were for the workers, not for him.

Gibbons's success brought him to the attention of organized crime elements in St. Louis. A successful union meant money to be skimmed, something Gibbons would not tolerate. Yet he was being threatened. He was told that either he put some of the mob people on the payroll or he would be killed.

Dick Cavener was second in command in Local 688 in 1953, and he suggested that Gibbons talk with Hoffa. They knew that Hoffa had worked successfully with the mob, though they didn't know that Hoffa was involved in various illegal and unethical scams.

Hoffa explained that there were two ways to handle the mob. The easier was to put a few of the mob men on the payroll and leave it at that. However, if he did that, within six months the mob would work its way into a controlling position and Gibbons would be out.

The alternative, Hoffa explained, was to buy a pistol and kill whoever came at him. Gibbons decided to arm himself rather than let organized crime take over his union.

Hoffa was impressed with Gibbons and the organization he had built. He gained permission from both the Detroit and Chicago organized crime families to move into St. Louis and help Gibbons fight the attempted takeover. Bodyguards were provided for Gibbons, and the St. Louis mob family was warned to lay off.

Eventually Hoffa persuaded Dave Beck to force the St. Louis area joint council into trusteeship. This would allow Beck, through Hoffa, to choose a new leader. Hoffa made Gibbons the man in charge.

Hoffa understood that he needed the St. Louis region beholden to him as he maneuvered for power. He also understood that there was no better man to have on his side than Harold Gibbons. He recognized that, although Gibbons was honest, he was also loyal. He would back Hoffa any way he could so long as he could maintain his ideals for the workingman. Hoffa, in turn, made Gibbons his major representative to the Central Conference and, eventually, made him his assistant. The men were so close that, eventually, they shared an apartment in Washington when they had to be at the international headquarters office.

Gibbons changed a bit after joining with Hoffa. He was still out for the rank and file, though he decided to take advantage of assistants who could serve as hired muscle. He first hired Bernard "Barney" Baker, whose weight varied from 325 to 500 pounds. He was twice convicted of various strong-arm crimes, was a former boxer, and had worked for Bugsy Siegel. His testimony before the McClellan Committee was a favorite of Robert Kennedy, who liked questioning him about such friends as Cockeyed Dunne and Squint Sheridan.

"Kennedy: Do you know Cockeyed Dunn?"

"Baker: I don't know him as Cockeyed Dunn. I know him as John Dunn."

"Kennedy: Where is he now?"

"Baker: He has met his maker."

"Kennedy: How did he do that?"

"Baker: I believe through electrocution in the City of New York of the State of New York."

Baker then explained that Squint Sheridan ("he was a friend of mine") had also "met his maker" through electrocution.

Other friends named during the testimony included Meyer Lansky, Siegel, Joe Adonis, Vincent "Piggy Mac" Marchesi, and "Trigger Mike" Coppola. Baker made it clear that, other than Hoffa and Gibbons, his primary work had always been with men who were convicted killers, narcotics traffickers, pimps, and other criminals. His size and history of violence were such that his presence in a room often was enough to intimidate anyone who didn't want to go along with either Hoffa or Baker.

Gibbons became a different personality after he became involved with Hoffa. He wasn't corrupted by Hoffa so much as he was exposed to a different life-style that enabled him to change the way he operated.

Gibbons began living in luxury on the road, taking advantage of all the perquisites his new position as Hoffa's aide allowed. His home life remained modest because his family had no interest in wealth. He also never cheated the union, detailing his expenses and using his own money for frequent womanizing. No one ever considered Gibbons capable of stealing anything, and there is no indication that he ever did. The only stress with Hoffa arose from his sexual activities outside marriage, activities of which Hoffa did not approve.

In theory, Harold Gibbons should also have been upset with Hoffa's Mafia connections. Such corruption violated his own code of ethics from his early years. But Gibbons, though claiming that Hoffa planned to rid the union of organized crime figures once he was in full control, recognized that Hoffa's statements were different from his actions. He even went so far as to refer to a number of major mob figures in the Teamsters as "tough unionists" or men who were "temporarily necessary" to gain control. He apparently remained too impressed with money and power to oppose Hoffa. At the same time, his personal integrity was such that he made a good legitimate front for Hoffa.

Hoffa, with men such as Gibbons, Tony Provenzano, and the others surrounding him, was ready to make his move for the top. Oddly, Robert Kennedy, the man who would eventually send him to jail, became his unwitting ally.

The McClellan Committee became interested in the ways in which the Teamsters were spending their money. Unions involved with the National Labor Relations Board (NLRB) had to file annual financial statements with the Labor Department. However, because of the Gold decision by the U.S. Supreme Court, the law did not require that any statements be accurate. It was enough to file them, no one bothering to check the books to see whether they were factual.

Unions were also tax-exempt at the time, so there was no reason for the U.S. Treasury Department to examine the books. Beck could have been stealing the union blind and there would be no proof.

Carmine Bellino was sent by the McClellan Committee to investigate Beck's actions. He found that Beck had essentially stolen $370,000 for personal use from the Western Conference of Teamsters. He used some of the money for friends, other funds to pay for home improvements.

There had also been earlier concerns about the money, including an IRS investigation into Beck's personal income in 1954. When that pressure occurred, he returned $200,000 to the union, claiming that the money was a portion of a loan that he owed. Later he returned another $170,000.

Investigators found that the "loans" were part of a carefully hidden scheme of kickbacks and probable frauds involving executives of companies such as Fruehauf Trailer Company and Associated Transport Company. Beck established a beer distribution company and obtained favors from Anheuser-Busch in St. Louis. Then he prevented the Teamsters from hauling any of the company's beer until his partner in the business allowed Dave Beck, Jr., to be president of the company.

In addition, Dave Beck sold his personal residence in Seattle for $163,000 in 1955. The purchaser was none other than Dave Beck, though in his position as union president. The union then agreed to give Dave Beck the use of the house at no charge.

The McClellan Committee's investigators uncovered repeated misrepresentations by Beck of the alleged loans he obtained. It was obvious that no one thought the money was a loan until Beck was caught in his lies. When Kennedy asked about the use of the money, including the payments made for gardening at his home, Beck stated:

"I must decline to answer the question because this Committee lacks jurisdiction or authority under Articles 1, 2, and 3 of the Constitution; further I decline to answer because I refuse to give testimony against myself and invoke the Fourth and Fifth Amendments; further because the question is not relevant or pertinent to the investigation."

Then Kennedy asked, "Do you feel that if you gave a truthful answer to this Committee on your taking of $320,000 of Union funds that that might tend to incriminate you?"

Beck said, "It might." He would give no details.

Additional testimony indicated that Beck had provided money to a close friend to make purchases ranging from a large food freezer for his home to outboard motors to five dozen baby diapers and a bow tie. There were dozens of different items, all paid for by funds that originally belonged to the Teamsters and had been misappropriated by Beck.

The destruction of Beck was completed by the McClellan Committee on May 16, 1957. That was the last time Beck appeared for questioning, again invoking the Fifth Amendment. Although there was still time before he would be indicted, it was obvious that he was going to jail. President Eisenhower no longer wanted him in the White House or anywhere else that they might be seen together. Senators and congressmen who had curried his favor now pretended that they had never been close to him. He was dropped by everyone in government and awaited the trial he knew he could not win.

In the end he was convicted of only two charges. One was that he sold a 1952 Cadillac that belonged to the Teamsters and kept the $1,900 involved. The other was that he helped file a false 1950 tax return for the Joint Council No. 28 Building Association. There was also an attempt to convict him for nonpayment of $240,000 in back income taxes for the years 1950 through 1953, though that case was dismissed.

Beck was later asked about his innocence of the Cadillac sale charges. John D. McCallum, writing in the book *Dave Beck,* quotes Beck as saying:

> State charges that I pocketed the $1,900 were farfetched. These are the facts: Guiry Marcella was my secretary in our Seattle office and she received a sales payment for the Cadillac, belonging to the Teamsters, which I had been using whenever I was in the Northwest. She promptly deposited the check in the International account. When she advised me of her action, I corrected her immediately. "No, no, no," I told her over the telephone from Washington. "That's not where it goes." So she changed it, but instead of holding the check until I got back to Seattle and putting it in the right account, she deposited it in my own personal account. As soon as I found out about her second error, I quickly reimbursed the union for the $1,900. That was the legal issue right there. Obviously, the grand jury

didn't believe my version of what really happened. In any event, they charged me with grand larceny and the indictment stuck. Guilty? Hell, no.

Dave Beck was sentenced to five years in jail. He was ordered to serve a minimum of two years and did his time at McNeil Island. With that conviction, it was time for Jimmy Hoffa and Bill Presser to make their move. The plans of the Mafia almost thirty years earlier, the work that took place with the Jewish Combination, and the careful groundwork laid by Jimmy Hoffa all came to fruition. The Irish were finished as the dominant power, and the Teamsters were about to start a new era in organized labor.

5

The Hoffa Era

From the day that James Hoffa told Robert Kennedy that he was nothing but a rich man's kid who never had to earn a nickel in his life, Hoffa was a marked man. When Kennedy became Attorney General, satisfying this grudge became the public policy of the United States, and Hoffa, along with Roy Cohn and perhaps other enemies from Kennedy's past, was singled out for special attention by United States Attorneys. This is, of course, the very antithesis of the rule of law, and serves to bring into sharp focus the ethical obligation of the prosecutor to refrain from abusing his power by prosecutions that are directed at individuals rather than crimes.

> *Monroe H. Freedman, "The Professional Responsibility of the Prosecuting Attorney."* Georgetown Law Journal *55, no. 6 (May 1967): 1035.*

The Teamsters Union is the most powerful institution in this country—aside from the United States Government itself. In many major metropolitan areas the Teamsters control all transportation. It is a Teamster who drives the mother to the hospital at birth. It is the Teamster who drives the hearse at death. And between birth and burial, the Teamsters drive the trucks that clothe and feed us and provide the vital necessities of life. They control the pickup and deliveries of milk, frozen meat, fresh fruit, department store merchandise, newspapers, railroad express, air freight, and of cargo to and from the sea docks.

Quite literally, your life—the life of every person in the United States—is in the hands of Hoffa and his Teamsters.

But though the great majority of Teamster officials and Teamster members are honest, the Teamsters Union under Hoffa is often not run as a bona fide union. As Mr. Hoffa operates it, this is a conspiracy of evil.

> *Robert F. Kennedy,* The Enemy Within.

THE McCLELLAN COMMITTEE investigation that brought down Dave Beck came about in a roundabout manner. Robert Kennedy, then chief counsel for the Senate Permanent Investigations Subcommittee, was interested in learning more about Johnny Dioguardi, not the Teamsters. Dioguardi was involved with the garment industry in ways that seemed to warrant an investigation.

"By controlling the unions, you can operate your own factory without having to worry about union pay scales and rules," Dioguardi was quoted as saying in 1953 (Ovid Demaris, *The Last Mafioso* [New York: Times Books], 1981). He was speaking to Sam Berger, Jimmy, and Louie Dragna in a meeting at the Roosevelt Hotel in Hollywood. "You get waivers on practically every point in the contract, while your competitors have to operate under strict union conditions. It gives you the edge you need in the market place. It used to be that this industry was all Jewish, but now the Italians are getting into it. Guys like Joe Stretch (née Stracci) control big companies like Zimmet and Stracci.

"To really make money you've got to get into the manufacturing end of it, and to do that, you've got to get some leverage with the ILGWU (International Ladies Garment Workers Union), from the needle trade to the pressers and truckers, every phase of it."

Kennedy had learned that Johnny Dio, as he was usually called, had owned several cheap dress manufacturing firms at the same time that he was a director of the United Auto Workers Union, American Federation of Labor. (the UAW-AFL broke with the CIO in 1939. Much better known was Walter Reuther's United Auto Workers, Congress of Industrial Organizations). Dio not only ran a nonunion shop, but sold it with the condition that the shop remain nonunion. His commitment to organized labor was obviously only as deep as that which he could gain for himself.

Johnny Dio was never a major crime figure. He had been convicted of income tax evasion from the sale of one of his garment manufacturing plants. He had been implicated in the Victor Reisel acid blinding incident. Yet most of his appeal for Hoffa was due to alleged contacts within the mob.

Hoffa helped Dio impress Dave Beck through the use of selective strikes by his UAW-AFL local back in 1953, including one by cabdrivers at a time when Beck was traveling. Beck was not impressed enough to give Dio a Teamsters Union charter, though Hoffa and Dio remained close.

The investigation of Dio and the garment industry problems he had allegedly created led to the discovery of the paper locals (union locals used to create the image of strength but which do not recruit members) mentioned earlier, and those connections led to Jimmy Hoffa and the Teamsters.

It is hard to know exactly what made Robert Kennedy push so hard to get Hoffa. There have been off-the-record insider accounts that indicate that Kennedy had little or no interest in or awareness of the Teamsters, that he started the investigative work because advisers said that labor would be the hot new issue for getting national attention. Kennedy did have plans to run for public office and this may have been true. Whatever the case, Hoffa and Kennedy eventually took an intense dislike to each other and Kennedy made convicting Hoffa for any crime he could find what amounted to a vendetta.

The reactions of both men to their first meeting have been recorded by each of them. In *The Enemy Within,* Kennedy wrote:

> Immediately, I was struck by how short he is—only five feet five and a half. We walked into the living room of Cheyfitz's [Edward Cheyfitz was a public relations man based in Washington who had begun supporting Hoffa after previously backing Beck] elaborately decorated house, but chatted only a few minutes before going in to dinner. The three of us were alone. Hoffa, I was to discover, can be personable, polite and friendly. But that evening, though friendly enough, he maintained one steady theme in his conversation throughout dinner and for the rest of the evening.
> "I do to others what they do to me, only worse," he said.
> "Maybe I should have worn my bulletproof vest," I suggested.
> From that first meeting, it seemed to me he wanted to impress upon me that Jimmy Hoffa is a tough, rugged man.

Then, in his book *Hoffa: The Real Story,* Hoffa commented: "Robert F. Kennedy was a man who always made a big thing out of how strong and how tough he was, how he had been a football player or something at Harvard, and how he always exercised and kept himself in top shape. . . ."

Hoffa continued: "I was sure, by this time, that Kennedy was a hard-nosed guy who was so spoiled all his life that he had to have his way in everything no matter who got hurt. The kind of a guy you had to be as nasty with as he was with you or he'd run right over you. But it's always been my theory that you keep the door open to your enemies. You know all about your friends."

The McClellan Committee began looking into the labor and management field on January 30, 1957. Dave Beck was one of the first targets, Kennedy focusing on the misappropriations of the $320,000 mentioned in Chapter 4.

The AFL-CIO was determined to respond openly to questions, the organization's Ethical Practices Committee insisting that union officials asked to testify cooperate fully, and not take the Fifth Amendment. The organization also stated that it would expel any groups found to be corrupt.

Johnny Dio and Hoffa were defiant, as were numerous others. Not only did they take the Fifth Amendment, Dio and Hoffa ate lunch together in an area where members of the committee would be certain to see them. Hoffa later claimed that he didn't care about Dio's background except where it affected his labor organizing. He stated that Dio was good with the UAW-AFL and that was what impressed him. It is probable that he knew about Dio's ownership of nonunion garment shops that exploited the workers, but this was not mentioned.

Hoffa saw the McClellan hearings as a way to accomplish two things. One was to begin tweaking Kennedy's nose: for example, eating with Dio in a restaurant where Kennedy and some of the committee members would also eat. The second was to get rid of Dave Beck so he could make his move to control the Teamsters.

The relationship between Hoffa and Kennedy was almost humorous in those early days. Newspaper accounts and various books, both by Hoffa and Kennedy and by others, indicate that both men acted like a couple of kids on the school playground. Robert Kennedy challenged Jimmy Hoffa to arm wrestle and both bragged about what good shape they were in. They compared the number of push-ups they could do routinely (thirty for Hoffa, forty for Kennedy). It was so adolescent that it would have been funny were it not for the power both men wielded.

The truth about Johnny Dio was that his position in New York was meant to provide power for Hoffa. Dio worked with Tony "Ducks" Corallo in setting up the six paper locals that Hoffa convinced Beck to charter. Then other members of organized crime, all the men loyal to Hoffa, were named as delegates to the Teamster Joint Council for New York City. As the McClellan Committee reported (Report 1417, p. 167):

"Dio and those with whom he formed alliances brought 40 men into the labor movement in positions of trust and responsibility—men who, among them, had been arrested a total of 178 times and convicted on 77 of these occasions for crimes ranging from theft, violation of the Harrison Narcotics Act, extortion, conspiracy, bookmaking, use of stench bombs, felonious assault, robbery, possession of unregistered stills, burglary, violation of the gun laws, being an accessory to murder, forgery, possession of stolen mail, and disorderly conduct."

The McClellan Committee did the opposite of what Kennedy expected. There were indictments of Hoffa, including one for wiretapping some of his business agents, but nothing came of them. The only man who would be destroyed was Dave Beck: it was precisely the scenario Hoffa had desired.

Hoffa took over the international presidency in a much more subtle manner than he had taken control of the Detroit Joint Council years earlier. He was nineteen then, seemingly just a kid who could only count on receiving four of the twenty possible votes. However, from the time he headed his first local he made a practice of employing newly released ex-convicts as organizers. They were meant to give him the force necessary to persuade antiunion businessmen to go along with the young local president. Their methods were generally violent, as was discovered years later on August 3, 1958, when Frank Kierdorf, an armed robber, improperly made a firebomb which he was planning to use to burn a cleaning and dyeing business that had refused to unionize. In fact, he was running a protection racket in which nonunion laundry and dry cleaning companies that did not wish to pay union wages had to pay Kierdorf to leave them alone. His mistake sent him to Pontiac, Michigan's, St. Joseph's Mercy Hospital with burns over 85 percent of his body and called attention to Hoffa's methods. When investigators sought a dying declaration that would implicate Hoffa in the racket, Kierdorf's last words were typical of the loyalty all of us felt to Jimmy. He said, "Go fuck yourself."

It was May 26, 1957, when Dave Beck stepped down from the presidency of the Teamsters. He knew that he was going to jail and he also knew that, even if he weren't, his arrogant image had cost him extensive support. He was no longer viewed as an assured victor and could have lost the election.

The contempt with which he was held became evident when he went to jail. Years later, when Hoffa went to prison, he was treated with as much respect on the inside as he had been on the outside. But Beck's arrival was greeted by such taunts as:

> Big Dave Beck
> Was a merry old soul
> With a buckskin belly
> But he had no soul.
> He rode it wide
> And he made it rich,
> Just another con now
> The son-of-a-bitch.

The convention was held on October 4, 1957, and I traveled to Florida with Bill Presser. I was not supposed to be present at the election. Bill wanted me along as a bodyguard, obtaining fake credentials for me since I wasn't an officer in any of the locals or joint councils.

We stayed at the Eden Roc Hotel, a luxury building right on the ocean. Naturally Bill had a suite, though I had no idea what power he held behind the scenes. I also was not fully aware of all the dramas being played out around me.

A month earlier, on September 17, 1957, the Ethical Practices Committee of the AFL-CIO attacked the corruption within the Teamsters. Both Beck and Hoffa were accused of using their union positions to aggrandize themselves. The committee pointed to John Dio and the paper locals that had given Hoffa control of New York as an example of the corruption.

No one is denying that the Teamsters were violent and corrupt. I've detailed too many of their crimes to be naive about what was taking place. What angers me to this day is the image the Teamsters has in comparison with other unions.

Most unions are corrupt and many are far more violent than the Teamsters. Embezzlements, bombings, arson, extortion, beatings, and other crimes have been committed by unions within the AFL-CIO over the years. Numerous union officials have gone to jail for their actions. But the Teamsters are the ones with the reputation.

Hoffa's election was planned, but not by the membership. There was opposition from Harold Gibbons and others, though the truth is that even if the election hadn't been rigged, as I will explain shortly, Hoffa probably would have taken the presidency without a problem.

I don't get excited by people. I've seen some of the most respected men and women in America take bribes and commit crimes to get or keep power. I'm not the type to cheer for anyone—except for Jimmy Hoffa.

There was something about that man when he walked to the podium. He was a little guy, built like a fireplug, and not particularly handsome. Yet I went crazy along with the seventeen hundred others who attended the convention. I was clapping and whistling. I was shouting Hoffa's name. I would have followed Jimmy anywhere.

Dave Beck had warmed up the crowd, talking about the accomplishments during his time as president. He spoke of raising the treasury to $12.5 million and attacked the government's investigations into the Teamsters.

Hoffa spoke after John English, the secretary-treasurer of the Teamsters. Both used the same theme. The Teamsters were under attack by the AFL-CIO, the FBI, the Senate Rackets Committee, and others. The implication was that the attacks were on the workingman. Never mind what crimes Hoffa may have committed. Never mind the funds that may have been misappropriated from the members. The image they were conveying was of the workingman under fire from outside forces. Hoffa and English presented their problems as the problems of all the members.

"I have no fight with the McClellan Committee," Hoffa said. "But when a Congressional committee concentrates on a personal attack or misuses its power, it can be dangerous for all of us.

"Something is wrong when a man may be judged guilty in the court of public opinion because some enemy or some ambitious person accuses him of wrongdoing by hearsay or influence. . . ."

The delegates who elected Hoffa, usually the business agents, trustees, secretary-treasurer, and president of various Teamster locals, had been carefully rigged. There were also stewards and rank and file members of locals who had been sent as representatives of those locals. Sometimes they were handpicked men whose locals were created for the purpose of supporting Hoffa, like Johnny

Dio's operations in New York. Some other locals were dominated by Hoffa loyalists who knew how to work with organized crime, such as Bill Presser, who had worked behind the scenes to influence other delegates. The few legitimate delegates got caught up in the excitement and also voted for Hoffa.

Once Hoffa had enough loyalists to support him, he had to make certain that he had control over who was seated and who wasn't. He took control of the convention credentials committee so that strong opponents, such as some East Coast dissidents who would later file suit against the election, could be stopped. Hoffa's actions had been anticipated by some of the dissidents so they arranged with congressional investigators to be present if anything improper occurred. Hoffa still won on the first ballot, something that would have been impossible in an honest election. Hoffa would have won. Of that I'm certain. He just would not have won on the first ballot without corruption.

Hoffa's men had meant to cover their tracks. They had stolen ballots that went against them and rigged both the seating and the voting so inappropriate voting took place. Then they tossed the documents into the incinerator, blaming the maid for the action.

The story might have been believed had the person assigned to dump the paper taken the time to check where he was throwing the ballots. Instead of the incinerator, he used the laundry chute. At the base of the chute, mixed in with sheets, pillow cases, and other items to be washed, were the minutes of the meetings where all the planning had been done. There was proof that a minimum of 561 delegates had been seated improperly. These men represented more than half the people who were there and obviously affected the outcome of the voting.

A lawsuit followed the discovery of the improper seating and the rigged election. Federal Judge F. Dickinson Letts ordered Hoffa not to take office until the charges of improper seating could be fully investigated. This was on October 14, 1957. Ten days later the AFL-CIO Executive Council suspended the Teamsters from membership. By the time their convention opened in Atlantic City, New Jersey, on December 5, it was a foregone conclusion that the Teamsters would be expelled.

Labor leader George Meany led the fight against the Teamsters. He said that his fight was not with the rank and file. He was hostile to the corruption at the top, to Hoffa and the others who had abused their positions and become involved with criminal activities.

The truth was different. Robert Kennedy was determined to destroy Hoffa any way he could. As chief investigator for the McClellan Committee he had an implicit power he knew how to wield. Messages were quietly spread to the AFL-CIO leadership, who, as I explained, had as much to hide as the Teamsters or more. Either the union got rid of Hoffa or they would be investigated in the same manner.

Meany and the others probably hoped that their threat would result in a revolt by the rank and file. What they did not realize was that the union members had no reason to view the expulsion as a loss. Everyone but the members of the AFL-CIO would gain by it. The Teamsters would save more than $750,000 in dues that went to the AFL-CIO. The Teamster leadership would have to answer to no one. And the rank and file would never know the difference when it came to their ability to win contracts. Membership was large enough to cripple any company they struck, regardless of whether or not other unions gave them their support.

Hoffa developed a plan with the approval of Judge Letts. He would become provisional president. A three-person monitoring board would be made up of a member of the rank and file, a Teamster official, and a third person to be appointed by the judge. Kennedy assumed that the monitor board would find the evidence to remove Hoffa from office. This did not occur.

The monitor committee did little except pass on union member complaints, most of which Hoffa handled. There was also a mood shift on the McClellan Committee, where it was felt that others should be investigated rather than keeping the focus on the Teamsters. Many of the members wanted to be certain that they were seen as impartial rather than risking a worker backlash in which the Teamsters were perceived as being singled out for attack.

Later that year Hoffa appointed Senator Bender, who, as has already been seen, was easily subverted. There was simply too much money available to Hoffa for anyone to stay "pure" when dealing with him.

At that convention in Florida I began to learn how Bill Presser was far closer to Jimmy Hoffa than I had imagined.

Ohio and Michigan are major centers for trucking and the Teamsters. The men who have their bases in Cleveland and Detroit are extremely important to the union operations. These are also strong mob areas and Bill, as I have explained, was closely associated with one of the families. He was known by mob figures in other areas of the country and managed to work his influence behind the scenes to help orchestrate Jimmy's improper win. Yet my first hint of that relationship did not come until after the balloting and the speeches, after the delegates cleared out of the hall.

"Aren't you going to congratulate Hoffa?" I asked Bill. He just smiled and took me back to our suite. Then, a while later, Jimmy Hoffa came to the door to thank Bill for all he had done. In many ways, when it came to behind-the-scenes political action, it was obvious that Bill was the more powerful of the two men.

THE CUBAN CONNECTION

One of the most surprising connections between Bill Presser and Jimmy Hoffa, at least for me, was the discovery that together they were selling weapons to Cuba. This was a period when the Cuban revolution was taking place and many of Jimmy Hoffa's friends had a financial stake in the events.

Havana, Cuba, was well known as a gambling and nightlife center. The casinos were extremely fashionable, much as Monte Carlo was in later years. Members of the Mafia invested heavily in both the gambling and the regime of Fulgencio Batista in order to remain welcome in Cuba. Yet the real reason for the interest in Cuba was quite different. The Mafia was using the country as part of its trade route for illegal substances.

The old-time Mafia leaders liked to perpetuate the myth that they were not involved with the drug trade. It was the one area where they were supposedly pure, the organization corrupted by younger men who were seeking fast profits and big money.

The truth was quite different. Charles Luciano had been a major drug trafficker and continued to work in the field after he was deported. Frank Costello was placed in charge of most of the American operation, though he did not see the profit potential that Luciano recognized.

Vito Genovese, next in line to Costello, was more far calculating. When Costello was convicted for income tax fraud in 1956, Genovese took control of the narcotics trade, delighted by its money-making potential. With the encouragement of other mob leaders who had been urging Costello to do more with drugs than he had been, Genovese arranged Costello's murder after the gangster was released on bail during his tax case appeal. The gunman made the mistake of shooting only once, inflicting a scalp wound that looked fatal but allowed Costello to recover fully.

While this was taking place, Giuseppe and Vincent Cotronis, two brothers from Corsica, were handling trade routes for the narcotics. They needed pathways that would allow them to send the drugs into the United States in as simple and direct a manner as possible. One route, already described, was through Canada. The second route they developed was through Havana.

Meyer Lansky and Santos Trafficante were heavily involved with the Cuban gambling joints when this was taking place. Lansky had a close working relationship with Genovese despite the fact that Luciano had grown to distrust him.

Lansky was the man who developed methods for taking large skimmings from the casinos and ensuring that the mobsters could retain most of the money. Prior to Lansky, most of the Italians in organized crime had no respect for the IRS. If they made a million dollars, they were likely to declare ten thousand dollars. They lived well beyond their means, their life-styles so conspicuous that they were likely to attract the attention of investigators. Jail was a certainty because they could not justify the money they spent in comparison to the money they declared.

The few Mafia members who were smart about taxes changed their life-styles. They hid their money, living as frugally as possible so that no one would suspect how wealthy they were. If they made a million dollars and declared ten thousand dollars on their taxes, they tried to live on the ten thousand.

Lansky showed the mob a different approach. He explained that if you made a million dollars, you declared 20 or 30 percent, enough to live like a king. You enjoyed the good life and still socked away more money than almost anyone could imagine making in a lifetime. The IRS would be satisfied because the taxpayers' life-styles would match their income. Their families would be satisfied because they did not have to watch every penny while having a massive net worth. And the men came to realize that they had one less hassle to face in getting from day to day.

Lansky's plans were so good that he helped the mob with their casino skimmings, pleasing everyone but Luciano, who remained in exile. Lansky shorted Luciano, a fact that would have gotten him killed had he not been close to Genovese.

The proof of the worth of Lansky's theories actually was found in Cleveland. During the years when the smoke shops and the illegal gambling casinos were in operation, men like Moe Dalitz and Morris Kleinman understood the risk of income tax evasion. They declared a high enough portion of their real incomes to appease the IRS, then used the rest of their money to invest in casinos in Las Vegas and elsewhere.

Because the Batista regime was close to Lansky and Trafficante, it was decided that the two gangsters would arrange for men to protect the heroin transportation through Havana. It was also decided that the men would make an effort to bring more of the mob into Cuba to boost the lucrative gambling operations there.

The Cuban narcotics and gambling activities resulted in a minor war among the gangsters. In addition to the attempt on Costello's life, Genovese and Carlo Gambino arranged for Albert Anastasia to be murdered while seated in a barber chair. Anastasia had earlier rejected the idea of becoming involved with the Cuban operations, then demanded to be let in at a time when others in organized crime had become more important.

The Anastasia hit was later found to be connected with an international movement to solidify Cuban narcotics, among other issues. Prior to the Genovese/Gambino decision, major Mafia leaders, including Joseph Bonanno, Vito Vitale, Luciano, Frank Coppola, and Carmine Galante, met in Palermo, Sicily, to discuss the case. Anastasia and Costello had simply gone too far in working against the direction the top leaders in organized crime wanted to take.

During this same period, the American public first became aware of the scale of organized crime in America. On November 13 and 14, 1957, a convention—known as the Apalachin Conference—of top crime leaders was held in New York State. Men like John Scalish, who would later control both Bill and Jackie Presser, attended. There were an unknown number of men attending, fifty-eight being caught on the grounds, their records noted by the McClellan Committee report (Report 1139, pp. 487–88). The report stated, in part:

50 had arrest records; 35 had records of convictions, and 23 had spent time in prisons or jails as a result of these convictions; 18 of these men had been either arrested or questioned at one time in connection with murder cases. Other illegal activity noted in the survey included narcotics (for which 15 had been arrested or convicted); gambling (for which 30 had been arrested or convicted), and the illegal use of firearms (for which 23 had been arrested or convicted).

As to legitimate business activities, a study of the men who attended the Apalachin meeting showed: 9 were or had been in the coin-operated machine business; 16 were involved in garment manufacturing or trucking; 10 owned grocery stores or markets; 17 owned taverns or restaurants; 11 were in the construction business. Others were involved in automotive agencies, coal companies, entertainment, funeral homes, ownership of houses and racetracks, linen and laundry enterprises, trucking, waterfront activities and bakeries, and one was a conductor of a dance band.

The organized crime figures were primarily from Pennsylvania (Joseph Barbara and Russell Bufalino), New York (Bonanno, Genovese, Gambino, and Joseph Profaci), Florida (Trafficante), and New Jersey (Gerardo Catena). Chicago and Detroit were conspicuous by their absences, though police officials believed that both Sam Giancana and Carmine Galante of Chicago were on the premises and escaped into the surrounding woods during the raid. In addition, Anthony Giacolone and Joseph Zerilli of Detroit were believed to be late, the only reason they were not spotted or arrested. Many of the men present had direct or indirect connections with both Detroit and Hoffa, one of the early indicators of the extent of organized crime's involvement with organized labor.

The main connection with Hoffa was believed to be Raffaele Quasarano, a man who was alleged to be an unseen partner in a Detroit lawer's jukebox business. He also acted as promoter for a boxer Hoffa owned along with Bert Brennan.

There were other connections between the mob and Hoffa during this period of interest in Cuban narcotics and gambling. Paul DeLucia, a man who, along with Anthony Accardo and Sam Giancana, had taken over the old Al Capone rackets in Chicago, needed money to pay off the IRS. Jimmy Hoffa arranged to buy DeLucia's home in Long Beach, California, so that it could be converted into a school for business agents. Not only was it illegal for any labor union to own real estate in Long Beach, but Hoffa had the Teamsters pay sixty-five thousand dollars more than the appraised value of the house so that DeLucia would have the money he needed. Then the union let DeLucia live in the house at no charge for more than a year.

The various Mafia connections may seem irrelevant to Teamster operations, but they were not irrelevant to interests of Jimmy Hoffa and Bill Presser.

Cleveland was a natural location for gun-running in the late 1950s. Two-thirds of the nation's population lived within five hundred miles of Cleveland. There were numerous ethnic groups in neighborhoods that were hostile to outsiders. Many had relatives and friends in countries such as Hungary and Czechoslovakia that either had been or were in active revolt against the Communist regimes. It was natural for them to seek ways to support their homelands financially or physically. This meant obtaining money and/or weapons which could be shipped abroad, then smuggled to the rebels in the countries with which the Americans were concerned.

Bill Presser and Jimmy Hoffa were aware of the Cuban revolution and the need for arms by both sides. They also knew that military surplus weapons were readily available through both legitimate and illegal sources. They decided to support both sides, making the most money possible.

Bill kept his plans fairly quiet. We talked about it at the dinner table a little, but this was not something with which I was to be involved. I knew it was going on, yet it was only years later, after extensive research and conversations with people involved on all sides, that I learned some of the details.

Bill and Jimmy were using Florida as their shipping base. They had guns and a few army surplus planes that they sent. In addition, allegations were made that a third man, a public relations executive in Washington, D.C., was also involved. However, although he discussed his sales of tanks and other weapons to Batista in 1959, it was never proved that he was linked with Bill and Jimmy.

Hoffa wanted to continue gun-running after Castro took control of Cuba. This time he wanted to utilize Teamster money, trying to obtain a $300,000 loan from the Central States, Southeast and Southwest Areas Pension Fund to aid friends involved with gun-running. The friends were a part of Akros Dynamics, an organization created to sell C-74 aircraft to Cuba. The action was Hoffa's way of trying to help organized crime figures whose incomes would be drastically reduced if Castro refused to allow the continuation of the casinos and other Mafia-run operations.

It is believed that Hoffa's main interest was in helping Santos Trafficante, the leader of the Cuban numbers game in Florida often called the "bolita lottery." Trafficante's Miami office was in Teamster Local 320, the local established by Rolland McMaster. This was at the same time that Hoffa and the Teamster leadership were attempting to take over the Miami National Bank, where one official allegedly laundered money for various criminal groups. That official took 10 percent of the money placed with him, then used the rest for legitimate investments in real estate, businesses, and hotels. He worked with Meyer Lansky, who developed the laundering procedures for the Mafia.

In addition to Trafficante, David Yaras was involved with both Cuban gambling operations and the organizing of Local 320. During investigations by the

McClellan Committee, Yaras was identified as being an assassin for Sam Giancana as well as having been involved with the pinball and slot machine business under Al Capone. He worked for the Chicago mobsters and, a year after founding Local 320, helped install Harold Gross as head of the union. This was done with both McMaster's and Hoffa's approval despite the fact that Gross had been convicted of extortion.

Richard Nixon was becoming involved with Hoffa's people and the Cuban connection at this time. He regularly visited Cuba before the election, visiting Batista and occasionally going to the casinos while he was a senator.

Later, Nixon became involved with Arthur Desser, a friend of Hoffa who was involved with the negotiations for the Teamsters' purchase of Miami National Bank. Desser bought 547 acres of land in Key Biscayne, Florida, using, in part, a $5 million loan from the Central States Pension Fund. Less than ten years later, just before the 1968 election, Nixon bought two of the lots owned by Desser in Key Biscayne. Although the lots were worth more than $75,000 in appraised value, Nixon paid only $50,000. Later there would be evidence of direct payments to Nixon in exchange for favorable treatment of the Teamsters.

The Teamsters' Cuban connection would eventually lead to a series of unresolved incidents that shocked the world. First there was Castro's decision to rid the island of the men and businesses so popular under Batista. This came as a complete surprise to Trafficante, who believed that no one would give up money for idealism. Yet Castro had announced: "I'm going to run all these fascist mobsters, all these American gangsters, out of Cuba. I'm going to nationalize everything. Cuba for Cubans!"

Trafficante saw only that gambling in Cuba was worth $100 million and generated ten thousand jobs. It was only when the casinos were shut down and Trafficante, along with Frank Cammarata, a Detroit rackets figure, were jailed that the mob fully understood Castro.

The second situation evolved from the first. The mob wanted to do something to rid itself of Castro at the same time that Allen Dulles, the head of the Central Intelligence Agency (CIA), began considering assassination of the Cuban dictator.

There were three men who essentially shared leadership in Cuba—Fidel Castro; his brother, Raul; and his friend, Che Guevara. Raul was more of an administrator and Guevara a guerrilla fighter. Neither man had the leadership appeal for the Cuban people that Fidel enjoyed. The assassination of Castro seemed a logical step in destroying the regime.

Nixon was established as the liaison to the CIA in this matter. Neither he nor President Eisenhower was involved in the original discussions. They were brought in when the CIA decided something had to be done.

What happened next seems ridiculous yet has been carefully documented, including through a committee headed by Democratic Senator Frank Church which investigated government assassination plots against foreign leaders ("Alleged Assassination Plots Involving Foreign Leaders," Report 94–465). From March to August 1960, the CIA planned a number of incidents that would destroy Castro without killing him. These would be laughed at if they were used on a television show, yet the agency was serious.

Various ideas were either tried or seriously considered: One was to wait until Castro traveled to a country where it was customary to leave your shoes outside the hotel room door so that they could be shined during the night. When that occurred, an agent would cover the inside of the shoes with thallium salts which would be absorbed through the soles of his feet. Then, some time later, all Castro's hair would fall off. Making Castro lose his famous beard seemed to be a good way to humiliate the Cuban leader.

Another idea was for someone to get close to Castro and spray him with a chemical that would be disorienting when he tried to give a speech. Castro was notorious for talking for several hours at a time so anything that hurt his speech would be instantly obvious to the public.

A second approach to disrupting his speech was a variation of the spray. This time the drug would be introduced in a box of Castro's favorite cigars. Each time he smoked one, he would become incoherent, much like someone on the drug LSD.

The various techniques did not seem very practical and the CIA turned to assassination approaches. There was talk of an assassination squad that would be paid a million dollars for each kill, Castro to be the first hit.

Finally it was decided to arrange the assassination of Castro. Robert Maheu, a man who worked for the late Howard Hughes, was asked to handle the matter.

Maheu was the logical choice to be a liaison. He had been involved with counterintelligence during World War II and a strongly anti-Communist. Also, he had worked as an FBI agent for a number of years, and had aided the intelligence community by breaking into a hotel room and recording documents relating to a Middle Eastern government, according to the Church Committee report.

Maheu, working in Las Vegas, contacted John Rosselli of Chicago. He had met Rosselli earlier, knew that Rosselli was with the Chicago mob, and realized that the Mafia had reason to want Castro dead. A new leader might allow the return of casinos and other businesses that had paid so handsomely. There was also a valid patriotic reason since an invasion of Cuba had been authorized by President Eisenhower. The death of the nation's leader would reduce the resistance, and American lives would be saved, an important consideration to Maheu, though it is doubtful that it was to Rosselli.

Rosselli had several thoughts on the murder. The simplest seemed to be to arrange to have two or more men with machine guns catch Castro in a cross fire. This would require recruiting men who could get close to Castro and would feel comfortable shooting the man, knowing that they might not get away. This combination of idealism and muscle did not seem possible to achieve without giving away the plot.

The next idea was a return to the treated cigar trick. This time the cigars would be tainted with botulin, perhaps the strongest poison available. All Castro had to do was touch his lips with the cigar, not even light it, and the poison would kill him.

Botulin was not found to be practical. Technical problems relating to how it could be added to cigars or anything else could not be resolved. Instead, the CIA's Technical Service branch found a liquid poison that would take two or three days to kill yet would not leave a trace.

The CIA offered $150,000 for the hit, a high price in those days. The invasion of the Bay of Pigs by anti-Castro forces was a secret operation scheduled for April 17, 1961, and the hit had to take place before that invasion.

The mob double-crossed the government, though. Santos Trafficante was supposed to be acting as a courier, coordinating the murder for Rosselli. He was establishing a series of assassination squads and passing on the poisons. Sam Giancana, the Chicago Mafia leader, was part of the group working in the United States on this hit, as were others.

Reports to Maheu were always frustrating. A restaurant was infiltrated because it was one Castro frequented. Yet for some reason Castro began eating elsewhere after the hit squad was in place.

Then there was a man who had been corrupted and was going to kill Castro, but he was fired before he could receive the poison he needed. There were men who misunderstood their orders and failed in that manner. And, finally, there was a squad that was supposedly captured after John Kennedy became president. The men were tortured, and revealed everything about the plot. Castro allegedly vowed revenge.

Much of the story was later garbled by skilled, well-meaning investigative reporters such as Jack Anderson and Drew Pearson in the late 1960s. Because of what should have been good information, they reported that the plot to attack Castro was probably instigated, in part, by Attorney General Robert Kennedy after his brother, Jack, became president. In reality, Robert Kennedy did not know of the plot until May 1962, long after President Eisenhower's orders had gone through. What is known is that Fidel Castro was determined to get back at Kennedy. There were allegedly three or four contracts on Jack Kennedy's life. Castro wanted revenge for the attempt on his own life. In addition, Santos Trafficante, along with Carlos Marcello of New Orleans, allegedly planned a

Kennedy murder. Johnny Rosselli and Sam Giancana were recruited to handle the job. The facts that Giancana was involved with the Kennedys; had dated Judith Exner, one of Jack Kennedy's girlfriends; and was later murdered add credibility to this scenario.

In addition, there were rumors that Hoffa or other top Teamsters wanted Jack Kennedy killed to stop the pressures on the union officials. And Peter Lawford, the late brother-in-law of President Kennedy, left notes indicating that he, apparently along with members of the Kennedy family, was convinced that the death was connected with businessmen involved with the Texas oil industry.

Whatever the case, the involvement of Bill, Jimmy, and the mob down in Cuba foreshadowed the eventual assassination of President Kennedy. Just who committed the actual murder in addition to Lee Harvey Oswald is uncertain. What is certain is that more than one group wanted to see the president dead.

THE NIXON CONNECTION

While Hoffa was still working under Dave Beck, he became involved in a new scheme to rip off Teamster members. Henry Lower, whose past business involvements included being a narcotics dealer and an escaped convict, spent $150,000 on some land in Titusville, Florida. He used a combination of bank loans and $6,000 of his own money, part of a $10,000 loan from Detroit Local 985. Hoffa hid his interest quite well, though it was found that the money Local 985 loaned came from a loan of the same amount of money provided by Jimmy Hoffa's Local 299.

The scheme was a simple one. The money purchased eight thousand lots at just under $19 each. The lots were then sold to the rank and file for $150 each. Only 25 percent of the lots were for union members, the remaining lots going to the general public for $550 each, giving the Teamster members the impression that the lots were a good investment.

This was a period when Florida had just been "discovered" by the American public. There was little business or industry adequate for drawing large numbers of people to the area. Land was extremely cheap and, often, worthless. Yet the climate was excellent and the location could be promoted as the perfect retirement area. Lower's sales efforts on behalf of what became Sun Valley, Inc., the parent company for the deal, utilized business agents who were in contact with the rank and file.

Land scams in Florida have been common since the 1920s. Some people never learn the lesson. Swampland was sold to some. Others bought land so isolated that getting water or electricity was impossible. Lower avoided that type of fraud, overpricing worthless land. Then needing to put in improvements he had hoped to avoid, he borrowed money to add paved roads and water.

Local 299, through the prodding of Hoffa, gave Lower $400,000 to use in the corporation. Lower, according to the McClellan Committee investigators, pocketed $90,000 as a finder's fee for arranging for the loan for Sun Valley, Inc. Then he deposited $250,000 into an account that was meant for business interests other than the Florida deal, Hoffa being fully aware of his actions. Only $60,000 could be earmarked for property improvements.

The beauty of the scam was that the lots were sold as spots for retirement homes. The members were young and healthy and would not be building for some time to come. The land was more accessible than most, though it was also known that most people would not check out the location, possibly for several years.

But members did take a look. They found that the lots were more isolated than they had been led to believe. There was no sewer or water system despite the Local 299 loan. Hoffa said that the loan he made was good and went on with business as usual.

The Board of Monitors group that had been established by Judge Letts was theoretically overseeing Hoffa's deals. Despite this, Hoffa was constantly trying to dominate them. He wanted everyone to think of them only as an advisory group. It seemed the only way he could fight the dissidents who had filed suit against him.

At the same time, Hoffa was trying to stop internal opposition by ordering that only members who had their dues paid on exactly the first of the month were eligible for office. There was a way to check that the money had been paid when they received their pay checks. The employers arranged for the dues notations on the paychecks. It was easy for Hoffa to convince them simply to delay the notation a day or two. This was not the fault of the rank and file but it was a way to control them. The management was happy to cooperate since this assured them sweetheart contracts.

Hoffa didn't count on Judge Letts, who stated that the monitors were not just advisers. They were "empowered to exert every known method of achieving the basic purpose set forth in the consent order, to wit: That a new convention would be free of corruption and in recognition of the rights of the membership." Letts also stated that rank and file members could not be prevented from running for office just because they were not credited with paying their dues on the exact date Hoffa and his aides demanded.

The monitors were taking their job seriously. They brought charges against Hoffa for allowing $400,000 in Local 299 money to serve as collateral for a $395,000 Sun Valley loan from a Florida bank.

By the fall of 1961, Hoffa knew that he had to replace the $400,000 used for the Sun Valley loan personally. The Central States Pension Fund had $200 million in its treasury so he arranged for real estate and construction loans with companies that might not be able to go elsewhere and receive such favorable terms. In exchange for his generosity, Hoffa was given kickbacks of 10 percent. In this manner, he was able to replace the $400,000 without hurting Sun Valley.

It was during this time that arrangements were made for Hoffa to meet Vice President Nixon. The arrangements were made by a third party who explained that Hoffa was a man innocent of the charges against him. In a follow-up letter, the friend told Nixon that Hoffa could easily win a court case related to the Sun Valley deal but that the cost of defending himself would be great. The friend stressed that "[Hoffa] has absolutely no worries because he leads a clean life, pays his taxes, and obeys the law."

Hoffa gave his support to Nixon for the 1960 election. He stated, through the Teamsters executive board, that Kennedy was a danger to the nation. There were also financial contributions including a million dollars for Nixon which Hoffa arranged through organized crime members in Louisiana, Florida, and New Jersey. All the support was covert, Hoffa knowing that if he personally made a public declaration for Nixon, the scheme might backfire.

As expected, the grand jury investigating the Sun Valley scheme requested Hoffa's indictment by the Justice Department. However, because Nixon was being supported by Hoffa, the Justice Department refused to indict him. Although no one is certain exactly what decision Nixon reached, it is known that after he lost the election by one of the slimmest margins in history, Attorney General William Rogers, in his last days in office, reversed his preelection decision not to indict Hoffa. He brought charges which seemed likely to result in a conviction.

Hoffa looked upon Nixon's actions as a double cross. He also decided to move ahead in an effort to maintain ultimate power within the union. A new Teamsters convention was scheduled for July 3 to 7, 1961, and Judge Letts allowed everything to proceed normally. More important for Hoffa, the Board of Monitors was dismissed.

Hoffa consolidated his power in a number of ways. Bert Brennon, the vice president for Michigan, died shortly before the convention. Hoffa replaced him with Frank Fitzsimmons, the vice president of Local 299, who was then elected to take the office at the convention, affirming Hoffa's power.

In addition to Fitzsimmons, Anthony Provenzano of New Jersey was a prominent vice president. Tony Pro, as he was known, started as president of Union City, New Jersey, Local 560, then moved to the presidency of New Jersey's Joint Council 73 and on to the vice presidency of the International Brotherhood of Teamsters in just three years. He was also a captain in the Genovese crime family and under indictment for extortion with New Jersey trucking companies.

Later he would go from being a friend of Hoffa to a man suspected of arranging Hoffa's murder.

Bill Presser was named one of the trustees for the international, as were Frank Matula of Los Angeles and Raymond Cohen of Philadelphia. Cohen had been indicted for embezzlement and Matula had a previous perjury conviction.

The Teamsters didn't care about any of the backgrounds of the men, though. They supported Jimmy as he told the two thousand delegates to the convention that they were going to succeed regardless of the attacks. Again he made what were personal problems seem to be attacks on the Teamsters in general, an action that was effective. Hoffa was allowed to do whatever he felt was necessary, including raising his own salary to seventy-five thousand dollars, a 50 percent increase, and giving himself an unlimited expense account. Henceforth, all Teamster officials would have their legal bills paid out of union coffers, even if they were charged with crimes that worked against the membership.

Hoffa made other changes. He had the right to put any local in trusteeship, he declared, removing any officials he did not want and replacing them with his own choices. He arranged procedures limiting who could become a convention delegate in the future, thereby assuring himself the opportunity for full control of everything that happened and giving him an easy way to reject the dissidents.

Hoffa was a big part of my life during this period. I was one of the men Jimmy used to handle special problems. There were a number of us who were willing and able to travel to any city he desired in order to firebomb a business, dynamite a porch, beat up a reluctant businessman or labor dissident.

For example, there might be trouble in St. Louis which Harold Gibbons either could not handle or with which he did not want to have his men connected. Or the difficulties might be in Detroit, Chicago, Youngstown, Toledo, or Pittsburgh. Whatever the case, even though the police might know that the violence was connected to the labor strife, they would not know the out-of-town men who were involved.

One of my specialties was arson. I'm not a guy who knows much about chemicals. Under normal circumstances I'd probably have started a fire like anyone else, trying to use gasoline or kerosene to burn papers, curtains, or other flammables, probably not doing a very good job of torching a place. But guys like me—thugs, hoods, gangsters, wise guys, whatever you want to call us— we're fascinating for a lot of straight people. Maybe they think we're celebrities. Maybe they secretly want to have the balls to do what we do. I really don't know. It's just that we're a little like these rock musicians with their groupies. Straight people want to do things for us, help us, maybe get a secret thrill from knowing that their suggestions resulted in something bad that took place. All I know is that a lot of straight men tried to become my friends over the years, and one of them, who had connections in the building trade, taught me about the chemical I used for years for torching places.

I don't remember the full name of the chemical. It was a phosphate of some sort. It came in a powder and it came in sticks, a little like dynamite, so that hunks could be torn off and tossed onto a building.

The part about this phosphate that was so important was that it burns hotter in water. In fact, you don't have to light it. You just toss a little water on it and it starts to burn. Toss more water on it and it burns hotter. Toss enough water on it and the heat is so intense that steel girders melt and buckle.

I used to test its potency in the days when I always kept a large quantity hidden in my house, carefully wrapped so that no moisture would get to it. I'd take a tiny spoonful, toss it into the toilet, then watch it burn. I would flush it down the drain before it got too hot, though, never thinking that the heat would damage the pipes as it went through the sewer system. As a result, for years there was a tiny leak in the pipe leading from that particular toilet, a leak that required my leaving a bucket beneath the pipe in the basement to catch the very slow drip.

There was one strike in the Midwest where a settlement just wasn't taking place. Harold Gibbons needed something done but could not handle the job himself. He asked Jimmy for help and Hoffa called me to do it.

I always either worked with a partner or went to a bar in a tough neighborhood and spread a little money with one of the harder-looking longshoremen. I found that for one hundred dollars or so, some of them would beat up or kill somebody without thinking twice. Most longshoremen were straight, but they were all tough men and frequently needed money because of the seasonal nature of their work. There were men who would do anything for their money and those were the ones I went after.

This time I took a partner I knew I could trust. There was a strike at a manufacturing plant where the owner was just not going along with the union's demands. The decision was reached to torch the place and I was told to do a good job. That was when I used my phosphate compound.

We went to the plant at night. The guards weren't around so I climbed onto the roof of the building and tossed pieces of the compound everywhere I could. Then I went back down the ladder, tossing a firebomb through the window.

I used to mix my bombs carefully. In addition to the chemicals I used, I stuffed the container with cotton balls that would become saturated with gasoline in a modified Molotov cocktail. I used a wick to light the firebomb, heaved it inside, and the container broke, spreading the gasoline and the soaked cotton balls. The phosphate-based chemical spread on the floor. The wick would set everything on fire at impact; the cotton balls spread the flames throughout the interior.

My action was important. If the fire was concentrated in just one spot, the fire department's water spray, when combined with the phosphate, would do less damage to the roof. Spreading things out would destroy the building.

You have to understand about firemen. Unless they know about the chemicals used at a fire, they assume that the flames can be doused with water. Because almost all fires can be put out that way, there is no reason for them to think otherwise. As I counted on, the firemen went to the plant and poured water inside the building and on the roof wherever they saw flames. The roof especially had to be cooled to prevent it from being ignited by the fire inside. What they did not know was that the phosphate, when struck by the water, would make the problem much greater. As a result, I learned the next day that the building had been destroyed by what the fire fighters considered to be an unusually hot fire.

You may be wondering how destroying a place helped the workers who were on strike. It didn't, of course. The boss was out of business, at least until insurance money could be used to rebuild what was lost, and that meant dozens or hundreds of workingmen without jobs.

Hoffa, Bill Presser, and others in leadership didn't care about the workers in a situation like that firebombing. They wanted to show their power. They wanted to prove that a boss either cooperated or lost everything. They were trying to show him that he could not fight them or the union because their beating him was more important than the contract won for the workers. This reality put fear in the man and also fear in the hearts of the other employers who understood the message we were sending.

Another time Hoffa wanted me to beat up a man who had been bad rapping him. The situation wasn't very serious because Hoffa didn't want him badly beaten. He just wanted him hurting enough so that he would stop what he was doing.

The pay was going to be seventy-five hundred dollars for the beating and I wanted to have some guys with me. This time, when I went to the city where the victim was living, I went to the longshoreman's area and stepped inside a bar. I began talking with some of the guys there, then settled on two men I thought would help me, no questions asked. I offered them two hundred dollars each and they asked who they had to kill. Remember that this was in the 1950s and I was offering them a good week's pay for the work they were going to do.

I explained that I just had to beat the shit out of a guy. I didn't tell them I was from the Teamsters or anything else about myself, and they didn't care. They just wanted some fast money, especially when I explained that I would be with them and would help.

Beatings had to be done carefully. I don't know whether Hoffa ever had anyone killed, though I don't see why he would. Labor was different from organized crime. You didn't want to lose somebody. What you wanted to do was get him thinking and acting differently. If I could break a guy up a little, send him to the hospital so he would be hurting for a few days and maybe not be completely recovered for a few weeks, that would send a message. The man would be on our side or at least afraid to continue knocking Jimmy Hoffa.

We tried to get a guy someplace where we could move in fast, break him up, and get out of there. We would punch him, knock the wind out of him, break a few ribs, maybe mark up his face or break an arm or two, then dump him. We might grab the guy in the doorway of an office building, as he left his home, in a parking lot, near a bridge, or anywhere else we could move in and out quickly without risk of being seen. We'd usually pick a spot where he would be found shortly after we got out of there.

I mentioned that it wasn't just the Teamsters who used violence. Once I began working for Bill and Jimmy, I was contacted by others. For example, the Ironworkers Union had a problem in a right-to-work state where a contractor was using mostly nonunion help for his job. There was nothing wrong with that, but the union wanted to fuck up his job. They sent me down to dynamite his place, again using longshoremen.

The one type of job I never liked was when we went against our own members, though if Babe Triscaro, Bill, or Hoffa said to do it, I would. For example, there was a problem with some steel haulers. There were twenty or thirty men who disagreed with the contracts Bill had negotiated. He asked Babe to handle them so Babe got me and twenty-five or thirty others, then gave each of us a golf club to use as a weapon. The steel haulers were on a high hill. We arrived in a half dozen cars, parked at the bottom of the hill, then began walking up together. The steel haulers knew that they were going to get the shit beaten out of them so they took off and ran the other way. I was happy about that because I didn't want to have to do any beating of our members.

Although I was doing work for the Teamsters, I actually started with the Hotel and Restaurant Workers Union along with Jackie Presser, who was able to get the charter. It was the early 1950s and Jackie asked me to work as his organizer.

The problem with the union is that it was actually split among five different groups. Anyone who organized a hotel or restaurant couldn't keep all the workers as members, and membership was the way we made our money. Instead, whichever union represented particular workers, such as bartenders, cooks, or waiters and waitresses, got that portion of the place I organized.

Maybe this system would have worked if all five of the unions were active, but they weren't. The organizer for the waiters and waitresses, for example, was an old woman who seldom went out. The bartenders weren't much better. Yet they all benefited from my work. If I organized a place with twenty-five employees, the waiters and waitresses union might take eight or ten, the bartenders might take one or two, the dishwashers would take three or four, the cooks would take some more, and so on, until Jackie and I had maybe five or fewer new members. I was building everyone else's membership at the same time that I was trying to build our own.

I was extremely frustrated by what was happening. I was making $139 a week, which was not enough for me to make ends meet. I asked Babe Triscaro to get me a soft night job, so he got me one driving a truck for a contractor who was working a cost plus profit job. The contractor's money increased the longer it took to complete the work so he did not mind that I took a magazine to read and a pillow for sleeping in the truck.

The work was for a steel company where a large shovel would dump a load of dirt in the truck, then I would haul it to a fill area. I made a trip a night or every couple of nights, working with a number of other drivers.

We also stole from the site. We'd stick copper, lead, copper wire, and other items in the truck, then cover it with dirt. We'd go to the dump site, where a man would separate the dirt from the scrap. Then the scrap would be sold and we drivers would split the money from it. Eventually some of the security police for Republic Steel got wise and arrested several of us. They claimed that they had photographs of our taking equipment and burying it under the fill dirt. I don't know how far they would have gone with prosecution because Babe arranged for all charges to be dropped in exchange for our quitting. I quit for Babe, though I didn't like the idea because I've never pleaded guilty to anything in my life and quitting was, in effect, admitting guilt.

The five unions were reluctant to join together at first. We had to talk with them and use a little muscle because we were fed up with being penalized by the inability to earn money from everyone we signed. A few of the leaders were pushed around, and the result was a single union where real money could be made.

It was during this time with the restaurant workers that I was involved with the start of the long-term corruption of a man who would eventually prove to be a federal judge. This began like all the bribes or seductions with which I would be involved over the years. A young, struggling attorney new in practice, his clothing frayed at the edges, came to me.

A lot of people believe in God and the devil. They like to think that everyone is pure, trying to do good until some evil force comes along and forces them to commit crimes against their wills. These people wonder how we could corrupt honest officials. They want to know what special offers we make that they cannot refuse. They act as though we force someone up against a wall and keep stuffing his pockets with cash, bringing him beautiful women for sex, and supplying him with favors until he can't resist anymore. Then they can go around being high and mighty, saying that the devil made them do what they did and we should have sympathy for them because they were worn down until resistance was impossible.

The truth is quite different. I never went after a cop, a politician, or anyone else in my life. So far as I know, when I was the bag man for Bill Presser, the money I delivered was not something Bill offered to the person getting it. The same was true with all the other Teamster officials.

We don't have to corrupt anyone. They come to us. They want our money. They want to be associated with our power. They want whatever we can do to make them more than they are.

Sometimes the corruption starts when they near the top. The candidate for mayor comes seeking an endorsement. The mayor who wants to be a senator needs our money and our backing. The senator running for president looks to us for help.

And they all do it. Jimmy Hoffa made certain that Richard Nixon was well provided with cash and behind-the-scenes support. Ronald Reagan sought Bill Presser's money. George Bush knew he needed the Teamsters and they gave him an official endorsement even though the Reagan administration had generally been anti-labor.

The Pressers created what they call DRIVE, a name that stands for Democrat/Republican/Independent Voter Education. DRIVE has a newsletter that supports candidates such as Bush. There are also campaign funds available for candidates through contributions by the rank and file and others. The Teamster members have no say in how their contributions to DRIVE are used, trusting in the heads of the union to select wisely, and give thought to which candidate will be strongest for labor. In truth, the candidates supported may have little interest in labor but may be making side deals with the Teamster leadership. Yet the impression of independence looks good and is seldom challenged.

The Teamsters learned a lesson from organized crime that worked with a struggling young attorney. You find a man early in his career and help him. You continue to help him as he grows in power, often not asking any favors in return. Then there will come a time when, with luck, the person reaches a position of significant influence and a favor can be returned.

For example, members of various organized crime groups like to cultivate friendships with individuals going through the minor crises that seem to occur early in a career. They might seek out the young police officer, new on the job, whose wife was working but had to quit to have a baby. Or they might go with someone who just purchased a new home. The "friend," actually a member of organized crime, will help financially, expecting nothing in return, yet knowing that there will come a time when that patrolman might be a detective or administrator, capable of ignoring a criminal action.

The Teamsters learned from this practice and took advantage of a man's needs early in his career just in case he might be helpful later. That was why I was delighted when an attorney called me during my days with the Hotel and Restaurant Workers Union.

The attorney I mentioned telephoned me at the office, identifying himself and offering to buy me lunch so he could make me a proposition he thought I would find interesting. We agreed to meet at the Theatrical Grill on Vincent, that once notorious street in downtown Cleveland I mentioned earlier. I didn't know the man, but apparently he knew what I looked like and assured me that he would have no trouble identifying me.

The first surprise I had was that the attorney took the bus to our meeting. He either didn't have a car or wanted to save the cost of parking.

His suit was frayed and he looked as if he didn't have a dime to spare. As we sat down together, he explained that he represented several ethnic restaurants. He also said that he was not making any money and needed a way to get some.

The attorney's idea was for me to go to each of the restaurants he represented, signing up the members so that he would have to be called in to negotiate the contracts. In exchange for his giving me the list of names of the restaurants involved, I would negotiate a "sweetheart deal" which wouldn't cost the restaurant owners very much more than they were already paying. It was a good arrangement for everyone, and the attorney would begin making a little money for his time.

I took the list of ethnic restaurants he gave me and went to each one in turn. I never bothered organizing the places because it really wasn't necessary. I just went in as though I had done the work and could usually bluff my way through.

The idea that unions organize workers isn't always true. With the big places we had to work hard to sign people to pledge cards, then present enough pledge cards to the boss to show that the workers were behind us. We'd ask the boss to sign a letter of recognition and begin negotiating with us for the workers' contract. If he didn't, we carried picket signs in our cars and arranged a strike.

With smaller places we didn't always bother to organize. We'd just tell the boss we had the members pledged to join, flashing phony cards, not all of which were even filled out by the employees. Sometimes we'd have two or three signatures. Sometimes we'd have none. It didn't matter. If we could bluff our way through, we would.

I worked with a partner from Local 10, which was created from the combined unions serving restaurant and hotel workers. We walked into the restaurant, flashed what were usually a bunch of cards that were either mostly blank or we had signed, and demanded that the union be recognized. The owner would yell at us and throw us out of the restaurant. Then we would go to the car, pull out the picket signs, and start walking back and forth in front of the business.

We probably turned some business away and startled some of the workers, but those weren't our primary goals. What we wanted to do was prevent the owner from functioning and that meant stopping his suppliers.

John Felice, an acquaintance of mine, headed the local that controlled the beer truck drivers. When the beer arrived, I'd tell the driver that he wasn't supposed to deliver the beer that day because John Felice sanctioned the strike. The driver would go on to his next stop without leaving any beer behind.

Then the milk truck would arrive, the driver a member of Local 336 headed by Russ Elmer. I'd talk with him the same way I talked with the beer driver and, again, he would leave.

I'd use the same line for produce drivers since I was close to Mickey Rini of Local 400. Within a short time the owner would realize that none of the essentials he needed to run his restaurant was being delivered and he would not be able to serve that day.

Usually we'd get another guy or two to join the picketing and we'd abuse the customers trying to go inside. Within an hour, I'd see a bus pull up to the nearest stop and the attorney would step off. He'd wink at me, then walk into the restaurant to talk with the owner.

The attorney would talk with the restaurant owner for about twenty minutes, then come outside and ask me to step in. We'd sit down together, then he would say, "Mr. Friedman, are you sure that these cards are legitimate?"

I'd be indignant, telling him that of course they were. The employees wanted the union and that's why I wanted the letter of recognition signed.

Usually no one had signed a pledge. If I was lucky, one or two might have signed. But that didn't matter. It was easy to organize those places. Stop the supplying of essential services and they're out of business. They'd recognize the union even though I never was speaking for the members.

Generally the meetings would be similar. The restaurant owner would start yelling, the attorney talking with him in his native language, quieting him. He then would explain that the owner should slip me a few hundred dollars and I would give him a sweetheart contract. The owner understood the bribe, paid it, and got a good deal. The employees didn't care because they kept their jobs and got a little better deal than they had had.

We signed up all their restaurants, the attorney and I getting along together. I decided to help him further, figuring that it would both be a payback and keep him in our debt. I went to Bill Presser, who by then had tremendous political influence within the city. I told him how cooperative the attorney had been and asked Bill to find a way to get him appointed to the first judgeship that opened up and for which he would be considered qualified. Bill agreed to do it.

Bill used his influence and the attorney received his first appointment to the position of Common Pleas judge. To understand how the corruption works, it is important to realize that several years passed without much contact between "our" judge and the Teamsters. It was the 1960s and I was part of the Teamsters by then, working as one of the heads of Local 507, the power base that launched Jackie Presser into the presidency of the International. I was trying to organize a place called Dolphin Seafood, which had twenty-one or twenty-two workers, but could only sign up eight or nine of them.

I decided that I might as well bluff my way to union recognition because I couldn't seem to do anything with the remaining employees I needed to sign. I faked a bunch of intent cards and tried to force the issue.

First I went inside the shop, though you're not allowed to do that. There was no union in the plant and I had no right to be there. But the workers like a tough union man. They want someone who is willing to stand up to the boss because they feel that he will do the same on their behalf. They can be fired; the union organizer can't. Thus the employees get a thrill out of watching someone get around authority.

That was the one attitude Jimmy Hoffa conveyed to the American public that the wealthier Americans never understood. Sure he was a crook. We all were engaged in dishonest, self-serving deals. But Jimmy gave the workingman a sense of power he never had before. The workingman saw that Jimmy was not afraid to stand up to anyone. He was tough. He and the other leaders were getting better contracts than the members had had in the past. And many of the people who were joining liked the idea that the Teamsters had the image of being mobsters at the top. They were fed up with feeling exploited or unappreciated. As Teamsters, they saw themselves as being with the toughest labor fighters in the nation. So long as they benefited from the association, they did not care who embezzled money or who went to jail. The accusations of violence and corruption, the venom with which government investigators attacked us, all helped us gain members. They never hurt us. And that was why I walked through what, in effect, were restricted areas in Dolphin Seafood.

The plant manager challenged my being there, so I told him to "get the fuck out of my face or I'm going to bounce you." It was all a show, the foul language, the threats, the hint of violence about to happen. The manager didn't know whether I was serious, but the employees like hearing that kind of talk. It makes them think that you're strong and I was able to sign up one or two more that day. Still, I didn't have enough and I told the manager I was going to put the place on strike the next day if I didn't get recognition.

That day, after I had been to the plant, Bill called me. He always knew the tactics I was using. He knew when I was lying and when I was straight. I was also one of the few people who could argue with him and get away with it.

Bill told me to come to the office immediately, a request you do not question. I arrived and he introduced me to an attorney who represented Dolphin Seafood. Bill asked me whether I had threatened the company with a strike and I told him that I did, that the company would be shut down at five o'clock in the morning.

The attorney knew Bill and was irate. "You see, Bill," I remember his saying. "You see what kind of relative you've got? He's a goon. He's threatening people. Why doesn't he go to an election?"

I told him that the reason I didn't go to an election was that the management was pulling too many tricks. They weren't, but I also knew that things would be done to force me to bring charges against the company management so that the issue of the union would go before the National Labor Relations Board for arbitration. Such an action would keep everything tied up for a year, giving the company that much extra time to avoid paying for unionization. "You're down!" I said. "Do you understand me?"

Bill asked the lawyer how he wanted to handle it.

The lawyer said that he wanted to go before a judge. He would produce the IRS forms of all the employees at Dolphin Seafood. I would have to turn over all the intent cards I claimed to have. Then the judge would determine whether or not the signatures matched so he could see whether the names were forged or authentic.

I wasn't about to let him get away with something like that. He suspected the truth and I wasn't about to give him the satisfaction of winning. "What do you think, the judge is a handwriting expert, pal?" I asked the attorney. "Besides, what judge do you want to go to anyway?"

The lawyer named the attorney who was now a judge, and then I knew I had him.

"Oh, no," I said. "Oh, no. Fuck that guy! I've had trouble with him."

It was just the reaction the lawyer wanted to have. "You see, Bill? You see?" The lawyer was certain that I was trying to avoid a confrontation with someone who wouldn't do things my way. What he didn't know was that Bill had put him in office. Bill was laughing inside, aware of my big act, knowing we had the guy in our pocket.

Bill became quite stern with me. "Listen here, Allen," he said. "Tomorrow morning you go to the judge." Then he told the lawyer to have the tax forms with the signatures of the employees. "And Allen, you have the cards. And if those are phony cards, don't go to the judge!"

"They're not phony cards," I said. "I've got seventeen out of twenty-one people." But I kept fighting the choice of judge, claiming that the one who was selected was a bad choice. Then, seemingly reluctantly, I told Bill to call up the judge to arrange for us to go to see him. I never let on that I knew that the judge would do anything I wanted him to do.

Bill called the judge and arranged for the lawyer and me to see him. Then I left the office, the lawyer apparently thinking that he had won a victory.

I knew that the judge liked cigars, though I didn't recall now whether he smoked them or gave them away to others. As soon as I left Bill's office I went to a store and bought a box of good ones. Then I called the bailiff and explained that I needed to see the judge right away.

"What did you get me into, Allen?" the judge asked when I arrived at his office.

"I need a favor, Judge," I replied. I explained that the cards I had were phony. "I did you a favor. Now I want a favor. I want this joint," I told him. "It's no big deal. Nobody's going to see the cards but you, and after that I'm going to rip them up so you can't get in trouble."

The judge said okay. He agreed to see me at 9:30 the next morning.

The judge was extremely formal when we arrived the next day. He was wearing his black robe and called the court to order to make it all look official. Then he asked the lawyer for the papers signed by the workers and he asked me for the intent cards. Finally, to protect himself, he explained that he was no handwriting expert. However, he said that he would go back into his chambers and study them. If he felt that the signatures on the cards were similar to the signatures on the IRS forms, he wanted the lawyer to agree to recognize the union. And if he felt that the signatures were phony, I was to walk away from the business and engage in no further organizing efforts there.

Both of us agreed.

The judge stayed in his chambers a good thirty-five or forty minutes. Finally he came back, and all of us stood as he came into the courtroom. Then he announced that to the best of his ability, he had determined that the signatures were authentic. He requested the letter of recognition from me, handed it to the lawyer, and ordered that the attorney sign it.

The lawyer was irate. He was trying to protest, certain that the signatures were no good yet hesitant to challenge the judge outright. The threat of a contempt of court citation quieted him.

The judge came into my life again when I was with my independent Local 752 in the 1970s, involved with an informational picket line around a manufacturing plant. There were eighty or ninety workers in the place and I had been able to organize only ten or fifteen of them, so the informational picket line gave us the chance to talk to the workers and hand out leaflets. Even though there was no strike, the picket line was engaged in quite a bit of violence. I figured that if there were enough violence, I could take the whole place without having adequate commitment by the workers.

We were stopping deliveries, cutting tires, and doing anything else we could. At the same time, one of the men who was on the picket line with us told me that the owner had another office on Superior Avenue. It was a first-floor office so I increased the pressure by going down there one night and throwing a firebomb into the place.

The police usually went along with labor during those days. However, this time the owner had police connections strong enough that they were coming down on us instead of looking the other way. They began harassing my pickets and, before we went to court, the cops looked up the records of the men who both worked for the plant and were actively engaged in picketing the place.

Several of the pickets had warrants out for their arrests, mostly for minor offenses. Several had unpaid parking tickets so they began handcuffing the men in the hallway of the courthouse.

I began screaming at the cops to take the handcuffs off the members. I told them that I would pay for the tickets. They threatened me and I threatened them, but it was really a standoff.

An informational picket line can only last thirty days. As soon as our picketing reached the thirty-first day, the lawyers for the plant went to the labor board to file charges against me.

The Labor Board agents all knew me. In addition to 752, a small union I created myself, I had been an organizer for Local 507, which I helped start along with Harold Friedman and Jackie Presser. I had also helped Local 416 and others. In fact, I worked with so many locals that one of the board agents used to ask me which hat I was wearing that day, a reference to an insurance company's advertising that they handled all types of insurance.

The hearing concerning my exceeding the thirty days was to be held before the judge. This time I was not trying to play any games. I never thought about the thirty-day restriction. The board members knew it and had to bring me up on charges when the company lawyers pushed the issue.

We went before the judge. The Labor Department investigators who were responsible for Teamster Local 507 told him the situation and I decided to bluff my way through.

"Your honor, there's a lot of violence on this picket line. The boss is creating it with the police, and because of the violence, I think I should have some extra days. I can't just pull the picket line off right now. I'd like to have ten days more."

I was given the extra time, but I still lost that strike. I firebombed his other office. I burned a roof on his manufacturing plant. But the owner stood up to me and beat me.

Another time the labor department gave me a subpoena to go to the Grand Jury. I asked what would happen if I didn't appear and I was told that I would go to jail for contempt of court.

I refused to show up, then was told that there would be a warrant for my arrest. I was supposed to show up at 9:00 or 9:30 the next morning so I arranged to spend the next couple of days in a motel room. The arrest warrant was issued to my house, and my wife accepted it.

Then I called the federal marshals from the motel and offered to turn myself in. I went down to the Federal Building, taking cigarettes, pills for my heart condition, and a couple of candy bars. I went to the federal marshals' office and was searched, fingerprinted, photographed, then put into a cell. It was lunchtime and I had left my pills in the office after the search. I asked the guard for my prescription, explaining about the heart condition, but the guard told me I would be getting nothing. I told him that I needed to go to the hospital because of my chest pains if I couldn't get my pills.

I began yelling at the guard. I told him that I would sue if I had a heart attack. I said that I had to be taken to the hospital rather than spending the night in jail, but he said there was no way. The guy then handcuffed me and pushed me toward the judge's courtroom, where I was to have my hearing.

The handcuffs, which were much too tight, were removed before we went into the judge's chambers, where the press, my wife, and the attorneys were waiting. He wanted to make things look good so he said, "Are you Mr. Friedman?"

"Yes, I am," I said, raising my voice. "And that marshal over there won't give me my heart pills. He handcuffed me too tight and he was pushing me and my chest is hurting me."

The judge laid into the marshal. He sent him to get my heart pills and the marshal was suddenly very helpful.

I started yelling about what was going on. I told the judge that he had signed an order to have the government prosecutor stop harassing me. I said that despite that, there were government agents outside my home, watching my kids go to school and generally still bothering me. The judge asked the prosecutor whether it were true, but all the prosecutor could say was that he did not think their actions were harassment and, really, they weren't. But by then the judge did whatever we wanted so long as he could protect himself so he ordered the prosecutor to put a stop to everything and said I did not have to go before that Grand Jury. Had I gone before the jury, I would have had to testify against Jackie Presser, which I didn't want to do at the time. It was only later, when the *Akron Beacon Journal* found out about his Teamsters connection and revealed the story, that he had to remove himself from conflicts of interest such as the ones we were involved with.

The lawyer was not our only federal judge, the reason I am not singling him out by name. We let several corrupt themselves in the Cleveland area alone. In fact, 60 to 70 percent of the judges in our area were beholden to the Pressers and the Teamsters. Nationally there are judges at all levels who are beholden to the Teamsters.

It is important to remember that these judges have personal codes of ethics that leave much to be desired. A judge is a man or woman in a position of the highest possible public trust. A number of judges are appointed for life, and their decisions have a greater impact on the American society than many of the laws passed by Congress. The fact that they are helped in some way early in their careers does not change this. There is no reason why this judge or any of the other judges shouldn't tell people like Bill and me to go to hell when it comes to cases heard before them. There is no reason why they should rule in our favor when we are obviously wrong. Such loyalty is the kind of ethics school children follow when they get into trouble playing childish pranks.

We never held a gun to the heads of the judges we supported early in their careers. We did not kidnap their spouses or their children. We certainly did not threaten to expose them to the media or ruin their careers. They choose to go along with us. They choose to act on our behalf at the expense of others who, by all rights, should benefit in our place. Such choices are wrong for people in positions of public trust, though we take advantage of them.

That is why I cannot stress enough that we don't have to corrupt politicians, cops, and judges. They come to us and corrupt themselves.

It was during this same period that Jackie was forced out of the Hotel and Restaurant Employees Union. He was moving to become powerful in the International and had moved near the top in Ohio, but he was doing things too fast and too openly dishonestly.

Part of the problem was the way Jackie was treating the people from the five unions we had merged. Many of them were old and they were just pushed out. They had friends within the organization and their friends did not like to see them mistreated, even though they went along with the consolidation.

The rest of the problem was a criminal one. Jackie was stealing from the union, embezzling money and cutting in a friend of his. I resented what he was doing because I was still working nights for Babe Triscaro, still trying to make ends meet on $139 a week from the Union. Even more important, Jackie was cutting in a friend of his on the skimmings, not me.

Jackie and I were involved with a lot of violence which other labor leaders objected to, though we were getting results faster than other organizers. We were using stink bombs in restaurants, beating people, and intimidating in ways that caused some of the other labor people to try to remove us from the labor movement. They weren't all that clean themselves, but we were getting the publicity and the reputation.

Jackie began spending a lot of money and didn't care how he got it. There were seven thousand members so we had a lot of dues. He also developed some scams to increase what we were getting.

There was a restaurant owner named Marie Schreiber who was expanding her business to include making the food trays for United Airlines. The airline food preparation division had more than 130 people and I wanted to organize the place.

The International for the restaurant business had a rule that your dues were four dollars per month and you had a per capita tax paid to the international of seventy-five or eighty-five cents a member. There were payments to all levels of the union hierarchy: the city, the state, and the big International.

I said to Jackie that we should organize the employees at Marie Schreiber's and tell the people that our dues were six dollars per month. This was what we did as soon as we organized the place.

Everything went fine for a few months. Then the International found out what we were doing and we were forced to give back two dollars per member for the months we had been collecting the extra money. They also discovered that he had been collecting special fees from part-time employees, then pocketing the money.

The International sent two representatives from Cincinnati to take away our local. There had apparently been a number of complaints from former leaders of the unions we had merged, though they were aimed at Jackie. I was considered a good labor organizer and the men wanted me to go to Columbus for them. But we would not be allowed to keep our local. The books and records were to be turned over to them on behalf of the International and Jackie had to go.

Our office was on the second floor of a building on East Seventeenth Street and Superior Avenue. They explained why they were there and I told them to get out. There were no outsiders who were going to take over our union. There were roughly twelve hundred to fifteen hundred members when we consolidated. I had been working hard, raising the number to more than seven thousand in four or five years. In fact, there would come a day when the Cleveland labor organization business agents would refer to me as "Mr. Organizer."

I may not have had a raise in my pay since I started. Jackie may have been stealing money and not cutting me in. But no outsiders were going to take over what I had built. "Are you for real?" I asked them. "You think I'm going to let two assholes come in here after all of the work I've done, and turn over the books and records to you people and we're just going to walk out of here?"

"No," they said. "We want to discuss something [a job for me] with you, but Jackie has to go."

"I'll tell you fellas something. Either you can walk down those stairs or I'm going to throw your fucking asses down those stairs. Now you got a choice, but get out of our office."

The International took Jackie to court, at which time Bill Presser called me to find out what was going on. I explained that Jackie and an associate were stealing all the money from the union while I was working two jobs and not even getting a cut.

Bill asked me what I would recommend now that the International was taking

Jackie to court. I explained that the moment the International got hold of Jackie's books, he was going to jail for embezzlement.

Jackie went to court on a Friday, at which time the judge ordered him to get his records and produce them in court the following week. The records would be turned over to representatives of the International.

Normally Bill liked to finesse a problem. If he caught a man stealing, he would arrange for a change in the guy's pension, cut him out of a little money as a punishment, then force him to resign. The books would be doctored in whatever way was necessary to prevent outsiders and the rank and file from knowing what had happened and everything would be kept quiet.

Jackie Presser came on like a bulldozer. He threw people out or arranged for them to go to jail. He just didn't give a damn about anyone and now he had gone too far. As I explained to Bill, the only thing left to do was to destroy the records by burning the entire building. Bill told me to go ahead and handle it.

It was a Saturday night when a friend of mine and I went to the building. There was a rug company on the third floor and it was there that I went to start the fire. I used that phosphate-based chemical so that everything would be destroyed when the water hit the structure. Then I covered the floor with gasoline to start the fire and left a lighted candle burning to start it.

Jackie was apparently notified by the fire department when the place was burning and he called me on the telephone. Jackie was all excited, shouting, "Come on down to the office! Come on down to the office!"

"What for?" I asked.

"The building's burning," he said.

"Fuck it. Let it burn," I said and went back to bed.

The next morning Jackie came by my house to see me. His face was anguished and he stuck out his hands, saying, "What did you do to me? I'm going to go to jail. What did you do?"

Calmly I said, "Jackie, I didn't do nothing. What are you talking about?"

"Let's take a ride. Come on down to the office."

We drove down to Seventeenth and Superior. The firemen were still there. The heat from the phosphate-based chemical had caused the beams to bend, but by then there was only smoke. The fire was out, the building so completely destroyed that it would eventually have to be replaced, ironically by a fire station.

Jackie was in shock as he looked at the shell of the building. "I got to go face the judge," he moaned.

"Jackie, I didn't do it," I lied. "Did you do it?"

"No," he said, shocked that I could think of such a thing. "I didn't do it."

"So just go tell the judge that a fire started. What are you coming running to me for?"

"I'm scared to go face the judge," he whimpered.

"You'd better go see your old man, pal," I said, and he agreed, provided I went with him.

Bill Presser never let on that he and I arranged to start the blaze in order to protect Jackie. Bill calmly explained, "If a fire started, a fire started. And if the books and records were burned up, I don't know if you were stealing or not, but now they don't have no proof if you were stealing. Just go face the judge."

Monday morning we went back to court and that judge laid into Jackie until tears were coming from Jackie's eyes. He was certain he was going to jail, though there was nothing the judge could do. There was no evidence remaining.

I just sat in the back of the courtroom, grinning as I watched the show. No one brought me up on any charges. No one thought I might have had a hand in the embezzlement, a fact that also convinced them that I was not going to be involved with burning the joint.

There was more going on behind the scenes, of course. Bill Presser was not going to let things stand with just the arson. He wanted to be certain that there was no chance that Jackie would do time so he called a friend who was connected with the judges. He arranged for the charges to be dropped regardless so long as Jackie agreed to leave the labor movement quietly.

I don't know whether the judge hearing the case was the one who was fixed, but it did not matter. After Jackie was raked over the coals, the judge told him to sit down and help the International piece together all the restaurants, delicatessens, and other places that were organized. There were too many for him to remember fully, but Jackie agreed to try.

Jackie had been making too much money to go quietly. The International learned that I was making approximately eighty-six hundred dollars per year and offered me the same money to go to Columbus and build membership the way I had in Cleveland. I agreed, but Jackie decided to cut himself in again. He explained that he could get an independent state charter so that again we could have our own union in Cleveland. I would not go to Columbus, and he would be right back in the labor movement, though working independently.

I did what I always did with Jackie. I went along with his scheme even though, once again, my organizing partner and I would do all the work while Jackie got fatter on the money we brought in. However, this time the scheme backfired against him.

My partner and I had organized about four hundred people when various mob-connected people in other cities learned what was happening. They sent word back through the International to Bill Presser that we had to give up the members to the Hotel and Restaurant Workers Union or we would be in serious trouble. We did. Jackie finally got out of the labor movement at that time.

Even though I had stayed with Jackie, creating an independent union, I could still be a part of union activity because no one other than Bill realized I was linked to the destruction of the records. Because of the fiasco with the Hotel and Restaurant Workers International Union in Columbus, I was out the money I had been promised I would earn if I had gone with the International. I was angry and Bill agreed to make certain I had work with the Teamsters. I went on the payroll of Joint Council 41 to act as a trouble shooter and organizer for whatever locals needed me.

The more crimes I committed for the labor movement, the more I was trusted to handle sensitive jobs for Jimmy Hoffa, Bill Presser, and others. One of the more important at the time involved a former milk truck driver named James Luken. Luken was from Cincinnati, the president of Local 98. But he cared about the members and he was against the corruption he felt existed with Hoffa. He was also part of the movement to leave the International Brotherhood of Teamsters and affiliate with the AFL-CIO.

Hoffa was outraged not only by his apparent inability to bring Luken into line but also by Luken's willingness to give the McClellan Committee information about corruption within the Teamsters. For example, it was Luken who provided information about forty thousand dollars that was spent for expenses for Babe Triscaro and Bill Presser during the time that they appeared before the Bender Committee.

Luken was just honest enough to be surprised by the extent of the corruption. He explained to Kennedy, "I wasn't shocked that a politician would take a bribe. I was shocked that somebody would be stupid enough to say so in front of seven people." He was referring to the Ohio Teamsters Joint Council's being told that the forty thousand dollars was meant to pull strings behind the scenes in order to have all charges dropped against Presser and Triscaro.

"I am sure that Senator Bender's name was mentioned but I want to make it clear that I am not saying that this man [George Starling, former president of Cincinnati Joint Council 26, the position which Luken eventually held as well] said the money went to Senator Bender. It may have; it may not." Of course, as I have already indicated, no matter what happened to the money, Bender was one of the many politicians who corrupted himself in exchange for Teamster support.

Bill Presser tried to handle Luken for Hoffa. Before Luken became president of the Cincinnati union, winning the position despite Bill's opposition, there was petty harassment against him. A funeral wreath was delivered to Luken's house in one instance. In another, an undertaker called the Luken home and asked where he should go to pick up Jim's body since he had just been called and told that Jim was dead.

Bill also tried to offer Luken a bribe. Before Luken won the joint council presidency on the strength of his popularity, Bill thought there was no way

Luken could take the post legitimately. He decided to bribe Jim, offering to force the resignations of the people in power and put Jim in charge, provided Jim stopped fighting Hoffa and Bill. Luken wanted nothing to do with such cooperation.

The more Bill and Hoffa pushed, the more information Luken passed on to the McClellan Committee. He even named my own brother, Harry Friedman, whom Bill sent to Cincinnati in the early fifties to take over jukebox Local 122. But Harry was never a man who could survive as a criminal. He never had the sense to be patient with his scams, to cover his tracks and keep the scores he made. Once Harry hit Cincinnati he began filing false affidavits related to the union activity and was caught. Once the court looked at his arrest record, which included auto theft, blackmail, illegal transportation of whiskey, and forgery, there was no way he would go anywhere except the Ohio State Penitentiary.

Bill also sent another Teamster organizer named Ralph Vanni to Cincinnati. Vanni's job was to undermine the strength of Luken's union by stealing contracts from him. Vanni was to offer employers contracts that would undercut Luken's. The only problem was that Vanni was greedy in his own right. He tried to make a few extra bucks by extorting money from the employers in exchange for giving them the sweetheart deals. He was forced to leave town or face possible charges.

There were other tactics used. In 1958, a man working for Luken was accused of rape. The trouble was that whoever set the man up—and this time I don't think it was anyone working directly for Bill Presser—chose the wrong woman. Under pressure she admitted that she had been paid $195 to lie about the attempted rape and was promised another $1,000 if she were convincing enough to get the man indicted.

Another alleged attempt to frame Luken and his staff came from Robert Morris, the man Bill and Hoffa used in Cincinnati to represent some of their interests. Morris's car was bombed, the bomber never found though Luken and his staff were the primary suspects. The Cincinnati Police Department gave polygraph (the so-called lie detector) tests to Luken and his men, all of whom passed. Morris, who then became a suspect in the bombing of his own car, refused to take such a test. The fact that Morris called his insurance company to make certain that he would be paid if his car were bombed added to suspicion against him. However, no one was ever charged in the matter.

Eventually I was sent to Cincinnati to take care of Luken. It was my job, along with the men I took with me, to give the man a beating.

Luken always went around with a couple of men to protect him. As a result, Bill Presser told us to grab one of the other union heads, beat him, and tell him that he was to tell his boss that if he didn't come around, he would be "planted in the ground." I don't know whether we scared him or not, but he didn't go for another term after his time in office was up that year.

Luken did not fade from the scene, though. He became mayor of Cincinnati, and, at least for a while, his independent union was quite successful within the AFL-CIO. What mattered was that Luken was no longer a problem for Jimmy Hoffa.

Although I used the phrase "planted in the ground," I never considered murder with all the jobs I did. There were killings within all the unions. Some were accidental when a firebombing or other violence got out of hand because the people involved didn't know what they were doing and didn't take proper precautions to make sure no one got hurt. Some were deliberate, contracts executed by pros who seldom had anything to do with the unions whose leaders hired them. But murder was not routine because, no matter how mob-connected the unions happened to be, killings were not appropriate for trade union leaders.

Union leadership might be corrupt in many unions, but the members are usually decent, hardworking people trying to gain a better way of life. All of American society has benefited from unions, though most people don't like to admit that, especially if they hold white-collar, high-paying management positions.

Take a look at the typical business person earning a substantial five-figure or low six-figure income. How many days a week does that individual have to work? Five days, though some may choose to work a part of a sixth just because they are dedicated. No one makes them do that. In fact, no one can legally force them to work more than a forty-hour week if they stand against it. What they forget is that there was a time when the six-day week was normal and many people worked all seven days. Instead of eight hours a day, ten or more hours on the job was common. Everyone was tired. Families were seldom together. Children, even from good homes, often were unsupervised more than anyone wants to admit today. There simply wasn't time.

Who changed all that? The men and women in labor unions. When they struck for better conditions because their pay was bare subsistence and their benefits nonexistent, they bettered life for everyone.

The membership of organized crime is quite different. Their actions are self-serving, criminal, anti-social. When they do business, murder may be as appropriate a tool for them as a picket line is for labor. The mob kills. Organized labor rarely does, though we threaten a lot, as I did when I talked of "planting" Luken or when I threaten to throw someone out the window. The greatest danger Luken or anyone else might face would be a broken collarbone, a broken arm or leg, or some other painful injury from which he would recover.

The one exception came with the death of President John Kennedy. A number of facts I uncovered while researching this book indicate that there may have been as many as four contracts on the president's life. There have been numerous books written on the matter of who actually ordered the fatal shooting in Dallas, and the scope of this book is such that that topic will not be covered. What will be mentioned is the fact that the Kennedy brothers, Jack and Bobby, generated so much hatred against them for various reasons that rumors from reliable sources indicate that there were elements within the Teamsters out to get him.

Earlier I mentioned the actions against Fidel Castro by the Kennedy regime. It is known that he wanted Kennedy murdered, and it is believed that he actually placed a contract on Kennedy's life. There were many of his supporters, most former military men with the training and skill to handle an assassination, already in the United States.

Jack Rubenstein, who later changed his name to Ruby, was a nightclub owner in Dallas, Texas, when Kennedy was shot. He was also alleged to be a police buff who often hung out at the Dallas Police Station. His visits were so commonplace that he was able to get inside during a time when Lee Harvey Oswald, the arrested assassin of Kennedy, was being transferred. Ruby murdered Oswald, then died in jail before anyone could determine his true motivation.

But there was more to Jack Ruby than his Dallas years. Ruby worked as an organizer for the Chicago Waste Handlers Union when it was taken over by Paul Dorfman after the shooting of its former president, Leon Cooke, by John Martin, a colleague of Ruby. Ruby was believed to be an accomplice in that murder, an issue rendered meaningless after Cooke was acquitted of murder and the death determined to be self-defense.

Dorfman was not close to Ruby. He found Ruby rather emotional and noted that Jack left the union two months after Dorfman took over. From there he went into what was then the Army Air Force, serving three years, then moving to Dallas in 1947.

Ruby's arrival time coincided with the movement of a number of Chicago gangsters into the same city. There was Sam Yaras, the brother of Dave Yaras, who had been involved with union activity in Miami and gambling operations in Cuba. There was also Paul Roland Jones, a man with conviction records for bribery of a police officer and involvement with drug trafficking.

Ruby had a connection with Castro's Cuba as well. Lewis McWillie, a Dallas gambler, paid for him to go there twice in 1959, both times after Castro had taken control and turned on the Mafia. The first trip occurred right after Santos Trafficante, the man for whom McWillie was working, was thrown into a Cuban jail. The second time, that same year, Ruby went to offer a twenty-five-thousand-dollar "ransom" to spring three unidentified but presumably mob-connected prisoners from jail. He offered the bribe to Robert McKeown, who was a gun-runner and a major supplier of weapons to Castro during the revolution. Later Ruby met McKeown in Houston and added several hundred Jeeps for Castro to the bribe, the vehicles apparently coming from the mob in Louisiana.

There were other connections among Ruby, the mob, and Hoffa's inner circle during the period from 1959 through 1963. Ruby was in contact with Irwin S. Weiner, the major bondsman for the Teamsters Union on October 26, 1963, though Weiner refused to talk about the nature of the call.

Other telephone contacts in the days just prior to the Kennedy assassination included those with Nofio Pecora (October 30, 1963), a man with convictions for his involvement in both the heroin trade and a call girl ring in the Louisiana-to-Mississippi corridor. He received a call from Hoffa aid Barney Baker (November 7), a giant of a man who was known both for being one of Hoffa's emissaries to the mob and for eating as much as thirty-eight pounds of meat at one sitting. At least that was the legend.

There was also a call to Murray W. Miller of the Southern Conference of Teamsters. Miller handled Teamster problems in Dallas, Nashville, and New Orleans, among other work. That call, on November 8, as well as the one from Baker, involved Ruby's requests for assistance with labor problems.

Miller, during this same period (November 7), contacted Walter Sheridan of the Justice Department, where efforts were being made to convict Hoffa for jury tampering. It was believed that Ed Partin was acting as a Kennedy informant, a fact that frightened Hoffa. Partin was the source of the information that Carlos Marcello, the mob boss of Louisiana, had paid $500,000 to Richard Nixon's election campaign in 1960 in order to eventually eliminate the land fraud charge against Hoffa. Partin was also knowledgeable about Hoffa's being asked to be a go-between with the mob in the CIA's efforts to murder Fidel Castro. Miller was apparently attempting to learn whether Partin were talking about matters that were about to send Hoffa to jail.

There were other connections among the various men involved with a number of alleged plots. One was with New Orleans investigator David Ferrie, who was also a pilot for Carlos Marcello. Another was Jim Braden (formerly known as Eugene Hale Brading), a man who had served several prison sentences. Braden and Ruby were both seen in the offices of the H. L. Hunt Oil Company on the afternoon of November 21, 1963. Men at the top of Texas oil companies were among those suspected of wanting President Kennedy murdered, adding to all the various theories. Braden was among the people detained for questioning after the Kennedy assassination, though he was released because he had no criminal record (his convictions had all been under the Brading name). His alibi for the time, that he was with his parole officer, was challenged by that same officer, Roger Carroll, who claims he did not meet with Braden that afternoon.

Ferrie had a valid alibi for the day, since he was in court, but he had been associated with the Cuban Revolutionary Council, 544 Camp Street, New Orleans, through the early part of 1963. The council was in the same building as Lee Harvey Oswald's Fair Play for Cuba Committee. In addition, Antonio de Varona was a cofounder of the council, and it was Varona who had been supplied with poison pills to kill Castro.

There were connections everywhere, yet what was the truth of the Kennedy assassination? The answer is unknown, but my research has revealed that regardless of who killed Kennedy, there were probably four contracts for his death.

The first contract, reported by an insider within the Kennedy family, came from men involved with American oil company interests. They perceived Kennedy as a threat to their business. They felt that enough money was at stake for them that ordering the assassination was a sensible business move. The insider claimed that, regardless of who actually committed the crime, this was the primary motive for the murder.

The second contract came from Fidel Castro in retaliation for Kennedy's efforts to have him murdered. However, the exact nature of who would carry it out and how has never been determined, and Fidel Castro did not respond to attempts to interview him for this book.

The third contract came from the mob. This is the most accepted theory of how and why Kennedy was killed on November 22, 1963, and ties in many of the elements related to Hoffa, the Teamsters, the attempt to kill Castro, and the Kennedy brothers. Santos Trafficante mentioned a plan to kill Kennedy before 1964 when talking with an FBI informant. Carlos Marcello, the New Orleans mob boss, suggested that Jack Kennedy would be murdered in retaliation for the problems his brother, Attorney General Robert Kennedy, was causing. Both the Marcello comments and the one by Trafficante were made in August 1962.

In conversations with men involved with mob families in Chicago, Las Vegas, Arizona, and New York, there was a pride in discussing the Kennedy hit, a pride that elevated the story to mythic proportions. This story, though undoubtedly based on facts, seems similar to a Mafia "folk tale" told about a turn-of-the-century mob hit.

The Mafia has two forms of "history" when you talk with both old-time members and elderly Sicilians sympathetic to its past. There are the stories of what occurred over the years and there are the embellished stories, with an added element of disdain.

For example, at the turn of the century there was a New York police officer who was disgusted by Mafia murders. One corpse, for example, had been found with the man's genitals cut off and placed in his mouth. The brutality and the symbolism of death disgusted and fascinated him. He decided to go to Sicily to investigate the origins of the Mafia.

The Mafia had only been a presence in the United States since about 1880. The officer made known his intentions to stop the violence before making his journey and a decision was made to have him killed. He traveled by ship, arrived in Sicily and went ashore. The killer approached him, shot him, and disappeared in the crowds. That is the truth of what happened to the officer, and the killer was never caught, though the Mafia took credit for the hit.

Simply being assassinated on the land does not show the proper disdain for the police officer who was murdered, though. Members of the Mafia changed the history to one that was more dramatic and symbolic. According to the story that would be repeated in the years to follow, the murder took place on board the ship before it docked. According to the myth, the police officer was sitting on the toilet, his pants down, when the assassin shot him. Such a death was revealing of the full contempt for the man. It also was a death that was less than honorable.

The same situation is true of the murder of John Kennedy. The idea that the Mafia was involved with the actual assassination remains the most likely. Robert Kennedy was after both the Mafia and the Teamsters at the time. Jack Kennedy was allowing the investigations within the Justice Department to take place and thus was ultimately responsible. Jack Ruby had Mafia connections. Lee Harvey Oswald, who may or may not have been a trigger man, had connections with men involved with those suspected of the murder. (Current writing about the case positively links Oswald's rifle and its position in the Texas School Book Depository with the assassination. It does not necessarily link Oswald as the trigger man, though it is presumed that he was probably one of the killers.) Oswald was also a man who could have been manipulated, turning him into yet another weapon for the mob. No matter what, more bullets were fired than originally thought, a fact determined by the discovery of an intact, spent bullet that was originally mistakenly believed to have passed through both John Kennedy and Texas Governor John Connolly, who was also struck at the time. (Journalist James Reston, Jr., author of *The Great Expectations of John Connally* [New York: Edward Burlingame Books/Harper & Row, 1969], believes that Connolly was the original target of Lee Harvey Oswald.)

The truth about Oswald remains unknown. That the Mafia had a contract on Kennedy and would like to take claim for the actual shooting is undisputed. However, a myth evolved within organized crime, a story that is often repeated today as proof of their strength and contempt for the Kennedy brothers.

According to the myth, the Mafia was irate over the treatment of Jimmy Hoffa, who was about to be sent to jail. They were tired of the vendetta against a man who had worked so efficiently with them and decided that both Kennedy brothers would have to die. The first assassination was of John Kennedy, a "proper" murder and a warning to Robert to back off further investigations. But Robert Kennedy would not back off, so, when he ran for president, he, too, was shot. Sirhan Sirhan fired the revolver. (He has not, at this writing, been linked to organized crime elements. In fact, one psychologist who interviewed him and was interviewed for this book explained that Sirhan Sirhan could not understand why he was treated so badly. He came from a country where political assassination is an accepted part of changing leadership and not a major crime. He expected to be treated either as a hero or with more respect than his life sentence indicated.) But there was a second man nearby who also shot, a man who was connected with the Mafia. Remember that this is Mafia myth, not fact, though it is believed by many of the older men within the mob.

Finally, with the two Kennedy brothers dead, the Mafia turned to the surviving son of Joseph and Rose Kennedy, the youngest brother, Senator Edward "Ted" Kennedy. According to the myth, Ted was told that he would not be murdered because he was not directly involved with the harassment of Jimmy Hoffa. However, it was felt that all three brothers should be penalized in some way. Ted Kennedy's punishment would be to never be president. It was explained that if he ran for president, he would undoubtedly win the election. It was also stated that if he did win, he would be murdered shortly after taking office, just as his brothers were killed. Instead, he was never to run, his punishment being the knowledge that he would have had the top political prize in the United States had Robert Kennedy not started the vendetta against Hoffa.

There is no proof that the Ted Kennedy story is true. There is ample evidence of a Mafia plot against Jack Kennedy. There was also evidence that some Teamsters were interested in murdering Robert Kennedy in retribution for his actions against Hoffa, at least one such incident possibly being known to Hoffa. But these were men who wanted to act on Hoffa's behalf, not Hoffa's orders. They were not connected with organized crime and they were talked out of making a serious effort to carry out their desires.

The fourth contract on President Kennedy's life was from within the Teamsters. So far as I can determine, it was not ordered by Jimmy Hoffa, nor was Bill Presser involved. It apparently involved one or more mob-connected higher-ups, hoping to win Jimmy's favor and stop the prosecution he was facing.

The Robert Kennedy vendetta against Jimmy involved the Test Fleet truck leasing business. It had been started back in 1949 and was in violation of the Taft-Hartley Labor Act related to conflict of interest since it did business with employers for Commercial Carriers, a Detroit Trucking firm. The relationship had resulted in $242,000 in gross business over several years, according to the indictment, a misdemeanor punishable by no more than one year in prison.

Hoffa, quoted by Victor Navasky in *Kennedy Justice* (p. 416), stated:

> Since Test Fleet didn't do its own trucking business or in any other way become involved with the Teamsters, I just couldn't see where there was a conflict of interest. Leasing trucking equipment to truckers was no more ominous to me, than, say, selling gasoline to truckers or selling cigarettes to truck drivers.
>
> Can an executive in General Motors invest his savings in a gas station? I

know several pharmacists and doctors who own stocks in drug-manufacturing companies, and no one complains. I even know of a doctor who owns an interest in an undertaking establishment, and it is likely that some of his patients have ultimately become patrons of the funeral parlor, but no one has ever suggested that he has deliberately created business for the latter.

The Test Fleet case ended in an eventual mistrial in which Hoffa was accused of jury tampering. The charges were several, all stemming from October and November 1962, when the case was being heard.

Hoffa men allegedly called several prospective jurors who were believed to be hostile to Hoffa. The caller claimed to be a reporter for the *Nashville Banner*, who induced them to discuss their attitude toward Hoffa. Those attitudes ultimately caused them to be disqualified from serving. This biased the prospective jury pool in Hoffa's favor.

On October 24, 1962, Lawrence "Red" Medlin offered prospective juror James C. Tippens ten thousand dollars to find in favor of Hoffa. Tippens reported the bribe attempt to the judge hearing the case and Medlin was eventually convicted for his action. However, no direct link between Medlin and Hoffa was ever made.

Another jury tampering effort was made against Betty Paschal, whose husband, James, was a member of the Tennessee Highway Patrol. Ewing King, the leader of the Nashville Teamsters, attempted to persuade the officer to influence his wife in Hoffa's favor. What he did not know was that the FBI had the meeting under surveillance.

The other proven allegation was the effort to influence Gratin Fields, a black juror on the case. Larry Campbell, also a black man, was a business agent for the Detroit Teamsters. He had an uncle named Thomas Ewing Parks, whom he used to contact the Fields family with the offer of a ten-thousand-dollar bribe. One of the children of Gratin went so far as to accept a hundred-dollar down payment. Parks, brought to court when Hoffa was present, looked over at Jimmy, who held up five fingers. Parks understood the message, taking the Fifth Amendment when questioned about the case.

There were other tampering allegations, including one involving Hoffa and Allen Dorfman, but the four mentioned were the most important. Much of the information initially came from Partin, a Teamster informant who was not trusted by the FBI. However, Walter Sheridan, who worked closely with Robert Kennedy, did believe him because independent checking of Partin's stories invariably supported them during this period. It was this case that allegedly resulted in the contract against Jack Kennedy. It was also this case that resulted in Hoffa and associates being found guilty on March 4, 1964, Hoffa receiving a ten-thousand-dollar fine and an eight-year sentence in the federal penitentiary. What was ironic about all this was that had Hoffa not tried to tamper with the jury, and had he been convicted in the Test Fleet case, he would have been convicted of a misdemeanor. Through actions that were unusually inept, Hoffa's case turned into a felony.

There would also be a second case against Hoffa, though this came after the assassination. Brought in Chicago on April 27, 1964, it charged Hoffa, Benjamin Dranow, and others with personally benefiting from loans from the Teamster Central States Southeast and Southwest Pension Fund. Hoffa was found guilty of fraud concerning four of twenty-eight counts, then sentenced to serve four concurrent jail terms of five years each.

I don't know whether the fraud charges were valid. They concerned kickbacks and a loan for a project in which Hoffa had a 45 percent interest. From what I know about the pension fund's operations through Bill Presser, I would not doubt the charges. However, it is interesting to note that it was believed that Hoffa may not have personally profited. Instead, he may have used the money to pay off congressmen. Whatever the case, there were eighteen trustees for the fund and Hoffa was the only serious target because he was considered to be the most important trustee.

So who killed John Kennedy? I have no idea, though rumors of mob involvement in the murder are undoubtedly accurate on the basis of the interviews that have been conducted and the documents that have become available. What is interesting is that, in part because of Robert Kennedy's vendetta against the Teamsters, the president was going to die before his term in office was ended. It was just a case of which assassin reached him first.

6

Teamsters in Transition from Hoffa

THE TEAMSTERS and the mob were never stronger than they were in the mid-1960s despite the fact that the "Get Hoffa" squad in Robert Kennedy's Justice Department finally sent him to jail. Hoffa negotiated the master contract for the nation that forced all trucking companies to negotiate as one. There was no more escaping to a state where management had the upper hand over the Teamsters as occurred in the past. Various locals no longer had the power to make deals on their own. Sometimes this worked against the members in an area where companies did too little business to be able to afford a master contract agreement. And other times this worked against the local union leaders who wanted to profit from sweetheart deals.

But the master contract was a major step in the labor movement. It was a vision of Farrell Dobbs that had taken more than twenty years to achieve. It also came at a time when unions probably had the most acceptance they had ever had in recent history.

The middle 1960s was a period of prosperity when many companies were making record profits while workers wages often soared with them. If anything, there were some contract settlements starting that were hurting individual businesses enough for them to consider closing, relocating to states with weaker or no unions, or reducing employees through robotics and other technical changes. There was also a recognition of discrimination against minorities, discrimination that led not only to the civil rights movement but also to the start of the demand for equal pay for equal work. There would continue to be bias against women in the workplace, but the public was beginning to clamor for minority group males to be paid equally with white males in the same job. Record new contracts were achieved for auto workers, bus drivers, transit workers, and others.

The National Master Freight Agreement, for example, established standards for working conditions, wages, and fringe benefits for both local drivers and over-the-road men. There were both increased benefits and a forty-five-cent-per-hour raise for the three-year life of the contract. The contract was created on January 16, 1964; for most of the rank and file it greatly overshadowed the jury tampering trial begun January 20. Again it was a case of the members wanting strong leadership and being willing to overlook everything else.

At the same time, organized crime members had such a strong position in some unions that bribes had to be considered a routine part of doing business. When the demands became too outrageous, as they would in the Cleveland building trades as a result of a man named Danny Green, ironically a leader of the longshoremen's union, most construction and meaningful redevelopment were completely stopped.

There was great hostility within the Teamsters when Jimmy Hoffa was convicted. Frank Chavez, a hotheaded Teamster official working from Puerto Rico, was especially enraged. He so hated the Kennedys that after the assassination of the president, Chavez sent a letter to Robert Kennedy which read:

Sir:
  This is for your information.
  The undersigned is going to solicit from the membership of our union
  that each one donate whatever they can afford to maintain, clean, beautify
  and supply with flowers the grave of Lee Harvey Oswald.
  You can rest assured contributions will be unanimous.

Later, in 1967, Chavez stalked Robert Kennedy, determined to kill him before Jimmy Hoffa had to begin serving his jail sentence after failed appeals for his convictions three years earlier. Chavez, accompanied by two men, arrived in our capitol on March 1, 1967, according to the Washington, D.C., Police Department. The three men stayed at the Continental Hotel and were armed with pistols.

The FBI issued photographs of Chavez to Kennedy personnel so they could be alert to his presence. However, before any arrests could be made, Hoffa confronted Chavez, raised hell with him, and took away his gun.

Tom Kennelly, a member of Robert Kennedy's staff during the McClellan Committee hearings, had become a bodyguard for Chavez. They began arguing one day, at which time Kennelly pulled out a gun and shot Chavez. So far as I could find, his reasons remain unclear to this day, but, oddly, nobody followed up on Chavez's threats.

Hoffa always maintained his innocence of jury tampering and of defrauding the Central States Pension Fund, but there was little question of his guilt. Ed Partin, the primary government witness, was a Teamsters leader from Louisiana who had been extremely close to Hoffa. Partin had been with Hoffa during periods that were an embarrassment to high government officials who were hostile to the Kennedys. For example, Partin had been present at the September 26, 1960, meeting with alleged New Orleans mob boss Carlos Marcello when Marcello showed a briefcase containing a half million dollars for the Nixon presidential campaign. He heard Marcello explain that the total mob contribution was a million dollars, the remaining money coming from rackets figures in Florida and New Jersey. Partin was also present two years later when Hoffa was talking about placing a contract on Attorney General Robert Kennedy.

Because of Hoffa's closeness to Partin, extensive efforts were made to discredit the man. Hoffa claimed that he was framed, that the information was false, that Partin was a liar. Yet Partin voluntarily took and passed a polygraph test. He also was subjected to intense investigations, all of which proved the substance of what he was saying. He later said that the reason he decided to tell the truth was because Hoffa turned against him in much the same way Jackie Presser eventually turned against me.

Another factor in the conviction was the extensive use of wiretap evidence. Many people in the Teamsters felt that no matter what Jimmy Hoffa had done, there should have been a better way to convict him. They disliked the tapping of telephone lines and invasion of privacy that were involved, yet the tactics were legal, and Hoffa was going to go to jail. It was just a matter of appealing the case to buy time.

One of the most blatant pieces of evidence confirming the integrity of Partin was the downfall of one of Hoffa's attorneys, Z. T. Osborn. Osborn was convicted of attempting to bribe a prospective juror, unknowingly working with Robert Vick, a Nashville, Tennessee, police officer who worked with Kennedy investigator Walter Sheridan. Sheridan was later quoted as explaining what happened in that matter, a case that eventually resulted in Osborn's arrest, conviction, disbarment, and suicide.

> He called me one day and said Osborn had called him that day and told him or rather asked him to offer a juror $10,000—$5,000 before and $5,000 after trial. Vick's reputation was bad. I believed him, but James Neal [the coprosecutor in both Tennessee trials] didn't and I think John Hooker, Sr. [the other government lawyer and a leading member of the Tennessee

bar specially recruited for the case] didn't believe it either. So we got an affidavit from Vick about his first conversation and went to the judge. He authorized the FBI to put a recording device on the small of Vick's back. That way we could find out if he was telling the truth. . . . He was this skinny little guy and when he sat down something went wrong with the recording device. But the second time, with the FBI surveilling him to make sure there was no funny business, it was as clear as it could be. Osborn told Vick to go tell the juror $5,000 now and $5,000 later. (Victor Navasky, *Kennedy Justice,* p. 433)

What Hoffa did not realize was that circumstances surrounding this period would lead to his downfall. Most people think that Hoffa was not in danger from the mob until he had a fight with Tony Provenzano while in prison. The truth was that he was losing face with some members of the mob for a reason that had nothing to do with the Teamsters or organized crime. Jimmy Hoffa's beloved wife was having an affair.

Hoffa liked the image of being a family man and, compared to many in the leadership, he was devoted to his wife and kids. I never saw him interested in getting a hooker when we were on the road. I never saw him go after women or encourage them to come see him in his hotel room. And I never talked with people who said that Jimmy ran around.

But Jimmy did have an occasional affair. They were quiet, as when Sylvia Pagano O'Brien Paris had been his mistress, and they were intense, not one-night stands. Eventually Josephine Hoffa felt lonely enough and betrayed enough that she sought companionship on her own.

It is hard to explain how shocking the idea of Josephine having an affair was to me when I learned about it. She was a wonderful woman whom we all adored. We had suspected something with Jimmy, but he was never an obvious womanizer. He went to his hotel room when on the road while many of us sought action with the girls. Yet there have been too many on-the-record testimonies in law enforcement investigations, too many books detailing the facts, to question the truth of the matter. It was still sad to see her driven to such a situation, something few of us ever suspected or wanted to suspect.

The man with whom Josephine had her affair was Tony Cimini, a friend of Anthony Giacalone, a man who, along with his brother Vito, was considered to be part of the Detroit mob. The two brothers owned Home Juice Company, a business they started with a half-million-dollar loan from the Central States Fund. They were part of the group of mobsters who viewed Hoffa as their connection with the fund whenever they wanted money for one of their projects. Sylvia Paris was also having an affair with Anthony Giacalone, and Giacalone used her to relay information about Hoffa. Sylvia remained close to Jimmy after their affair was over though she did not tell him that Giacalone's friend Cimini was having an affair with Hoffa's wife. She also did not say that frequently she and Tony Giacalone double-dated with Cimini and Josephine Hoffa.

The few people who knew about the affair blamed Jimmy, not his wife. They saw her as extremely lonely and long-suffering, much like the wife of a politician who is expected to raise a family, make appearances, and always pretend not to know what her husband does in hotel rooms when he travels. They felt that her one affair was the fault of Jimmy's indifference and double standard. He could bring his mistress, Sylvia Paris, to his home. His wife had to tolerate the seemingly intolerable.

Hoffa discovered that his wife was having an affair and the knowledge shattered him. He could have had Cimini beaten or killed. He could have beaten Cimini himself. He could have attacked Josephine. Any such action would have helped him maintain the mob's respect. Instead he turned to Joseph Zerilli for help.

Joe Zerilli was the head of the Detroit mob family and a man quite willing to help Hoffa because of all Hoffa had done for him. He called in Cimini and Anthony Giacalone, then ordered them to give up their lovers. There was an implied threat of violence if they failed to act as requested, though the exact penalty was never mentioned.

Shortly after the meeting, when Cimini refused to give up Josephine Hoffa, he found himself arrested for selling stolen securities. Although Cimini had been involved with the crime, the impression was that the arrest occurred either because evidence was provided to law enforcement people or because no effort was made to cover up the crime. Only Giacalone was unpunished, though Giacalone was better situated with the mob. He had been connected with Peter Licavoli, worked as one of Zerilli's enforcers, and was married to the cousin of Anthony Provenzano.

Hoffa became a joke to some of the members of the mob because he had failed to handle the problem with his wife personally. However, he remained in favor with Carlos Marcello and Santos Trafficante, who helped finance his effort to avoid serving time. (More than $1.2 million, most of it Teamsters money, would eventually be spent for Hoffa's defense and appeals before he went to jail in 1967.) Ed Partin later identified Charles O'Brien as the bag man for Marcello, claiming that he put up money to free Hoffa.

There was no question that Hoffa was going to jail in 1964. The only issue was when he would have to start doing time. As a result, efforts were made to determine who would run the union in his absence. The general consensus was that Frank Fitzsimmons would be the perfect man to take over.

Fitzsimmons was not under investigation or indictment for any crimes. He either was honest or had not gotten caught, in the eyes of law enforcement officers investigating the Teamsters during this period. He had worked long and hard for the Detroit Teamsters, was loyal to Hoffa, and had enough friends in organized crime that he seemed to be a "safe" choice. He also was fortunate enough to be present when Cimini was arrested, the mob suggesting that in return, Hoffa make certain that Fitzsimmons move into power.

Frank Fitzsimmons had an easier life growing up than many of the labor leaders with whom he worked. He was born in Jeannette, Pennsylvania, in 1908, his father part owner of a brewery. The family was large, five children in all, and the beer business was not as good as everyone had hoped. The family decided to move to Detroit in search of greater opportunities when Frank was sixteen, but shortly after the move, his father suffered a severe heart attack. Frank had to quit high school and take a job in a manufacturing plant to help support his family. He stayed there for eight years, then became a city bus driver.

Fitzsimmons enjoyed driving but temporarily quit in favor of working at a loading dock for twenty-two cents an hour. He was twenty-seven years old, ambitious, and a hard worker, getting himself promoted to an over-the-road driver traveling throughout the Midwest for the CCC Trucking Company. He also became interested in the Teamsters Union and became a shop steward, the spokesperson for his fellow workers, when he was twenty-nine years old.

Fitzsimmons was six years older than Jimmy Hoffa, yet the younger Hoffa looked upon Frank as a potential assistant on his rise to the top. They met soon after Jimmy had been named president of Local 299. Hoffa was already quite experienced with strikes and political action within the unions. He was job hopping, working his way into power positions that would take him to the top, in sharp contrast to Fitzsimmons.

Hoffa seemed instinctively to sense those qualities in Fitzsimmons which would make him an excellent second in command. Fitzsimmons was heavyset, methodical, and lacking in any desire for power. He was the type who seemed loyal, satisfied to take orders rather than give them. Although Fitzsimmons became the vice president of Local 299, he acted as the "gofer" for Jimmy during various meetings. He went out for coffee and sandwiches, then became nervous about whether or not he got the orders right.

Despite Fitzsimmons's seeming meekness, he was as skilled as Hoffa, the Pressers, and the other leaders of the Teamsters in arranging deals for himself. For example, during the McClellan Committee hearings, Robert Kennedy's staff discovered that Fitzsimmons had been paid seventy-five dollars a week for two years by a Chicago beer distributor for whom he did no work. Fitzsimmons claimed that he was a consultant on union matters. In reality, he had taken a weekly paycheck in exchange for negotiating a contract with the Teamsters that was more favorable to the management than the employees.

In another instance, Fitzsimmons and four other Teamster leaders were indicted in 1953 on charges of extortion. The men arranged for construction firms to pay them fees in exchange for their agreement not to enforce the union contracts. The leaders made money, the companies made money, and the rank and file earned less than was specified for in their contracts. However, when the prosecution started, Hoffa arranged for the four leaders to plead guilty in exchange for Fitzsimmons's not being prosecuted. To ensure the protection of his assistant further, Hoffa had the judge paid twenty-two thousand dollars. To hide the bribe, it was given in the form of a thirteen-week series of television political ads which aired during the judge's reelection campaign.

Hoffa also ordered the prosecutor to lay off Fitzsimmons in the extortion case. He explained that the prosecutor could be framed for a crime if he did not back off. However, if the prosecutor settled for the convictions of the other four men, he might find himself a member of the executive board of Teamsters International.

Obviously Fitzsimmons, though corrupt, was involved with petty activities compared to Hoffa. Again this solidified the relationship between the two men. Fitzsimmons was corrupt enough not to work against Hoffa, yet honest enough not to want to challenge Hoffa's power.

Hoffa was convinced that he would run the Teamsters from jail. He would give orders to his lawyer, William Bufalino, and Bufalino would relay them to Fitzsimmons.

The formal announcement was delayed, but the decision was passed to his friends on March 6, 1966. During a meeting in Baltimore, Hoffa made Robert Holmes president of the Michigan Conference of Teamsters, Dave Johnson head of Detroit Local 299, and Fitzsimmons leader of the International. There would have to be a formalization of the arrangement, but Hoffa knew that his desire would be rubber-stamped.

The Teamsters held their nineteenth annual convention in July 1966. It was the same year that Jackie returned to the labor movement and none of us, other than Bill, was actively involved with the International Brotherhood of Teamsters (IBT) gathering. However, the convention was to prove important because Hoffa arranged for handling his forthcoming prison term. He created the new post of general vice president (Hoffa was general president) and promoted Frank Fitzsimmons to that position. He also arranged for his personal salary to be increased by a third, to $100,000, and for the union to pay the $1.25 million he had spent on his defense. Dues were raised by 20 percent that year so that Hoffa could enjoy the benefits.

(Note: There is now a law that does not allow union dues to be spent for a criminal defense. I don't know if Hoffa violated this law or hid the way the money was allocated so that no one knew he was using it for his lawyers. I personally know of instances where a lawyer's fees were paid by giving a higher salary to a cooperating official of the Teamsters, letting him pay taxes on it, then having him kick it back for the lawyer. Everyone but the members and the government investigators knew what was happening.)

Hoffa surrounded himself with his immediate family the day before he had to go to jail. Barbara Hoffa Crancer, his beloved daughter, flew in from St. Louis to be with him. She was the delight of his life: she had a sociology degree, a Phi Beta Kappa key attesting to her brilliance, and a twenty-thousand-dollar wedding that was an unexpected extravaganza when held in 1964. Hoffa, who wore cheap clothing and avoided the flash that his money and position allowed, had gone all out for the wedding. It was an event that helped law enforcement officers determine where the power connections existed.

The wedding guests included not only Michigan politicians and legal officials but also members of several organized crime families. Johnny Dio was invited but was in prison serving an extortion sentence. However, Tony Jack Giacalone and New Jersey's "Tony Pro" (Anthony Provenzano) attended. The latter two were also among the favored guests invited to a special dinner with the Hoffas and the immediate family of Robert Crancer, his new son-in-law.

Jimmy Hoffa, Jr., was also present. He had recently graduated from the University of Michigan Law School and was working as an intern with the Michigan State Legislature. The three ate breakfast together, Josephine Hoffa sleeping in rather than joining the family. She had suffered a heart attack a few days before and, though home and recovering, was not very well.

Hoffa and his children drove to his Washington office in Jimmy's Pontiac convertible. It was a nice car but not flashy. Dave Beck had been chauffeured to jail. Jimmy, more image-conscious, refused to allow himself such a luxury because he knew that it could lead to a rebellion by the members. He was proud of the fact that he had increased the union by 50 percent almost immediately after he took control—from 1 million to 1.5 million members. He was determined to add another 500,000 before he eventually left the labor movement. (He actually reached approximately 2.2 million members.) Making his life-style radically different from that of the members was not something he wanted to do.

Hoffa's day was spent both getting his affairs in order and meeting with well-wishers who wanted to see him. Harold Gibbons, the vice president, was there, along with Bill and Jackie Presser.

Bill had gone to see Jimmy because he genuinely cared for the man. Bill had himself served eight months in prison a few years earlier when he was convicted for destroying evidence of gifts paid to various politicians and judges. The gifts were sterling silver ice buckets, nothing really big, but indicative of the little ways in which he maintained his influence. When the practice was investigated, he destroyed the list of judges, city and state officials, and others to whom they were given. That list was easily recreated through a subpoena of the shop from which they were purchased. Having served time gave him some understanding of what Jimmy was about to endure.

Jackie was there for a different reason. It was a year after he had returned to the labor movement as the head of his own local. Bill was thinking of grooming

Jackie to take over as a behind-the-scenes broker working with the mob, the politicians, and the Teamsters. Johnny Scalish had to give the okay for Jackie to move into position when Bill moved on, but there was little doubt that he would do so. Thus Bill wanted Jackie to know all the connections around the country, including Hoffa, and also to be aware of where there were safe deposit boxes and other sources of income Jackie would eventually inherit or control.

Others present included Salvatore Provenzano, the brother of "Tony Pro." Tony was in Lewisburg, awaiting Hoffa's arrival the following day. Salvatore was under indictment for allegedly counterfeiting food stamps, though that indictment was dropped. Frank Chavez was also present, along with his lawyer and friend, William E. Bufalino, a stenographer, and others. It was a gathering that showed a wide range of Hoffa acquaintances, special interests, and friends.

Hoffa surrendered to the U.S. marshals on March 7, 1967. He was taken to Pennsylvania's Lewisburg Penitentiary, where he faced the next thirteen years in jail. He was given a job stuffing and repairing bedding. He also lifted weights, took walks in the prison yard, and was determined to mark his time and get out.

The one problem Hoffa faced was that Lewisburg had two rival mob figures running the place. The top man was Carmine Galante, also known as Lillo. Almost equally powerful was Anthony Provenzano, who was serving time until 1970. Tony Pro was an old friend of Hoffa. He had also been a supporter of the Genovese family during a war with the Bonanno family with whom Galante had been allied. Tony Pro and Galante both waited to see where Hoffa would become connected.

Hoffa had little choice. He was a short man, tough, but not so tough as many of the more violent men in Lewisburg. Violence is relatively common and Hoffa recognized that if he chose the wrong side he was going to be a target. Carmine Galante had the power to provide protection from such assault. In addition, he was allied with Santos Trafficante and Carlos Marcello. Tony Pro may have been an old friend, but he could not keep Hoffa safe. Hoffa became allied with Galante for survival, an action that Tony Pro took as an unforgiveable insult.

The year was 1966 and there were any number of unusual circumstances taking place. Fitzsimmons had moved into a power position he would soon assume. Steel hauling truckers were feuding with the Teamsters, forming a dissident group that would eventually stage a wildcat strike that paralyzed the industry. And Jackie Presser decided to get back into the labor movement.

Both Harold Friedman and Jackie were hostile to their fathers in the 1960s. Harold pushed his father, Harvey, out of the bakers' union early in that decade. It was a time when George Meany sent ten or fifteen organizers to Cleveland to start a rival bakers' local in order to block Harvey Friedman. The fight involved two internationals, and Harvey lost 35 percent or more of his membership.

Harold hired me to beat the shit out of one of the rival organizers, but it didn't prevent a loss in the power and income Harvey Friedman had known.

Harold then had me go from shop to shop with him to try and retain bakers for Harvey's union. We weren't allowed to go into the shops, but I had a friend who owned Kaase's Bakery so I arranged to enter that shop to talk with the people.

The owner of Kaase's asked whether Harold would give him a break on the contract if he let me in. I assured him that he would, but when contract talks came about, a year or so later, Harold was trying to give him a rough time. Harold refused to give the man the sweetheart deal so the owner closed his business, opening another bakery later, though under a different name.

Harold just wanted to take all the power he could in the bakers' local, moving his father out. The problem was that with all the fighting and all the losses, the building in which the union was located was too expensive. Because they couldn't pay the mortgage, they were going to lose their lease unless something changed.

Jackie decided to get a Teamsters charter from his father. He would move into the same building as Harold and he wanted Harold and me to work with him. We would be partners, we would make a lot of money, and Harold could stay in the same location.

I didn't want anything to do with Jackie and the labor movement. He hadn't been straight with me when we worked with the hotel and restaurant workers' union. All the deals the Pressers had ever made gave them the best return. And I certainly didn't want to be involved with Harold. He was good at management but he was terrible with everyone who worked for him, a man I used to call Genghis Khan because he had the personality of a violent warlord.

The more Jackie talked, the more I understood what was happening. Harold's bakers' local was in trouble. There was too little money to pay the bills for his building, located on what would become the campus of Cleveland State University. In fact, had we not started a Teamsters Local with Harold, he probably would have gone down as a failure in the labor movement, losing everything because of a lack of cash flow. He offered to give Jackie and me offices and the use of telephones, copy machines, printing equipment, and everything else needed to help with the organizing. We would even be able to have Harold's business agents and stewards so that we could have men in the field working for us at no cost to us.

We needed $25,000 to begin operations. Jackie could come up with $12,500 and Harold would match the money. Then the Teamsters would match whatever we spent organizing. The gift of matching funds from the Teamsters was not dishonest. In order to expand the union membership, the Teamsters had a program of giving anyone who was organizing for them $1 for each dollar that person or local spent. Our $25,000 in seed money would become $50,000 as we spent it.

I thought that Harold's losing his building would be funny. I hated the man and was delighted to see him fail because he couldn't bring in enough members for his union.

I explained to Jackie that I certainly did not want to work under Harold, something I thought would happen since he and Jackie would be financing the local's charter. Harold liked the trappings of power. He enjoyed sending out high-paid business agents to get his shoes repaired or to cut his grass on union time. And if he wanted to eat dinner at eight or nine o'clock at night, he informed eight or nine of the business agents that they were going to eat with him. Later Jackie and I forced him to reduce the number to just two or three, still an imposition for the men.

Most of the men had wives and children. Staying out late with the boss for a dinner that had no connection with business caused stress within their families and angered the men, who didn't want to be separated from their loved ones. But Harold would hear none of that. If you wanted to keep your job, you pleased Harold, and your family be damned. Since the men might have to be at work at seven in the morning, this meant that they often put in fourteen-hour days. They would be home too late to see their children off to bed and up too early to help their children get ready for school. They became strangers to their wives. They were owned by Harold and he reveled in the power.

Even when Harold wanted to reward a man for something he did, the reward would be destructive. For example, after he was active with the Teamsters, Harold would think nothing of flying to California with several leaders for rest and recreation during the winter holidays. The men could not take their families nor even their wives. Resentment would build at home, destroying marriages.

I didn't mind working when I had to work. I didn't mind working around the clock because I had three shifts of workers I had to see. There were times I would get two or three hours' sleep at a time, then go see the men and women on a different shift. I might get the same total number of hours rest that I would have received had I been able to sleep right through the night and I might not. But always my sleep was interrupted so that I could stand at yet another factory gate.

I didn't like this, of course. It was an unnatural way to live. But if that's what it took to organize workers on three shifts, then that was what I did. What I could not stand was Harold's ordering me not only to do a rough job but also to go to dinner with him, to do his chores, and generally to act as a servant. I simply would not get into a new union local where Harold and Jackie were in charge and I had to do their bidding.

Jackie explained that there would be a deal whereby Harold would be president, I would be vice president, and Jackie would be the principal officer: secretary-treasurer. He said that the arrangement would be such that if any one of us said no to something, the other two had to go along with that decision.

I was tired of the idea of being in labor full-time. I was not even certain I liked helping Bill and Jimmy when they needed a favor. I was still hurt about the way I was treated by Jackie and Harold in the past, and about some of the things I had done for Bill that went against what I thought was right.

There was a wildcat strike in Akron, Ohio, for example. There were some Akron Teamster haulers who owned their own "horses"—the cabs that were hitched to trailers for hauling loads. These people were similar to the owner-operators that Jimmy Hoffa had to fight over the years.

I got a call from Bill explaining that there was a problem with the owner-drivers. They weren't going along with Hoffa's contract. They had a wildcat strike going against one large company and the owner needed to move the merchandise out or face financial ruin. An unauthorized picket line had been established and the owner wanted it crushed.

I always said that unions were my religion when I was organizing. I believed in the rank and file. I worked for the rights of women and minorities. I stole a lot, but I tried to better the lot of the members. Yet the truth was that there were times when I had to serve two masters and Bill Presser was the one who dominated.

Bill learned that the Akron strikers were not negotiating as asked and were not willing to go along with their local leadership. This type of thing usually happened when the rank and file had a legitimate grievance, but that did not matter to Bill right then. He was going to stop the strike and I was going to help him.

Bill rallied both Teamsters and men from the Murray Hill area who were willing to act as strikebreakers. These guys were mostly sluggers who enjoyed breaking heads. Then we formed a convoy to Akron, all of us armed with baseball bats, golf clubs, brass knuckles, and other weapons.

As I've said before, I don't believe in Teamsters' fighting Teamsters, but I also never opposed Bill's wishes. It had been many years since Bill was in action, yet he went in the lead car with me, the one that would take the worst of any retaliation when we arrived.

Bill told me not to slow down. We had a caravan and had to break through the line, go through the gate, and drive onto the grounds of the plant. There were more than a dozen rigs waiting to be driven out for delivery, trucks and trailers that had to go regardless of the men on strike. Some of the approximately two hundred guys in our caravan would move the rigs. Others would fight the strikers, sending as many of them to the hospital as necessary. No matter what happened, I was to keep moving. I was to sound my horn and roll into people if that was what it took to break through the line.

It was a violent day. The police were out in force, but they could not keep us separated. Weapons were used, then tossed, before arrests could be made. Both sides saw men going to the hospital, but we got to the rigs and moved them out, just as Bill said he would.

I may have been disgusted by having to hurt our own members, but I also took advantage of the confusion that day. A friend of mine and I each took one of the rigs, separating from the caravan and emptying them of their load. We had television sets and tires that we unloaded and sold, then abandoned the rigs where they would be found undamaged. We made quite a bit of money from selling the merchandise.

No matter how much money I made, that strike soured me a bit. I didn't mind doing special jobs for Bill or Hoffa. It was the idea of going back full-time, especially working with Harold Friedman, that bothered me. Yet in the end, as with everything Jackie ever wanted me to do which his old man supported, I agreed to help them.

Ironically Cleveland State, at this writing, has not exercised its right of eminent domain, although the building is on its grounds. Sources within the university have revealed that there is a fear of a backlash by union members if the building is taken since it now houses both the bakers' local and the Teamster Local 507 that we started. What they do not realize is that the violent image of the Teamsters has nothing to do with a situation such as eminent domain by a university. The union members have always believed in education to better their families' lives. Cleveland State is an inner-city university that is affordable and has an excellent teaching staff. The rank and file can afford the tuition and never feel as though their children will be receiving anything other than a first-rate education. Yet the university's fear prevents the very action Harold hoped for when he returned the members' money.

I told Jackie that Harold would personally have to confirm all that Jackie was promising about the way the union would be run. I wanted to learn more because I knew that Harold had strengths that made him an asset. He was a good office manager, understood contracts, and ran a tight ship.

Harold Friedman came over, whining and carrying on. He reminded me how skilled he was with contract negotiations, and I had to admit that Harold knew more about efficient office management, labor law, and the other technical aspects of a union than anyone I had ever known. He talked about how good an organizer I was and pointed out that Jackie had the Presser name, which was a powerful one in organized labor. I had to admit that he was right.

I finally said that I would only go along if he repeated the arrangements he had made to me to Bill Presser, especially the arrangement that any one of us who said no to an arrangement would have the power to veto it. I also would not work as Harold's errand boy, nor would I be expected to eat dinner with him at whatever time of the night he wanted to go.

Harold was always scared of Bill Presser. He wanted Jackie and me to talk with Bill. I insisted that he go, too. Otherwise there would be no deal. I would simply get the money to open my own auto body and paint shop.

On Monday of the following week the three of us arrived at Bill Presser's office.

"What's going on?" asked Bill.

"Your kid wants to go back into the labor movement," I told him.

"No way!" Bill shouted. "No fuckin' way! I don't want him in the labor movement. You saw what he did with the hotel and restaurant workers." Yet no matter how much Bill yelled and carried on, the truth was that Jackie Presser was the apple of his father's eye, not his other son, Marvin. Conversely, Faye didn't like Jackie but liked Marvin. Marvin could get anything he wanted from Faye. Jackie could get anything from his father.

I said, "Bill, your son wants to go back in the labor movement. Harold's losing his building. We made a deal and if they stick to the deal, I'm willing to give it a shot. I think we can make more money in the union than a $29.95 paint shop. And this way it isn't going to cost you any money. All you're going to do is get us a charter."

"No fucking way, Allen. You go into the paint shop. Let my son run that truck and auto repair shop."

Jackie started arguing. He said that we'd make a good team and have a good local with my organizing and Harold's watching the books. There would be no stealing.

Finally Bill looked at me and said, "Okay, Allen, it's your funeral. Give me a week and I'll get you a charter."

We didn't get a charter right away. First we received the right to organize and I immediately went after a place called Swiss Laboratories, which had eighty people. We needed the names for the charter, so I went into Swiss Laboratories and got signatures from an Indian, a Puerto Rican, some black guys, and others. The names of those men and women went on our first charter, which we received in April or May 1966.

In July of that year, Harold asked for a new charter so he could have different names on it. I really thought that he did it because he didn't like Puerto Ricans and blacks, because he certainly didn't. However, when he changed charters, some of the same names stayed on and I never did find out his motive in making the change.

Everything moved quickly and I brought in the first twenty-eight hundred members for our Local 507. Then, through 1969, I was considered the greatest person in the world. Jackie did no work and didn't even have an office. In fact, when I'd go in and ask where he was, Harold would say, "You mean, the fat boy?" then burst out laughing. Jackie just came in around 11:00 A.M. and left around 2:00 or 3:00 in the afternoon.

Jackie liked to claim he was an organizer who built 507. Yet he did nothing until after I was struck down with a heart attack at the end of 1969. However, in the meantime, much was taking place on a national level with Hoffa, Fitzsimmons, and others.

Jimmy Hoffa's time in jail was turbulent for everyone involved. As Hoffa wrote in his autobiography: "My cell was seven and a half feet wide and ten feet long. My bunk bed was twenty-eight inches wide. There was a chair and a locker twenty-four by twelve inches. That left three and one-half feet to move around."

He also talked about the staff's hostility and its effect on his health. "When they put me away I was a fringe diabetic and had to go to the doctor every two weeks. When I went in, I took along my medicine and a letter from one of the finest doctors in Georgetown Hospital explaining my condition. The first thing they did was tear up the letter and flush the pills down the toilet."

Lewisburg was relatively new, having been built in 1932. However, it was housing 750 more convicts than it was designed to hold, which meant that all facilities were overcrowded. The food was also of poor quality, and, as I realized during my first time in prison, the quality of the food determines the attitude of most of the men.

But Hoffa was different. He had connections. The delivery men to the prison were Teamsters who liked to call out to Hoffa once they knew the location of his cell, his work assignment, and the time he spent in the yard. The warden had only eighteen months to go before retirement and feared any violence that might be initiated by the labor leader. And there were enough mob-connected men drawing sides that Hoffa continued to have protection. Life was difficult compared to that on the outside, though nowhere near the hell it would have been without his position.

Tony Provenzano knew the best that Lewisburg had to offer. He did not have a cell, but rather a room in the "honor unit." This was a section of the prison that were previously used as apartments by bachelor members of the prison staff. He had a bed, not a cot. He had regular doors, a bathroom, and the same dining privileges as the guards.

At first there was a closeness between Tony Pro and Hoffa, which arose from their common problems. Tony even arranged for Hoffa to obtain better food and to learn how to take advantage of the honors unit. Hoffa was angry about his situation and had difficulty adjusting to change. He had emotionally decided to mark time, but he did not realize the tension that isolation, separation from family and friends, and deprivation of privileges to which he had grown accustomed would bring. Were it not for Tony Pro, during this period, Hoffa would have been murdered.

In return, Hoffa's bullying of the prison administration officials saved Tony

Pro's life. Provenzano had power over the lower-level inmates and guards but was not particularly feared by the men at the top. He developed a stomach ailment that almost cost him his life. He had been a big, barrel-chested man. Then his weight had dropped to ninety pounds and the prison officials had refused to do anything to help. Hoffa threatened to expose all the conditions in the prison if Tony Pro were not taken to a hospital outside the prison for surgery. The officials, fearing exposure, complied and the operation saved Provenzano's life.

The break with Tony Provenzano, a break that allegedly led to a murder contract on Hoffa, came for reasons I was never able to learn with certainty. Guys would talk about a fight between the two men, a fight that ended with Tony's allegedly telling Hoffa that he would see to it that Hoffa would never return to the labor movement.

However, the Hoffa family believes that the break with Tony Pro came when Hoffa approved a loan for a restaurant that Provenzano was involved with. The pension fund did not authorize the money despite Hoffa's recommendation and Tony Pro felt betrayed.

Whatever the truth about the break, there were other stories concerning Jimmy during those early months in prison. Most of them concerned his seeming disenchantment with the mob. Whether the rumors were true or not, most people came to believe that Jimmy planned to rid the union of the mob. He was going to take the Teamsters not only to record numbers of members but also to a level where they would be respected. The criminal element would be removed. The leadership would become respectable, working solely for the benefit of the rank and file.

No matter what the real facts were, and so far as can be determined, Jimmy died without revealing the details to anyone. Jimmy was being set up to die. There were power struggles on the outside and a break developing with enough members of the mob that the jail sentence was the beginning of the end for Hoffa.

Local 299 in Detroit experienced the first rebellion. It was actually an outgrowth of a pattern that had been seen around the country, a pattern that had frightened Hoffa before he went to jail.

Jimmy recognized that the leadership of the Teamsters was always vulnerable to the rank and file. A well-organized rebellion could not be stopped. The members could be manipulated and made to feel powerless. They could be cheated in planning contracts, strikes, and other economic issues. Balloting could be rigged during elections. But if they ever truly joined together, Hoffa knew he could do nothing.

Jim Lukens of Cincinnati provided a good example of a successful rebellion. We did everything we could to stop him short of killing the man and he still succeeded, though in a small way, with his Local 98. Earlier, in 1959, Dominic

Abata of Chicago cabdrivers' Local 777 formed a rebel group called the Democratic Union Organizing Committee. Within two years he was able to lead a successful rebellion against Hoffa's leadership.

Even a revolt that failed, involving Philadelphia's Local 107, was a success. The only way Hoffa was able to lure the rank and file away from the rebel leadership was by increasing pension benefits, something he did not want to do. He had to use a similar method to retain control in Detroit, buying Teamsters jackets for each member of his local for a cost of fifty-eight thousand dollars when rebels wanted to attack him while he was being investigated by the Senate. This was still a period when no one much cared about the workers, neither the union bosses nor the employers. A little thing like a jacket was enough to make the membership think that Hoffa personally cared about them. They never thought about the fact that he bought the jackets with money from their own treasury.

The one serious threat to Hoffa came from Larry McHenry and Andy Provenzino (no connection with the Provenzano brothers of New Jersey). McHenry became anti-Hoffa after being fired from his job with a hauling company, Theater Trucking Services, owned by the Fitzsimmons family. Provenzino, a militant union steward working at Merchants Forwarding Company, united with McHenry just after Hoffa was convicted. Both had had run-ins with Hoffa and both had remained militant without directly challenging Hoffa's power. When his power base weakened, they felt that they could make their move. They formed a group called the Teamsters Betterment League (TBL).

The complaints they had were little different from those in other parts of the country at this time. The dissidents did not like the Teamsters' gangster image even though they liked the respect they received as the toughest union in the country. They wanted to elect business agents and stewards; to have a better system for handling grievances, a credit union, greater democracy within the union hierarchy; and to gain better benefits—hospitalization, retirement, and soon—among other economic considerations. The dishonesty within the leadership became their rallying cry.

Provenzino was head of TBL in 1965, McHenry having lost his job and thus his eligibility to run for union office. McHenry was hated by Hoffa, who threatened to ruin the man financially, a threat that had not been carried out by the time new elections took place in 1968.

With Hoffa in jail and Fitzsimmons in charge of the International, Rolland McMaster was placed in charge of Local 299, a power position from which, among other services, he was expected to stop the TBL.

McMaster had been convicted of labor extortion and thus was an excellent target for the TBL. In addition, Provenzino was the ideal man to stand up to him. He had a reputation for being a "good old boy" who liked to drink, fight, and drive trucks. He was the father of seven children, a natural leader, and a man truly dedicated to reform. In addition, he had been injured by a hit-and-run driver who was never caught early in the days of his leadership, a fact that added to his image of toughness.

McHenry, equally dedicated to reform and also a family man (eleven children), had no leadership abilities. He was a loner, withdrawn, poor at communicating. He was extremely stubborn about any issue in which he believed strongly; his detractors said that he was bullheaded regardless of the facts.

Both men were determined to stop McMaster's crusade against corruption. Some of the attacks were direct, using their own union newspaper to fight for issues within the union. Others were more subtle, such as the circulation of a song meant to be sung to the tune of "McNamara's Band":

Oh, my name is Frank Fitzsimmons,
And I'm the leader of this band;
299's my local,
The Most Corrupt One in the Land.
We steal from drivers and warehousemen,
We laugh and have a ball;
And to make it even better,
We do it in their union hall.

Oddly, McHenry's anger was directed toward Hoffa. He was a friend of Richard Fitzsimmons, Frank's son, and he liked Rolland McMaster personally. They had a mutual respect and McHenry claimed that, unlike Hoffa, McMaster always told you where you stood. He might like you or hate you, but he would not lie to you as McHenry felt that Hoffa did.

By 1968, the dissidents had renamed their group Unity Committee 299 and assembled a full slate of candidates for office against the leadership backed by Hoffa and Fitzsimmons. Dave Johnson, whom Hoffa preferred to stay in power in Local 299, had become little more than the financial adviser and bookkeeper for the local. McMaster wanted to consolidate his power over the money to be spent in order to gain as much personal autonomy as possible. Fitzsimmons seemed to back the thinking of McMaster, which put him at odds with the jailed Hoffa.

Jimmy was still running for the presidency, though, from prison. His plan was to take office from jail. Fitzsimmons was running for vice president with the understanding that he would be the acting president. And McMaster was running the local without an election. All these facts seemed to strengthen the rebels' position.

The defeat of the rebels was a foregone conclusion because the voting was rigged enough to assure that everything went the way Hoffa wanted it to go.

There were twenty-five observers: twenty-three Hoffa loyalists and two rebel partisans. There were unexplained power outages during the counting of the ballots and numerous other irregularities, all in favor of Hoffa's people.

The rebel group then tried to show that McMaster was cheating the members. Having lost the election when they used the issue of McMaster's criminal record, they turned to his actions supposedly in behalf of the rank and file.

McMaster had the idea of buying a recreation area for the members of Local 299. City dwellers who were members of the Teamsters could not afford to get away into the Michigan countryside as the wealthier often did during the summer. He told the members that he wanted to buy Saline Valley Farms, a 637-acre property west of Detroit. The land cost $483,788 and would serve as a country place for the members.

McMaster purchased the land using union money, making a deal with a farmer who wanted to work 350 acres of the property. Only 300 acres would actually be given over to the members, a fact of which the members were not informed. In fact, much was concealed from the rank and file when McMaster held a meeting and convinced them to approve his decision to purchase the property. McMaster lied, stating that the land, which he claimed had not yet been purchased, cost $800,000, the difference between the purchase price and the money the local approved going into his own pocket. He also didn't mention the farmer who would be working a portion of the land.

McMaster also had the nerve to charge each member $2.00 a month for the privilege of being taken: $1.50 was for the purchase and $.50 was to cover administrative expenses. When the land was dedicated in 1969, the members saw for the first time that it was swampy and not very good for development. McMaster just explained that the project was still rough, that facilities were being developed for recreation. Everyone was uneasy about what was taking place and Provenzino's group had more criticism for the leadership.

John R. Ferris was appointed administrator for the recreation area. Ferris and McMaster had found black walnut trees on the land, wood that had great value. As preparation for developing the land, Ferris had the woods cleared, selling the timber for a substantial profit. Although Local 299 owned the land and thus the trees, the money allegedly never made its way back into the union treasury. McMaster claimed it did, but Johnson, the man who kept the books, claimed that it was never deposited in any account related to the local.

McMaster was not all bad for the members. He developed "Operation Upgrade," which, among other things, created a credit union, a retiree's organization, a training program for shop stewards, and a Miami, Florida, school for business agents. No one knows how many of these actions were meant to give him personal gain and how many were meant to serve the members so they would not look too closely at his other actions.

The dissidents' timing was poor. The previous year, in 1968, the nation had witnessed unprecedented violence by political protesters. There was violence in the civil rights movement, with some demonstrations turning into brawls. There was violence on the streets of Chicago, where Mayor Daley let the police club and beat men and women who had rallied in order to be heard during the Democratic National Convention, where the 1968 candidates for president and vice-president of the United States were being selected.

Teamsters are generally patriotic. They don't like to see people attack the country. They're uneasy when someone wants to change society, and they may not look all that closely at the issues. Even when they recognize that their leaders are dishonest, they accept that fact as a part of the price they have to pay for getting ahead in life through union negotiations.

McMaster knew all this about the members. He began circulating leaflets pointing out that a small minority of members were trying to manipulate twenty thousand others. Instead of dealing with the corruption, he ignored the attacks and made the attackers seem to be misguided anarchists who wanted their own way at the expense of the members. It was only by siding with the leadership that the members could end the tyranny of the minority. The fact that the rebels wanted to make life better for everyone in the union was an issue that was not discussed.

The members of Unity added a magazine called *Teammate* to their weapons against McMaster. The attacks ranged from satire to carefully investigated pieces relating to the corruption. Oddly, not only did it solidify some of the members into a strong group, it also cost Unity the support of McHenry. McHenry had been a source of information for the Justice Department in its fight against Hoffa. Suddenly he was back with McMaster, declaring the man to be inherently honest and decent, supporting him against the hostility in *Teammate*.

The Unity Committee was gaining enough attention from the rank and file to be an embarrassment. The members were trying to force an injunction against the use of their dues to pay for Saline Valley Farms. Their ridicule of McMaster was impressing some of the members (Example: A full-page advertisement for a "Mister McMister Doll." The ad copy read: "IT WALKS! IT TALKS! TAKE IT HOME, FEED IT MONEY, AND MARVEL AT THE WAY IT PICKS YOUR POCKET, STEALS THE FOOD OFF YOUR TABLE, AND THE CLOTHES OFF YOUR BACK. . . . JUST LIKE THE REAL THING!"). And the Unity Committee idea had spread to Indianapolis and Cleveland. The magazine had to be stopped.

On November 2, 1969, the *Teammate* office was professionally bombed. An explosion shook the office at 12:16 A.M., causing a fire that destroyed most of the interior. The firemen arrived quickly, assumed that the bomb was the only danger, and began fighting the blaze. What they did not realize was that the bomber wanted to be certain that nothing was left. Two explosive devices were used, the second timed to blow twenty minutes after the first. It was also placed in an area where the first explosion would not set it off prematurely. By the time the blast occurred, several firemen were in the nearby area and all of them were severely injured. The bombers were never caught.

The bombing terrified the publisher and editor. They claimed that they would not be intimidated or defeated. They bravely put out one more issue. Then they shut down.

Sunday, November 9, a noon protest rally was ordered by Provenzino. Most of the rank and file stayed home to watch football on television. The few who did show up were greeted by a goon squad and inevitable violence. By the time the bodies were cleared away, McHenry was spotted standing with the goons. Provenzino learned that he had truly lost his former partner in the reform movement.

McHenry, now firmly with McMasters, tried another tactic to stop the Unity Committee 299 he had helped found. He incorporated the name on his own behalf, then ordered Provenzino to stop using it. However, because of the unusual circumstances, the judge refused to go along with a restraining order against Provenzino's group.

During this same period, the rebel steel haulers among the Teamsters had formed the Fraternal Association of Steel Haulers, (FASH). Again there was dissension within the Teamsters with Jimmy Hoffa in jail and Fitzsimmons not firmly in control of anything.

The Teamster locals where FASH groups were active were determined to stop them. And nowhere was this so violent as in Youngstown, Ohio, where John Angelo ran Local 377.

Angelo was the sworn enemy of Mike Boano, the FASH national treasurer. Boano was convinced that Angelo had placed a bomb in his backyard the year before and was determined that his group would not be defeated by the Teamsters.

Boano was president of the Youngstown FASH and had called a strike of his members against the Republic Steel Company. The strike did not concern Republic Steel as such, it was the result of what FASH considered the improper firing of one of its members who worked for Stony Trucking Company, a firm whose primary client was Republic.

Local 377 decided to use the FASH strike of Republic Steel as a way of breaking the dissident union. Boano gathered business agents and sluggers in the same way Bill Presser had in Akron. With guns, bats, and golf clubs they traveled to Republic in a caravan to break heads. They were determined to hurt anyone who was in their way, assuming that a show of force would stop most of the dissidents.

This time the men who were a part of FASH decided to not be intimidated.

They were scared, probably as scared as the rebels in Akron, who mostly avoided challenging us. But Boano had been through too much personally to allow himself to yield to the threats. Although his group was outnumbered two to one, they stood their ground, the men also armed with bats, clubs, and a few handguns.

The Teamsters came prepared for war. Their windshields were covered with wire mesh and they were wearing steel helmets to protect their heads from clubbing. They traveled in a caravan of cars followed by a convoy of trucks whose job it would be to smash through the picket lines. John Angelo was in the lead and the police helped the group travel directly to the area of the plant where the FASH members were waiting. Then the police disappeared.

The confrontation was brutal. Pistols and carbines were fired. A firebomb was hurled into Angelo's car. Rocks were thrown and men fought each other with clubs. Bodies were dropping everywhere, some of the men seriously injured. A Teamster brought out a machine gun, firing into the crowd of strikers before he, in turn, was shot. And when the bullets were gone, the clubs broken, the men went after each other with fists.

The police allowed the battle to continue for half an hour before moving in with tear gas. They arrested FASH members but generally ignored the Teamsters, making individual arrests of the union men later. Surprisingly, only one man was killed and eight seriously wounded, though dozens had to receive hospital treatment. What mattered, though, was that FASH had beaten the Teamster leadership.

Bill Presser took on FASH next. He declared that a member of Teamster Local 377 could not be a member of FASH. The men holding joint membership had to renounce one or the other.

Bill privately was hostile to what had taken place. He disagreed with the decision to fight FASH at Republic Steel, blaming McMaster for the violence. He felt that Hoffa would not have tolerated the handling of the incident in such a manner and knew that the violence had been encouraged by Fitzsimmons as a way of beginning to dissociate himself from Hoffa. To Bill, the incident was a foolish attempt to assert independence from Jimmy.

In 1970, Fitzsimmons and his men negotiated a new Master Contract. The men had expected a $3.00 an hour raise, but in the end got just $1.10. Numerous working conditions, including those that effectively forced owner-operators of rigs to work as much as four or five days around the clock, having time only for naps of a couple of hours each whenever possible during a twenty-four-hour period, were not addressed. In fact, the money and benefits were so much lower than anticipated that some of the men were losing money by comparison with what they had earned under the former agreement.

The hostility triggered a second wildcat strike, this time by the Unity Committee in Detroit that lasted approximately a week and a half, then spread to other cities. Again there was more violence, including the dynamiting of the home of one of the Detroit rebels in an effort to murder his wife and child.

Everyone's power was eroding in the Teamster leadership except for that of Frank Fitzsimmons. Jimmy Hoffa had broken with Tony Provenzano by 1970. Carmine Galante had become extremely close to Hoffa while Bill Bufalino changed his support to Fitzsimmons. Many of the mob leaders on the outside also switched loyalty to Fitzsimmons, recognizing his growing power within the union.

Hoffa recognized which way his support was going during the 1968 presidential election campaign. Hoffa had been a supporter of Richard Nixon behind the scenes. He was counting on Nixon's giving him a pardon in 1969 if Nixon won the 1968 election. Yet the primary way for Hoffa to help Nixon was through the Teamsters, and Fitzsimmons decided to make a power move with the aid of a number of former Hoffa men, including Bill Presser.

Fitzsimmons discovered that he liked the perquisites of being one of the leaders of the Teamsters. He had his own jet plane in which to travel, three homes for his use, and a six-figure salary. On the domestic front he had more benefits and almost as much power as the president of the United States. It was a job he wanted to gain in his own right when elections for president were held in 1971. And this meant that he could not allow Hoffa's release from jail.

The first effort to stop Hoffa's release came with the endorsement of Hubert Humphrey for president. The Teamsters leadership felt that such an endorsement would cause the rank and file to vote overwhelmingly against Nixon, an event that did not occur.

Once Nixon won, strategies had to be changed. Nixon announced that he was going to be a law-and-order president and he appointed John Mitchell as attorney general to carry out this program. Mitchell, who would eventually go to jail, was still considered a tough legal fighter who could not be swayed by special interests.

Bill Presser, recognizing that the Nixon election could only help Hoffa, guided Fitzsimmons in his effort to regain favor with the White House. Fortunately Fitzsimmons was a close friend of John Mitchell, so the labor leader immediately made contact with the attorney general to defuse the tension that existed.

Mitchell had been Nixon's law partner before the election and had more influence on the president than any other adviser. If he felt comfortable with Hoffa's release, that would have been one of Nixon's first acts after being elected to office. But Mitchell agreed to support Fitzsimmons within the White House.

Mitchell was willing to keep Hoffa, a Nixon loyalist, in jail because of the battles taking place within organized crime groups. Jimmy had once been able to walk a tightrope stretched between the mob families of the North and the South. Through his financial clout with pension fund loans, there were few Mafia leaders who would go against him. He offered the best source of risk-free money in the country.

Jail had eroded some of Jimmy's power. Bill Presser, working with the Scalish "family," had moved into a strong position with the pension fund. Fitzsimmons was solidifying his own power base with the guidance of Bill and others. And Jimmy was being criticized both for the way he handled the discovery of his wife's affair and for his inability to maintain his power in jail. He was also being fought by Tony Pro and other East Coast mob figures who felt that they had been betrayed when promised money did not appear.

The hostilities were clearly defined. Hoffa was connected with Carlos Marcello and Santos Trafficante, both of whom had been trying to gain his release. There were also attempts to bribe Ed Partin to change his testimony in order to undermine the government's case against Hoffa. Both men were favorably aided by high contacts, Trafficante never being connected with organized crime when it came to Nixon's "war" on the mob and Marcello having only minor problems. Marcello had been convicted of assaulting an FBI agent in 1967. He was officially to be sentenced to two years in jail when Nixon took office. Intervention came from a number of people in high places who never forgot a man whose money had helped them, including U.S. Supreme Court Justice Hugo Black. Marcello's sentence was reduced to six months in a prison hospital.

Working against the southern mob leaders like Marcello were men such as Provenzano and the Bonnano family in New York. If Hoffa stayed in jail, there was no reason for violence to come to a head. Hoffa was not to be released.

There were payoffs for the mob, however. Allen Dorfman had been placed in control of the Central States Pension Fund as well as being a "special consultant" to that financial resource before Hoffa went to jail. It was understood that he would be neutral in handing out loans for new businesses. All factions of the mob could go to him for money and he would handle their requests impartially. The action appeased both pro- and anti-Hoffa forces within organized crime.

The loans given during the period of 1969–1970 reflect Fitzsimmons's and Allen Dorfman's efforts to solidify support from the special interest groups that could cause problems. Morris Dalitz, a Hoffa ally who had earlier received Teamster loans for his La Costa resort and his Las Vegas casino interests, was given $27 million to expand his California resort. Fitzsimmons and Jackie Presser would eventually be regulars there as well.

Frank Ragano, a Trafficante attorney, received $11 million for a Florida real estate deal. Irving Davidson received approximately $7 million (added to a previous loan of $6.5 million) for a California real estate project. These loans eventually proved scandalous because Ragano was convicted of income tax evasion and Davidson was convicted of bankruptcy fraud in relation to the loans.

Bill Presser and Frank Fitzsimmons were not content to let matters stay as they were, though. Hoffa had been denied a parole during a hearing in October 1970. He was coming up for parole again on March 31, 1971, roughly three months before the Teamster convention where Fitz was running for president. A Hoffa release would mean a Fitzsimmons loss of power. Eleven of the thirteen members of the Teamster executive board were in favor of Hoffa, a strong enough force to stop all opposition.

The U.S. Parole Board is designed to be independent of all political pressure. But it is still not clear whether anyone from the White House applied influence. All that is certain is that the board sent an investigator to Lewisburg the week before the March 31 hearing to learn Hoffa's plans upon release. Hoffa claimed that he would resume his presidency of the Teamsters.

No one knows what happened next. Hoffa had been expected to be released in October of the previous year. He and his family had been assured that they would all share Thanksgiving together. Yet that had not happened, Josephine Hoffa was seriously ill, and the children were anxious to arrange for their father's release.

Both of Hoffa's children went to the parole board and discussed the humanitarian reasons for releasing their father. The investigator reported on Hoffa's plans to return to power. And Hoffa's White House advocate, Murray Chotiner, a lawyer and adviser to the Nixon campaign, privately lobbied with government officials who might be able to influence some of the board members. In the end, nothing worked. The parole board denied parole and members of the Justice Department, speaking off the record, explained that Hoffa should come back when he agreed to abandon his union positions.

Josephine Hoffa continued to decline. Over Easter in 1971 she was admitted to the University of California Medical Center in San Francisco for treatment of her heart problems. Hoffa was granted a four-day humanitarian leave to visit her. He used the time not only to see his wife but also to meet with as many Teamster officials as possible, including Fitzsimmons.

Suddenly Fitzsimmons was a changed man. He had been a nobody within the Teamsters, a man who was given position without authority. He had had a good salary, but he had been a follower, not a leader.

Power changed Fitzsimmons. He was in the presidency, no matter how tenuous his position. Hoffa was in jail, his White House influence eroded. Fitzsimmons, through Bill Presser's urging, had thrown his support to Nixon after previously going along with the Teamster endorsement of Humphrey. By the time Hoffa was up for parole, Fitz was the only major labor leader backing Nixon, reinforcing Mitchell's efforts on his behalf.

Self-assured for the first time, Fitzsimmons asked Hoffa to resign from the Teamster presidency. Such a resignation would result in Fitz's winning the office easily. Then, or so Fitz claimed, a special election would be called once Hoffa was free. Hoffa would be nominated for president and returned to office.

It is impossible to know whether Hoffa realized how dangerous a step his resignation would be. Frank Fitzsimmons was not as bright as Hoffa, nor as skilled at handling the details of the union general presidency. However, Fitzsimmons discovered that he liked power and had a previously unrecognized facility for maintaining it.

Fitz recognized the power he had through his ability to make political contributions with the money the union raised. The Teamsters also spent $2 million a year on lobbying and public communication, including a special interest magazine with a circulation of more than 2 million. He had a vehicle for influencing both union members and politicians that was denied to Hoffa.

The Fitzsimmons management style was also in his favor. There were 742 locals during this period, their representatives gathering every five years to elect three trustees, sixteen vice presidents from designated regions throughout the United States and Canada, a secretary-treasurer, and a general president. There were also five area councils and forty-eight joint councils, each consisting of several area locals. At the lowest level, there were business agents and shop stewards, all of whom were expected to have power.

The size of the International was so great that only an organizational genius could control all aspects of it, the reason for the breakdown in power. Hoffa was the one man who had the brilliance to run everything, exercising such control that it was not unusual for him to be seen taking a telephone call from one of the rank and file with a grievance. The member may have been a "nobody" and the matter minor, yet Hoffa, if he felt the problem needed to be resolved, would then call the employer, no matter how small, and settle the matter.

Fitzsimmons lacked the organizational skill to do what Jimmy did. He had to rely upon the efforts of the various lower-level leaders to accomplish the goals of the union. There could be no more blanket endorsements of the general president's wishes. Board meetings became genuine forums, not rubber stamps.

The change that had occurred enabled Fitzsimmons to be less involved with union activity. Hoffa worked a seven-day week, his main recreation being push-ups when matters were tense. Fitz was an avid golfer who managed to play the game three or four times a week. He kept himself somewhat separate from the rank and file, though not so aloof as Beck had been. As a result, even lower-level leadership was no longer hostile to Hoffa's being out of labor. As much as Jimmy was loved, they knew that they had more freedom, responsibility, and personal power with Fitzsimmons's weaker leadership.

Hoffa did not understand these matters. He was frustrated, angry, bitter, and concerned about family pressures. His wife was ill. His children wanted him out of jail. And though he would have to give up the Teamster presidency, he trusted Fitzsimmons to carry out the plan they had agreed upon. Jimmy went to his cell, took a piece of paper, and wrote: "I agree not to be in organized labor as a [sic] officer." The note was taken to Fitzsimmons by Hoffa's lawyer, Morris Shenker. It was two and a half weeks before the convention where Fitzsimmons would run for president. In the meantime, the board named him as the interim holder of that office.

During this period other events were taking place that would have an impact both on my life and on the Teamsters. Jackie Presser agreed to become an FBI informant, providing the government with information concerning organized crime members within the Teamsters Union and those who worked with the union.

Bill Presser and Frank Fitzsimmons were involved with taking kickbacks from the Central States fund. Millions of dollars were allegedly involved and the IRS was going after Bill. Yet suddenly all charges were dropped. There were no indictments, there were no prosecutions, and Bill did not have to return any money. It has long been my belief that this was why Jackie became an informant, to save his father and, because Bill did not have to return all that he stole, to protect his own inheritance. Yet if this was the reason, it would have happened during the Nixon administration, but the official investigation of Fitzsimmons did not occur until the mid-1970s, long after Presser was working as an informant.

There are some other possibilities based on Nixon's closeness to the Teamsters and the mob figures connected with them. In addition, as greedy as Jackie Presser was, as much as he wanted to take over his father's power position, he worshipped Bill. Jackie would do anything to help his father.

The story about the IRS investigation is credible in general. Criminal prosecution of IRS fraud is handled by the Justice Department. The attorney general decides whether or not to file criminal charges, which, in the case of the stolen millions, would usually be automatic. The IRS recommends, but they do not have the final authority.

Nixon, as president, had control of both the Justice Department and the IRS. He also knew how to manipulate their power to attack his enemies.

For example, there was a mid-western mayor who was extremely aggressive in making changes. He had two goals: power and the good of the community, though not at the expense of his personal fortune.

The Teamsters backed the mayor, who publicly separated himself from the "criminal elements" of the union. He denigrated our attempt to give him money, then walked the Teamster representative to his car, reaching through the window and removing the envelope of cash when his supporters were not looking.

The mayor won the election, supported the Teamsters, and did work for the betterment of the community, where problems of community job loss, racial bias, and poverty were of great concern. He was also an extremely vocal critic of the Nixon administration.

The mayor, who must remain nameless because of the lack of indictments, began to steal money from a program that was meant to help rebuild the inner city. During the researching of this book, a number of law enforcement sources active at the time have come to me and explained, off the record, that the embezzlement reached $1 million. This was given to a legitimate investment broker, who put the money into a variety of real estate deals in the Bahamas.

Time passed and there were rumors that the mayor might run for higher office while Nixon was in the White House. Nixon had already established an "enemies list" comprising politicians, newspaper columnists, and others he felt were against him. The enemies were to be blacklisted wherever possible. He reacted to criticism viciously and vindictively and was determined to stop the mayor.

The mayor's investments should have made him quite rich. The only problem was that his business partner was in a car accident in the Bahamas and died unexpectedly. Fortunately for the mayor, the man's family knew about the deals that had been arranged. Unfortunately for the mayor, there had never been any agreement in writing. When the mayor flew to the Bahamas to arrange for the family to buy out his holdings and provide him with the money, they demanded written proof of the arrangements. He did not have any.

The family of the dead man essentially told the mayor that he had cut his own throat. There were no written records of the investments. The mayor could sue, establishing his claim to the property in question, but proof would also serve for an indictment for stealing the money used in the first place. The standoff was a no-win situation that left the mayor broke and unable to complain.

Somehow the Nixon White House learned of the Bahamian investments and the million-dollar theft. Nixon called the mayor and told him that he, the mayor, was going to stop being a Nixon critic. If the mayor complied, leaving office at the end of his term, then leaving the city immediately afterward so he would not be a continuing political force, the IRS would not be called in. However, if the mayor continued to criticize Nixon or tried to run for another term in office, then the full power of the government would be released against him. He would be charged with income tax evasion on the basis of the stolen million dollars.

The mayor understood that shutting up was in his best interest. He agreed to the terms, leaving the city without even personal funds. He also vowed not to return until the statute of limitations for his crime was over and he could not be prosecuted, regardless of who was in power in the White House. In addition, he became a Nixon supporter, quite vocal in public despite his personal hostility.

Yet Nixon was equally generous with his friends. Bill Presser and Frank Fitzsimmons were major supporters of the president. There was as yet no Watergate, no public awareness of improper taping, theft, and other criminal acts by the Nixon administration. It is doubtful that Nixon and Mitchell would have allowed either Bill or Fitz to take a fall for any actions that might be investigated during the early years of his first term in office.

Jackie's actions may also have been attempts to win favor with Bill and Fitz. It is possible that he agreed to serve as an informant to help solidify Nixon's refusal to let Hoffa, the former supporter, back into the labor movement. Whatever the case, Jackie began betraying everyone with whom he worked from that time forward.

In late June, after Hoffa resigned and Fitz had been elected interim president, Nixon paid a visit to him and the other members of the Teamsters' executive board. The board was meeting in the Key Biscayne area, the same location as the winter White House where Nixon was staying. Nixon deliberately went to Fitz to offer his congratulations and to explain that his door would always be open to President Fitzsimmons.

As I said earlier, we don't need to corrupt people: They come to us. Here was the president of the United States—a man who had been given under-the-table money by the mob back in 1960, a man caught in the cross fire of money and politics that resulted from the jailing of Hoffa—seeking out Frank Fitzsimmons. He was paying homage to Fitz in the same way Jimmy Hoffa had with Bill. It was a subtle action, but it established the hierarchy of power.

Chuck Colson, Nixon's special counsel for labor affairs, was also alleged to be behind many of the actions taken to keep Hoffa in jail, though this is subject to question. John Mitchell appears to have been the driving force, acting both with and without Colson's involvement.

Murray Chotiner was Hoffa's primary supporter within the Nixon circle of friends and advisers. He pointed out that despite corruption and despite the strength Fitzsimmons had gained, Hoffa was still beloved by the rank and file. Typical of the power that Hoffa retained was a petition Senator Norris Cotton of New Hampshire took to Washington. The petition, requesting that Hoffa be freed, was signed by 250,000 Teamsters. The names appeared genuine.

There were also power plays taking place within the lower level of the Teamsters. David Johnson, the president of Detroit Local 299, agreed to let Hoffa become his assistant after his release. However, Richard Fitzsimmons was vice president of the local and learned what was happening.

Frank Fitzsimmons realized that he had to change his strategy. There were too many people clamoring for Hoffa's release to be ignored. It was decided to arrange for Hoffa's release with conditions that would prevent him from returning to union activities.

There have been various rumors and allegations concerning who did what in planning the release of Hoffa. One story has Fitz's calling Chuck Colson and orchestrating the release solely on the condition that he would not seek office or be involved with the labor movement in any way.

Colson denied the story when it first began circulating. However, when the Teamsters fired one of their lawyers, Edward Bennett Williams, who was on a $100,000 a year retainer, Colson was hired in his place. Williams had sued Nixon's Committee to Re-elect the President (CREEP) on behalf of the Democratic National Committee as a result of the Watergate break-in. The settlement was for a half million dollars.

Williams had worked for the Teamsters for sixteen years. Firing him was a way for Fitzsimmons to show his loyalty to Nixon. It also proved to be a way to reward Nixon's people for helping Fitz. That was the reason Colson got the job.

The Teamsters' convention in July saw the start of a number of important changes. Roy Williams and Joe Morgan were named to the position of vice president after pressure was brought by Santos Trafficante and Carlos Marcello. Salvatore Provenzano replaced his brother, Tony Pro. And a resolution carefully worded to allow the executive board to destroy the power of the dissident owner-operators was passed.

A new group of dissidents evolved after the elections: Teamsters United Rank-and-File (TURF). The TURF group included many of the former dissidents, including the Unity Committee organizations.

TURF campaigned for a number of causes. They tried to prevent Hoffa from receiving a $1.7 million lump sum pension on the grounds that such a pension could then be claimed by other leaders and bankrupt the union. They also investigated the Central States Pension Fund loans and learned the truth about what was then a $917.9 million holding. Whereas normally in a pension fund only 5 percent of the money should be committed to real estate, in the Central States fund 89 percent was committed, and more than 36 percent of those loans were in default. Even worse, many of the others were not properly secured. On July 22, 1975, *The Wall Street Journal* ran an article by Jon Kwitny which stated, in part:

> Through such loans . . . the fund has passed millions of dollars to companies identified with Mafia members and their cronies. It has also lent millions of dollars to employers of teamsters; and according to . . . rank-and-file teamsters, the union has sometimes deserted members' interests in favor of the employer-borrowers.

The trouble with TURF was that increasingly nobody cared. The Teamsters had long ago come to accept the fact that the union was corrupt. Most of the members lived from paycheck to paycheck, their only concern being to try and get a little bit ahead with each new contract negotiation.

There were also scandals within the TURF leadership. One extremely vocal member resigned from his position after pleading guilty to stealing ninety-eight bars of nickel from interstate shipments in June 1971. Then he took a job with Bill, who most people knew to be connected with the corruption within the Teamsters leadership.

On December 23, 1971, Nixon could put off the pardon of Hoffa no longer. He wanted to use the incident as a humanitarian gesture that would impress the Hoffa supporters among the rank and file. He also paid off Fitzsimmons by declaring that Hoffa would not be allowed to lead a labor union in any capacity until March 6, 1980. The penalty for not obeying the restriction would be a return to jail.

The official wording of the pardon did not detail the condition that Hoffa not return to union activity. The parole board personnel also were not aware of such a restriction. They did not realize that Nixon was going to make an end run around the board by commuting Hoffa's sentences to six and a half years, then barring him from the labor movement until 1980 as the condition of that commutation.

Hoffa was shocked. Had he chosen to stay in jail until the likely release date based on his original sentence and time off for good behavior, he would have been out without conditions in 1974. All he had to do was mark time and he could have had everything again. Instead, he went for a deal that seemed strong on the surface, only to discover that he had been tricked when he was released.

The restrictions shattered Jimmy. Everyone was working against him. Attorney General Richard Kleindienst warned Hoffa that to go too far in fighting his situation would result in immediate jailing. Kleindienst was a regular golfing partner of Frank Fitzsimmons.

By 1972, deals within the Nixon administration were becoming public knowledge. On May 28, 1972, the Seattle, Washington, *Post Intelligencer* broke the story that Dave Beck was excused from paying the $1.3 million in back taxes he owed in exchange for his support of Nixon's economic and military policies. John B. Connally, the secretary of the Treasury, was alleged to have negotiated the deal.

There were other stories of mob contributions, none of which could be proved for that year. However, Fitzsimmons and his friends contributed large sums of money to the Nixon reelection campaign ($4,000 from Fitz alone, with other contributions from men such as Salvatore Provenzano). Allen Dorfman was alleged to have been the conduit for contributions totaling the high six figures at least, though others claimed the money was something less than $100,000 in all.

At the same time, Fitzsimmons was using his close contact with the White House to attack mutual enemies. He would alert White House officials to problems with any Hoffa loyalist Teamster official who was also hostile to Nixon. One such alert was against Harold Gibbons, who was a supporter of George McGovern, the Democratic opponent of Nixon. Fitzsimmons sent a memo alerting the government to check Gibbons's income tax returns for irregularity.

While all this was taking place, Bill and Jackie Presser were becoming even fatter and richer from their positions as Fitzsimmons supporters. In 1975, the U.S. Department of Labor decided to investigate Bill Presser's earnings. They found that he held five jobs, each of which should have been considered full-time employment. Jackie held an equal number of union positions, then added two more.

The Pressers were taking advantage of a program Jimmy Hoffa had caused. Hoffa believed in rewarding himself and his loyal followers in whatever way would be appropriate. He had set the precedent for raising salaries and expenses that others would follow.

Bill's income in 1975 was typical of what the men at the top enjoyed. He earned $10,800 as president of Cleveland Local 555. He was also president of Cleveland Joint Council 41, which added $72,659 to his annual take. Then he was president of the Ohio Conference of Teamsters ($45,296) and an International vice president and general organizer ($38,484). He had also been a trustee of the Central States Pension Fund the previous year ($28,930 for three months of work), though that job ended because of the Pension Reform Act of 1974.

The salaries were not the only benefits. The union was so concerned about Bill's health that he was authorized to take Faye, secretaries, and aides of his choosing and travel anywhere in the world for "periodic rest." He was also allowed to travel anywhere in the United States for rest or business, all travel, apartment or hotel accommodations, gas, car expenses, utilities, entertainment, and anything else that came out of pocket being covered by the union. For Bill, this usually meant his condominium in Florida, which the Teamsters obviously supported.

Jackie earned more than his father that same year, though he had fewer benefits. His salaries from the Teamsters totaled $193,749.

Oddly, Harold Friedman managed to draw even more money than Jackie or Bill. Harold earned $115,982 from his bakers' local and $117,432 as president of Local 507. The difference was that Harold lived within his income. Jackie and Bill believed in stealing whatever they could from wherever they could. Harold's attitude was that you should be honest but arrange for the biggest income you could take from each union job you were allowed to hold.

All of the money came from rules and regulations Hoffa created when he was still in power. Yet Bill's gratitude left much to be desired. During a dinner in his honor after he had switched allegiance, Hoffa was described as being "just a bum not worth writing about."

During this same period, the other Teamster vice presidents all earned multiple incomes with the exception of Harold Gibbons. He was not permitted to hold extra jobs because he remained loyal to Jimmy.

The money that was coming into the Teamsters at that time provided other benefits. Dues totaled $51 million that year, along with the money from investments. Of that money $5.8 million was set aside for what was listed on the books as "organizing." In reality, much of it could be spent in any way necessary, from buying muscle to paying bribes.

On June 16, 1974, the Cleveland *Plain Dealer* showed just how far Bill Presser had come in his support for Fitzsimmons. During a testimonial dinner in Bill's honor, Bill stated of Fitz: "Wherever he goes, I'll be one step behind him. No matter who runs against him."

Hoffa struck back at the disloyalty. He claimed that Fitz was seeing a psychiatrist, the reason he was making crazy statements about the man who had taught him the union business. And *Overdrive* magazine conducted a poll of the rank and file which found that 83 percent would support Hoffa's return to power.

Nixon was the next concern. The investigation into the Watergate break-in and the discovery of Nixon's privately made tapes of all conversations were rapidly creating a situation in which impeachment of the president seemed likely. Hoffa decided to play both sides against each other in order to assure his power.

Publicly Hoffa supported Nixon at a time when few others bothered. He called the Watergate affair a "second-rate burglary" and declared that the case was being blown out of proportion. Yet privately he was delighted with the way the courts were going against Nixon.

Gerald Ford, the man who would move into the presidency if Nixon stepped down, was from Michigan. Hoffa had known him, felt close to him, and figured that Ford would help him return to union activity.

There were other scandals taking place during this period, scandals that would not be investigated. Nixon had had underworld connections for many years. One of these was Santos Trafficante, who was also believed to be involved with the theft of millions of dollars from funding meant for overseas service clubs. Government agents had quietly begun investigating not only Trafficante but also the man they felt was receiving some of the money in the form of kickbacks. That man was President Richard Nixon. However, the investigation was dropped after he resigned from office on August 9, 1974, and was given a blanket pardon for past crimes by President Gerald Ford.

Hoffa was concerned about major changes in the unions. He looked to Local 299 for a power base, but Richard Fitzsimmons was going to challenge him in any fight for the presidency. He was also at odds with the Mafia figures who had supported him in the past.

Perhaps the major danger to Hoffa was from Anthony Provenzano. Tony Pro was considered the deadliest man in the Teamsters Union. For many years, the Provenzano brothers had ruled New Jersey Local 560, one of the biggest locals in the country. They were considered good leaders, but they were also violent. Anyone who criticized Tony Pro would get beaten. In the extreme, the man would die.

For example, Anthony Castellito was the Local 560 secretary-treasurer in 1961. He decided to run against Tony Pro for president and was a threat either because he had enough potential votes to win or because it was necessary to make an example of anyone who dared challenge Tony Pro. Whatever the case, Castellito disappeared in 1961. It was not until 1976 that Tony Pro and Salvatore Briguglio were indicted for the murder. Provenzano was accused of ordering the death and Briguglio of carrying it out.

Apparently it was thought that Tony Pro could beat the rap if he did not have to contend with Briguglio. Or perhaps someone just assumed that. Whatever the situation, twenty-two months after the arrest, Briguglio was standing outside a New York restaurant when two men approached him. They knocked him to the ground, then fired five shots into his head and one into his chest. Despite one less witness, Tony Pro was sentenced to life in jail.

Many in the union were relieved when Tony Pro was convicted. It had always been dangerous to run against him. George Phillips took Tony on in an election in 1962, then was beaten with a claw hammer. A year later, while campaigning against Tony Pro, William Glockner was killed. That he had planned to testify against Tony Pro in an extortion trial added to the suspicion that the murder had been ordered.

Tony Pro was a free man when Hoffa was making his move and a definite physical threat. Bill Presser was another one, though Bill would not have attacked Hoffa.

Bill had hoped to retire from union activity in 1974. He wanted to name Jackie to the head of Joint Council 41, but John Scalish said no. The Mafia didn't want Jackie in power then. Scalish's brother-in-law explained to Bill that he would not be retiring until the boys on the hill gave word that he would be retiring. And at that time Jackie still would not take over, Sam Busaca, Babe Triscaro's son-in-law, would replace him. Bill agreed with his orders. This confirmed that the Cleveland mob and the people to whom they answered were against Hoffa. However, Sam's Local 436 proved to be the only one in town that had stickers demanding that Hoffa be released. They also spent a lot of money trying to get Hoffa out of jail.

Fitzsimmons had Bill Presser in his corner for several years. Suddenly Tony Pro was courting him as well. Then Detroit's Tony Giacalone and Tony Milano, Jerry Catena of New Jersey, and New York's Tony Corallo, all former friends of Hoffa, turned against him.

There was also high government support for Fitzsimmons and his friends. For example, in 1973, the government had discovered a Mafia plan to establish a prepaid medical program that would be financed by the Teamster welfare funds. This was actually a scam to steal millions off the top. Involved in the setup were, allegedly, such men as Fitz, Peter Milano, Tony's son, and members of the old Capone gang in Chicago. Allegedly the details were to be developed with Allen Dorfman, who would shortly go to jail for extortion related to one of the recipients of a pension fund loan. The investigation was dropped on the grounds that there was no probable cause to continue it, a statement of which most Justice Department officials were skeptical.

Then there was the case of a recorded bribe related to Miami Local 390. Despite the recording proving the allegation, the case never went anywhere.

Bill Presser solidified his position during this period. He took over for Allen Dorfman as the man to see when you wanted a pension fund loan after Dorfman's 1973 imprisonment. This was a perfect position for obtaining kickbacks and other "benefits."

Bill also helped major mob figures earn extra money. A year before he took primary control of the pension fund, Bill arranged for Tony Liberatori to become the public relations consultant for Fitzsimmons. The primary work experience Liberatori had had during the previous twenty years was not in public relations but in prison. That was the term he had served as the result of killing two Cleveland police officers.

Liberatori gave work to his friends as well. Harry Haler (aka Harry Helfgot) was contacted and arranged for Duke Hoover to have the job. Hoover, a former disk jockey, was provided with a contract worth a gross of approximately $1.3 million, at which time he formed his own company, Hoover-Gorin. Over the next twenty months, more than a third of the money was returned to Harry Haler in the form of commissions and consultant fees.

Hoffa must have known that he was finished. Politicians who had previously been friends began to shy away from him. He had nothing more to offer them, and Fitz was constantly sending his people to see them, reminding them who controlled money and votes. The president of the United States occasionally invited Fitz to travel on Air Force One.

Hoffa knew that the rank and file loved him. He inspired loyalty. He gave the impression of being incorruptible and caring only for the underdog. He was a man who did just enough good to be seen as far better than those who had gone before. And even when he was dishonest, he got the workingman a better deal than had been experienced in the past. The leaders may not have liked Hoffa, but the workers adored him and would have welcomed him back into the union.

Hoffa's obstinacy, the changing power positions in the Teamsters and the mob, and other factors all contributed to the decision to kill Jimmy.

The issue of who killed Jimmy Hoffa is not a particularly important one. His death did not alter union history as many people would like to think. The balance of power had already shifted away from him, though his influence remained strong.

I have my own theories, of course. But I was never involved with a planned hit, nor was Bill Presser, so far as I know. There have even been those who take credit for it in ways that seem quite probable.

The standard theory is that Tony Pro was behind the murder. Tony Pro had a history of violence, was active in union politics, and was feuding with Hoffa. It is also thought that Chuckie O'Brien, a man who was like a son to the Hoffas and whose mother was Hoffa's girlfriend for a while, was involved with a setup. Yet there is also the story told by Tony "Dope" Delsanter to Jimmy "the Weasel" Fratianno and related by Ovid Demaris in *The Last Mafioso:*

> Forget that bullshit in the newspapers about Tony Pro or Chuckie O'Brien or Russ Bufalino. Detroit don't need no outside help to clip their own fucking guy. They owned this Hoffa. Period. Tony Giacalone was in tight with Hoffa and he's the one that set him up. Tony Zerilli and Mike Polizzi gave the order and that was all she wrote.

There was a connection between Chuckie O'Brien and Anthony "Tony Jack" Giacalone. Chuckie played with Tony Jack's son, Joey, when the two were growing up. In addition, Sylvia Paris was Tony Giacalone's mistress from the time her husband died until her own death in 1970.

Whatever happened, the known facts begin in July 30, 1975, when Hoffa had scheduled a meeting with Tony Provenzano and Jack Giacalone. He was in the midst of a court case that might help him return to union work despite the conditional pardon he had received.

Hoffa was staying in his summer home in Lake Orion, working on his property until close to noon that morning. Then he changed into a pullover knit blue shirt and knit slacks, telling Josephine that he was going to meet with Tony Jack and a "couple of other guys." He had met with Giacalone the week before to talk about the mobster's forthcoming trial for tax evasion so there was nothing unusual about what was happening.

Hoffa stopped off in Pontiac, Michigan, to see Louis Linteau. The two were friends and business partners. Linteau headed a Teamsters local in Pontiac until he was convicted of extorting a bribe from an employer. Hoffa had kept him in the Teamsters after Linteau got out of jail, then had secretly gone into partnership with him to create a limousine service. It was Linteau who had arranged for Giacalone to meet with Hoffa at Giacalone's urging. But Linteau was not expecting Hoffa to stop by on his way to the Machus Red Fox Restaurant, and the employees explained that he was not in.

Hoffa talked freely at the limousine service. He explained that he was going to meet with Tony Jack, Tony Pro, and someone the employees could only identify as "Lenny." Later investigators decided that it was probably Lenny Schultz, another convicted extortionist who was involved with the unions as a labor consultant.

The problem with the meeting was that nobody came. Hoffa called home at 2:30 P.M. to find out whether anyone had called. An hour later he called Linteau to learn what was happening. So far as anyone knows, he was never seen away from the area of the restaurant again.

Chuckie O'Brien has always been a prime suspect, at least in setting up Hoffa. O'Brien was probably the most trusted person around Hoffa. Chuckie was often considered closer to Hoffa than his own son, Jim, Jr. He became a business agent for Local 299 when he turned seventeen and told Jimmy that he was tired of school. He acted as a bodyguard for Hoffa, a troubleshooter, and a companion. They were so close that there was speculation that O'Brien was actually an illegitimate child, though that was never determined.

When Hoffa went to prison, O'Brien was a regular visitor. He was also likely to be the person who drove Josephine Hoffa for visits. In addition, Hoffa named Chuckie to the position of general organizer with the International. He received twenty thousand dollars per year in pay, unlimited expenses, and a pension program that could make him quite rich. In addition, O'Brien maintained his position with Local 299.

O'Brien was always an inside man. When there was an attempt to bribe various Louisiana officials to stop Ed Partin, Chuckie was allegedly the man who passed out more than $1 million.

By the time of Hoffa's murder, O'Brien was no longer quite so beloved as he had been. He was more interested in money than serving Hoffa. There were stories that when given money to buy kitchen hardware for the Hoffas' summer home, he pocketed the cash instead. Another time O'Brien took the Detroit Red Wings' hockey team to dinner at a cost of a thousand dollars, then charged the bill to Local 299. The local refused to pay, but Hoffa covered the cost. Hoffa also protected O'Brien from prosecution for both bad checks and failure to pay alimony and child support payments.

After Hoffa's murder, trained dogs were used to check O'Brien's borrowed maroon Mercury automobile for any sign of Hoffa. The dogs were owned by the FBI and had a reputation for never missing a scent. They indicated that Hoffa had been in both the backseat and the trunk of the car, though there was no way of knowing when. This information coincided with a businessman witness who claimed to have seen Hoffa and three other men leave the Machus Red Fox Restaurant parking lot in a maroon car. Hoffa, in back, seemed to have his hands bound behind him. The driver was identified as O'Brien, though the witness had to be shown photographs before identifying Chuckie. That ID was not considered credible enough for a court case.

Shortly after Hoffa's disappearance, O'Brien tried to create an alibi for Tony Giacalone with a reporter friend of his. He discussed places Tony Jack had been but changed his statements later. He did not mention that the car he had borrowed belonged to Giacalone and that Hoffa had noted on his calendar that he had an appointment with "T.J."

During a grand jury investigation of Giacalone concerning the day of the murder, he had a perfect alibi. Literally every minute was accounted for by credible witnesses who knew his precise time of arrival and exact moment of departure. Some were people whose services he had used for years. Others were strangers who still managed to give precise times for his coming and going.

During the investigation into the murder, the Newark, New Jersey, FBI office received a call from the New Jersey State Prison indicating that an inmate wanted to provide information concerning Hoffa's murder. Ralph "Little Ralph" Picardo (aka Ralph Birche) claimed that Hoffa was abducted and killed by Salvatore and Gabriel Briguglio and Thomas Andretta, the brother of Steve Andretta, business agent for Tony Provenzano's Local 560.

Sal Briguglio first entered labor as secretary-treasurer of Local 560. He had a conviction record for counterfeiting food and postage stamps (and may have taken the fall for Salvatore Provenzano, who was under indictment for the same crime until Sal's confession), robbery, and extortion. He also had a reputation for violence.

Gabriel Briguglio headed Teamster Local 84. At the time of the investigation, Local 84 was believed to be a phony local, set up strictly as a way of handling drivers for sweetheart deals in which the men were paid less money than the national master contract demanded. He also had taken a fall for counterfeiting.

Thomas Andretta was the driver for Sal Briguglio and a hanger-on at Local 560. He had what was apparently a phony paper trucking business, because, at the time of the Hoffa murder, investigators found that he had no trucks and did no carting. There were allegations that his business was a front for receiving bribes and payments from loan-sharking.

Picardo was of questionable credibility because he had been in jail since May

1975. However, he had been involved with rackets at Local 560, kept in contact with friends there, and was the man responsible for handling kickbacks and "commissions" from carefully placed pension fund loans.

Picardo had proved an accurate informant concerning other crimes including an interstate stolen truck business and providing loan shark records. When the men he fingered for Hoffa's murder were brought before a grand jury, they all took the Fifth Amendment. However, after being given immunity from prosecution and serving sixty-three days in jail for contempt of court, Steve Andretta finally said that he spent the day at the union hall, playing cards with his brother, Tony Pro, and the Briguglio brothers.

Further indication of Tony Pro's involvement was the similarity between the Hoffa disappearance and that of Anthony Castellito, the man Tony Pro had killed back in 1961. The Castellito death had involved Sal Briguglio, along with a man named Harold "K.O." Kongsberg. Yet all the allegations were meaningless. The killers may be known. The statements made by the mob may be correct. But no one has ever been successfully prosecuted for the murder as of this writing.

There is no question that Tony Provenzano's motive was probably the strongest. Hoffa was insisting upon all locals' following the National Master Freight Agreement. Tony Pro, however, developed a way of getting kickbacks by arranging for companies relying heavily on large volumes of trucking services to get around it. Instead of having their own trucks and drivers, they would use labor leasing companies. These would work for a set fee, hiring drivers for far less money than required by the Teamsters contract. This meant that union drivers were put out of work by the leader of one of the locals that should have been looking after their interests.

Hoffa had vowed to end sweetheart deals. This seemed a publicity stunt in his fight against Fitzsimmons to many in the mob. What seemed more likely was that Hoffa would simply ask to be cut in for a piece of the action. Should that occur, profits would be down for everyone else, a situation that no one wanted.

There was other pressure as well. Just before the murder, the court of appeals that was hearing Hoffa's request to return to union activity seemed likely to agree to let him go back to work. In addition, a memo had been prepared for Attorney General Edward Levi by Justice Department lawyers concerning the restrictions. That memo would have indicated that the restrictions on Hoffa were probably unconstitutional and should be dropped.

In addition, there was the threat that Hoffa would run someone in his place. His son or another man, obviously meant to serve as a spokesperson for Hoffa, could be elected easily by the rank and file.

Whatever the details, Giacalone and Provenzano remain the primary suspects in the murder of Hoffa. The death scenario has Hoffa arriving at the restaurant at two, being picked up, forced into the backseat by one of his murderers, being knocked unconscious, then strangled or shot. He was eventually placed in an incinerator to be certain that no positive evidence would ever be found.

What none of us realized was that the death of Hoffa was only one major change in the Teamsters. Jackie was an informant for the FBI along with a number of other top Teamsters. And in Cleveland, a mob war would soon mark the beginning of the end for not only the Teamsters as union independent of the AFL/CIO, but also the older leaders of the Mafia.

7

The Beginning of the End

WHILE JIMMY HOFFA was fighting for his future and his life, union leadership was going too far. The 1960s was perhaps the strongest period in history for labor unions and also the time when their power, the corruption at the top, and other factors were coming together to reduce their membership and influence.

I have been too dedicated a labor man not to recognize that the bosses started the problems. When I was organizing for Local 507, I still ran into businesses where underpaid workers had to endure sweatshop conditions. There were often inadequate heat and ventilation in warehouse operations, unsanitary toilet areas, unsafe equipment, often with whatever safety devices existed rigged so they would not work, among other problems. The employees felt helpless and never had enough money put aside so that they could quit and look for work elsewhere.

Harold Friedman was always hostile to the workers. He used to say that if a Teamster didn't like what was happening, he could vote with his feet. He meant that the worker could go elsewhere, get a different job: that he did not have to be involved with the same boss or union.

Harold's attitude—common among the bosses—was unrealistic. The average workers of the 1960s earned more money than at any other time. They received medical benefits, unheard of in the past. Yet they remembered hard times and feared the loss of their jobs. They would not go elsewhere because they were frightened of losing all they had gained.

Non-union businesses, often a throwback to the past, were often hard to unionize. Some places paid their workers so little, they could not afford to lose even a day's pay.

The places that were hard to unionize were not the ones with the best pay and benefits program. Even where the workers were treated fairly, being able to get a little money ahead each year, there was hostility toward the boss if they had no contact with the man who owned the place. Instead, it was the shops where the boss was friendly, visible, accessible to everyone where the workers were hesitant to organize.

Sometimes it was a little thing such as the boss's walking the shop floor each day, talking with the workers, encouraging them, letting them know that they were appreciated. Or the boss might buy doughnuts and coffee for everyone. Or there might be a Christmas party where inexpensive gifts or small bonuses were given to the workers. All that was required was anything that seemed to indicate an appreciation of the efforts of the staff who helped the company succeed.

That the time on the floor might be minimal compared with the rest of the day when the boss was holed up in his office did not matter. The workers did not compare the cost of the gifts and bonuses with the price of increasing wages and/or benefits. The boss became loved, seeming to care for his workers, and they were reluctant to cause trouble by joining a union.

Since the bosses did not treat the workers fairly at most places, it was easy to make workers enthusiastic about unionizing. What they did not realize was all the games that we were playing, some of which cost them money or jobs.

I've already explained that we frequently organized places without the consent of an adequate number of workers. If we could fake the pledge cards and force the boss to sign a letter of intent, we'd do it. But there were more things that we did.

By the end of the sixties both strikes and contracts were often carefully planned in advance. Sometimes strikes were arranged with the bosses as a way of balancing the books at the end of the year or as a way of forcing the workers to accept a contract. The contracts were usually set in advance of presenting them to the workers.

For example, we would meet with the bosses and work out a contract so that the workers received a "one dollar twenty-cents an hour" raise over three years. (Remember that this was the 1960s, when wages were much lower than they are today.) They would get an extra forty cents an hour immediately, forty cents an hour a year and a day later, and forty cents an hour more at two years and a day following the time the contract went into effect. There might be other benefits, such as insurance or extra days off, as well.

Next I would go to the members who thought that we were in the process of starting negotiations for their new contract. We would not tell them that a contract had already been written. Then we would lie to them.

I might start off attacking the employer. "That damned boss wants to give you only a twenty cents an hour raise over each of the next three years," I would tell them. "And that SOB wants to take away two of the holiday days we won for the last contract." I would work the members up until they were hot for blood.

"I'm not going to stand for that and I don't think you should either. I want to fight him. I want him to know that you're going to strike if he can't do better than that. I want your support to really stick it to him!" The speech would vary with the group and the specifics, but that would be the general attitude I would use with the workers. I wanted them angry, backing me and thinking about a contract that was not so good as they hoped.

This negative thinking worked great. They were so angry with the boss, so certain that they were not going to be treated fairly, that they would back anything I suggested.

Then I'd give them the impression that I was going back to take on the boss. By the time I returned with the contract I had negotiated in the first place, one that had better terms than I told them about, I was a hero. I had stood up to their boss on their behalf. I had shot down his efforts to prevent them from getting ahead. And I had won concessions from him that he had not planned to give. Or so they believed.

Many strikes are meant to help the boss force a contract down the throats of the workers, even though they think that they are in control. For example, suppose a contract is worked out and the money involved is all the boss can spare with his profit/loss picture. Or, with Jackie in control, suppose a sweetheart contract has been developed with the understanding that we will get a kickback. Whatever the case, the contract must be accepted by the workers or we have a problem. The trouble is that the workers want more and are unwilling to budge. In such a circumstance we would arrange for a strike to hurt the workers.

Strikes are never very good for anyone. I used to have a chart that showed how many days you could be on strike before the wages lost during the strike were greater than the money that would be earned during the life of the contract. A strike of a day or two might be all right. A strike of a couple of weeks could cost the workers more money than they would gain from their raises over the next three years. A long strike might result in the workers' coming out behind for several years.

More important is the fact that workers cannot afford to be on strike at all. They are living from paycheck to paycheck, and most locals do not have adequate strike benefits to cover the money they're losing. When I had legitimate strikes, I'd try to get my workers welfare, food stamps, or whatever other government services I could. But the strikes that were set up to force a contract acceptance would entail as little assistance as possible.

Jackie or Harold would go to the employer and explain that I was having trouble getting the workers to accept the contract we agreed upon. I would ask the employer whether he could handle a strike of a week or two without any problems. Often there were enough items warehoused or already shipped that the strike would not cause any problems so long as it did not last very long. In many cases the strike would provide benefits for the boss because he would not be paying wages, pension fund contributions, and other expenditures during the time the workers were out. Workers rarely realize how profitable for a company a strike can be, given the right advance planning and timing.

Workers without a paycheck for a week or two are much more willing to agree to a contract. They are hurting and a little scared, and I can talk them into a deal they would not have accepted before they lost a couple of paychecks.

We also rigged the voting. Harold and I would always open the ballots for various issues in front of the members. What they did not realize was that the ballots and the envelopes they mailed in were designed so that they could be held up to a light and their vote seen clearly. If the voting went against whatever we wanted, we would dump all the ballots. Then we would take fresh ballots, mark them so we'd win, stick them in envelopes, and mail them from as many different parts of the city as we could. When they arrived, the postmarks were the same as the ones that were on the legitimate ballots. We opened them in front of the members, who had no idea that we were doing anything improper. Naturally, we won.

Some of our actions caused us to destroy companies. For example, Harold always delighted in getting ever higher contracts, then bragging about the terms in newsletters to the members. This raised the members' expectations no matter where they worked. They always wanted more than other workers got, never looking at what the company could afford to pay.

The trouble is that different companies in the same business have different overheads and profit margins. A small bakery, for example, cannot pay what a massive chain can. Yet publicizing the contract terms made someone who worked in one bakery decide that he should make at least as much as someone with the same job description in a larger facility. To make himself a hero, Harold would sometimes force the contract down the throat of the owner, then the company would either go out of business or move away because it could not meet the terms. Some companies automated procedures for this reason, taking on an expense they did not want and might otherwise not have accepted. A large number of businesses either folded or closed their Cleveland area offices because of Harold's trying to get ever larger contracts. He took the unions too far in a desire for power and money.

Not that the Teamsters and the bakers' unions were alone. There were so many union problems in the 1960s that new construction in the city seemed to come to an end for a while.

One of the key players in the problems of the city, a man who also would affect Jackie Presser, was Danny Greene. He was considered one of Cleveland's leading racketeers until his death of "unnatural causes" in October 1977. Greene also headed the union that was most responsible for the stopping of construction in the city. The Greene murder would be the beginning of radical changes in both the mob and the Teamsters Union, helping to weaken the criminal stranglehold that once dominated.

Greene moved quickly in the union business. He was twenty-eight years old in 1957 when he became a stevedore on the waterfront. He was a member of Local 1317 of the longshoreman's union and was quickly elected its president. Always looking for a way to make money, he began taking kickbacks from the men who were given assignments as casual labor. By 1964 Greene was convicted of embezzling eleven thousand dollars from the union, a conviction reversed on appeal. However, he did lose his union position in 1970 after he pleaded guilty to violating union laws.

Danny Greene was an unusual character. He was tough and his speech pattern reminded some of the people who encountered him of Marlon Brando in movies such as *On The Waterfront*. Those who knew him say that it was as though a rather nice man decided to be a gangster and, from then on, behaved as he felt a gangster would behave. His language was coarse and he was constantly threatening to beat up people. Yet he was highly likable, even to those who were trying to put him in jail.

Danny had developed a scheme to extort money from cities for providing essential services. He created the Solid Waste Trade Guild, which was to be an association of independent rubbish haulers. He was allegedly using Johnny Dio (Dioguardi) as an adviser since Dio had been involved with organizing solid waste disposers in New York. *I* am not sure Dio was involved.

The city of Cleveland had its own rubbish and garbage disposal. They owned the equipment, had the men who were trained for such work, and could do it extremely cost-effectively.

The Solid Waste Trade Guild planned to divide the city into zones, then to lease the zones to independent trash haulers. They would bid at levels that undercut the cost of a city operation until the organization controlled all waste disposal. Then they would wait until the city sold all of its equipment. At that time the city would be totally dependent upon the organization. They could charge any price they wanted, raising the rates to an extortionate level, knowing that there would no longer be competition. The only way such a plan would work would be to involve all of the independents, as Dio did in New York.

The independent hauling companies were too independent for Danny. He knew he needed greater persuasion, and arranged for attacks against those who would not cooperate. Shootings were reported by the drivers and, occasionally, a bomb exploded one of the trucks. Despite the terrorist-type attacks, Danny failed.

During this same period, Greene headed Emerald Industrial Relations. I remember Danny Greene as a man who was hated by all labor leaders except Babe Triscaro. I feel he had nothing to do with the construction field. Yet police investigators, contractors, and others interviewed claim Danny was responsible for the end of much of Cleveland's revitalization in the 1960s. Their story has Danny demanding bribes to assure that materials such as glass would not be delayed at the docks. The materials were needed for high rise construction projects that had schedules to meet. Only after the bribes were paid would the materials be moved.

In one instance, according to investigators, Danny arranged for a wildcat strike at one site where bribes had been paid to assure a shipment of window glass. The strike allowed the glaziers to use an outside elevator that otherwise would have been in use by the wildcat strikers. This saved the contractor who needed the glass in place three days' idleness and was a payback for meeting the original bribe. However, despite the integrity of the sources, I am not convinced it happened. Danny could not get the cooperation of the building trades, his only real power being on the docks.

Whatever the truth of the allegations, someone—the investigators say it was Danny—was creating serious problems in the construction industry. And Danny was the man who has historically been given the credit for what took place.

Further investigation into Greene's operation revealed that Emerald Industrial Relations was allegedly a conduit for moving the payoffs to the mob. Even worse, the payoffs were far higher than anyone was used to paying. Money was routinely slipped under the table to ensure that a project would move smoothly. The money might buy union cooperation, prevent "accidents" on the docks, or otherwise ensure that the project would be completed on time and without problems. But Danny had raised the stakes. He was demanding higher payoffs than the contractors had ever had to pay. They were nonnegotiable demands that forced most contractors to stop building. So long as Emerald Industrial Relations was in power, outside builders decided that the city was not worth the effort. Construction came almost to a stop and the city went into a serious financial decline.

Danny Greene was a good friend of Alex Shondor Birns, the longtime rackets figure whom the press dubbed "Public Enemy Number 1," much to Birns's delight. He was so pleased with the "respect" the reporters gave him in their stories that he regularly treated them to free meals when he owned the Alhambra Restaurant. The free meal courtesy was also extended to judges, off-duty police officers, and others from whom Birns either needed or might need favors.

Shondor had been raised in one of the few Cleveland neighborhoods where there was enough of a mix of racial and ethnic groups that he was known and respected by all. When he entered the rackets, one of his major activities was handling problems with the numbers houses. These houses had a loose association which controlled payoffs. If one place paid a little better than another, there was a chance that that house would take away many of the customers from the others. Whenever that occurred, Shondor was sent as an intermediary to discuss the problem. Usually, the payoffs voluntarily returned to the same rate. Force helped other operators decide to reduce their rates.

The union did other things as well. For example, Danny would have twenty-five men on a site payroll, all of whom would show up early in the morning, clocking in. Then perhaps two would stay on the job site and the rest would go to another job, go to a bar, or just take a nap somewhere. They did not work and they did not stay near where they could be called to work. At the end of the day, they would return to clock out, usually with two or three hours of overtime on their time cards.

This type of padding has always existed, especially in businesses in which pick-up labor is used. For example, a convention center might have one staff for daily operations and a larger one for setting up, running, and dismantling displays for a big event. If the man who handles the hiring knows from past experience that twenty-seven men are needed, he might fill out forms for thirty, claiming that that is the number the job requires. Then he works the twenty-seven men as hard as he can, making certain that the work is done effectively and on time, keeping the company happy. The salaries for the other three go through payroll as though they are genuine. When the numbers are small and the work is completed on time, there are no complaints. In most instances the companies involved don't realize what has happened. In others, they do not care so long as the work is completed.

The Cleveland Police were actively investigating Danny Greene, building a case for prosecution. The investigation alone was enough to change Danny's fortunes, especially since reporters for the Cleveland newspapers learned what was happening and printed stories about it. The constant inquiries into his dealings by both law enforcement and press gave courage to both his enemies and some of the men from whom he was trying to extort money. His business was going bad and he was in financial trouble. Police investigators suddenly found themselves being asked by government agents to back off.

It turned out that Danny Greene was an FBI informant. The bureau was allowing him to make money committing crimes in exchange for information he was able to provide about organized crime.

No one has yet been willing to talk freely about the FBI's involvement with organized crime after the death of its founding director, J. Edgar Hoover, in 1972. Hoover was a man obsessed with power. He created a public relations division that made the FBI seem like supermen. (Oddly, the most successful government crime fighting organization during this period was the investigative arm of the U.S. Postal Service, a law enforcement agency few people knew existed.) They conveyed the idea that they always got their man, never mentioning that they avoided certain types of crime. In fact, into the late 1960s, the official FBI policy on organized crime was that it did not exist, at least in Cleveland. They concentrated on the easier or more dramatic cases, avoiding those in which the agents were most likely to fail or be corrupted.

After Hoover's death there seemed to be a rush to improve their image by tackling white-collar crime in America. Succeeding directors and newer agents recognized the Mafia and similar organized crime groups. They became involved with the fight against computer crime. And they sought to gain inside information as fast as—and, seemingly, in any way—they could, even if that meant allowing crimes to take place. Danny Greene committed extortion, bribery, and murder without anyone's being allowed to build a case against him. Whether or not the FBI realized the extent of the crimes is uncertain because they have never been made accountable for their actions.

This type of approach to law enforcement has been repeated in other cases. Jackie Presser was not called into account for crimes for years because he was giving the FBI information. This information ranged from facts that could convict Mafia partners of his to details of employee theft that sent his niece to jail. The same was true for others. It was as though the FBI were trying to make up for its incompetence in white-collar crime under the Hoover administration by allowing criminals to practice their profession, no matter how violent, so long as they were turning in other criminals.

One of the reasons Danny Greene, an informant for the FBI, was interested in Shondor Birns was Birns's ability to work with many different groups. Shondor moved freely among the Irish, the Italians, the blacks, and the Jews, the only independent to do so. And when he went to jail, as he did periodically, he eventually asked Danny Greene to work with Shondor's girlfriend in handling the numbers racket houses.

It was March 29, 1975, Easter weekend, and Shondor was in a bar on West Twenty-fifth Street and Detroit, his car parked nearby. He had been talking with a criminal from out of town; the conversation continued as they walked to Birns's car. Then the man left, walked around the corner, and suddenly a violent explosion destroyed Birns's car, killing him instantly. His body was blown apart, his leg flying into the air and landing directly in front of a group of parishioners as they came from services at St. Malachi's Church.

Later it was learned that Shondor's "friend," Danny Greene, was the one who killed Birns as a result of a numbers racket power struggle. He had used a radio-controlled device to set it off, waiting until no one was around who might be physically hurt by the explosion. What he did not realize was that this murder set into motion a series of events that would effect the Teamsters, the mob, and the nation.

There is a myth about organized crime that was about to be punctured by one of the most ridiculous mob wars ever fought. This was the myth that the old-style mobsters only killed each other. They do not involve innocent people in their wars.

Car bombing became the murder weapon of choice for organized crime in Cleveland and, to a lesser degree, in other parts of the nation. It was simple and it involved a vehicle in which most people feel safe. Equally important, a car is a giant gasoline container, adding an explosive liquid to the impact of the bomb itself.

The debris from a car bomb can kill for many yards. The best car bombs are those that do not even go into the victim's automobile. Instead they are installed in the car parked next to the one owned by the intended victim. They are detonated as the victims are about to get into their own vehicle. The force of the explosion could also result in the unfortunate death of anyone nearby. Despite Danny's precautions when he murdered Shondor Birns, it was just a miracle that the debris did not injure or kill one of the people emerging from the nearby church. The fact that a flying leg landed near them was adequate proof of how possible are "unintended accidents."

Shondor knew that he might die as a result of the Greene power struggle and arranged for twenty-five thousand dollars to be available for a contract on Danny Greene's life if he was murdered. The contract was taken by a local hired killer who was assisted by some of Danny's enemies from the days when they lived and fought in the Collinwood section of Cleveland as teenagers.

Danny was a study in contrasts during all this. Part of him was good-hearted, willing to help anyone in need. There were many people whose children he helped with their education or other needs. He never wanted to turn anyone away. He also liked maintaining the image that he could afford to help someone even when he was broke. One story was that Danny was in a bar, leaned over to a friend, and borrowed twenty dollars. Then Danny slapped the twenty-dollar bill on the bar and announced that he was buying drinks for everyone in the house.

Danny was also quite violent. There was a period when Shondor Birns went to jail and Danny was handling the muscle for Shondor's girlfriend who was involved with the numbers rackets in Birns's place. Danny wanted to bomb a house that was not cooperating with Birns's policies. Art Sneperger, a Birns associate, built a bomb with a military explosive that had a thirty-second fuse. For some reason Danny thought that he had three minutes between the time he lit it and the time that it would explode.

Danny tossed the bomb out of his car window into a heavy wind. The bomb bounced onto the car's surface, then was sucked back inside. The fuse was burned almost to the end as Danny bailed out of his moving car. He rolled away from the car as it exploded just far enough past him that he was not killed. Rather than admitting what had taken place, Danny claimed that someone had tossed the bomb into the car in an attempt to murder him.

Danny eventually became convinced that Sneperger was a traitor to him. He decided that Sneperger was carrying information about his activities to Michael Frato, a former member of the Solid Waste Trade Guild. Frato had abandoned the guild before Danny had been able to tell whether or not it might be successful and the two men went to war.

Danny decided to kill Frato, but he also wanted to kill Sneperger, whom he considered disloyal. He suspected that Sneperger was a snitch for one or more of the Cleveland Police detectives. Sneperger asked Danny what he would have to do to get back in Danny's good graces, and Danny told him that he would have to bomb the longshoremen's union hall. He was feuding with that union and wanted to get back at them. Sneperger did as he was told.

What happened next is uncertain because there are two different stories. Danny wanted to murder Frato with a bomb; of that there is no question. He also had Sneperger prepare it, again an issue that is certain. One report indicates that before the bomb could be placed on Frato's car, Danny, who was holding the detonator, deliberately set it off. He had never trusted Sneperger after he learned the man was a snitch and he was also fairly certain that he was supplying information to Frato.

The other story is that the bomb exploded by mistake. Sneperger made an error while assembling it and the result was an accidental death.

Even if the story of the accidental death is true, Danny was probably the man who spread the rumor of the deliberate murder. It would have been the type of story he would like to tell, to add to his "tough guy" image.

The feud between Frato and Greene ended on November 26, 1971, when Greene was out jogging along the beach. Frato who felt that Greene would be most vulnerable at that time, drove alongside and fired a gun at him. Because the car was moving, Frato was unable to hit Greene, who proceeded to pull out his own gun and killed Frato instantly. The shooting was ruled to be self-defense.

There were other attempts on Danny's life because of the twenty-five-thousand-dollar contract left behind by Shondor Birns. One hit involved the placing of bombs, one at the front and one at the back of the apartment in which he lived. The bombs used a military explosive that required a special triggering device because the explosive was meant to take a lot of abuse. A bullet could be fired into it without setting it off, a necessary condition during wartime.

The triggering devices are numbered: the higher the number, the greater the power of the explosive. This particular bomb required a number 8 blasting cap, but the gang apparently only had one of them. The bomb for the front of the building used one but the bomb for the rear of the building had three caps—a number 6, a number 4, and a number 2. This had a number 12 total, which, in theory, would have made for a stronger blast. However, the three caps failed to explode simultaneously. The number 6 went off first, separating the other two caps on the second bomb and sending them into the backyard, where they were eventually retrieved by the police bomb squad.

Danny and his girlfriend were on the second floor of the apartment building when the bombs exploded. He grabbed for her, protecting her from the falling debris, as they rode down with the collapsing floor. Death would have been certain had both bombs exploded. But the way the explosion took place, Greene settled to the ground almost as gently as if he had been riding an escalator.

Danny was hurt enough to be sent to the hospital, where he was visited by John Nardi, Bill Presser's associate and the nephew of Tony Milano. Nardi, not directly involved with the Mafia, was a practical man, willing to work with anyone who could help make him money. Danny, on the other hand, had a history of being biased against the Italians. However, he seemed to recognize that they had enemies in common, that he could use the extra muscle and political clout that John Nardi offered, and thus he was willing to work with him. Danny also needed to make money, and he was given a loan-sharking collection business by Nardi.

The bombings continued, as Danny fought his enemies and as other rival gangs found bombs to be the weapons of choice for settling disputes in Cleveland. We in the Teamsters used firebombs and stink bombs. Explosive devices were used so commonly that Cleveland became known as the bombing capital of the United States during this period.

Danny was both frightened of attack and defiant enough to make himself available. He flew an Irish flag in front of his home and sat outside, defying anyone to come after him. This made him an easy target, but it also made those who did not realize his state of mind quite vulnerable to unexpected trouble.

For example, there were two men who bought a high-powered hunting weapon from a legitimate gun shop. These men wanted a Colt .45-caliber rifle, and the one they selected looked very much like a Thompson Submachine Gun. The actual weapon they purchased was legal. Their intentions were honorable. Unfortunately the gun shop was only a couple of blocks from Danny's place.

The two men got into their car and drove from the gun shop, excited about their purchase, which was wrapped in its case. They decided they wanted to look at it once more, stopping, by chance, in front of Danny's place. The weapon was unloaded and they were not handling it in a threatening manner. Yet all Danny knew was that there were two men and a gun in a car. He pulled out a concealed handgun and began chasing the terrified rifle owners down the street.

Danny was irate about the "attack" because he thought that he had made peace with the mob. He was also going legitimate, or so he claimed. He had a new business that he felt would make him rich.

The business Danny developed was the purchase of Texas cattle, which would then be taken to a meat processing plant, butchered, and sold on the docks to the longshoremen and others for 20 to 30 percent less than any other dealer in the country. Even with the overhead of shipping and processing, he was certain he would make a fortune.

What Danny forgot to mention was that his plan was workable only because he had bypassed the middle man—the legitimate cattle owner. The cows were going to be rustled in a large-scale operation, driven across the border into Mexico along one of the rural stretches of unguarded and unfenced territory that were so common there, then brought back into the United States. They would be transferred to another ranch, where all identification could be changed as necessary. After that they would be sent to a Mafia-owned meat packing plant in Pennsylvania before being shipped to the docks, where the Mafia controlled the workers. The sale price would be high enough to seem legitimate and low enough to undercut everyone else. Rustling cows eliminated overhead.

Danny signed his own death warrant because of his relationship with John Nardi. No matter how well connected Nardi was with organized crime, he was not a member of the Mafia. He thought, however, that he should take over from Johnny Scalish. Instead, Jack Licavoli (Jack White) was given the power, and Nardi decided to kill anyone connected with Licavoli. This included Leo "Lips" Moceri, a made member of the Mafia from Akron, Ohio, whom he arranged for Danny to kill.

No one alive who might know what happened to Lips was willing to talk. What is certain is that Moceri's car was found in the parking lot of a Holiday Inn just outside Akron. Moceri was missing and there was blood on the seat. He was never seen again.

The Mafia knew that Greene and Nardi had planned what was obviously a murder. They liked John Nardi, considered him their friend, and generally liked Danny Greene. But what they had done, without permission, without proper justification in their minds, required that they be punished by death. It would just be a matter of time before both men were murdered.

The bombings were bringing a strong hostile reaction from both the police and the public, yet they seemed to have the greatest potential for success. There had been too many failed shootings, too many cross fires set up in which the guy got away.

The trouble was that most of the bomb makers were not as good as they thought they were; certainly they were not always successful. For example, a bomb was planted in Danny Greene's car when he and John Nardi flew from Cleveland to Texas on business. The car was parked in the airport lot and it was easy to plant a device controlled by a radio trigger in the hands of the killers.

The two men returned to Cleveland, got into Greene's car, and started driving from the lot. The killers, standing in the airport hotel with their remote control device, flipped the lever the moment the car started past. Nothing happened. They flipped the lever again with the same result.

The car picked up speed, the would-be killers leaving the hotel and chasing after it, working the switch on the remote control trigger. Nothing happened.

The car left the airport, traveling down the street, the men still trying to make the remote control work. Then the car went over a bump, and the bomb fell off. The would-be assassins picked it up and sadly returned home.

Eventually Nardi and Greene were both killed the same way. The mob followed the assassination technique of the Irish Republican Army and a number of Middle East terrorist groups. They had failed to explode the cars in which Nardi and Greene were driving. Both men had become wary of starting their vehicles without checking. But no one looked at the cars that might be parked next to theirs in parking lots. As a result, on May 17, 1977, when John Nardi left the Teamsters Union offices and entered his Olds, the car parked next to him exploded, killing him instantly. On October 6, 1977, Danny Greene was murdered after a dental checkup. The bomb used to kill him had been placed in the car parked next to his in the dentist's lot.

What no one realized during this period were all the behind-the-scenes activities that would have so much impact on so many people.

The war against Nardi and Greene involved a mobster who was known in the Cleveland area as Jack White but whose real name was James Licavoli. He had a woman working for the FBI in the Cleveland area who was supplying him with information concerning confidential informants and others. Two of these informants, Curly Montana and Tony Hughes, were allegedly connected with the Teamsters, though I have never known Curly to have any such connections. Two others had been located by confidential file name but were not yet identified. Licavoli was determined to stop information from destroying the mob.

Licavoli was the man coordinating the killing of Greene. He had placed a wiretap on Greene's telephone. A total of $15,900 in bribes was spent on Jeffrey and Geraldine Rabinowitz (he was a car salesman; she worked for the FBI; both were eventually sentenced to five years in jail) in order to gain government information. Ray Ferritto had been hired to commit the murder, and a number of men, including Jackie Presser, were running scared about the possibility of being caught in the middle.

Jackie was afraid of being hit after Leo Moceri was killed. Word was out that Nardi wanted Jackie dead since Jackie seemed to be too well connected with

Licavoli and his side in the feud. If Jackie could be killed, Nardi felt that he could put his own man into the Teamsters in a power position. Then he would have a personally loyal source of information about both the union and the mob.

Jackie and a friend went down to Florida to hide out. I moved them among several hotels for a little over a month before Licavoli sent word that Jackie was safe. Nardi was dead.

Jackie's survival meant that Jack White trusted him and his loyalty to the mob. Bill had been partners with John Nardi in the past, and Jackie was obviously connected with him. However, Bill always went with the mob, an action that Jackie did not necessarily understand. He might have felt that he would be seen as a Nardi loyalist and thus would get caught in the cross fire. Bill was still alive during this period, yet Jackie never gained the respect within the families that Bill had. The family connections would do no good.

Jackie had increased his activities with the FBI, giving them information on John Nardi. Jackie also arranged for Jack Nardi, John Nardi's son, to go on the Teamsters Union payroll at three hundred dollars per week with the understanding that he would do no work. This hiring was supposed to be a sign of respect for the elder Nardi. It was also supposed to keep peace in the mob since it would appease all factions. However, Jack Nardi was fired immediately after his father was killed.

The war among the factions created other problems. Jackie, though remaining an FBI informant, was eventually able to return to work. He also gained the support of the Chicago mob leaders such as Joey Aiuppa who would be instrumental in placing both Roy Williams and Jackie in positions as head of the Teamsters. However, other men involved with the power fight were turned into informants by the FBI. Everyone was fearing for his life, it seemed, and the fallout from the bombing included such key witnesses as Jimmy "The Weasel" Fratianno and Angelo Lonardo becoming informants for the FBI. In fact, the fear that drove men such as Lonardo, a trusted stand-up guy in the past, into the hands of the government would eventually destroy the older leadership among the five Mafia families who dominated American society. Those who lived eventually went to jail.

There were other events causing radical changes in my life during this period. In 1969, after having brought twenty-eight hundred new members into Teamster Local 507, I suffered a heart attack. I was at home at the time, living near Jackie in an apartment building. My wife, Nancy, had Jackie help me to the hospital, which was poorly equipped to deal with such an emergency. After three weeks of care I was still in great pain and, I later learned, near death from an aneurysm on my heart. The nurses told me, off the record, that I needed to get to a better hospital so I arranged for a transfer, found a new doctor, and eventually recovered.

Jackie was actually quite good to me during this period. He stayed at the hospital with Nancy, sitting with her during the time I was in surgery. Then he had the union buy me a new car and hired a man to drive my wife, my daughter, and me to Florida. I thought he really cared about me, and I still think that was one reason for his action. However, there was more taking place than I realized.

By the time I returned to Local 507, everything had changed. If I did a favor for someone, getting the person a job through my influence with the employer, that new employee would be let go. If I talked about a contract, Harold Friedman would put me off. I was supposed to be one of the people in charge, yet there was obviously an increasingly successful power play taking place and I was coming out on the short end.

For example, my wife had a relative who needed a job. I was certain from what I knew of the woman that she was sincere and hardworking. I arranged for her to go to work for a company I organized, explaining that she should not reveal our connection. Then, not long after she started working, she was fired.

I found the woman a second job and the same thing occurred. I did not understand what was happening until I got her a third job, this time with a paint company. I explained to the boss that he was not to fire her without telling me. I wanted to know whether the woman was incompetent, not doing the work, or otherwise giving him valid reason to get rid of her. I made the owner promise me that he would take no action against her without first checking with me.

A short time later I received a call from the man who ran the paint shop. Nancy's relative had made the mistake of telling the business agent that she was related to my wife. He reported that fact to Harold, who ordered her fired. The owner called me to explain that he had to listen because Harold was the one who negotiated contracts and could hurt him badly if he didn't do what Harold wanted.

The forced firing was typical of Harold. He didn't care whether or not someone put a friend or relative on the payroll of some plant we organized, even though there wasn't an employer anywhere who was going to refuse. In fact, Harold used to find all sorts of ways to hurt the workers.

For example, there were jobs for which a worker could not get hired unless he joined the union. He had to pay fees, such as a five-dollar DRIVE program fee up front, something only Local 507 rigidly enforced. At the end of the first week or two, the person might be unsuccessful and have to be let go. Instead of refunding his fees, which the worker might need to pay his bills, Harold laughed at him and kept the money. He never gave a damn about the worker, only what the worker would have to spend to be a part of the union.

Both Harold and Jackie also found ways to pay bonuses, buy gifts, and otherwise cheat on union finances. For example, they would give a man a much higher salary than he should receive with the understanding that he would pay taxes on the money, then kick back the difference between his proper pay and what he had been given. That difference might buy a new car for someone, pay for some legal bills the union had no right to pay, or otherwise be used for an improper purpose. Yet the government never caught on because all taxes were paid.

Harold and Jackie cheated in every way they could when holding elections, as well. For example, when we were having a vote in a Polish neighborhood, we'd set up a tent at the grounds of the business, just off their property. We'd have free food and drinks, perhaps some polka players. We'd encourage everyone to have a good time before and after they'd voted.

Wherever we were, we treated the workers in ways that would ensure their thinking we were the greatest people who had ever come into their lives. Forget the fact that we might have a sweetheart deal with their bosses. Never mind that all we wanted was their money. We treated them like friends in ways their bosses never had and they went for it. The actions were illegal under the various labor rulings controlling organizing, but we didn't care, the workers loved the attention, and the bosses seldom pursued the matter far enough even to have us reprimanded.

The problems I was facing had nothing to do with morals or ethics. Harold was getting back at me, playing power games that I could not win.

I began complaining to Bill Presser, who had always sided with me. He told me to take the charter off the wall, an action that was within his power to order. He would give me space and not let Jackie and Harold continue to lead the union. However, every time we would get into such a fight, I would let myself be talked back into working with them, and they would promise not to continue their behavior.

I did make one mistake with Harold, though. During one of the confrontations I acted in front of the business agents. You have to remember that Harold seemed to look upon the business agents as his private servants. He would send them to cut his grass or pick up his clothing from the cleaners. This was not part of their job, nor was it the work they were supposed to be doing for the members. They were working on union time, being paid high union salaries, but performing personal services, and I was sick of it.

This one day he had pulled one of his power plays on me so I confronted him during one of his morning meetings with the business agents. I forced him to admit that we were equals. I forced him to admit that he could not fire me. I forced him to admit just how impotent he was in any confrontation with me. I humiliated him in front of his business agents, an act that gave me great pleasure at the time. Unfortunately, it made him all the more determined to get rid of me in any way that he could.

During this time Jackie was also turning against his father. It was around 1970 when Bill had to go into the hospital for surgery of his own. He was extremely ill and at risk of dying. Bill had cancer in addition to his troubles with the government. He was planning to step down as soon as the mob would let him pass power on to Jackie.

I say that Jackie loved his father, yet it was odd that he visited me in the hospital but not Bill. Maybe he had never faced the fact that Bill might die one day. Maybe seeing his father sick terrified him because he could be next, and ironically Jackie would die of cancer. And maybe Jackie didn't have the feelings I always thought he had. I just don't know.

All I remember was going to Mt. Sinai Hospital in Cleveland, where Bill was facing surgery. It was very early in the morning, not normal visiting hours, but a visit was allowed because of the high risk of the surgery he was about to experience. Bill had not had any sleep that night because he knew it might be the last time he was alive. Jackie was nowhere to be seen.

I walked in and Bill said, "You know, Allen, I knew you'd be the only one here."

Bill started crying and then we both were crying, hugging, and kissing. This was the man who was my friend, my mentor, and my father, all at once. The surgery was so risky at that time that only one in ten survived and Bill did not think he would make it.

Bill, knowing he was going to die, had prepared Jackie before the surgery by taking him around the country. Bill introduced his son to all the mob figures, the politicians, the business people, bankers, contractors, and others with whom he would be doing business. He showed Jackie the hidden sources of money and information, the safe deposit boxes scattered throughout the states, and everything else he needed to know about. And then Bill survived the surgery.

Giving up when he did was the greatest mistake in his life, Bill told me. Jackie turned against him, working to solidify his power with the mob, the politicians, the government agents, and the others. He talked about Bill as though Bill no longer had any brains. He tried to make people think that Bill was senile as a result of the illness and surgery. He worked to make it impossible for Bill ever to return to the labor movement or have power over his son again.

Not that Bill was treated unfairly. Bill had always accumulated money slowly, building his wealth in subtle, seemingly safe ways. Jackie, on the other hand, was bolder, perhaps because he felt that the FBI would cover his ass to keep him as an informant in much the way his father had bailed him out in the past. Or perhaps Jackie was shrewder than any of us realized. Whatever the case, Bill bragged that as much as he didn't want to see Jackie go for power in the Teamsters, he had to admit that he had made more money going into deals with Jackie than he ever had on his own. Still, the last ten or eleven years of Bill's life, until his death in 1981, were filled with many regrets.

Between 1970 and 1973 I seemed to be constantly fighting with Harold. Increasingly Jackie was taking Harold's side. He was actually going into the office and earning a part of his ridiculous pay. Yet "Uncle Allen" could no longer reason with him. Worse, I lacked Bill's muscle.

Finally Jackie came up with a compromise: I would start a new local. I would draw my pay from 507 and have some support, but not much. Harold had printing on credit, telephones, and other things. I had a single organizer to help me and no Teamsters charter.

The idea behind this plan was probably to drive me out of organized labor. However, I loved what I was doing and did it well. I built Local 507 from nothing and now I was building what I called Local 752. Eventually I would have a thousand members, seemingly overnight.

I have been a lot of things in my time—a con man, a thief, an arsonist. I have been to jail and I have been lucky to avoid jail perhaps more often than I should. I see religion as something people believe in because they have no faith in themselves. I am cynical, angry, and ready to punch you out if you cross me. Yet my involvement with organized labor has been something special for me. As I said before, it is the closest I have ever come to a personal religion.

I know I have taken advantage of people. Certainly I have forced unions on employees just as often as I have on employers. I have declared strikes in order to force contracts. I have made sweetheart deals in which both sides benefited despite the fact that my loyalty should have been to the workers, who could have had a better deal had I been strictly on their side.

Yet there has always been an excitement about unions I cannot fully describe. I guess that it is the one way I truly like helping people. I may have my own racial and ethnic prejudices when it comes to my daily life, but none of that matters when I am working with labor.

For example, there was a manufacturing company in which women held the menial jobs and had the lowest pay. Men did fairly well because they were allowed to drive the heavy equipment, work that required more skill and paid higher hourly rates. Yet there was no reason why a man had to work the equipment. Sure, it was often big and heavy, but you did not have to be strong to operate it. Even a child can work an electric lift truck, for example, given adequate training and practice. The controls are designed to be simple even if the equipment itself lifts hundreds or thousands of pounds.

The women were frustrated because they could not advance. The employer seemed sympathetic but rightfully noted that he could not promote someone if she could not do the more sophisticated job. As a result, when I found a female worker interested in meeting the challenge, I arranged for her to receive training on the equipment separate from her regular job. She put in her full day, then learned to use the equipment. Soon she was promoted to the first available opening, did well, and all the jobs began to be open to everyone without regard to sex, race, or anything else.

I had a black man who came to me when I was organizing a place. He wanted to learn to be an organizer and a business agent. I couldn't afford to pay him and knew that, though he might be fine working with other blacks, there was a chance he would be overwhelmed by ethnic bias in some areas. However, he persisted, telling me that his wife earned enough for them to get by and that he trusted me to pay him fairly when I could afford to do so, if he worked out.

I hired that man and he did work out. His color did not matter to most people, and he did not let the occasional racist interfere with the work he loved. I also gave him money as soon as I could, then eventually helped him obtain an extremely well-paid job as a business agent for another local, where he remains successful.

I say that unions have gone too far today, but I don't mean the workers. If they understand what is happening, if someone shows them how their actions or lack of actions affects their future, they accept changes and setbacks. The problems have come from the union leadership, who have caused the decline in membership by demanding too much in order to gain the support of their workers who only want a decent job and fair pay.

Perhaps the unions are the best side of Allen Friedman. All I know is that organizing and helping the workers have always been activities where I am happiest. The idea that a good worker has kept his or her job because of me, that a boss has not been able to fire someone supporting a family just because he has a nephew who wants the job, brings me pleasure. I feel good when someone is in crisis and is given a few days off to deal with a death in the family, serious illness, or some other problem without being fired. Although we forget this fact, in the recent past the extent of employer concern in such a situation might be excusing the person from overtime. There was exploitation. There were unsanitary and dangerous conditions. There were arbitrary hiring and firing practices having nothing to do with the quality of the worker or the time on the job. And all these problems have been reduced or eliminated through the labor unions.

But labor unions were also killing me. When I was organizing my little union, nothing else mattered. I smoked all the time, ate the wrong foods, and got my exercise yelling at some boss who didn't want to see his employees get a fair deal. If I had an election at a plant, I made certain I was present for all three shifts, grabbing a nap for an hour or so whenever I could. And I did this after having nearly died from the heart attack and subsequent aneurysm.

The heart is a wonderful muscle. I recovered enough to lead a normal life. But organizing the way I did was not normal. Soon I experienced a second heart attack, and I would not recover so quickly from this one.

I was driving my car, concerned about getting to where the votes would be

I was also breaking the law, something I did not know. I was being paid for not working, which was not and had never been my intention. In a sense, I was what is known as a "ghost" employee every week that I collected my paycheck but was not permitted to perform substantial service for the union to earn it. What I did not know was that what Harold and Jackie were doing to me would eventually send me to jail despite my desire to earn my money and my efforts to do so.

Nationally there were changes for the Teamsters Union, though the scandals were not major for the moment. The concern was over the disappearance of Hoffa and the usual number of trials related to extortion, sweetheart contracts, and violence on the picket lines.

Frank Fitzsimmons had decentralized power, letting the union operate in the way it was supposed to operate. There were almost 750 locals meeting every five years to choose the general president, the secretary-treasurer, sixteen vice presidents, and three trustees. There were five area conferences and forty-eight joint councils. All of these groups had varying powers and responsibilities under the union's constitution. However, Hoffa and his immediate following tended to dominate all operations. He would take a grievance from a member of the rank and file. Fitzsimmons was different.

Frank Fitzsimmons insisted that the chain of command operate as originally intended. He lacked the ability to organize on a grand scale. He was unable to keep track of everything as Hoffa had, relying, instead, on the organization to function as designed. As a result, there was no centralization of power, no single voice against which the opposition could rally. It was easy for the dissidents to attack Hoffa because he was the union. It was almost impossible to rally a group against Fitz because decisions that affected the dissidents might be made at any level of the rank and file.

These changes were reflected in Teamster headquarters in Washington in the mid-1970s. Under Fitzsimmons the offices were filled with bureaucrats who went about their chores like any other headquarters staff for a large organization. The people didn't carry guns, blackjacks, or other weapons. There was no talk of secret deals and power plays. The idea that any of them could be violent or even consider violence was viewed as ridiculous. These were nice people who resented the gangster image the union had gained as a result of the actions of Hoffa, Bill Presser, and the others who had helped build the organization.

Many of the staff workers were frustrated when the old Teamsters image was mentioned. They often avoided talking about where they worked, discussing labor law in general and not mentioning the Teamsters. They did not wish to be seen as a part of the past.

Hoffa had been like Harold Friedman. He expected the underlings to do his bidding, no matter what they were paid, no matter what their job might be.

Fitzsimmons was so accustomed to being a toady for Jimmy that he had no desire to treat his staff with disrespect. He may have been criticized for having limited leadership ability, but he was loved for his lack of arrogance toward others.

Bill Presser and Allen Dorfman controlled what happened with the Central States Pension Fund during this period. Roy Williams, the vice president from Kansas City, dominated the negotiations for the nationwide trucking contract. Yet none of them controlled the union as such. As casual as Fitzsimmons was, he still was head of the union.

Fitzsimmons probably had a better political sense than Hoffa. He knew that he could use his position to back the leadership of various locals, then call upon them for favors when he needed them. For example, in 1971 New York City Local 237 arranged for fifteen thousand municipal workers to walk off their jobs. To create chaos, they left drawbridges open, stopping commuters on their way in or out of Manhattan Island. This resulted in a number of lawsuits and Fitzsimmons loaned Barry Feinstein, the local president, ninety thousand dollars to cover the resulting legal problems. Later Feinstein was also asked to be a part of a constitutional committee for Fitz, a position that paid a two-thousand-dollar bonus for his time. To no one's surprise, Feinstein became an ardent Fitzsimmons loyalist.

Fitz also knew how to give out jobs. For example, he helped Vincent Trertola became an International "general organizer" in 1976, a job that paid $35,600. In addition he earned $13,800 for working with a New York Teamsters local, $3,600 for being involved with New York Joint Council 16's pension fund, $17,000 from Joint Council 16, and $14,000 for working for the Eastern Conference of Teamsters. He also earned an average of between $200 and $300 a week selling insurance to various locals within Joint Council 16. Obviously the total from the lower-level jobs resulted in far more money than he needed or earned, so why had Fitz bothered to give him almost another $700 for a bullshit position as "general organizer"?

Vincent's father was Joseph Trertola, an International first vice president and president of Joint Council 16. He was a man who was in a position to overthrow Fitz. He had been approached toward this end by Harold Gibbons in a carefully planned power play. However, Fitz had bought the elder Trertola's loyalty by throwing money at the son.

Fitzsimmons also knew when to remove a man from one of his extra jobs, instantly reducing his earning power. Thus he used financial muscle rather than the threat of violence to control his followers and maintain support for his presidency.

The one thing Fitzsimmons did do during this period was to proclaim that labor had become a business. This was an idea Hoffa expressed and Fitz reinforced it. No longer were the unions a social movement. No longer were a group of men and women united in demanding fair pay for a day's work from an abusive boss who was deliberately keeping them in bondage to unnecessarily bad wages and vile working conditions. The union had become a business requiring expert attorneys: people who understood economics, the cost of living, pension laws, health and safety laws, and numerous other factors that never previously had to be considered.

The Teamsters were poor in this regard under Fitzsimmons. He used far fewer experts than the other unions, and many of the higher-paid employees were of marginal competence. He believed too strongly in using family members, his own and those of other high-level officials, regardless of their competence. His son, Donald, was an auditor for the International, though he was not a certified public accountant. In all, fifteen family members of the top eighteen men in the Teamsters were on the payroll. Numerous other family members of lower-level officials were also employed by various locals, conferences, and other groups.

The only problem Fitzsimmons had was with the White House. Once Jimmy Carter was in power, Fitz was no longer an influence in government.

Fitz had been an ardent supporter of the Republicans, even going so far as, in 1974, giving twenty-five thousand dollars to Rabbi Baruch Korff's anti-impeachment organization. He delighted in the time he spent in the White House and the gifts that Nixon gave him, such as golf balls with the presidential seal. Such support kept him out of the Carter White House and reduced his national influence. However, that occurred when there were no more threats to his power position, Hoffa long since dead.

Fitzsimmons was also involved with charitable works. He supported a home for retarded children (including those who were both blind and retarded), agencies working with children addicted to drugs, crippled children, and others. If children were in need and an organization were legitimately attempting to help them, Fitz was a soft touch.

At the same time, Fitz maintained his own organized crime contacts. Often they met in California during trips he took to play golf at La Costa, the country club largely financed by Teamster money. Their topics allegedly included a prepaid health plan for Teamsters in several states, the money going to a Los Angeles physician who would establish a clinic specifically to serve the members using the plan. The doctor agreed to kick back a percentage, the money being laundered through an organization to be called the People's Industrial Consultants. Apparently there would be legitimate medical care available, the rates set being adequate to meet the needs of the rank and file at the same time that kickbacks were made to both Teamsters and organized crime figures.

The investigation was thwarted thanks to the corruption of various government officials. The FBI requested wiretaps, but Attorney General Richard

252 POWER AND GREED

Kleindienst refused permission for them. He was aware of the relationship between Fitzsimmons and Nixon and did not want to jeopardize either man. This cover-up went so far as the sending of a memo to California law enforcement agencies letting them know that Washington would not be pleased with any investigations into misuse of Teamster funds or illegal activities by the Teamsters. Later Kleindienst would be convicted of failing to testify fully before a congressional committee, a plea bargain arrangement after he was found to have lied under oath in the ITT antitrust case.

The medical plan never went into effect, though. The *New York Times* reported the story and the publicity forced the dropping of the scheme.

There were other accusations, including an investigation into kickbacks from the Central States Pension Fund. Yet Fitz was firmly in control and until the late 1970s, facing no major crises that would gain him the publicity that Hoffa had had. The only dark spot in his life came with fears of retaliation for an action he had to take through no fault of his own.

In 1974, Congress had passed the Employee Retirement Income Security Act. This required the Department of Labor to regulate the trustees of pension funds to make certain that they handled the money properly. By January 1976, investigators were in the Chicago office of the Central States fund in order to examine their records. However, the timing was off because Daniel Shannon was running the fund. Although hired as administrator by Bill Presser, Shannon was straight. When he began managing all investments in 1975, he stopped making loans to mob fronts. The loans were made to legitimate enterprises only.

A greater concern was a separate investigation being conducted by the Internal Revenue Service since they revoked the fund's tax-exempt status retroactively, back to 1965. That action took place in June 1976 and came as a result of all the allegations of corruption, mismanagement, and poor record keeping.

The IRS action was halted almost as quickly as it began. Although the government's suspicions were well founded, the penalties would have been too great for people to endure. First, the fund would have had to pay taxes on all earnings and interest for the previous eleven years. Then all employers who contributed to the fund would have had to declare their contributions nondeductible, an action that would affect eighteen thousand companies. And most serious of all, the total penalties would have destroyed the fund, eliminating critical pensions for retirees who were innocent victims of both sides.

The Labor Department action was not stopped, though, and Fitz had to fire eleven of the sixteen trustees of the pension fund. He also had to appoint five individuals whose backgrounds were as clean as that of Shannon.

It was not until October 26 that Fitzsimmons rid the fund of the eleven members as requested. He had been running scared about the way some of them would react, fearing that they might retaliate for his actions in trying to force them out. However, the IRS was only letting him have time while trying to figure out how to handle their investigation and bring sanctions, without hurting the pensioners. And the Labor Department's investigation was uncovering enough problems that he had to continue management reforms.

The only person who was still coming out clean was Shannon. He had also begun reforms of his own prior to the goverment pressures.

The change of administration brought a change of pressure on Fitzsimmons. He had dominated the Republicans but he was unable to manipulate the Democrats. Labor Department investigators had discovered blatant abuse of the fund and no one was willing to protect Fitz. The press delighted in exposing loans in which interest had been miscalculated, costing the fund millions of legitimate dollars. They also pointed out such abuses as a loan for several million dollars which had been backed by a gambler's IOUs. The Labor Department decided to force Fitz and Roy Williams to resign from the Central States Pension Fund. In addition, the fund would be turned over to a legitimate private company.

On June 30, 1977, Fitz, Williams, and the others were out. The assets were to be managed by the staff of Equitable Life Assurance Society. In addition, by the middle of 1978, even Allen Dorfman would lose his contract to manage the insurance claims for medical reimbursement. And this occurred despites winning a power play against Shannon, who was angry with Dorfman's failure to provide documentation that would allow for effective financial planning by the fund in relation to the various health claims.

By 1978 it was obvious that Fitz was on the way out. His health was bad and there was pressure on him from Labor Department and FBI investigators. Jackie Presser was telling him that he needed to step down, to allow a new, cleaner image to be presented. And the rank and file were turning against him. There was no question that a new president would take his place sooner than he desired.

8

And Then It Was Over

IN A SENSE, it will never be over. Not the greed. Not the corruption. Not the power plays.

There will always be new politicians on the make, men and women who will sell their souls for the money necessary for just one more television spot, another radio commercial, a few dozen more handbills to pass out. There will always be the established old pros who know what it is to head congressional committees, dine at the White House, command respect wherever they go, yet still crave another young woman for discreet sex, a piece of a business that will guarantee them a retirement in luxury, or some other previously unattainable sensual delight.

A cop with a new baby, a new house, and a wife who no longer works to supplement the family income will still have his price to look the other way at the right time and the right place. Employers who pay themselves under the table will remain interested in schemes allowing them to pay their employees less than the standard union contract for similar business in exchange for splitting the extra profits between themselves and union officials.

People aren't honest, and when they know you're with a powerful and wealthy labor union like the Teamsters, they come to you. That isn't going to end.

Yet for me and for the world I had known, there was an end. It occurred during the decade following Fitz's troubles, and it saw changes that now seem as impossible as our dreams for the success we came to have when we were tough, struggling Jewish kids fighting for a buck against the ethnic hold on organized labor. Lucky Luciano is dead. Bill Presser is dead. I went to jail again, then lived to be able to piss on Jackie's grave, just as I told him I would. But there is no satisfaction.

We survivors are mostly old men now, telling stories of the past over breakfast, remembering the violence that dominated so much of our lives. Organizing labor has become a business that is far more respectable than in the past. The violent era that we knew will probably not be seen again.

Only the corruption lingers. In fact, as I write this a trial is taking place revealing just how far men on both sides will go to gain power.

But I am getting ahead of myself.

It was 1978 and Frank Fitzsimmons was on his way out. He was under investigation. He had lost his White House power base. He was suspected of at least knowing about the disappearance of Jimmy Hoffa and, possibly, helping arrange for Hoffa's murder.

Jackie Presser had become an International vice president in 1976, replacing Bill, much to Bill's disgust. Bill never wanted Jackie to go for ultimate power in the Teamsters. He wanted him to stay behind the scenes, a wheeler-dealer, using his connections with politicians, judges, and the mob to wield power and make money. He felt that Jackie was incapable of handling life at the top, that it would destroy him. But Bill did not realize how determined and ruthless Jackie could be so long as he did not seem to get his own hands dirty. That was why Jackie was spreading the word about his father's incompetence. And that was why Jackie was letting the FBI take out his enemies through the information he was passing on to them.

Oddly, I helped Jackie gain power in the International. There were a lot of sons of high officials, including those of Fitzsimmons. But all of them were viewed as leeches, incompetents, or worse during this period. Jackie was seen as a man who had been a union organizer and hard worker since he was twenty-two years old. No one realized that he couldn't organize anyone. He could only take credit for the work of others, charming men and women alike with his personality.

I still remember when I brought twenty-eight hundred new members into Local 507 and Jackie went around talking about how he had made the local what it was. Talk with any of the members and you'll find that most knew nothing about Jackie, had never met him, or had seen him briefly making a speech, sweating like a fat hog. He didn't know the law, relying upon Harold for analyzing contracts, and he was uncomfortable trying to do the legwork and the behind-the-scenes actions needed to force a company into accepting the union.

Jackie also worked on the image of the Teamsters, something he understood well because he was almost all image. He developed a public relations campaign. He encouraged newspaper interviews that would show the Teamsters in a new light, implying that the corruption of the past was long over.

Bill knew that he was dying the year before Jackie moved into power. He had cancer, diabetes, and a stomach that seemed to be barely held together by all the skills of the surgeon's trade. Traveling to a pension fund meeting in Chicago, he was embarrassed to find that he had bled from the rectum while riding in the car. Moving Jackie into power seemed the only logical act, much as he hated the idea. He wanted to have a family member follow him, and Jackie was the only one of his two natural sons who was interested in the unions.

The one area in which Jackie excelled on his own—and it was a major factor in gaining Fitz's support—was his idea for mobilizing the pensioners into a political force. He recognized that the retirees had money and time, and that they could be used to force political change. It was an idea that would eventually be similar to what the American Association of Retired People was able to do, though on a larger scale. Jackie convinced Fitz that this concept should be adopted by the International, not just the Ohio Teamsters.

In October 1976, Jackie proposed a public relations campaign for the International based on what was developed for Ohio. At the same time, Bill announced that he had become too ill to continue with his International duties and proposed Jackie as a vice president. It was an emotional period that made for an easy transition.

Bill was as smart as ever with the change. He could have stepped down during the June convention, during which time the delegates would have voted on his successor. But there was no way that the delegates were going to back Jackie.

There were protests concerning the changes, yet Bill and I had done our work well. We had covered Jackie's crimes. Bill had pulled him out of financial binds that would have showed his skimming and his inability to manage effectively. Even Harold had protected him in a sense by handling the management end so effectively. Jackie looked good. There was no way to know how dishonest, incompetent, and lazy he was unless one of the three of us talked.

Jackie even had an answer for the mob connections. He pointed out that the mob figures were in the unions. They had power and position. If you wanted to advance your union, to be able to help your members, then you had to work with the Triscaros, the Milanos, the Provenzanos, and all the others.

Jackie was changing history, of course. The Jews and the Italians made a concerted effort to go for power. In some instances they saw the union as a money machine through which both the management and the rank and file could be exploited. In other instances they just wanted to be at the top, taking the power that had once belonged to the Irish. The crimes they committed and the deals they made were often designed to make them successful, all others be damned. That's why they went after the legitimate informers, attacking men like Jim Luken.

But no one knew that. They also did not know that both Jackie and Roy Williams were closely connected with Nicholas Civella of Kansas City, and Joey Aiuppa of Chicago. These two organized crime leaders wanted to control Teamster leadership, Roy and Jackie being their key to such power now that Fitzsimmons's health was failing.

The truth did not matter. Jackie knew that he was the cleanest Teamster leader in the country in the 1970s who also had a chance to take control of the top. He understood the media and public relations. The mob considered him a good front and made certain that he was seen in a positive light.

Jackie worked behind-the-scenes miracles in Cleveland for both himself and his father. In June 1974, Bill was honored by the *Cleveland Press,* once an opponent of his, for his fifty years in the labor movement. The Israeli government honored him with its Tower of David award. He had received blessings from Pope Paul. A dinner held in his honor included judges from the Common Pleas Court, the Eighth District Appeals Court, the Supreme Court, and the federal judiciary—thirty-nine judges in all. He was able to obtain letters showing his good character from the mayor of Cleveland, the governor of Ohio, and the chief justice of the Ohio Supreme Court.

Jackie sold Israel Bonds and raised money to build a children's home in Israel. He also convinced the Teamsters rank and file to buy such bonds, the union leaders and locals buying more than 25 percent of all the bonds sold in the United States in 1977. Two years earlier, after even the Provenzano Local 560 bought huge quantities of bonds, law enforcement agencies checked to see whether skimming were taking place. To their surprise the effort was sincere. Jackie had seen that it was a way to win respect and reduce the heat that might come to them from crimes they were committing.

Jackie eventually was named to the boards of directors of numerous charitable and business organizations. Many were meaningless positions, but a few involved genuine power or allowed for important contacts, such as those through the Cleveland Convention and Visitors Bureau. The Cleveland Teamsters also sponsored charity fund-raisers and direct contributions to various organizations. He also used the publication *Ohio Teamster* to praise area politicians, knowing that they would support him, rather than risk alienating the 150,000 men and women who received the newspaper.

Jackie mentioned salary reforms during this period, taking a line he really did not believe in but thought would make him look good. He said that high salaries were justified, that the work the men did warranted them, and that they should pay their taxes. He said that the idea of stealing to supplement was something out of the past and would not be tolerated. Harold Friedman actually felt that way. Jackie was still a product of the past, but he knew when to take Harold's idea, present it as his own, and gain the glory. He also kept one hand under the table for any deals he could make.

Jackie expanded his public relations efforts. The publication he had developed in Ohio went nationwide. He placed ads on radio and television and sponsored college football games. He arranged for a full-page ad in numerous larger city newspapers to congratulate Jimmy Carter when he was elected president, the ad actually discussing the Teamsters and their goals. He still attacked dissidents and often got into arguments with hostile news reporters, yet his efforts were the most sophisticated anyone had seen from the Teamsters, and they served a dual purpose, by also making Jackie Presser a national name.

Jackie could see that Roy Williams was the likely successor to Fitzsimmons so he began setting him up for failure, even before Fitz's time as president came to an end. He leaked word that Williams was trying to have Kansas City union members sign up for a prepaid legal plan in which the fees would be high enough to allow for kickbacks to organized crime. He also let the reporters know that Williams was trying to keep the Central States health and welfare fund in the hands of the nationally discredited Allen Dorfman. Perhaps he could not prevent Williams's taking office, but he could ensure that the path would be difficult and the time in power brief.

As I mentioned, the Carter years were bad ones for Teamster influence in the White House. We didn't dominate White House labor policy as we had under Nixon and as we were about to under Ronald Reagan.

Bill Presser was four years out of top office when Reagan ran for president of the United States. Bill was a sick man, dying, yet he was determined to continue to influence the nation as he had with Nixon. On his own, separate from Fitzsimmons, he arranged for a private contribution.

I don't know where the money came from. I don't know how much was involved. I do know that in the world in which Bill operated, a contribution of less than a half million dollars would not have been taken very seriously. A million-dollar donation, such as the money sent to Nixon by the Teamsters and the mob, was normal.

All I know for certain was that in 1980, Bill called me in to his Cleveland office. (He retained his Ohio positions after giving up the International posts.) He had a suitcase that he said was filled with money. He told me to take it to a Washington hotel, where I was to give it to Edwin Meese for Ronald Reagan. This I did, meeting both Meese and another man only long enough to pass on the case, explaining who sent it. I never opened the case, nor did I ask Bill how much money I was carrying.

If my deliberate ignorance of the contents seems odd, you have to remember the life I had led and the type of people with whom I worked. There are two ways to stay alive when you are involved in any way with organized crime. One is to obey orders without question, to be known as a stand-up guy who is always as good as his word. The second is to know as little as possible. That way, no matter who asks you questions, you can protect the people with whom you work.

For example, there were many times Bill would take me to some other city to act as muscle. Often I was armed and always I was ready to fight. The meetings were usually fairly social, everyone being friendly because he respected Bill, had something to gain from him, and did not want to cause trouble. But the men we met were like a "Who's Who" of organized crime. I would later see some of their faces in news stories, sometimes after what was described as a major criminal arrest and sometimes when the person had been a victim of a knife, a bullet, or a bomb. Only then would I put a name to a face. Bill would never introduce me by name or tell me the names of the men we met, nor would they introduce themselves. And I liked that best. You can't tell the cops and the feds what you don't know.

The reason I know the money must have been a large amount was what happened later. First Reagan appointed Jackie to his transition team. He was to be a senior adviser to the economic affairs group, as the *New York Times* reported on December 15, 1980.

Now it might seem that Reagan's actions were innocent ones, a tribute to a man who had a reputation as being important in the labor movement. After all, I have already admitted that I covered Jackie's ass over the years. The truth is quite different, though. The FBI knew all about Jackie Presser. They had been using him for years. They knew how well connected he was with the mob. They even encouraged him to keep me on the payroll, even though he and Harold wouldn't let me do anything, because there was a chance I would add to their information about organized crime through my conversations with Jackie.

The FBI knew about Jackie's support from the Chicago and Kansas City crime families. They knew that you don't get that kind of muscle unless you have already proved your worth by doing them favors. In other words, they knew that Jackie Presser was completely "mobbed up," and that was the reason they had him as an informant. In fact, some of the details had long been public record through the writings of men such as Steven Brill, who laid out some of the connections of both Bill and Jackie in his book *The Teamsters* (Simon & Schuster, 1978).

There was no way this information could not be known by Reagan through the routine investigations into anyone closely affiliated with the new presidency. The FBI makes a check. The Secret Service makes a check. And the information is returned to the new president and his aides.

Jackie was no exception, as the papers reported. In fact, on December 24, 1980, the *New York Times* reported that Edwin Meese knew that Jackie was connected with the mob. However, he felt that Jackie's labor expertise was too important to ignore. In addition, the Teamsters was the only major union to endorse Reagan. What was not said was that the bribe I took to Washington, along with whatever other money might have been spent in the same manner by other Teamsters leaders or organized crime figures, made Jackie someone to reward.

Once Reagan took office, numerous stories began appearing in the newspaper about White House aides' demanding that Reagan break his connection with Jackie. They did not want to see Reagan tainted by the connection. Yet loyal Ronald Reagan, understanding how the game is played when you go for ultimate power, ignored everyone and requested that Jackie be given the position of under secretary of labor. To the White House staff, that was going one step too far. More rational heads prevailed and Jackie's potential appointment was dropped because of the staff pressure.

The national power struggle for the Teamsters presidency ended quickly. On May 6, 1981, the same year that Bill Presser died, Frank Fitzsimmons succumbed to cancer. Roy Williams was made interim head on May 21, then officially made president at the convention in Las Vegas in June.

Williams's background was that of a teamster who entered the union. He was born on March 22, 1915, in Ottumwa, Iowa. His family was extremely poor, Roy being one of twelve children. He became a trucker in 1935, hauling livestock to Chicago. Thirteen years later, Roy was a Wichita, Kansas, business agent. He rose to being a trustee of the Central States Pension Fund in 1955, became a vice president in 1971, and was appointed director of the Central Conference of Teamsters, an organization giving him power over Teamsters in fourteen states, in 1976.

Williams learned the Teamster business, including the methods for working with the mob, from Jimmy Hoffa. He had been charged with embezzlement in the past and would be forced to resign from the pension fund, but he did not have convictions. His resignation in 1977 came, in part, because he was found to have provided a pension fund loan to the Landmark Hotel in Las Vegas back in 1966 in a manner that resulted in a kickback to Nicholas Civella. Civella was the Kansas City organized crime leader who was both Roy's and Jackie's mentor in their bid for the Teamster presidency.

Roy Williams lasted only about eighteen months in office. He, along with Thomas F. O'Malley, Andrew G. Massa, Allen Dorfman, and a Dorfman assistant, Joseph Lombardo, were convicted in December 1982 of conspiring to bribe Senator Howard Cannon of Nevada.

The bribe was a clever one. There was no actual cash involved. Instead, they offered to sell the Senator 5.8 acres of land the Teamsters owned on the golf course of the Las Vegas Country Club back in January 1979. The sale seemed legitimate enough. The land could be sold. The price of $1.4 million seemed high enough to be legitimate. And no one mentioned that Senator Cannon was a key vote concerning a measure deregulating trucking company rates that was pending in the Senate.

The true value of the land was at least $1.6 million, even in a quick sale, and that was the price for which it later sold to developers. The idea was to have Cannon legally buy the land, then legally sell it, taking the quick profits as his bribe.

The deregulation bill was an important one for the Teamsters to defeat. The Teamsters knew that the bill would aid consumers and hurt union membership. This was because, after the law was passed, ten thousand new companies were formed, all of them nonunion, and all of them able to provide jobs at wages that were 20 to 30 percent below union scale. Cannon voted against it, but the bill still passed. Deregulation increased the number of jobs available. The bill decreased unemployment in the industry. And despite the lower-than-union wages, the pay scales were generally fair and opened work to men and women who would otherwise be unemployed. However, whereas the union membership was 2.8 million members before deregulation, shortly thereafter it began to drop until it was between 1.6 and 1.8 million. The workers were not suffering, but the union officials had a lower base of income, and that, with the salaries and perquisites they desired, made them very nervous.

On April 23, 1984, after all the appeals related to Williams's conviction were ended, he was replaced as president of the International by Jackie Presser. By now Jackie was widely known for his connections, but his importance in the Reagan administration had not diminished. It had only taken a lower profile.

According to a study by the *New York Times* on November 25, 1984, Jackie had a major say in all appointments related to the National Labor Relations Board and the Interstate Commerce Commission. There were even allegations that he had veto power, though that was not certain. He also publicly supported Reagan by opposing imported goods and favoring the Strategic Defense Initiative. Jackie, despite the publicity, had made it to the top.

I guess it was fated for Jackie never to face any penalties for his crimes over the years. He was dead four years later, in 1988, after returning the Teamsters to the AFL-CIO in order to stop a takeover bid by the Justice Department. He was under indictment for federal charges, facing disgrace, fines, and jail, yet still at the top of the Teamsters, still a friend of Reagan, when he died of brain cancer. And most galling of all for me is that I was never able to haul that fat bastard into court to gain revenge for what he did to me.

Remember that I said that after my heart attack and the merger of my little independent local with 507 I wanted to work but Harold and Jackie wouldn't let me? What I didn't know was that I was being set up by Jackie, by Harold Friedman, and by the feds for whom Jackie acted as an informant.

It was July 1983 when the government indicted me for embezzling $165,000 from the Teamsters. This was the money paid to me as an alleged "ghost employee."

I suppose some people would say that I finally got what I deserved. I was involved with arson, theft, and numerous other crimes over the years without ever getting caught. What difference would it make how I went to jail so long as I spent some time behind bars for something, even a trumped-up charge?

There isn't a good answer to that. I did commit crimes. I was not caught and convicted during the legal time limit known as the statute of limitations. I beat the system for years, in a sense. But the charge of embezzling was the result of a serious violation of civil rights by the government.

The FBI, in its efforts to stop organized crime, became a version of an organized crime group itself. The FBI encouraged Jackie Presser to add to his payroll people who could provide him with information about mob-related people and activities. They not only told him to break the law, they told him to use money from the Teamsters Union to pay them, stealing from hardworking taxpaying citizens.

The FBI did not want anyone to know Jackie Presser was an FBI informant. There had been rumors. There had been statements made in books and articles that implied that Jackie, and perhaps Bill, was involved with the FBI. But no one took those statements seriously. Jackie knew that such a situation would result in his murder and everyone assumed he was too smart to do something like that.

Oddly, in 1986, when Jackie first became seriously ill with a variety of problems including cancer, the mob decided that they had had enough of Jackie Presser. A number of the older men were going down, either through criminal convictions or death from "natural causes." A member of organized crime revealed privately that there was a contract out for Jackie, a contract that would be fulfilled within two years if he did not die of natural causes. There was talk of shooting him, but one insider said that they would probably inject him with a lethal dose of potassium chloride. It was explained that when a person has a heart attack, potassium chloride is released naturally into the bloodstream in unusual quantity. It is a normal sign of death and shows the coroner that there was no foul play. However, an overdose of potassium chloride causes a fatal heart attack. There is no way to determine after the death whether any was injected to cause the fatality.

Obviously, had the mob known the truth, that Jackie had been setting them up, he would have been immediately hit: another reason the FBI did not want the truth about Jackie to be known.

Under the law, when a person goes on trial, any information known to the prosecution that can affect the case must be given to the defense. It does not matter whether the information helps or hinders the prosecution's case. In order to have a fair trial, such information must be provided. Not providing it constitutes grounds not only for a new trial but, depending upon the circumstances, potentially severe sanctions against the prosecution. In order to protect Jackie, the prosecution never revealed the government's ghost employee scheme developed with Jackie, the fact that he was an informant, or anything else. The government could have proved that I was an innocent man but, instead, chose to prosecute me and send me to jail to protect their informant.

Both Jackie and Harold became greedy as well. They saw that my going to jail removed the one remaining thorn in their side. They would do anything to prevent me from having a fair trial or to protect themselves by helping me, even though I knew all their dirty little secrets. They kept witnesses from coming to testify on my behalf.

Remember that once you are in a union, you owe your livelihood to the men at the top. The organizers, for example, are well paid and respected. The only other job skills many of these men have will let them earn only a fraction of what they get as business agents and in other positions. If Jackie or Harold told them that they would be fired for helping me, they could not risk the loss of pay. Likewise, the rank and file could be dismissed from their jobs because of the pressure by union leaders. The bosses would go along because they would not want strikes. And the other members cannot afford to lose their jobs by complaining.

The pressure that was put on the men prevented all my witnesses from coming forward. I was sold out and determined that one day the truth would be known, making Jackie and Harold pay.

I don't know how to describe what it was like to go to the penitentiary again. I was in my sixties. I had a wife and two daughters still at home. I had a heart condition and had been warned that I probably would not be able to survive the stress of jail, even though I was going to be placed in a hospital ward in a federal facility, the easiest time you can do.

No one cared. There were careers to be saved. The FBI cannot condone or authorize crimes under our laws. Cleveland agents had to cover their asses. Jackie Presser had to be protected. Washington officials had their careers to be concerned with. What difference did one person make?

I served eleven months before it was learned that Jackie had set me up, that the government had withheld information, and that I would be released. The government did not want a new trial for me because they were frightened about what might come out. It was already known that Labor Department investigators had had their careers shattered for trying to pursue the truth and other heads were about to roll. The judge who had sent me to jail was not about to let me remain behind bars under the circumstances. Yet no one connected with the prosecution was ready for what was going to be revealed.

The situation that caused Harold's downfall and, I am convinced, would have sent Jackie to jail had he lived was caused by the corrupted government agents and the greedy Teamster leadership. As soon as I was released, I went to court in Akron, Ohio, where I insisted upon a new trial to vindicate myself.

The prosecutor from Washington was so arrogant that he pointed his finger at Federal Judge Bell, who was hearing the case, an action considered improper, and said, to the best of my recollection, "Your honor, if we, the government, don't want to prosecute Allen Friedman, you have no case to try."

Judge Bell became extremely angry, dismissing my case with prejudice. Then he ordered an investigation into all aspects of the case, including the revelation that Jackie was an FBI informer. It was that investigation, which never would have happened had Jackie and Harold helped me in the first place, that eventually resulted in the conviction of Harold Friedman and Anthony Hughes. I talked with anyone who would listen, fighting the efforts of Harold, Jackie, and the government to discredit me.

The American people admire strong leadership. They also have a love of gossip and a delight in seeing the rich and famous revealed in all their humanness. After my release the press uncovered any number of facts that showed government officials with their pants down.

First there were the revelations of Jackie's corruption and his influence in the White House. A memo by White House counsel Fred Fielding had warned Reagan, at least as far back as 1983, that Jackie was trouble and should be avoided. It was found that Secretary of Labor Donovan had been so close to Jackie that he coached him on how to testify before the Senate Labor Committee when Jackie had to appear before it back in 1983. Vague allegations of some sort of improper relations between Presser and Edwin Meese began spreading, one of the factors that would eventually lead to one of the special investigations into the former attorney general's conduct. And the role of the Mafia in Presser's rise to the top was uncovered.

By the end of 1988, many lives were in shambles. Top Mafia figures such as Cleveland's Angelo Lonardo were talking freely, sending both mob leaders and Mafia-related Teamsters officials to jail. Harold Friedman, an International vice president, president of the Ohio Council of Teamsters, president of Teamsters Local 507, and president of Bakery Workers Local 19, was convicted of racketeering and embezzling on Friday, January 13, 1989. He was found guilty of one count of embezzlement, one count of filing a false report with the Labor Department, one count of labor racketeering, and one count of conspiring to commit labor racketeering. U.S. District Judge George W. White was given the option of sentencing him up to a maximum of forty-six years in jail and a seventy-thousand-dollar fine. Also convicted was Tony Hughes, the recording secretary for Local 507. He had been an FBI informant as long as Jackie and possibly longer. Had he agreed to testify against Harold in exchange for immunity from prosecution, he probably would have gone free. Instead he was convicted of one count of labor racketeering, one count of embezzlement, and one count of conspiracy to commit labor racketeering. I must admit taking pleasure in these convictions.

During the trial, one FBI agent was jailed for contempt of court. Others refused to testify on the grounds that they might be incriminated. And none of this would ever have come out had Jackie and Harold not decided to screw me when I was under investigation.

In addition to those changes, Ronald Reagan left office beloved by the American people, yet the scandals connected with him and his staff were becoming so blatant that he may eventually be discredited in much the same manner as Richard Nixon. I am divorced, my older daughter married, my younger daughter is finishing school and planning for college, and the family's relationships are strained.

There are still men and women involved with the Teamsters who were part of the past corruption. And the money the union generates will still bring willing supplicants to trade their souls for what the Teamsters can provide.

The government's efforts to put the Teamsters into trusteeship has received extensive press. It seemed that a compromise would be reached when three of the International Vice-Presidents resigned and efforts to bring criminal charges against them were dropped. The government asked for free elections of the General President and the Secretary/Treasurer. It also requested additional resignations from among the Vice-Presidents, some of whom are so strongly politically and criminally connected that they have the clout to avoid being removed.

The rebel Teamsters For a Democratic Union (TDU) joined with the Teamster leadership in fighting most other changes. The TDU wants the free elections by the rank-and-file, while recognizing that a government take-over would weaken the union to the point where it would not be so effective for the average working man.

At this writing, the Teamsters are back with the AFL-CIO and the government is trying to work out a compromise that will change the election procedures while avoiding the Trusteeship approach that is unwanted by both the dissidents and the entrenched, old time leadership. Yet even if the trusteeship occurs, I foresee few changes. As Senator Bender's story showed, corruption is just too easy. The government got its headlines with Jackie's death and Harold's conviction. If they also gain free elections, elections which may still be rigged through a ballot box scam such as Harold, Jackie, and I pulled, outsiders will be impressed while the leadership continues business as usual.

The investigation did lead to an attempt to whitewash Jackie Presser's role as an informant. The FBI claimed that Jackie agreed to work for them because of a "genuine desire" to rid the union of mob influence. The truth was that he was protecting himself from the various mob wars and developing a power base by ridding himself of his enemies. Even Oliver B. Revell, the FBI's executive assistant director for investigations, admitted to the Los Angeles Times in February of 1989 that Jackie was a key to the 1982 prosecution of his rival, former president Roy Williams.

On a regional level, things were different for a while. New Jersey's Local 560, Tony Pro's former union, was placed into trusteeship by Federal Judge Harold Ackerman. The incident occurred in 1986 after fifty-one days of testimony concerning beatings, extortion, murder, and numerous other crimes. The trusteeship for the nine-thousand-member local was handled under the Racketeer Influenced and Corrupt Organizations (RICO) Act, the result of allegations that the union was actually a labor racket run by a Mafia unit identified as the "Provenzano group."

Local 560 did all it could to stay in the hands of the Provenzanos over the years after Tony Pro went to jail. First Nunzio Provenzano took over, though he was identified as a member of the Mafia by Judge Ackerman and went to jail for extortion. Then Sam Provenzano, the third brother, took over, going to jail for mishandling the fund for dental benefits. Eventually Tony's daughter, Josephine, became secretary-treasurer for Local 560 and Mickey Sciarra became the president. It was Sciarra who was the first person to lose his job when the union went into trusteeship.

The union rank and file remains bitter over the takeover. Some claim that there was no connection between Local 560 and the mob, that Tony Pro and his brothers were dedicated advocates of the workingman. Others say that Tony Pro was unquestionably mob-connected, violent, and all the other things the judge had said. However, they feel that despite all that, he was good to the workingman who wanted to do his job, go home to his family, and not have to worry about bills.

And this is one of the other truths about the Teamsters Union membership. The majority of the rank and file are concerned with their personal lives. So long as they are helped to earn higher wages, have their medical expenses covered, and can retire with a predictable income high enough to keep them from poverty in old age, they are happy. Few of them care about the leadership. Many of them see the government intervention, as in Local 560, as a challenge to their rights to select their own leadership and run their own affairs. And among these are people who see no difference between the corruption of Tony Pro and his successors and the corruption of government overseers.

Aside from the Local 560 issue, I have had the pleasure of seeing Harold in the courtroom, though I am saddened by the loss of Jackie. He was my nephew and I loved him, but he also hurt me badly, abandoning my wife and kids while I was jailed. I am disappointed that his death deprived me of the pleasure of seeing him in court. I said that I wanted to piss on his grave, but first I wanted him to pay for all the things he did to me.

I have sued Jackie's estate, the government, and others, hoping to make them pay a penalty for what they did to me in the wrongful jailing. And I have written this book to provide the historical perspective that has been lacking. Yet I wish that it had not all been necessary.

Perhaps the saddest fact of all is that the union movement seems on the decline, the membership down, no strong leaders on the horizon. The Teamsters, especially, went too far under Jackie Presser and Harold Friedman. Their demands were unrelated to the realities of doing business, and many companies were forced to fold or move to areas where unions had less power. The Teamster leadership, along with bosses of some of the other unions, asked too much, too fast, without seeing what management could truly afford.

Bosses are still a problem. Job security, harassment, racial and sexual bias, and all the other problems the working person has faced over the years remain. The work of the union has not ended, nor is it likely to do so.

At the same time, when a boss is good, obviously caring about the employees, letting them know what they are truly earning in wages and benefits, making them recognize that they are respected and appreciated, no one wants to organize. A caring boss, a friendly boss, an honest boss does more to destroy a union than all the violence in all the labor wars in the country.

As for me, I can only reminisce. This is a new era for everyone. The older ones, like me, are mostly outsiders now, those who aren't in jail or on trial. Obviously a few old timers, like the new president, remain. The children of the labor leaders of old have sometimes pursued other professions, sometimes stayed in the movement, where most have shown themselves to be singularly underqualified for the modern business structure. The other new leaders are less likely to have ever been sluggers, to know the down-and-dirty violence which shaped our early history.

I have gained great satisfaction in seeing Harold fairly convicted in a court of law. He was guilty as charged, as was Jackie, whose professional life was also put on trial with Harold, despite his death. I am convinced that had he lived, Jackie would also be facing a jail sentence.

All my life I have made certain that anyone who wrongfully hurt me paid the price. Sometimes this has meant returning a beating I received. Sometimes it has meant getting the best of them in a business deal. And when I went to prison because Jackie and Harold deliberately hurt me, I vowed that I would use the truth about their pasts to make them pay. Jackie died too soon, but I had the pleasure of facing Harold in court, revealing his past, and watching as the judge ruled that he would pay the price for his past actions. I know that when I die, I will die happy because of that.

There have been changes in the labor movement, of course. From the murder of Danny Greene to the present time, most of the old-time leaders have died, gone to jail, or been moved out of office. Many high-level individuals in the Mafia and the Teamsters became government informants. After Hoffa, none of the Teamster presidents had the leadership skills to control all the locals and so they became far more independent than in the past. By the time Jackie died and William McCarthy of Boston took over the International presidency, the extreme abuses of the past were no longer possible. The world that Bill and I both knew and helped to shape, the world I shared with Jackie and, to a lesser degree, Harold, no longer existed.

Yet the greed, the desire for power, the lust for the pleasures of the flesh—these do not change among the politicians, the judges, and other American authority figures. Perhaps the Teamsters of tomorrow will not actively seek favors or attempt to bribe anyone. But they won't have to any more than we did. The people on the rise will continue to approach them, hats in hand. The union leadership has what they want and they will sell their souls to get it.

One era is over. Another era has begun. The faces have changed. The leadership has become more educated, sophisticated, street smart in the ways of Wall Street rather than the loading docks and truck stops of the nation. Yet the power and the greed continue. It is what has kept us going. It is what has kept us strong. And, for me and others like me, it has been our lifeblood, our religion, and our downfall.

BIBLIOGRAPHY

BOOKS

Alinsky, Saul David. *John L. Lewis: An Unauthorized Biography*. New York: Putnam, 1949.

Brill, Steven. *The Teamsters*. New York: Simon & Schuster, 1978.

Brooks, Thomas R. *Toil and Trouble: A History of American Labor*. New York: Delacorte Press, 1971.

Condon, George E. *Cleveland: The Best Kept Secret*. J. T. Zubal & P. D. Dole, Publishers, 1981.

Demaris, Ovid. *The Boardwalk Jungle*. New York: Bantam Books, 1986.

Eisenberg, Dennis, Uri Dan, and Eli Landau. *Meyer Lansky: Mogul of the Mob*. New York: Paddington Press Ltd., 1979.

Exner, Judith, as told to Ovid Demaris. *My Story*. New York: Grove Press, 1977.

Gage, Nicholas. *Mafia, USA*. Chicago: Playboy Press Books, 1972.

International Brotherhood of Teamsters, Chauffeurs, Warehousemen and Helpers of America. *Teamsters All: Pictorial Highlights of Our History;* compiled by the International Brotherhood of Teamsters, Chauffeurs, Warehousemen and Helpers of America for Its 21st Convention Celebrating the United States Bicentennial. Washington, D.C.: Merkle Press, 1976.

James, Estelle, and Ralph C. James. *Hoffa and the Teamsters*. New York: Van Nostrand, 1965.

Jedick, Peter. *Cleveland: Where the East Coast Meets the Midwest*. Cleveland: Jedick Enterprises, 1980.

Kennedy, Robert F. *The Enemy Within*. Westport, Conn.: Greenwood Press, 1960.

Kidner, John. *Contract Killer*. Washington, D. C.: Acropolis Books, Ltd., 1976.

McCallum, John D. *Dave Beck.* Mercer Island, Wash.: Writing Works, 1978.

Messick, Hank. *The Silent Syndicate.* New York: Macmillan, 1967.

Messick, Hank, and Burt Goldblatt. *The Mobs and the Mafia.* New York: Thomas Y. Crowell Company, 1972.

Moldea, Dan. *The Hoffa Wars.* New York: Charter Books, 1978.

Mollenhoff, Clark R. *Tentacles of Power: The Story of Jimmy Hoffa.* Cleveland: World Publishing Company, 1965.

————. *Game Plan for Disaster.* New York: W. W. Norton & Co., 1976.

Mustain, Gene, and Jerry Capeci. *Mob Star.* New York: Franklin Watts, 1988.

Navasky, Victor S. *Kennedy Justice.* New York: Atheneum, 1971.

Peterson, Virgil W. *The Mob: 200 Years of Organized Crime in New York.* Ottawa, Il.: Green Hill Publishers, 1983.

President's Commission on Organized Crime. *The Impact: Organized Crime Today.* Report to the President and the Attorney General. Washington, D. C.: U. S. Government Printing Office, 1986.

Reston, James, Jr. *The Great Expectations of John Connally.* New York: Edward Burlingame Books/Harper & Row, 1969.

Time-Life Editors. *This Fabulous Century,* vols. 3, 4, 5, 6, 7. New York: Time-Life, 1971.

Van Tassel, David D. and John J. Grabowski, eds. *The Encyclopedia of Cleveland History.* Bloomington: Indiana University Press, 1987.

Velie, Lester. *Desperate Bargain: Why Jimmy Hoffa Had to Die.* New York: Reader's Digest Press, 1977.

Vincent, Sidney Z. and Judah Rubenstein. *Merging Traditions—Jewish Life in Cleveland.* Cleveland: Western Reserve Historical Society and Jewish Community Federation of Cleveland, 1978.

Zuckerman, Michael J. *Vengeance Is Mine.* New York: Macmillan, 1987.

NEWSPAPERS AND MAGAZINES

Akron Beacon Journal: April 7, 1988.

Cleveland News: numerous issues, 1920–1960.

Cleveland Plain Dealer: numerous issues, 1920–1988.

Cleveland Press: numerous issues, 1920–1982.

Detroit News: August 1, 1976.

New York Times: numerous issues, 1970–1988.

Oakland Tribune: September 21–28, 1969.

Washington Star: December 5, 1976.

Life: May 15, 1964.

TRIAL TRANSCRIPTS

United States of America vs. Jackie Presser, et al; Case No. CR 86–114; Judge George W. White.

United States of America vs. Allen Friedman; Case No. CR83–188; United States District Court Northern District of Ohio, Eastern Division.

United States of America vs. Jackie Presser; Harold Friedman; and Anthony Hughes; No. 87–3896, United States Court of Appeals for the Sixth Circuit, 844 F.2d 1275; 1988 U.S. App.

United States of America vs. Robert S. Friedrick; No. 87–3001, United States Court of Appeals for the District of Columbia Circuit, 842 F.2d 382; 1988 U.S. App.

United States of America vs. Allen Friedman; No. 83–3815.

William Presser, Appellant vs. United States of America, Appellee; No. 15,697, United States Court of Appeals, District of Columbia Circuit, 284 F.2d 233; 41 Lab. Cas. (CCH) P16, 597; October 27, 1960.

Raymond J. Donovan, Secretary of Labor, Plaintiff vs. Frank Fitzsimmons, Roy Williams, Robert Holmes, Donald Peters, Joseph W. Morgan, Frank H. Ranney, Walter W. Teague, Jackie Presser, Albert D. Matheson, Thomas J. Duffey, John Spickerman, Herman A. Lueking, Jack A. Sheetz, William J. Kennedy, Bernard S. Goldfarb, Andrew G. Mass, William Presser, and Alvin Baron, Defendants; No. 78 C 342, United States District Court for the Northern District of Illinois Eastern Division, 32 Fed. R. Serv. 2d (Callaghan) 1630, October 7, 1981.

United States of America vs. Allen Friedman; No. 83–3815 nl; United States Court of Appeals for the Sixth Circuit; Slip Opinion; July 31, 1984.

MISCELLANEOUS SOURCES

Sixty Minutes (transcripts) 20, no. 22, February 14, 1988; 19, no. 50, August 30, 1987.

Freedom of Information Act files related to *United States of America vs. Friedrick;* No. 86–0188 (DDC, Revercomb, J.).

Interview of Robert S. Friedrick by the Department of Justice in Washington, D.C., September 18, 1985.

Files of the Western Reserve Historical Society of Cleveland, Ohio: various files including those for Bill and Jackie Presser, Teamster Local 407, the Elliot Ness collection, and collections relating to various ethnic groups (Jewish, Irish, Italian, and others).

Interviews are not listed because of the confidential nature of many of the sources. They include law enforcement personnel, Teamsters Union officials, Teamsters, members of the Mafia, and friends of the Presser family. Technical information concerning the legal cases involving Allen Friedman came from Robert S. Catz, Professor of Law at Cleveland State University, Cleveland, Ohio.

Most of the research materials, including court cases, used for this book are in the Ted Schwarz and Allen Friedman archives of Arizona State University's Special Collections Division, Tempe, Arizona.

INDEX

273